D1084610

CHINA'S RURAL ECONOMY AFTER WTO

The Chinese Economy Series

This series examines the immense importance of China within the global economy. Books in the series view the Chinese economy in many ways, such as: a transition economy; a bridge between the developing and developed nations; a vital member of the WTO; and even as a potential rival to the US.

Providing readers with high quality monographs and edited volumes by authors from East and West, this series is a truly global forum on one of the world's key economies.

Series Editors

Aimin Chen, Indiana State University, USA
Shunfeng Song, University of Nevada-Reno, USA

Recent Titles in the Series

Chinese Youth in Transition
Edited by Jieying Xi, Yunxiao Sun and Jing Jian Xiao
ISBN 0 7546 4369 7

Grains in China
Edited by Zhang-Yue Zhou and Wei-Ming Tian
ISBN 0 7546 4280 1

Critical Issues in China's Growth and Development
Edited by Yum K. Kwan and Eden S.H. Yu
ISBN 0 7546 4270 4

Urban Transformation in China
Edited by Aimin Chen, Gordon G. Liu and Kevin H. Zhang
ISBN 0 7546 3312 8

Urbanization and Social Welfare in China
Edited by Aimin Chen, Gordon G. Lui and Kevin H. Zhang
ISBN 0 7546 3313 6

China's Rural Economy after WTO
Problems and Strategies

Edited by

SHUNFENG SONG
University of Nevada, USA

AIMIN CHEN
Sichuan University, People's Republic of China

ASHGATE

Published by
Ashgate Publishing Limited
Gower House
Croft Road
Aldershot
Hampshire GU11 3HR
England

Ashgate Publishing Company
Suite 420
101 Cherry Street
Burlington, VT 05401-4405
USA

Ashgate website: http://www.ashgate.com

British Library Cataloguing in Publication Data
China's rural economy after WTO : problems and strategies.
 - (The Chinese economy series)
 1.Agriculture and state - China -Congresses 2.Rural
 development - China - Congresses 3.Rural-urban migration -
 China - Congresses 4.Rural women - China - Economic
 conditions - Congresses 5.China - Rural conditions -
 Congresses
 I.Song, Shunfeng II.Chen, Aimin
 330.9'51'0091734

Library of Congress Cataloging-in-Publication Data
China's rural economy after WTO : problems and strategies / edited by Aimin Chen and Shunfeng Song.
       p. cm. -- (The Chinese economy series)
   Selections from papers presented at the international symposium on "China's Rural Economy: Problems and Strategies," organized by the Chinese Economists Society in Hangzhou, China on June 25-27, 2004.
   Includes bibliographical references and index.
   ISBN 0-7546-4695-5
   1. China--Rural conditions--Congresses. 2. Agriculture and state--China--Congresses. 3. Rural development--China--Congresses. 4. Rural-urban migration--China--Congresses. 5. Rural women--China--Economic conditions--Congresses. I. Chen, Aimin. II. Song, Shunfeng. III. Series.

   HD2097.C4628 2006
   330.951009173'4--dc22

                                                                                    2006003898

ISBN 0 7546 4695 5

Printed in Great Britain by Athenaeum Press, Ltd.,
Gateshead, Tyne & Wear

Contents

List of Figures

List of Tables

List of Contributors

Bina Agarwal Professor of Economics, University of Delhi, India.

Gene H. Chang Professor of Economics, University of Toledo, Toledo, USA.

Aimin Chen Professor of Economics, Indiana State University, USA and Vice President, Sichuan University, China.

Shaoqiang Chen Research Fellow, Research Institute of Fiscal Science, Ministry of Finance, China.

Yuyu Chen Assistant Professor of Applied Economics, Peking University, China.

Alan de Brauw Assistant Professor of Economics, Williams College, USA.

Xiao-Yuan Dong Professor of Economics, University of Winnipeg, Canada.

Shenggen Fan Senior Research Fellow, the International Food Policy Research Institute, USA and Class-one Scientist, the Chinese Academy of Agricultural Sciences, China.

Nico Heerink Beijing Office Coordinator and Research Fellow, International Food Policy Research Institute, China office, Beijing, China.

Zhaohui Hong Professor of Economic History, Purdue University, Calumet, USA.

Zuhui Huang Professor of Agricultural Economics, Center for Agricultural and Rural Development, Zhejiang University, China.

Puqing Lai Ph.D student of Agricultural Economics, Zhejiang University, China.

Ligang Liu Senior Research Fellow, Hong Kong Monetary Authority, China.

Mingxing Liu Associate Professor, School of Government, Peking University, China.

Xiaoyun Liu Associate Professor of Agricultural Economics, Center for Integrated Agricultural Development, China Agricultural University, China.

Ding Lu Professor of Economics, Sophia University, Japan.

Zhigang Lu Associate Professor of Information System, Tianjin University of Finance and Economics, China.

Fiona MacPhail Associate Professor of Economics, University of Northern British Columbia, Canada.

Scott Rozelle Professor of Agricultural and Resource Economics, University of California, Davis, USA.

Futian Qu Professor and Dean, College of Land Management, Nanjing Agricultural University, China.

Wei Shan Ph.D. student, Texas A&M University, USA.

Xiaoping Shi Associate Professor, College of Land Management, Nanjing Agricultural University, China.

Terry Sicular Professor of Economics, University of Western Ontario, Canada.

Shunfeng Song Professor of Economics, University of Nevada, Reno, USA.

Yu Song Ph.D. student of Agricultural Economics, Zhejiang University, China.

Guanghua Wan Senior Research Fellow, World Institute for Development Economics Research, United Nations University, Finland.

Wenbo Wu Assistant Professor of Public Policy, National University of Singapore, Singapore.

Xian Xin Professor of Agricultural Economics, China Agricultural University, China.

Chunbing Xing Ph.D. student, Guanghua School of Management, Peking University, China.

Xu-Chu Xu Associate Professor of Agricultural Economics, Center for Agricultural and Rural Development, Zhejiang University, China.

Xianguo Yao Professor of Economics, Zhejiang University, China.

Linxiu Zhang Professor, Institute of Geographical Sciences and Natural Resources Research, Chinese Academy of Sciences, China.

Qi Zhang Ph.D. student of Political Science, Northwestern University.

Xiaobo Zhang Senior Research Fellow, the International Food Policy Research Institute, USA.

Introduction

Chapter 1

China's Rural Economy after WTO: Problems and Strategies

Shunfeng Song
Aimin Chen

Before 1978, China was one of the poorest countries in the world with 60 percent of the one billion people living below poverty, earning less than $1 per day. Almost all of the poor were in the agricultural sector, which provided livelihoods to nearly 75 percent of the total population. Since 1978, the world has seen a different China—a China with an economy growing consistently at red-hot speed. The growth started in 1978 with the implementation of the household responsibility system and was later fueled by the development of rural township-village enterprises.

Agriculture, however, which was a clear leader in reform, is now lagging behind other sectors. China's rural economy faces many serious challenges. The gains of economic growth have not been fairly shared between urban and rural residents. Many parts of the agricultural and rural sector remain underdeveloped. Rural residents confront tremendous barriers when they enter the non-farm sector and find jobs in cities. Women assume a disproportionate share of those rural residents who have to rely on agricultural production for a living. Land holdings are so small that farming cannot raise enough income for most rural households. The improvement of agricultural productivity is further hindered by the lack of well-functioning credit, land rental, and insurance markets. Managing the post-reform rural development needs to change the role and organization of the government. Establishing efficient governance at the local and regional levels while increasing accountability, however, remains a major challenge.

As China enters the 21st century, the major measure of success in the nation's push toward modernization will depend upon the extent to which the aforementioned concerns about the rural population, rural areas, and agricultural sector—termed "*sannong wenti*" by the Chinese media—can be properly addressed. What measures can China take to raise farmers' income so that the income disparity between rural and urban residents can be reduced? What changes should China make to help farmers smoothly migrate to non-farm sectors? How could China improve the size and efficiency of public finance to rural areas?

The book is divided into four parts. The first part, "Gender Inequality in Rural Areas," discusses the inequalities rural women face in the labor market and their households, and how these inequalities affect China's rural development. The second part, "Poverty and Income Inequalities," examines the inequality problem from the perspective of the increasing income gap between rural and urban residents. The third part, "Rural-Urban Migration and Labor Market," investigates the massive migration movement that is taking place in China and analyzes the motives that are driving farmers to migrate or work in non-farm businesses. The fourth and final part, "Government's Rural Policies and Rural Governance," analyzes how the Chinese government at the local level handles various rural problems, such as debt and financing, and how rural grassroots organizations deal with economic development and government regulations. The content of each section is briefly reviewed below.

Part 1 begins with Chapter 2, contributed by Bina Agarwal, who discusses the often neglected—or hidden—inequalities existing in rural women's access to agricultural land and property, their social perceptions and norms, and their interactions with emergent institutions for natural resource management. Drawing examples largely from South Asia, the author raises issues that are of general relevance and connections to rural women in China. The author argues that rural development and the formation of new governing institutions can create new inequalities on the bedrock of pre-existing ones, that inequality can be constantly recreated unless direct measures are taken to mitigate them and that enhancing women's bargaining power in all these areas is important in order to reduce persistent gender inequalities.

In Chapter 3, Fiona MacPhail and Xiao-Yuan Dong examine the relationship between women's market labor and their status in rural China. Based on a 1999 to 2000 survey of more than 750 men and women working in township and village enterprises (TVEs), the authors find that women have a heavier work burden and greater responsibility for often undervalued domestic tasks and that they also have little say over household decisions compared with men. The authors conclude that the broad economic changes and policy reforms going on in China have increased the gender wage inequality and that the intensification of market work conditions is troubling from a gender equity perspective.

In Chapter 4, using household data, Linxiu Zhang, Alan De Brauw, and Scott Rozelle analyze the role of women in labor markets by studying employment trends and how women's participation in agriculture has affected farm output. The authors observe an overall increase in non-farm participation, most of which has been driven by young migrants with female participation rates equal to or higher than those of their male counterparts. The authors also find that when women are left in charge of farm work, crop productivity does not fall.

Xiaoyun Liu, Sicular Terry, and Xian Xin conduct a probit regression model in Chapter 5, using the China Health and Nutrition Survey dataset. They find that gender is a significant factor in determining the non-agricultural occupation. Being female reduces the probability of non-agricultural employment by 16 to 17 percent. Moreover, women's probability of participation in non-agricultural employment decreased from 1989 to 1997, suggesting that the gender gap widened during this period. The regression results also reveal that as income grows the gender inequality of non-agricultural employment increases.

Part 2 expands the discussion of inequality from gender to income. Chapter 6, contributed by Zhaohui Hong, contends that the deficiency of Chinese farmers' land rights takes precedence over their lack of other rights. The author finds a causal relationship between the poverty of farmers' rights in land property and their economic poverty overall, seen in the massive number of landless, jobless, homeless, and uninsured farmers in China today. The author proposes three basic directions and alternatives in dealing with the farmers' lack of rights in regard to land property. The first direction is to establish an institutional standard of eminent domain with land that is designed to maintain the principles of justice, transparency, and mutual-benefits. The second direction is to marketize land to promote the free choice of land cultivation as well as the free transfer, mortgage, and consolidation of land. The third direction is to diversify land ownership in order to encourage the development of different formats of land property.

Chapter 7 takes a closer look at income inequality. Using a combined Box-Cox and Box-Tidwell model specification, Guanghua Wan examines regional inequality in rural China. He found that income inequality is greatly influenced by TVEs, education, the rural credit system, and levies on land. To reduce regional inequality in rural China, the author argues that China must promote TVEs in less developed areas, maintain education provisions to the poor, develop a viable rural credit market to attract capital input to the poor regions, and convert fees and levies into transparent taxes to make farming a profitable business so that land can become an equalizing contributor to regional inequality.

Gene H. Chang, in Chapter 8, reviews both theoretical and practical issues involved in the decomposition of China's aggregate income distribution into three components: the rural intra-group distribution, the urban intra-group distribution, and the rural-urban income disparity. The author finds that the recent increase in the aggregate income inequality in China is mainly due to intra-urban income inequality, rural-urban income disparity, and rural migration to urban areas.

In Chapter 9, using panel data of provincial economies, Ding Lu investigates the factors affecting urban-rural household income disparity in China between 1998 and 2002. The study's findings suggest a divergent trend across regions in the development of urban-rural disparity. The study also reveals evidence of deteriorated trade openness and inefficient local governance. The author believes that the increase of fiscal support to agriculture has less to do with the need to curb the rising urban-rural disparity than it does with the excessive growth of the bureaucracy's size and administrative costs and that price subsidies may have a role in containing urban-rural disparity, but its significance is moderate.

Part 3 is dedicated to examining the migration movement in China and China's labor market. Based on a 2003 survey in Tianjin, Zhigang Lu and Shunfeng Song examine the pulling and pushing forces and the barriers of rural-urban migration in Chapter 10. This research also looks at the characteristics of migrants and compares the employment and social conditions of migrants with those of permanent urban residents. The authors argue that efforts such as reforming the household registration, employment, education, and social protection systems will help prevent social exclusion against rural migrants and promote social justice and rural development.

Chapter 11 analyzes the relative importance of four sub-categories of non-farm employment and the factors that are driving the participation of individuals in these sub-categories. Using data collected during a 2000 survey in Jiangxi Province, Xiaoping Shi, Nico Heerink, and Futian Qu find that migration is the most important type of non-farm employment. Agricultural non-farm employment is just a minor activity. The gender bias in terms of non-farm employment is largest for agricultural employment and local non-agricultural employment. Land scarcity stimulates migration and local non-agricultural employment, while possibilities to rent land out to other farmers stimulate only migration.

In Chapter 12, Xianguo Yao and Puqing Lai analyze the wage and non-wage welfare differentials between urban and rural workers. Using enterprise survey data and rural workers survey data, the authors find that the great gap is the result of human capital disparities between urban and rural workers as well as hukou discrimination. The results indicate that rural workers suffer great discrimination in such areas as wage, ole-age insurance, medical insurance, unemployment insurance, and union membership. The findings imply that the real welfare gap between urban and rural workers is far higher that the gap in wage.

In Chapter 13, Yuyu Chen and Chunbing Xing discuss the return to education in the forms of wage and job opportunity return. Using the Heckman two-step model, the authors find that the return rates of education for those wage earners are not significant, but one more year of education does increase the probability of being employed in a non-farm sector. The research also finds that education increases one's employment opportunity by the high-wage sector within the non-farm sector and that more education also may protect workers from unemployment risks.

Chapter 14, written by Aimin Chen, compares the economic conditions and modes of urbanization in five Chinese provinces. The author finds that urbanization in Zhejiang and Jiangsu provinces, China's manufacturing bases and forerunner of economic development, has been driven primarily by rural industrialization through the development of TVEs. The geographical and economic conditions of the Hainan province make it more efficient to urbanize through developing areas along the coastal lines and migrating the poorer rural population from the inland to the coasts. The author thinks the Fujian province shares the characteristics of both modes. The development of southern areas resembles that of Zhejiang and Jianagsu, but northern inland areas should migrate poorer rural residents out of their native villages. Inner Mongolia, being geographically unique and less developed in many aspects, needs to urbanize through developing specialty agriculture, promoting trade with Central Asian nations, and most importantly, attracting outside investment and talent.

The last section, Part 4, examines the roles played by local government in handling various issues in rural development. In Chapter 15, Wenbo Wu looks into the local government role of financing rural health care. The article analyzes the tradeoff relations faced by a local government in choosing its own consumption level and the level of spending in health care. The author finds that a fundamental dilemma in reforming China's fiscal system exists between preserving the incentive of local government to promote local prosperity and motivating them to provide meaningful social services. The author thinks that the current fiscal system needs to be fundamentally reformed and a rule-based fiscal system needs to be eventually established.

In Chapter 16, Shenggen Fan and Xiaobo Zhang investigate the importance of infrastructure in rural development. Using data on rural infrastructure from the Agricultural Census and other official sources, the authors take a traditional source accounting approach to identify the specific role of infrastructure and other public capital in explaining productivity differences among regions, throwing new light on how to allocate limited public resources for the purpose of both growth and regional equity.

Chapter 17, contributed by Ligang Liu and Shaoqiang Chen, focuses on the local government's role in debt issuance. This paper shows that just banning local governments from issuing debts has not eliminated local government debt in many Chinese provinces. Instead, the authors advocate that local governments should be allowed to issue debts subject to some stringent fiscal rules and that such rules can only be made effective if they are accompanied by parallel institutional building efforts such as a transparent budget process and budget institutions, independent credit rating agencies, a proper accounting and auditing process, and other inter-governmental agencies aimed at alleviating information asymmetry of local government finances.

In Chapter 18, Xiaobo Zhang examines the local government's role in providing public finance for rural development. The author argues that due to the large differences in initial economic structures and revenue bases, the implicit tax rate and fiscal burdens to support the functioning of local government vary significantly across jurisdictions. Regions initially endowed with a broader non-farm tax base do not need to charge heavily on existing and new firms to finance public goods provisions, thereby creating a healthy investment environment for the non-farm sector to grow. In contrast, regions with agriculture as the major economic activity have little resources left for public investment after paying the expenses of bureaucracy. Because of its relatively high transaction cost of tax collection from the agricultural sector, the local government tends to levy heavily on the existing non-farm sector, thereby greatly inhibiting its growth.

The next two articles of Part 4 discuss how rural organizations are governing themselves. In Chapter 19, Zu-hui Huang, Xu-chu Xu, and Yu Song examine one of those organizations: farmer cooperatives. The authors find that as the risks and uncertainties of farmer production increase, the desire of farmers to be united in order to enhance their market competitiveness becomes more urgent. Therefore, the special cooperative economic organizations of farmers—cooperatives being the major form—achieved very rapid development, especially in the coastal areas.

In Chapter 20, Qi Zhang, Mingxing Liu, and Wei Shan examine the effect of central regulations on the reform of village self-rule in China. The authors argue that because of information asymmetry between the central government and local governments, local governments can find good excuses to under-supply grassroots democracy and even seek their own self-interests in the name of implementing central regulations. Local governments can levy taxes and fees higher than the level that is necessary to implement regulations. In order to have the regulations implemented, the center will to some extent permit the non-democratic behaviors of local governments, and in such case, there exists the phenomenon of legal soft-constraint.

In summary, this book provides an up-to-date review and in-depth analysis of some of the most pressing issues facing China's rural economy, such as rural-urban income inequality, gender inequality, migration and urbanization challenges, and the inadequacy of government help with rural development and rural governance. The authors recommend that China must enhance women's bargaining power to reduce gender inequalities, accelerate the pace of rural-to-urban migration to narrow the urban-rural divide, develop the rural credit market to attract capital to the poor areas, provide public investment in the less-developed areas to mitigate regional disparities, and encourage the emergence of advocacy organizations for rural residents.   The success of China's modernization drive will depend on maintaining a healthy agricultural economy.

Acknowledgements

We thank all the participants of the international symposium on China's Rural Economy: Problems and Strategies for contributing their quality research. We are grateful to the Zhejiang University, the Ford Foundation, and the International Development Research Centre, Canada for their financial support. We appreciate many referees for their constructive comments and suggestions. Finally, we acknowledge Qingmiao Hu, Caren Roblin, Kelly Wilkin, Cindy Zhao, and Zishi Zhao for their helpful research and editorial assistance in preparing the volume for publication.

Part 1
Gender Inequality in Rural Areas

Chapter 2

Gender Inequalities and Rural Development: Some Neglected and Hidden Dimensions[*]

(China)

Bina Agarwal

J16 Z13   P36
O15 O18 R23 P25

1 Introduction

Mainstream economics has paid rather inadequate attention to gender inequality, but even within gender economics, some issues are especially neglected or hidden, such as women's rights in land and property and social norms and perceptions. This essay focuses on these dimensions. The examples are drawn mostly from South Asia, but many of the issues raised here would also have relevance for China. On occasion, the Chinese context has also been explicitly discussed.

2 Gender Inequality

Rural women in northwest India, married to strangers miles away from their birth villages, use folk songs to decry their estrangement from the green pastures of their childhood homes—homes to which their brothers, who inherit the ancestral land, have automatic access. I quote excerpts from two folk songs:

> To my brother belong your green fields,
> O father, while I am banished afar.
> Always you said
> your brother and you are the same.
> O Father. But today you betray me…

---

[*] This paper was delivered as a keynote address at the Chinese Economists Society Conference, Hangzhou, Zhejiang, China, June 27, 2004. A somewhat different and earlier version was also presented by the author as the Malcolm Adiseshiah Memorial lecture, at the Madras Institute of Development Studies (Chennai, India), in November 2002, and as a public lecture at Barnard College, Columbia University, when based there as their Hirschorn visiting professor.

> My *doli* leaves your house, O father
> My *doli* leaves your house.
> These dowry jewels are not jewels
> but wounds around my neck, O father,
> my *doli* leaves...[1]

Women in Sri Lanka, by contrast, traditionally inherited immovable property and sometimes their husbands moved in with them. But according to folklore, such a husband was advised to always keep a walking stick, an umbrella, and an oil lamp handy. Why? In case his wife evicted him when he was ill, and in the rain, in the middle of the night! And some wives indeed did so.

Both examples depict gender inequality. In the first, the woman has no property, and social norms require her to join her husband—a dislocation she sees as banishment. In the second, the man has no property, and social norms allow him to join his wife, but in a home from which he can easily be evicted. In the first example, the woman is the less equal, in the second the man.

These examples illustrate several things. They highlight that gender inequality and indeed gender in general, is a relational category, and even though most times we are grappling with women's disadvantaged position, in rare cases men too might occupy that position. In particular, these examples highlight the importance of women's property status and enabling social norms in determining gender relations.

Compared with other inequalities, such as those of class or race, gender inequality also has some distinct features. For one, it dwells not only outside the home but within it as well. Mainstream economic theory has long treated the household as a unitary entity in relation to both consumption and production. The unitary household model assumes that all household resources and incomes are pooled, and family members either share common interests and preferences, or an altruistic household head (who represents the household's tastes and preferences and seeks to maximize household utility) ensures equitable allocations of goods and tasks (Agarwal, 1997).

Most people know from personal experience that this is not how real families behave, but in recent years within academia, virtually every assumption of the unitary household model has been challenged effectively through empirical evidence, including assumptions of shared preferences and interests, pooled incomes, and altruism as the guiding principle of intra-household allocations. Gender, in particular, is noted to be an important signifier of differences in interests, preferences, endowments, and allocations. In addition, the alternative of "bargaining models" of the household—bargaining power rather than altruism is seen as guiding intra-household allocations—developed.

---

[1] These verses are taken from folk songs sung by rural women in northwest India when the bride leaves her parent's home on marriage. *Doli* means palanquin, which traditionally carried the bride to her husband's home. I am grateful to Veena Das for sharing the second song with me some years ago.

Secondly, gender inequalities stem not only from differences in economic endowments between women and men but also from social norms and perceptions, meaning that the inequalities are also ideologically embedded. While norms and perceptions also impinge on other social inequalities like race and caste, gendered norms and perceptions cut across these categories and exist additionally.

Thirdly, gender inequalities not only pre-exist, new ones can arise from the foundations of the old ones, and people with prior advantage can set in place rules that perpetuate that advantage, such as rules governing new institutions now being promoted to manage common pool resources. Although based on principles of cooperation, such institutions can effectively exclude women from decision-making and any benefits. In other words, gender inequality can be in the process of constant recreation in new forms.

Gender inequality is thus a vast subject with a vast amount of literature on it, but some aspects are more neglected and hidden than others. It is on these aspects that I will now focus, namely:

1. Inequality in command over property – a notably neglected dimension;
2. Inequalities in social perceptions and social norms, the workings of which are often hidden but which have visible economic outcomes;
(the former is a significant material form of inequality, the latter a significant ideological form); and
3. How both of these dimensions can interactively create new inequalities. This will also throw light on the *process* of inequality creation.

In addition, I will illustrate how gender inequalities are simultaneously constituted in several arenas: the family, the community, the market, and the state. The bargaining approach provides a promising analytical framework for understanding how both the material and the ideological aspects of gender inequality can be challenged.

3 Gender Gap in Command Over Property

3.1 The Nature of the Gap

Consider first the issue of property. Economists have long emphasized the importance of property rights for incentives and efficiency, but relatively few have looked at the gender gap in command over property. Economic analysis and policies concerning women continue to be preoccupied with employment and education. In the process, inequality in command over property has largely been neglected, yet it is this aspect that remains one of the most important forms of persisting economic inequality between women and men—one which has a critical bearing not only on women's economic well-being but also on their social and political status.

The idea of "command" over property is more complex than it appears on the surface (for a detailed discussion, see Agarwal, 1994). First of all, it takes us away from the narrow legalistic way in which many think of property rights. Command over property implies not merely rights in law, but effective rights in practice. Equality in legal rights to own property need not guarantee equality in actual ownership. This is especially true of inheritance where the gap between law and practice can be vast.

In India, for example, women enjoy significant—and legal—inheritance rights, even if they are unequal to those of men (Agarwal, 1994). In practice, only a small percentage of women inherit. A sample survey of rural widows in 1991 by development sociologist Martha Chen found that only 13 percent of the surveyed women with landowning fathers inherited any land as daughters. And only 51 percent of widows whose deceased husbands owned land inherited any. Thus 87 percent of daughters and 49 percent of widows with legal claims did not inherit (cited in Agarwal, 1998).

Secondly, property advantage stems not only from ownership but also from effective control over it. Ownership alone does not always guarantee control. In many countries, even when women inherit something, they do not fully control what they receive. Some obstacles are social. For example, some cultures restrict women's public interactions in the public sphere and hence their ability to manage their property effectively. Other barriers can be legal. For instance, in Sri Lanka's Jaffna Province, a married Tamil woman, under local law, needs her husband's permission to lease out or sell her own property. Similar laws prevailed earlier in parts of Europe. The distinctions between law and practice—as well as between ownership and control—are thus especially critical for women.

Thirdly, property advantage can arise not only from private property but also from public property. For instance, in most societies today, control over wealth-generating public property is largely in male hands, be they managers in large corporations, or heads of government bureaucracies. Even in the former socialist USSR, although private property ownership was abolished, decision-making over public property remained mostly with men.

Fourly, men (as a gender, even if not all men as individuals) also largely control the instruments through which existing property advantages get perpetuated, such as institutions that enact and implement property laws (such as Parliament and the law courts) and the mechanisms of recruitment into bodies which control property.

Lastly, command over property can also significantly influence the institutions that shape ideas about gender, such as the media and educational as well as religious bodies. Predominantly male control over these institutions can thus affect the persistence of certain ideological assumptions about women's needs, work roles, capabilities, and so on.

Seen in this broad way, gender inequality in regard to command over property is thus important in both developing and developed countries. However, which form of property is important can differ by context, and in large parts of the developing world, arable land has a pre-eminent position, as outlined below.

3.2 The Importance of Land

In largely agrarian economies, arable land is the most valued form of property. It is wealth-creating, livelihood-sustaining, and status-enhancing. For most rural households, it provides security against poverty. Traditionally, it has been the basis of political power, social status, and even personal identity. That is why people often end up spending more on litigation over ancestral land than its economic value would justify. It is notable that even in parts of central Europe today, as urban labor markets stagnate, people are returning to land and rural livelihoods for survival, as recent work on Uzbekistan shows (Kandiyoti, 2003).

While the links between the access to land, economic well being, and social status are well recognized at the household level, their importance specifically for women has largely been neglected in both research and policy. The United Nations has long claimed that women own only 1 percent of the world's property, but they provide no data to back this claim. In fact, in most countries, large-scale surveys do not collect gender-disaggregated data for land or other assets. (Nepal is a recent exception where gender-disaggregated census data are now being collected.) Hence, in order to estimate women's access to land, we still have to depend mostly on small-scale surveys. These show, as noted, that few women own arable land and even fewer effectively control some. Why would this be the case?

First of all, there are the noted biases in inheritance. Second, even government transfers of public land instead of narrowing the gender gap in private property, are actually widening it by transferring titles almost only to men. This is true not only in India but in many other countries. In the Latin American agrarian reforms of the 1960s to the 1980s, for instance, less than 15 percent of the beneficiaries across eight countries were women. Recent shifts toward joint-titling remain regionally uneven (Deere and de Leon, 2001).

In China, although the law promises gender equality in use rights in the distribution of household responsibility land, in practice, a range of gender inequalities can emerge. For instance, since most women leave their village upon marriage and land re-adjustments are infrequent, many have to wait long periods for land to be allotted for them in their husband's village. They also face special problems on divorce or widowhood (e.g. Li, 1999). These problems could get compounded following the 1998 Land Management Law (LML) which has restricted readjustments by extending the duration of the household responsibility contract from 15 to 30 years (Li, 2003; Brown, 2003). According to Li (2003), figures derived from a survey undertaken by the All-China Women's Federation and the State Statistics Bureau of 2000 showed that 70 percent of people without their own land were women, and among these women, 20 percent had never held land, while the rest had lost their land due to marriage, divorce, or reallocation. It is as yet unclear to what extent the 2003

Rural Land Contracting Law (RLCL) can redress these gender inequalities.[2] Studies also show that typically officials get the husband to sign the contract for the family's land use allotments, embodying the assumptions of the unitary household model (Li, 1999).

The third source of land is potentially through the market. However, in many countries, rural land markets are limited, and in any case, given women's fewer financial resources, their access either by land purchase or lease is substantially more restricted than men's. Support from the state can enhance this access, say, through the provision of subsidized credit to groups of women, but only to a limited extent.

3.3 Implications of Women's Unequal Access to Land

The social and economic implications of this inequality can be wide-ranging. Millions of women in Asia, Africa, and Latin America depend critically on land for a livelihood. The process of agrarian change under which labor shifts from agriculture to non-agriculture has been slow and gender-biased. In many countries, more men than women have moved to non-farm jobs. Hence, a disproportionate number of those left dependent on land are women. In India today, relative to 53 percent of male workers, 75 percent of female workers are in agriculture, and the *gender gap is growing* (Agarwal, 2003).

As more men shift to non-farm work, *de facto* female-headed households also grow. Estimates for India and Bangladesh range from 20 to 35 percent. Many of these women bear growing responsibilities for running the farm, but could be seriously constrained by inadequate land rights.

Indeed a lack of effective land rights affects both welfare and productive efficiency. This is discussed in depth in my land rights book and recent papers (e.g. Agarwal, 1994; 2003), so I will only touch on some aspects here.

Welfare

Consider first, the welfare effects. These can be both direct and indirect. There is ample evidence that a household's property status does not automatically define the well-being of all its members. First, there is persistent gender inequality in the distribution of gains from household resources. In South Asia, this impinges even on allocations for food and health care. Land solely in men's hands, therefore, does not guarantee female welfare.

---

[2] For instance, on the one hand the RLCL further limits the practice of land readjustments, especially on account of population change. On the other hand, under this law, a collective cannot reassign land that is allotted to a woman if she later marries out of the village, unless the collective in her marital village allots land to her. Similarly, a collective cannot reassign land allotted to a woman during her marriage, if she divorces, unless she receives a new allotment in the village where she lives after divorce (Brown, 2003).

Women without their own land also face high risks of poverty in case of desertion, divorce, or widowhood. In parts of South Asia often widows deprived of their property shares by family members are found doing wage labor on the farms of well-off brothers or brothers-in-law. In Bangladesh, widows living as dependents of male relatives are found to face much greater mortality risks than those heading their own households and presumably owning some independent assets.

In China, I understand that in practice (even if not in law) divorced women lose their land allotments in their husbands' villages and may not easily get land allotted for them in their parental village when they return there, leaving them effectively landless and poverty prone. This is especially likely following the above mentioned 1998 Land Management Law which restricts the frequency and scope of land readjustments. This is likely to have negative implications for women marrying into another village or returning to their birth villages because of divorce or widowhood (Brown, 2003; Li, 2003).[3]

Indeed, in most countries, to the extent that women even of propertied household's own none themselves, their economic position remains vicarious: a well-placed marriage can raise it, but divorce or widowhood can lower it. Direct land access would provide a more certain means of welfare improvement and poverty reduction.

Second, land access would increase women's entitlement to family welfare. For elderly women, owning land can improve support from kin. As many elderly people say in India: "Without property children don't look after their parents well."

Third, land access has interlinked livelihood effects. For instance, it can improve credit and employment access. In South Asia, those with land are more likely to obtain credit and put it to viable use. In rural labor markets those with land are found more likely to get employment and higher wages. Also even a small plot is found to be a critical element in a *diversified livelihood system*. It can be used not just for crops, but also to grow trees for fruit or fuelwood, or fodder for animals, or a vegetable garden. In addition, it can be used to set up a micro-enterprise. The landed are found to do very much better than the landless, even in terms of rural non-farm activity.

Fourth, assets in women's hands can have inter-generational benefits. For a start, women are found to spend a much larger part of their earnings on family needs than men (Dwyer and Bruce, 1989). Several studies also show a positive link between children's welfare and the mother's assets. In Brazil, the effect on child survival probabilities was found to be almost 20 times greater when asset income accrued to the mother than when it accrued to the father (Thomas, 1990). In rural India, children were found more likely to attend school and get medical care if the mother had assets (Duraiswamy and Duraiswamy, 1991and 1992). On children's education, similar results obtain for Bangladesh, Indonesia, and Ethiopia (Quisumbing, 2003). It is no coincidence that in South Asia the best social indicators on health, education, and fertility are found in Kerala in India and Sri Lanka in general—regions where women historically enjoyed notable rights in land and other property.

---

[3] As elaborated in footnote 2, it is as yet difficult to say if these problems will get mitigated to some degree by the RLCL 2003.

Efficiency

Welfare aside, in several contexts there can be efficiency gains from gender-equal land access for several reasons. First, there is the issue of incentives. These are found to matter not only at the household level but also at the intra-household level.

In Kenya, for instance, the introduction of new weeding technology was found to raise crop yields on women's plots by 56 percent—plots from which women controlled the output—but it raised yields only by 15 percent on the men's plots where too women weeded but men got the proceeds (Elson, 1995). Second, there can be gender differences in preferences and efficiency of land use.

In Burkina Faso, due to their choice of cropping patterns, women achieved much higher values of output per hectare on their own plots than did their husbands on theirs (Udry et al., 1999). Similar research is needed in other regions.

Empowerment

Last but not least, land is found to empower women socially. It adds to their voice, their sense of identity, and their self-confidence. This is perhaps most graphically revealed in the voices of women themselves. In the Bodhgaya movement in Bihar (eastern India), when landless women in two villages received land for the first time, after they and their households had participated in an extended land struggle, they movingly recounted how having land of their own had empowered them (Alaka and Chetna 1987, p. 26):

> We had tongues but could not speak,
> We had feet but could not walk.
> Now that we have the land
> We have the strength to speak and walk.

I believe women in China responded in similar ways when the Agrarian Reform Law of 1947 gave them separate land deeds for the first time, as described by William Hinton (1972) in his book *Fanshen* (on this, see also, Croll, 1978).

Also, in recent analysis of a sample of 500 households in Kerala, a colleague and I found a dramatically lower incidence of marital violence where the woman owned land or a house than where she owned neither (Agarwal and Panda, 2003).

Indeed in mainly agrarian economies there are many pointers that enhancing women's land access would help improve not just equity but also family welfare, production efficiency, and women's bargaining power and sense of empowerment.

Having said this, however, I need to emphasize four points. One, there is scope for more empirical analysis in different regions of the world on the welfare and efficiency effects of women's property status. For instance, are the links between women's land access and incentives noted in Kenya also found in Asia or Latin America where the pattern of family-based farming is different? Are the links between mother's assets and child survival found in Brazil as important as in

Africa or Asia? Does women's ownership of property serve as a deterrent to domestic violence also in other countries? Two, although for illustration I have focused on land, my general purpose is to highlight the importance of property as such. In other contexts, a house may be as critical for economic and social security. Three, ownership confers only one form of right, but use rights, or rights of control, are also important. Indeed, in public property, what matters is not ownership but managerial control – the ability to make rules, be it for government-run enterprises or for the management of local common pool resources, such as forests.

Four, it is imperative that countries formulating new property laws do not repeat old biases. In post-apartheid South Africa, as well as in Central and Eastern Europe, Russia, and China, scholars are already expressing concerns about the creation of new gender inequalities in land and other assets (Verdery, 1996; Kandiyoti, 2003; Li, 2003). To move toward such equality often requires taking into account the social context within which the laws will be implemented, since many laws which might in principle be gender-neutral can become unequal due to pre-existing social biases.

4 Social Perceptions

The second form of gender inequality I will explore today is ideological as embedded in social perceptions and social norms. Although difficult to quantify and often hidden, these inequalities can affect economic outcomes for women in virtually every sphere, be it property rights, employment, or intra-household allocations. These inequalities remain understudied and under theorized.

First consider perceptions. There can be, and often is, a divergence between what a person actually contributes, needs, or is able to do, and perceptions about her contributions, needs, or abilities. In particular, a person's contributions and needs may be undervalued because of her gender or race, or both. This affects outcomes in the market, the family, the community, and the State (Agarwal, 1997).

In the labor market, for instance, gender, like race, often defines perceptions about abilities. The work that women do is often labeled "unskilled" and that which men do as "skilled," even if the tasks require equal skill. Or women are perceived as having lesser ability or commitment; or as being supplementary earners and men as being the breadwinners. Such assumptions often underlie discriminatory hiring and pay practices. Women on account of their gender may thus be paid less than men with the same abilities, for the same tasks.

Perceptions also guide intra-family allocations. For example, who gets what is often justified by referring to a person's contributions or needs. But a person's contributions may be undervalued because of gender, or because the work is less "visible." Home-based or unwaged work done mostly by women is often less valued than work which is more "visible" in physical or monetary terms.

Female members would thus receive less than males because their contributions to the household are perceived as being less—what Amartya Sen terms "perceived contribution response" (Sen, 1990). Equally, women and girls may receive less because they are seen as needing less—what I term "perceived need response" (Agarwal, 1997). Systematic undervaluation of women's contributions or needs in systems where these are important distributive principles can thus reinforce gender-related deprivation. Such undervaluation is not confined to developing countries. Research on American households indicates that women doing paid work have more bargaining power than housewives because housework is culturally devalued (England and Kilbourne, 1990).

Perceptions, similarly influence community responses, and hinder women from participating in collective activity. For instance, in my current research on forest management in the villages of India and Nepal, men typically exclude women from decision-making because they perceive them as making little contribution. Some characteristic responses are: "Women can't make any helpful suggestions," or "Women are illiterate. If they come to meetings, we men might as well stay at home ..." I found that often the men who said this were themselves illiterate. Hence, their response clearly had more to do with their *perceptions* about gender differences in abilities rather than with *actual* gender differences in abilities.

The government's public policy is similarly affected by perceptions. For instance, that governments transfer land almost solely to men, even when women are significant farmers, has much to do with perceptions about, rather than the universal fact of male responsibility and female dependency. Similarly, perceptions can make women's public presence invisible. For instance, in matrilineal Meghalaya, when I asked officials why even in this society where traditionally women had property claims, they did not allot plots to women, I was told: "Women can't come to our office to fill out papers." Yet outside their windows, numerous women traders were selling their wares!

Indeed perceptions underlie many assumptions in economic analysis and policy. On the one hand they constitute gender inequality in ideational terms; on the other hand they can lead to gender unequal material outcomes.

5 Social Norms

Like perceptions, gendered social norms embody an important form of ideological inequality. Conventionally, few economists explicitly recognized the importance of social norms. Recent literature on social capital emphasizes the positive side of social norms. Norms are seen to reduce transactions costs and enhance economic efficiency.

But are all social norms good? Not at all. Many social norms can also have a "dark" side, especially for women. Within the home, norms define the gender division of labor and goods. For instance, everywhere norms define housework and childcare as mainly women's work, and in many rural areas this is also the case for firewood collection and cattle care. Hence, firewood or fodder shortages adversely affect women more than men. Domestic responsibilities also undermine women's ability to participate in public decision-making, which may involve lengthy meetings at inconvenient times. Hence, a common response by rural women is that they don't have time to sit around for several hours in a meeting in the middle of the day.

Again, in north India, norms determine that males should eat before females and/or get more and better quality food. This makes for gender differences in nourishment and growth (Agarwal, 1994). I believe this is also the case in parts of China. For instance, Elizabeth Croll in her recent book, *Endangered daughters*, quotes a young girl as saying: "My mom, no matter what happened, always considered my elder brother first and ignored me. At the table, she kept putting food into my brother's bowl and not mine, as if I were not her own child" (Croll, 2004, p. 145).

Outside the household, social norms restrict women's earning options by discouraging (or even preventing) them from working outside the home, limiting the range of tasks they may perform, placing double burdens of work on them, institutionalizing lower wages for them, and so on. For instance, in many societies, norms restrict women's mobility and public interaction. In northern South Asia, women of *good character* are expected to avoid village spaces where men congregate. Hence, while male farmers can sit in teashops and strike deals with other men for hiring labor or selling their crop, women farmers cannot do the same (Agarwal, 1994). Similarly, a fear of reputation loss or reprimand from families makes women uncomfortable going to public meetings, unless men invite them. As a group of women in north India told Britt (1993): "The meetings are considered for men only. Women are never called" (p. 148).

Social norms also govern female behavior: in many societies, women are usually expected to be soft spoken and to sit on one side in public meetings where they are less visible and audible. All this makes them less effective in public forums. Again, in most societies, norms dictate that women rather than men relocate on marriage or job shifts. In both India and China, it is women who typically go to the husband's village or home under the *cong fu ju* marriage custom.

Basically, gendered social perceptions and social norms embody inequalities which are hidden, sometimes difficult to name, often impossible to quantify. Yet they centrally affect material outcomes for women, impinging both on their employment and property status.

6 Emergent Inequalities: Community Forestry

Gender inequalities in property endowments, norms and perceptions form the bedrock of pre-existing material and ideological disadvantage and their persistence can create new inequalities. Consider examples from community forestry and collective action in India and Nepal, where I have done detailed fieldwork (Agarwal, 2000; 2001).

Forests and commons have always been important sources of basic needs such as fuel wood, fodder, and other items for rural households, but because women often lack private property resources such as land and since social norms make firewood and fodder gathering mainly women's responsibility, their dependence on the commons is greater than that of men.

Traditionally, rights in local forests were based on village citizenship. Access to these communal resources thus mitigated, to some degree, inequalities in private property. However, to reduce deforestation, governments in many countries today (including developed ones, such as the Scandinavian countries and Canada) are involving communities in local forest management. Certainly, community forestry groups (CFGs) are mushrooming across South Asia today. Most are state-initiated under the Joint Forest Management (JFM) program launched in 1990, in which government and villagers share the costs and benefits from protection. There are over 64,000 JFM groups in India alone, in addition to self-initiated groups.

The JFM groups have a two-tier management structure: a general body (GB) which can draw members from the whole village and an executive committee (EC) of nine to15 persons. Both bodies interactively define the rules for forest use, the punishments for abuse, and the methods of protection and benefit distribution. Who has a voice in the GB and EC depends on who gains or loses from these initiatives.

These groups are based on modern ideas of cooperation and participation and are meant to include all villagers, but many have excluded significant sections, such as women, from their decision-making and main benefit-sharing. For instance, in many Indian states the criteria for GB membership is one person per household. Although technically gender neutral, it is usually men alone who join, since they are seen as the household heads.

But even where women can become members, few attend meetings or speak up at them due to restrictive social norms and perceptions. Women often explain this as follows (quoted in Agarwal, 2001):

> Men don't listen. They feel they should be the spokespersons.
> When we open our mouths, men shout us down.

Or take a male response:

> I am a man, I attend the meeting. If I am prepared to make the female members of my family act according to what I say, why should they attend the meeting?

These "participatory exclusions" as I term them—meaning exclusions within seemingly participative institutions—have other negative consequences. Without women's participation, the rules framed for forest use tend to take little account of their concerns. Typically CFGs ban forest entry. This affects women more than men. Men mostly use the forest for small timber for agricultural implements or house building – both are sporadic needs, and purchase is also an option. Women need the forests almost daily for firewood and fodder, and for most women, the firewood purchase is not an option because they have limited control over cash, and firewood is not easily available for purchase in the rural areas. Hence, women are the worst affected by a ban on entry.

In some regions, women who spent 1 to 2 hours for a head load of firewood before a forest closure ended up spending 4 to 5 hours after the closure. Journeys of half a kilometer grew to several kilometers. Even though the forests have regenerated over time, the strict restrictions on extractions often continue. Firewood extractions are sometimes as low as 10 to 15 percent of sustainable limits (Agarwal, 2002). Hence, even several years into protection, firewood shortages persist in most cases. Paradoxically, as some poor women in one Indian village told me: "Earlier too there was a shortage but not as acute."

Most women have switched in varying degrees to using crop waste, and some even use weeds as supplementary cooking fuel. These firewood substitutes take more time to ignite and keep alight, thus increasing cooking time. They also seriously increase smoke-related health risks both for women and for infants playing in smoky kitchens.

Benefits from the regenerated resource are, however, largely male-controlled. To begin with, any cash generated typically goes into a community fund controlled by men and is mostly used for purposes from which women tend not to benefit, such as for purchasing rugs, drums, or community utensils which the men use or lease out, or for travel to other villages, and so on. Where benefits are distributed in cash or kind, entitlements are usually linked to membership and to contributions toward protection. Thus, non-member households—mostly the poor—are excluded with this exclusion especially affecting poor women. Also, implicitly embodying the assumptions of a unitary household, benefit shares are on a household basis. Hence, even if both spouses are members, they get only one share.

Inequities arise too from the distributive principles followed. Distribution can be market determined (willingness to pay) or by contribution, or need. While seemingly neutral, these principles have notable gender (and class) bias since people differ in their ability to pay or to contribute, or in their needs. In practice, distribution is usually by contribution and sometimes by sale. Sales adversely affect women more than men, since women have fewer financial means. Although, even distribution by contribution can prove inequitable where social norms bar women from critical forms of contribution, such as doing patrol duty to guard the forest.

Not surprisingly, women, especially the poor, often resent the closures. Some common responses are: "What forest? ... Since the men have started protecting it, they don't even allow us to look at it!" Or "The community forest belongs to the men. We own nothing." The new arrangements are thus creating a system of property rights in communal land which—like existing rights in privatized land—are strongly male-centered and inequitable.

Here new gender inequality is being created through male control of public property and the rules that govern its use. All the rules are gender neutral on the surface. But they become unequal when filtered through the prism of pre-existing inequalities.[4] And much of this remains hidden—most evaluations deem the CFGs to be success stories of decentralized management and participative community involvement.

7 Reducing the Inequalities

How can the noted inequalities be reduced in both their material and ideological forms? A promising analytical framework for examining the prospect for change is that of bargaining. In terms of this framework—women's ability to change rules, norms, perceptions, and property distribution in a gender-progressive direction— would depend especially on their bargaining power with the state, the community, and the family, as the case may be (Agarwal, 1997).

Traditionally, economists have applied ideas about bargaining within the game-theoretic mode and with little attention to gender. Recent interest in intra-household gender dynamics has yielded some interesting formulations of bargaining models. However, these ideas have been applied very little to gender-related bargaining in extra-household arenas. Inadequate attention has also been paid to qualitative factors that can affect bargaining outcomes.

In my discussion, at least two types of shifts from the standard approach appear necessary: first, taking account of qualitative factors, such as social norms and perceptions, that have particular gender implications; and second, extending the framework to include non-household, non-market arenas, such as the state and the community. Both extensions need a less restrictive formulation than that of a formal game-theoretic model. Here it is useful to distinguish between a bargaining *approach* and formal models. A bargaining approach that is not constrained by the structure that formal modeling requires would allow us to more freely apply concepts, such as bargaining power, to new arenas and also allows us a freer engagement with qualitative factors.

In the present discussion, applying the bargaining approach to interactions within three major arenas—the state, the community, and the family—is especially relevant. It is relevant whether we are concerned with land rights, social norms, or community forestry. The question, then, is how we enhance women's bargaining power in these different arenas. As I have discussed both in a theoretical paper and in another work, the determinants of women's bargaining power could vary by context

---

[4] There is an interesting parallel with the Chinese context. Under the new rural land management and contract laws, for readjusting arable land or grassland under special circumstances during the contract period, approval is needed from two-third of the members of the village assembly or two-thirds of the village representatives, as well as from the township government and the county government responsible for agriculture (Brown, 2003). These public decision-making bodies are noted to be male dominated (Li, 2003, p.3), so that women's need for land readjustment are less likely to get adequate attention, thus compounding existing gender inequalities.

and could include their group strength, their command over economic resources, their support from external agents, such as the state and NGOs, and their enabling social norms and social perceptions (Agarwal, 1997; 2001). However, at least two factors appear important for all three arenas for different contexts: external agent support and the women's group strength. For illustration, again consider community forestry.

Community forestry experience indicates that pressure from external agents such as NGOs, donors, and key individuals can prove significant in changing the initial rules of entry at the state level. For example, several states in India have now made their membership rules more gender-inclusive by instituting that one man and one woman can be members of the GB, instead of only one person per household. Here village women did not need to bargain explicitly for change. External agent support and the larger women's movement gave village women implicit bargaining power vis-à-vis the state.

However, bargaining with the community to ensure that women have more voice in CFG forums is more difficult. Here again external agent support has helped to some extent. For instance, some NGOs have used their bargaining power on women's behalf to insist that meetings would be held only if men invited the women. Women on being so invited often turn up in strength. Not all regions, however, have external agents committed to gender equality. A larger and sustained impact needs women's own input.

Ground experience suggests that to have more voice in mixed forums and to challenge restrictive social norms, women would need—for a start: (1) a critical mass of vocal women; and (2) a sense of group identity.

In many villages, the women I interviewed stressed: "without a good majority of women present, it is impossible to express opinions." The importance of a critical mass has also been noted in the western context. A study of Scandinavian women politicians found that as women became a significant percentage (say 30 percent or more) in Parliament or local councils, there was less stereotyping and open exclusion by men, a less aggressive tone in discussions, a greater accommodation of family obligations in scheduling meetings, and more weight given to women's policy concerns (Dahlerup, 1988).

However, in South Asia, an additional step appears necessary: namely, building women's self-confidence in public interactions and increasing their sense of group identity. One way by which this is being attempted in India is by women's credit and self-help groups. Such groups are found to enhance women's self-confidence and collective identity. They also tend to improve male perceptions about women's capabilities and weaken restrictive social norms. The following responses from women I interviewed are fairly typical: "Initially men objected to our going to meetings, but our women's group helped men understand better. When we women became united in the women's group and men saw we were doing good work, that also helped."

These factors also help in bargaining within the family. Again, I quote from my interviews with rural women in India:

> There were one or two men who objected to their wives attending our meetings …. But when our women's association came to their aid, the men let their wives go.
> My husband feels I contribute financially, take up employment, obtain credit for the home. This increases his respect for me.

In fact, these experiences are common to many women's groups across South Asia, namely that women's collective strength and visible contributions, along with external agent support, can change at least some norms and perceptions. Of course, certain norms, such as the gender division of domestic work and gender inequalities in property, are more difficult to alter. To have an impact on them, a deeper structural change would be needed.

8 Concluding Remarks

Gender inequality takes both material and ideological forms. A critical yet neglected dimension of the material form is embedded in who commands public and private property, especially land. A critical hidden dimension of the ideological form involves social norms and perceptions. The interactive effects of these gender disadvantages can lead to the creation of new inequalities.

Of course, which type of property is central, or the specific nature of norms and perceptions, can vary by country as well as culture. However, the fact of their importance everywhere is indisputable, as is the need to enhance women's bargaining power through collective action for mitigating such inequalities. In academic terms, understanding how such collective action among women and among progressive groups can emerge and sustain is a challenge both for gender economics and for the social sciences more generally. In policy terms, there is a challenge here for outlining new strategies for social change and forging new alliances to carry such change forward.

References

Agarwal, B., *A Field of One's Own: Gender and Land Rights in South Asia* (Cambridge: Cambridge University Press, 1994).

———, ' "Bargaining" and Gender Relations: Within and Beyond the Household', *Feminist Economics*, 3 (1) (1997): 1-50.

———, 'Widows versus Daughters or Widows as Daughters? Property, Land and Economic Security in Rural India', *Modern Asian Studies*, 32 (1) (1998): 1-48.

———, 'Conceptualizing Environmental Collective Action: Why Gender Matters', *Cambridge Journal of Economics*, 24 (3) (2000): 283-310.

———, 'Participatory Exclusions, Community Forestry and Gender: An Analysis and Conceptual Framework', *World Development*, 29 (10) (2001): 1623-1648.

————, 'Gender Inequality, Cooperation and Environmental Sustainability' (paper presented at a workshop on 'Inequality, Collective Action and Environmental Sustainability', Working Paper 02-10-058, Santa Fe Institute, New Mexico, 2002).

————, 'Gender and Land Rights Revisited: Exploring New Prospects via the State, the Family and the Market', *Journal of Agrarian Change*, 3 (1&2) (2003): 184-224.

Agarwal, B. and Panda, P., 'Home and the World: Revisiting Violence', *Indian Express* (August, 2003): 9.

Alaka and Chetna, 'When Women get Land - A Report from Bodhgaya', *Manushi*, 40 (1987): 25-26.

Britt, C., 'Out of the Wood? Local Institutions and Community Forest Management in two Central Himalayan Villages' (Ithaca: Cornell University, monograph, 1993).

Brown, J., 'Protecting Women's Land Rights through RLCL Implementing Regulations' (mimeo, Seattle, Washington DC: Rural Development Institute, 2003).

Croll, E., *Feminism and Socialism in China* (London: Routledge and Kegan Paul, 1978).

————, *Endangered Daughters: Discrimination and Development in Asia* (London and New York: Routledge, 2000).

Dahlerup, D., 'From a Small to a Large Majority: Women in Scandinavian Politics', *Scandinavian Political Studies*, 11 (4) (1988): 275-298.

Deere, C., Deere, D. and de Leon, M., *Empowering Women: Land and Property Rights in Latin America* (Pittsburg: Pittsburg University Press, 2001).

Duaraisamy, P. and Malathy, R., 'Impact of Public Programs on Fertility and Gender Specific Investment in Human Capital of Children in Rural India: Cross Sectional and Time Series Analyses', in T. Schultz (eds): *Population Economics*, Vol. 7 (Greenwich, CT: JAI Press, 1991), pp.157-187.

Duncan, T., 'Intra-household Resource Allocation: An Inferential Approach', *Journal of Human Resources*, 25 (4) (1990): 635-663.

Duraisamy, P., 'Gender, Intrafamily Allocations of Resources and Child Schooling in South India' (Economic Growth Center Discussion Paper No. 667, New Haven, CT: Yale University, 1992).

Dwyer, D. and Judith, B., (eds) *A Home Divided: Women and Income Control in the Third World* (Stanford: Stanford University Press, 1989).

Elson, D., 'Gender Awareness in Modelling Structural Adjustment', *World Development*, 23 (11) (1995): 1851-1868.

England, P. and Kilbourne, B., 'Markets, Marriages and other Mates: The Problem of Power', in R. Friedman and A. F. Robertson (eds), *Beyond the Market: Rethinking Economy and Society* (New York: Aldine de Gruyter, 1990).

Hinton, W., *Fanshen: A Documentary of Revolution in a Chinese Village* (Harmondsworth, Middlesex: Penguin Books Ltd, 1972).

Kandiyoti, D., 'The Cry for Land: Agrarian Reform, Gender and Land rights in Uzbekistan,' *Journal of Agrarian Change*, 3 (1&2) (2003): 225-256.

Li, Z., 'Changing Land and Housing Use by Rural Women in Northern China', in I. Tinker and G. Summerfield (eds), *Women's Rights to House and land: China, Laos, Vietnam* (Boulder and London: Lynne Rienner Publishers, 1999).

————, 'Women's Land Tenure Rights in Rural China: A Synthesis' (mimeo, Ford Foundation, Beijing, 2003).

Quisumbing, A.R. and Maluccio, A.J., 'Resources at Marriage and Intrahousehold Allocation: Evidence from Bangladesh, Ethiopia, Indonesia, and South Africa,' *Oxford Bulletin of Economics and Statistics*, 65 (3) (2003): 283-328.

Sen, A.K., 'Gender and Cooperative Conflicts', in Irene Tinker (ed.) *Persistent Inequalities: Women and World Development* (New York: Oxford University Press, 1990), pp.123-149.

Udry, C., Hoddinott, J., Alderman, H. and Haddad, L., 'Gender Differentials in Farm Productivity: Implications for Household Efficiency and Agricultural Policy', *Food Policy*, 20 (5) (1995): 407-423.

Verdery, K., *What Was Socialism, and What Comes Next* (New Jersey: Princeton University Press, 1996).

Chapter 3

Women's Status in the Household in Rural China: Does Market Labor Matter?

Fiona MacPhail
Xiao-Yuan Dong

1 Introduction

China had achieved considerable gender equality in the workplace in terms of a relatively high female labor force participation rate and a lower gender wage gap, compared to other countries during the Mao era (Croll, 1995). The rapid economic growth in the reform period has brought new choices and opportunities to women, especially rural residents. The township and village enterprises (TVEs), which employed 54.4 million women in 1996, about 41 percent of all TVE workers (UNDP, 1999), have been a major source of new wage employment for women in rural areas. Economic diversification of the rural economy has also increased opportunities for self-employment in agricultural sideline activities and there has been considerable migration to urban areas (de Brauw et al., 2002; Jacka, 1997).

While "holding-up half the sky" in the workplace, women in China, like women around the world, perform the majority of domestic labor contributing to the general welfare of their families and society. Domestic labor, however, tends to be not only invisible in economic accounting schemes but undervalued even by the people benefiting directly from the labor. Despite women's responsibilities for both market and domestic labor, men still have control over household decision making (Bao, 2002).[1]

The gender division of domestic labor in China has been remarkably resistant to change. The Maoist revolution improved Chinese women's status (Li, 1995; Rofel, 1994), but failed to bring about a change in the gendered division of labor despite increases in women's participation in waged work and educational campaigns designed to encourage men to undertake domestic labor (Croll, 1983; Wolf, 1985; Stacey, 1983). Traditional views of gender roles in the Chinese society have re-emerged in public in the post-reform era. For example, in a recent survey, the majority of men thought that "a man should devote himself to building up a

---

[1] Also, as Elson (1999) notes in general, the unequal division of responsibilities for housework also affects the amount of leisure women have and weakens women's positions in the labor market in terms of earnings and occupations.

career while a woman's role should be at home," and yet, the majority of women reported being opposed to the traditional idea of the family (China Daily, 2002).

There have been constant calls for returning women to the home (Beijing Review, 2001); women are reported to have experienced disproportionate layoffs and greater difficulty entering or re-entering the labor market than men (Maurer-Fazio, Rawski, and Zhang, 1999). The market reforms have also eroded state protections for female employees and consequently, while the gender gap in work hours has narrowed,[2] the earnings gap has increased (Ho et al., 2002).

In this chapter, we investigate how women's market work affects their status in the household in rural China within a bargaining view of the household. While bargaining models of the household predict a positive link between resources and well-being (Alderman et al., 1995; Agarwal, 1997), the narrowing gender gap in labor force participation does not automatically lead to a reduction in gender inequality.[3] The evidence from time budget studies, for example, indicates that the gendered division of housework often does not adjust adequately to changes in the time allocation between men and women in the workplace (Elson, 1999). The result is that women in the labor force have less time for leisure than their male counterparts (UNDP, 1999).

We examine the relationship between market labor and status in rural China, where status is reflected by domestic labor time, responsibility for domestic tasks and household decision-making influence. We first examine women's and men's views about the status of women, market labor, and domestic labor, as well as how domestic work is shared between men and women in the context of rural China where there has been growth in wage earning opportunities for both men and women. We then empirically assess the impact of women's participation in waged work in the TVE sector on their domestic work burdens (time and responsibility) and decision-making influence in the household. With respect to domestic labor time, our analysis focuses on two particular questions: (1) are female workers able to substitute market labor time for domestic labor time? And (2) does market labor, which generates visible financial resources, enable women to reduce their domestic labor time? Related to this second question, we ask whether financial resources derived from paid work also enable women to affect responsibility for domestic tasks and enable them to gain greater control over household decisions.

The chapter draws upon a specially designed survey of over 750 people working in TVEs in rural areas of the provinces of Jiangsu and Shandong in 1999 and 2000. Given that the survey was designed with these research questions in mind, the data set offers a rich source of information and permits an analysis of not

---

[2] According to a nation-wide urban household survey by the National Statistical Bureau, during 1997 to 2001 when the state industry underwent labor force restructuring, weekly work hours increased from 42.9 to 45.0 hours for women and from 43.9 to 45.7 hours for men (Yang, 2003).

[3] This hypothesis has been quite widely supported in various countries (for micro level studies, see, Hoddinott and Haddad 1995, and for a macro level study see, Sen 1990).

only the absolute amount of time allocated to domestic labor (and market labor) but also the gendered division of responsibility for domestic tasks and household decision making, along with a useful set of control variables such as living arrangements, presence of children, and socio-economic characteristics of key household members. Second, the sample size is quite large compared to other case studies; and third, the relationship between market labor and financial resources and household status has not been widely explored in China.[4]

In the next section, we selectively review the literature on domestic and paid labor in China and features of household bargaining models from the broader literature, which guide our analysis of the relationship between market labor and women's status. The data are described in section 3. In section 4, we discuss perceptions of women's status and the meanings of market and domestic labor reported by men and women. In addition, we develop and estimate a model to explain the absolute amount of domestic labor, gendered division of responsibility for domestic tasks, and household decision making. The significance of the key finding, that market labor is important to women and affects their status, is discussed in section 5.

2 Overview of Domestic Labor, Paid Labor, and Status of Women

Women in China and around the world undertake the majority of domestic labor. While some domestic tasks can be personally satisfying, many domestic tasks are unrewarding and time consuming, leaving little time for leisure. The adverse implications for women's status is accentuated in a situation where domestic labor is undervalued compared to other forms of labor. Thus, the greater amount of domestic labor time, greater responsibility for domestic tasks, and lower household decision-making influence of women (compared to men) are viewed as indicators of women's lower status in the household. In this chapter, the relationship between resources and status is viewed within a bargaining perspective of the household where access to resources, constrained by a broader system of norms, may enable individuals to influence household decisions and domestic labor.

In order to develop a framework for this case study of domestic labor and the status of women in Shandong and Jiangsu, we selectively review the literature on market labor, domestic labor, and household bargaining models in the following sub-sections.

2.1 Market Labor

China has one of the highest female labor force participation rates in the world with about 84 percent of women (between the ages of 15 and 60) in the labor force,

---

[4] For an exception, see Song (2000), which focuses upon consumption patterns and gender within a bargaining perspective.

and women comprise about 45 percent of the entire labor force (Liu, 2000). Although women participate in great numbers in the labor force, they tend to work in lower levels of the hierarchy and many authors argue that discrimination against women has increased in the reform period in terms of recruitment, layoffs, and required early retirement in the state-owned sector (Summerfield, 1994; Zhou, 1997; Howell, 2003; Dong et al., 2002).

In rural areas, people have increasingly become involved in productive activities outside of agriculture including wage employment in the TVEs, agricultural sideline businesses, and wage employment gained through migration (de Brauw et al., 2002). TVEs were originally owned by township and village governments and underwent privatization in the late 1990s. While the TVE sector has been a growing source of wage employment for women in the rural sector, within the TVEs considerable industrial and occupational segregation by gender exists; in terms of occupation, for example, women are most likely to be employed as production workers and disproportionately excluded from the higher-skilled and -paid occupations.[5] Whether women maintain these jobs in rural TVEs after marriage varies across locations. Privatization of TVEs is reported to have accentuated gender divisions within the workplace by widening the gender gap in income, wealth, and decision making, and increasing discrimination against women in terms of earnings and employment opportunities (Dong et. al., 2004).

In summary, women have been involved in market work to a greater extent than in other countries, although it has often been in lower levels of the hierarchy compared to men, and the TVEs in rural areas have been an important employer of women. With ongoing market reforms, women's positions have been jeopardized through disproportionate layoffs and discrimination. Thus, we examine aspects of market labor, namely, income generated from, and hours of market labor in, the TVE sector, as well as views about the importance of the market labor. Market labor, while being important in its own right, is considered here because it may influence the gendered division of labor within households and patterns of household decision making, if the resources derived from market labor enable women to negotiate changes within the household, as discussed further in Section 2.3.

2.2 Domestic Labor

Despite dramatic changes in women's paid labor since the 1950s, there has been little change in the sexual division of labor in the home, and women remain responsible for domestic tasks (Croll, 1983; Thakur, 1996; Wolf, 1985). Jacka (1997) reports that there is only mention of a male in the family doing any domestic labor in about one-third of households in her sample in rural China. Women are much more likely to report undertaking the main household tasks such

---

[5] Liu (2000), for example, reports that only 8 percent of women are employed in occupations requiring "skill" and not physical labor.

as cooking, looking after children and elderly, and cleaning (Sun, 1995, reported in Yu and Chau, 1997; Croll, 1983). While the nature of domestic work varies across contexts, Jacka (1997) suggests that, for rural women in China, the main domestic tasks are viewed as cooking, cleaning, washing, shopping, and tending to domestic livestock, with child care and sewing and mending being considered either domestic work or closely associated with domestic work.

In terms of time, women allocate considerably more hours to domestic work than men. For example, women and men report 5 and 2.8 hours per day, respectively (Cheung and Tao, 1993, cited in Yu and Chau, 1997).[6] The actual reported amount of time will depend, however, upon the categories of tasks considered and how simultaneous tasks, such as cooking and childcare, are aggregated. A study undertaken by the All China Women's Federation (ACWF) indicates that 85 percent of all housework in China is undertaken by women (Donohoe, 2001). The amount of time spent is likely to vary with a point in an individual's life cycle and family composition, and in general, the amount tends to be underestimated.

Women have increased their role in decision making in the family, compared to the past when men made all the decisions. A recent national survey conducted by the ACWF shows that 57 percent of wives have greater control than their husband on daily expenditure items. However, on bigger items only 7 percent of wives have the greater control of the decisions (Bao, 2002). Decision-making patterns of married men and women are further complicated by the influence of fathers and other older relatives. Zhang (2002) argues that the proportion of family income controlled by women is greater for young generations than for older ones and that women are increasingly involved in making decisions about selling agricultural products, investing, and purchasing large items such as houses and consumer durables.

Despite the substantial amount of time allocated to domestic labor, it is generally argued that the contributions are not highly valued in the family (Yu and Chai, 1997). Jacka (1997), reporting on interviews with peasants and rural cadres in China, indicates that domestic work is viewed as less important than other work, because it is unproductive and unremunerated, and conducted in the inside, rather than the outside sphere. So while women are generally perceived to have social status within the family and men in the public sphere, women's contributions are undervalued. Jacka (1997) notes that women themselves recognize the value of their own domestic labor to the household (see also Wolf, 1985).

The state, in different periods, has tried to influence the gendered division of labor. The socialist economic revolution and anti-Confucianism campaign under Mao resulted in women being incorporated in the productive sphere (although not on equal terms) and some collectivization of domestic tasks; there was an education campaign to encourage men to participate in domestic labor (Croll,

---

[6] A study by Xia (1989), cited by Bu and McKeen (2000), reports that female workers average 3.7 hours per day on housework in contrast to 2.2 hours per day for male workers.

1983). In the reform period, there has been a shift in state ideology and the state has promoted more traditional gender roles. As White, Howell, and Shang (1996, p. 75) state, "the new construction of women's role in society looks backwards to the pre-liberation models and yet is parcelled in the rational jargon of the market." The state appears willing to accept women's double burden as indicated by policies of the ACWF which promote women's responsibilities for happy, healthy, and harmonious families. Further, the state may be actively encouraging the return of women to the home to reinforce traditional roles (Hooper, 1998).[7]

The gendered division of labor within the household may also change over time, as a result of family size, composition, and household technologies, although not always in obvious ways. Decreases in the number of children may reduce the amount of childcare and overall domestic labor. Since it also reduces the number of carers and domestic workers, it can increase the domestic burden for individual women. The decrease in overall family size due to increase in prevalence of the nuclear family (Zhang, 2002; for exceptions, see Davis and Harrell, 1993) may actually increase the domestic work of women if grandmothers are no longer available to share domestic responsibilities. Also, the amount of time may decline for those women with access to electricity, running water, and appliances (Jacka, 1997). Although, studies in industrialized countries suggest that the availability of appliances has changed norms of domestic labor more than it has reduced the time commitments.

In this study, we examine the gendered division of labor in which women perform the majority of undervalued domestic labor and have lower decision-making control as influenced by patriarchal norms. While the gendered division of labor changed little in urban China under Mao, despite educational campaigns and women's access to paid employment. We examine the relationship between paid labor and domestic labor in selected rural areas during the reform period, in a time when family size is smaller and labor-saving technologies are more available.

2.3 Household Bargaining Models

The allocation of individuals' time and commodities within households have been analyzed within economics using bargaining models of the household. Within neoclassical economics, bargaining models have increasingly replaced the unitary model of the household (Becker, 1981), given the theoretical limitations of the unitary model (Folbre, 1986a; 1986b) and the lack of empirical support for its hypotheses (Thomas, 1990; Hoddinot and Haddad, 1995; Phipps and Burton, 1998). While bargaining models postulate that individual household members may

---

[7] For example, campaigns of the AWCF have focused upon women's roles in the home as mothers and wives.

have common and separate interests, they vary as to the proposed mechanism underlying the allocation of resources.[8]

It is also recognized that the relationship between the intrahousehold allocation of resources and economic factors, the success of bargaining, is affected by a wider system of norms, structures, and ideology (Sen, 1990; Agarwal, 1997; Kandiyoti, 1998). Kandiyoti (1998, p. 136) argues "that bargaining always takes place in the context of 'rules of the game' implicit in different systems of kinship defining the nature of conjugal contracts (Whitehead, 1981), residence and inheritance rules." The basic hypothesis is that, within a given context of rules defining the conjugal contract, increases in women's bargaining power enable them to attain greater gender equity or a more favorable outcome for themselves and their children. For example, in rural China, Song (2000) shows that women's bargaining power affects household consumption decisions; more specifically, the higher women's education relative to her partner's, the greater the share of household income is spent on children's education and clothing, and the lower the share on alcohol and cigarettes. Norms, as Agarwal (1997, p. 15) argues, can limit what can be bargained over, act as a constraint to bargaining power, be the "subject of negotiation," as well as influencing "how the process of bargaining is conducted."

In this study, we view women's ability to use their financial resources to negotiate more favorable outcomes in the household as being constrained by the overarching patriarchal system; for example, similar increases in resources for men and women are unlikely to bring about equal improvements in outcomes.[9] Further, the impact of a change in resources on an outcome such as the gendered division of domestic labor may be negligible, given that it may require altering perceptions of appropriate gender roles which may be strongly held, particularly with the rise in Confucianism. While we do not directly analyze the nature of the rules of sharing within the household, we do explore whether differences in economic circumstances of women and men affect their domestic labor times, domestic labor responsibility, and household decision-making control.

---

[8] The models can be categorized into one of two groups depending upon the mechanism assumed for how resources are allocated. In earlier cooperative models, resources are allocated in accordance with individuals' relative threat points or fallback positions (Manser and Brown, 1980; McElroy, 1990). Later noncooperative models take more account of gender roles and how individuals respond to each other's contributions (Lundberg and Pollak, 1993; Hoddinott and Haddad, 1995; Chen and Woolley, 2001).

[9] As Katz (1991, p. 42) states "a feminist household theory would thus contend that gender 'impinges' on households in such a way as to limit the bargaining power that women in particular can derive from access to resources outside the family."

3 Data and Approach

The data used in this chapter are derived from the fieldwork undertaken in three counties in the provinces of Jiangsu and Shandong in 1999 and 2000.[10] Both provinces had been leaders in the development of collective rural industries prior to privatization in the late 1990s. The three counties, Penglai and Yanzhou in Shandong, and Wujin in Jiangsu, are above the national and their respective provincial average per capita income levels, although the income levels of the three counties vary, with Wujin being the highest and Yanzhou the lowest. For a variety of reasons, including slowing output and employment growth and increased competition from the private sector, the local governments, in conformity with national policy, undertook major privatization programs of their TVEs in the period 1996-98.

The fieldwork reported in this chapter involved a survey of workers in 45 TVEs.[11] Approximately 25 employees (mainly production workers but also some technical, sales, and mid-level managerial personnel) in each of the enterprises participated in the worker survey; while this generated 1125 questionnaires, our sample size is 770 because we focus only on those workers who are married.[12]

Based upon a survey questionnaire, we obtained information on workers in four broad categories. Demographically, we gathered data on each worker's age, marital status, number of children, years of education, and work history. For market labor we collected data on the number of hours of paid labor in the TVE, which contributed toward an estimate of total work burdens.[13] For domestic labor, the data collected included the distribution of household tasks among household members, hours spent on household tasks, and how household decisions are made.

The main strength of the data is that we have responses from both men and women, and thus are able to make gender comparisons. There are several limitations of the data viewed from the purpose of this study.[14] First, the sample is comprised of workers in the TVE sector, therefore there is less variation in

---

[10] This project on the impact of TVE privatization is a collaborative project between Chinese and Canadian researchers. The two groups discussed the fieldwork methodologies; however, the actual surveying reported here were conducted by researchers from Shandong University and the Jiangsu Academy for Social Sciences, in part because of a policy implemented in 1998 by the Chinese government which prohibited foreign researchers undertaking primary research.

[11] We selected the 45 enterprises from a list of about 50 enterprises presented to us by the local governments. We, therefore, had some control over which enterprises were included in our sample but, obviously, the sample cannot be said to be random.

[12] The sample size for our results varies from 593 to 763 depending upon whether the questionnaire provided complete information for the question being analysed.

[13] For descriptions of the data collected about wages, share ownership, and job characteristics and analyses of these data, see Dong et al (2004).

[14] In these data, and survey data in general, there is a tendency for respondents to provide the sort of information they think the interviewer wants to hear (see Chen 1994).

earnings among the respondents than if the sample was comprised of people with work in the agriculture sector, sideline activities, and those with no income-generating work. As a result of this more limited variation in income among respondents, the relationship between market labor and domestic labor may be underestimated. Second, the sample is not constructed of matched husbands and wives, therefore it is not possible, for example, to explore within a given household gender time gaps of a matched husband and wife, and we rely upon differences between married men and women in general.[15] Third, we can observe only whether a relationship exists between market and domestic labor, not the mechanism through which it occurs. Also, if a relationship is not observed, we cannot distinguish between a negotiation which was unsuccessful and a decision not to pursue such an outcome while pursuing another one which is of more interest.

Descriptive statistics for this sample are presented in Table 3.1. Statistical results reported in this chapter were generated using TSP. Female workers comprise 39 percent of the sample, which reflects their representation in the TVE workforce. Nearly half (46 percent) of the workers live in extended households either with parents or parents-in-law. Women and men in this sample have similar levels of education on average. In terms of income, female workers contribute, on average, 44 percent of the household income.

4 Results

In this section, we present the results of the case study of the relationship between market labor and women's status based on a sample of married female and male TVE workers in rural Shandong and Jiangsu. The results are organized into three sections, namely, perceptions of women's status and meanings of market labor in 4.1, domestic labor in 4.2, and household decision-making patterns in 4.3.

4.1 Perceptions of Women's Status and Meanings of Market Labor

To provide a context for our analysis of domestic labor and household decision-making, and because we are specifically interested in the possible relationship between market labor and domestic labor, we first analyze men's and women's perceptions of women's status and the meanings they attach to their market labor in the TVE sector. Male and female workers were asked about the status of women (compared to men) in the areas of society, family, and workplace generally, and five specific workplace issues. In assessing women's status, workers were asked to respond, using a three-point scale where a "1" indicates women's status is less than

---

[15] We examine the intrahousehold allocation of time and decisions only among workers who are married and thus, the contributions and positions of unmarried or widowed individuals who work in the TVE sector are not examined.

men's, a "2" indicates status same as men's, and a "3" indicates women's status is greater than men's. The results of these questions are reported in Table 3.2.

Table 3.1 Descriptive statistics of the sample of married TVE workers[1]

	All	Men	Women
Age (years)	35.39	36.16	34.10
	(8.21)	(8.72)	(7.08)
Number of Children	1.19	1.27	1.06
	(0.62)	(0.68)	(0.47)
Living with parents	46	46	45
or in-laws (%)	(0.50)	(0.50)	(0.50)
Education	9.12	9.34	8.76
(years of schooling)	(2.19)	(2.24)	(2.07)
Spouse's education	8.12	7.82	8.89
(years of schooling)	(2.24)	(2.21)	(2.13)
Relative education (%)[2]	53	54	49
	(0.085)	(0.09)	(0.06)
Annual income	6,833	7,701	5,486
(1998 *yuan*)	(4,430)	(5,173)	(2,367)
Spouse's annual income	5,204	3,634	7,843
(*yuan*)	(5,443)	(3,048)	(7,267)
Share in family income	58	68	44
(%)[3]	(0.18)	(0.14)	(0.14)
Observations	717	436	281

Notes:
1. Figures in parentheses are standard deviations.
2. Relative education is the years of schooling of a worker divided by the sum of his/her and his/her spouse's years of schooling times 100.
3. Share in family income is the annual earnings of a worker divided by the sum his/her and his/her spouse's annual earnings times 100.
Source: Calculated from the Survey of TVE workers.

In society, women are perceived to have a lower status than men, however, there are also differences in the perceptions of men and women. In terms of social status, the average score of all workers indicates that women have a lower status than men; the average score is 1.98 and this is a statistically significant difference (at the 10 percent level) from the score of 2.00 (equality with men). Note, however, that perceptions of women's relative status reported by women is on average 1.94 and reported by men is on average 2.00, indicating that women perceive that they have a lower status than men, and men perceive that women have the same status as men. In the workplace, women's perceptions of lower status than men are even more pronounced. On average, women score their status at 1.89, although men report women to be equal to men in the workplace.

Table 3.2 Perceptions of the status of women[1]

	All	Mean Score[2] Women	Men
Status in society	1.98	1.94	2
	(-1.77)*	(-3.48)***	(0.48)
Status in family	2.05	2.01	2.07
	(4.75)***	-1.192	(4.90)***
Status in work place	1.95	1.89	2
	(-3.24)***	(-4.58)***	(-0.14)
Specific workplace issues			
Opportunity to receive training	1.91	1.89	1.91
	(-5.01)***	(-3.30)***	(-3.77)***
Opportunity for promotion	1.75	1.69	1.79
	(-12.54)***	(-9.75)***	(-8.29)***
Opportunity to participate in	1.78	1.69	1.83
enterprise's decision-making	(-12.52)***	(-10.07)***	(-7.89)***
Benefits from privatization	1.88	1.77	1.96
	(-6.33)***	(-7.31)***	(-1.97)**
Costs of privatization	1.94	2.08	1.84
	(-3.34)***	(2.40)**	(-6.88)***
Observations	759	300	459

Notes:
1: Workers' perceptions of the condition faced by women in each situation with 1 indicating less (or lower) than men, 2 indicating same as men, and 3 meaning greater (or higher) than men.
2: Figures in parentheses are the t-statistics testing the null hypothesis that the mean score is equal to 2; *, **, and *** denote, respectively, the significance levels of 10, 5, and 1 percent for a two-tailed test.
Source: Calculated from the Survey of TVE workers.

The perception of women's lower status (compared to men) in the workplace is even more striking when we examine the results of perceptions about women's condition in specific workplace issues, as shown in the lower part of Table 3.2. For the first three issues, workers (men and women combined) report that women experience a lower status than men. Examining the results separately for men and women indicates that women perceive a lower condition for themselves, compared to men's assessment of women's situation.

Since the TVEs have recently been privatized, we also had the opportunity to ask about the benefits and costs of privatization. In terms of both the benefits and the costs of privatization, women viewed their situation more negatively than men's. For example, the mean scores are 1.88 for the benefits of privatization, which indicates that for men and women combined, women are perceived to have benefits from privatization which are lower than for men. While men view the costs of privatization as being less for women than for men, women view the situation in the opposite manner.

We turn now from perceptions of status to the meanings workers attach to their paid labor in the TVEs. Workers were asked to evaluate the meaning of their jobs in the TVE with respect to three issues, using a three-point scale, from "1" (not important) to "3" (very important); results are presented in Table 3.3. Of the three issues considered, contributing to family income is viewed as the most important reason for working for both men and women. The average score was 2.19 for female workers and 2.42 for male workers, which is a statistically significant difference. While contributing to family income is important to women, the higher score for men may reflect prevailing gender norms about appropriate gender roles and specifically, the association of men with the outside sphere and women with the inside sphere.[16]

Table 3.3 Meaning of market labor[1]

	Mean scores	t-statistics[2]	
	Women	Men	
Contribution to family income	2.19	2.42	-5.56***
Increase your ability to purchase things for yourself	1.79	1.75	0.47
Raise your status in society	1.96	1.99	-0.74
Observations	300	459	

Notes:
1. Workers assessment of the importance of their jobs for each reason with 1 indicating not important, 2 somewhat important, and 3 very important.
2. The t-statistics test the between-group differences with *** denoting the significance level of 1 percent for a two-tailed test.
Source: Calculated from the Survey of TVE workers.

We also wondered about two other motivations for working, namely, whether working would increase one's ability to purchase things for oneself or raise one's status in society. The estimates indicate that ability to purchase things is less important than raising one's status, but the gender differences in views are not statistically significant. For example, regarding the importance of market labor for raising status, the mean scores are 1.96 for women and 1.99 for men, indicating

---

[16] While the results of this chapter are based upon married workers, data from unmarried migrant workers, also collected in this project, show the importance of contributing to family income. In the survey, over 87 percent of the unmarried migrant workers reported, on average, sending 3,548 *yuan* per year to their parents, which represents about 52 percent of the average annual income of (married) workers. Thus, unmarried workers are making a large contribution to family income.

that both groups view paid work as being somewhat important for raising status in society.

We turn now, from women's status and the meaning of market labor, to an analysis of domestic labor time and the gendered division of domestic labor.

4.2 Domestic Labor

Since domestic labor tends to be undervalued and tends to be undertaken at the cost of leisure, the amount of domestic labor time undertaken by an individual is viewed to be negatively related to his/her status. In considering domestic labor, we start by examining the amount of time spent on market labor and domestic labor in order to assess overall work burdens; we also examine the division of responsibility for selected domestic tasks between married men and women. We then analyze the determinants of the amount of domestic labor time and the determinants of the division of responsibility for domestic tasks in a multivariate manner.

4.2.1 Work Burden and Division of Responsibility for Domestic Tasks

Estimates of annual hours of market labor are derived from questions on usual weekly hours worked and number of months worked. Estimates of weekly hours of domestic labor are derived from a question which asks about the number of weekly hours spent on housework (cleaning, shopping, cooking, laundry, and care of children and elders). The results are presented in Table 3.4.

Overall, women have heavier work burdens than men. First, in terms of market labor, women and men both work a large number of hours per week in the TVEs. Specifically, on average, women work 56.61 hours per week and men work 55.42 hours per week, although the difference is not a statistically significant one. Second, in terms of domestic labor, women reported undertaking on average 22.43 hours per week, compared to men's reported contribution of 14.93 hours per week; the gender time gap for domestic labor is about 7.5 hours per week, and this is a statistically significant difference.[17] Thus, women have comparable hours of paid labor but because they perform more hours of unpaid domestic labor their overall work burdens are higher.

---

[17] On a daily basis, this converts to 3.2 hours for women and 2.1 hours for men. These estimates of time spent on domestic tasks are comparable to studies reported in the literature (see discussion in Section 2.3). However, these estimates do not provide the level of detail and accuracy associated with estimates derived from time use diaries. See Bianchi et al (2000) for analyses of the impact of different data collection methods on time use estimates in the US context. Bianchi et al (2000) note, however, that the ratios of married women's to men's housework time are similar for data collected from time use diaries compared to surveys using one question on housework.

Table 3.4 Time allocated to market and domestic labor

	Women	Men	t-statistic[1]
Market labor			
Hours per week	56.61	55.42	1.43
	(12.81)	(9.63)	
Months per year	11.56	11.62	-1.11
	(0.91)	(0.74)	
Hours per year	2,632.87	2,584.14	1.09
	(682.96)	(516.91)	
Domestic labor			
Hours per week	22.43	14.93	11.42***
	(11.47)	(8.95)	
Observations	303	460	

Notes: 1. Figures in parentheses are standard deviations. The t-statistics test the between-group differences with *** denoting a significance level of 1 percent for a two-tailed test.
Source: Calculated from the Survey of TVE workers.

In addition to gender differences in the amount of time allocated to domestic tasks, we are interested in whether a gendered pattern in the allocation of various domestic tasks exists. To further our understanding of the gendered division of domestic tasks, people were asked to assess who in their household did various household tasks. Respondents used a five-point scale where a "4" indicates self, a "3" indicates mostly self but with some help from spouse, a "2" indicates equally shared between self and spouse or by all family members, a "1" indicates mostly spouse but with some help from self, and a "0" indicates spouse alone or parents or in-laws. The results of this question are presented in Table 3.5, in terms of both frequencies and mean scores.

The frequency results indicate that, for the majority of respondents, the various household tasks are reported to be shared equally. Notice that the highest percentages are reported for option number two, which refers to equal sharing of tasks between self and spouse. At first glance, this result is somewhat surprising because the previously reported estimates of hours spent on household tasks showed that, on average, men performed about two-thirds of the domestic labor time as women.[18] Despite the quite large percentages of workers reporting equal sharing of tasks (option two), there is still a greater percentage of women, than men, who report undertaking primary responsibility for these household tasks, represented by option four by themselves or option three mostly by themselves. For example, with regard to the first task, namely, food shopping, cooking,

---

[18] The finding that the majority of workers report equal sharing of domestic tasks and yet women providing more hours of domestic work may also be due to the grouping of tasks into categories.

laundry, and housecleaning, 33.4 percent of women report doing these tasks by themselves or mostly by themselves (options four and three), compared to 4 percent of men.

Table 3.5 Division of responsibility for domestic tasks[1]

	Women	Men	t-statistics[2]
Food shopping, cooking, laundry, and housecleaning			
Frequency (%)			
0	1.8	10.5	
1	0.4	29.7	
2	64.3	55.7	
3	19.4	2.7	
4	14	1.3	
Mean score[2]	2.22	1.41	12.65***
	(1.12)	(0.87)	
Caring of elderly and children			
Frequency (%)			
0	3.6	6.7	
1	0.7	15.8	
2	76.5	75	
3	13	2	
4	6.1	0.4	
Mean score	1.94	1.58	6.14***
	(1.02)	(0.95)	
Work on private plot and care of livestock			
Frequency (%)			
0	15.4	16.9	
1	4.6	18.7	
2	69.1	59.6	
3	6.7	4.2	
4	4.1	0.5	
Mean score	1.65	1.45	3.25 ***
	(1.03)	(0.89)	
Observations	303	460	

Notes:

1. Workers' assessments of who does each household task, with "4" indicating self, "3" indicating mostly self but with some help from spouse, "2" indicating equally shared between self and spouse or by all family members, "1" indicating mostly spouse but with some help from self, and "0" indicating spouse alone or parents or in-laws.

2. Figures in parentheses are standard deviations. The t-statistics test the between-group differences with *** denoting the significance level of 1 percent for a two-tailed test.

Source: Calculated from the Survey of TVE workers.

There are differences in the responses of women and men in the survey. For example, 18.7 percent of male workers report that tending private plots and livestock is undertaken mostly by their spouses with some help from them (option one). However, only 6.7 percent of female workers reported that this task was undertaken mostly by self with some help from spouse (option three). This difference in the reports of men and women may reflect the composition of this specific sample which is comprised of TVE workers who are not necessarily married to other TVE workers. It may be the case, for example, that the male TVE workers do not have spouses who are also waged workers, and therefore these female spouses are more available to carry out the agricultural labor than the female TVE workers.

Mean scores are also used to summarize the frequency distributions which is possible because moving from zero to four represents increasing amounts of work performed by oneself. Thus, a higher mean is interpreted as indicating that a larger percentage of people are taking primary responsibility for the task. For each of the three categories of tasks, the mean score for women is higher than that for men, and the differences are statistically significant; the highest mean score for women is for the food shopping, cooking, laundry, and housecleaning set of tasks.

Thus, in terms of the gendered division of domestic tasks, women are more likely than men to have primary responsibility for domestic tasks and this is particularly the case for the food and cleaning set of tasks. This gendered pattern of responsibilities for domestic tasks is consistent with the time-use data, reported previously, indicating that women provide greater amount of domestic labor time.

4.2.2 Determinants of Domestic Labor Time

We now examine empirically the determinants of domestic labor time. We are particularly interested in whether women's resources enable them to negotiate a lower domestic labor burden and whether women are able to substitute market labor time for domestic labor time to the same extent as men. In our model, an individual's domestic labor time, measured by average weekly hours spent on domestic labor (reported in Table 3.4), is a function of the person's predicted wage rate, share in family income, predicted number of hours of market labor, spouse's income, number of children, living arrangement, and age; in addition to this large set of variables, we also include regional variables.

The wage rate and share in family income are introduced as proxies for an individual's access to financial resources and potential contribution to household income. The wage rate reflects the opportunity costs of leisure and home production time, and an increase in the wage rate is expected to reduce the number of hours the person allocates to leisure and home production by inducing her/him to supply additional hours to the labor market (assuming a dominant substitution effect); thus, we expect a negative relationship between the wage rate and domestic labor time.

We use the predicted market wage rate rather than the actual market wage rate in order to avoid potential endogeneity between market wage rate and domestic labor time. The endogeneity problem arises because the market wage rate is calculated as total annual earnings divided by annual market labor hours, and the number of market labor hours may be determined simultaneously by the amount of domestic labor time.[19]

The individual's share of family income, defined as the ratio of the individual's earnings to the sum of the earnings of that individual and his/her spouse, is introduced as a proxy for access to financial resources. An increase in the individual's visible financial contribution is expected to raise his/her ability to bargain for a reduced domestic work burden, at a given market wage rate; thus, we expect a negative relationship between the share of household income and domestic labor time.

The number of hours of market labor is introduced in order to test for the substitutability of market labor time for domestic labor time. Neoclassical economic theory considers home production a close substitute to market work (Gronau, 1986). However, in the view of the institutional school, the allocation of time between housework and market work is dictated by social conventions in the short run. Therefore, the substitution effect may be observed only for men; women who allocate more time to market work may do so at the expense of their leisure instead of domestic labor. The number of hours of market work is measured by the predicted market labor hours rather than the actual hours of work in order to avoid simultaneity between domestic labor time and market labor time.[20] When market labor hours is controlled for, the effect of financial resources on domestic labor time reflects the reallocation of time between domestic labor and leisure.

To evaluate the impact of resources and market labor time on domestic labor, we control for other socio-economic factors related to domestic labor time, including the presence of children, living arrangements, spouse's income, and locality. The presence of children is expected to increase the amount of domestic labor required, thus, married workers who live in households with children will undertake a greater amount of household labor. Living in an extended family situation with older adults increases the possibility of sharing domestic labor, and consequently, married workers who live with their parents or parents-in-law may undertake less household labor if these tasks are performed by parents. Thus, we

---

[19] Based upon a Mincer human capital model, the wage rate is predicted from a function of the individual's years of schooling, years of experience, squared years of experience, and regional dummy variables.

[20] The predicted value of market labor hours is obtained from a reduced form regression for weekly work hours in which years of schooling, experience and experience squared, age, number of children, spouse's income, and dummy variables for living with parents or parents-in-law, locality, and enterprise that is profitable or could improve its financial performance by laying-off 10 percent of the existing workers. The dummy variables for enterprise characteristics, which are statistically significant in the reduced form regression, perform as instruments for the variable of market labor time.

expect that the variable for the number of children will be positive and the variable for living with parents or parents-in-law will be negative.[21] However, these factors, namely, the presence of children and living in an extended family situation, may not affect the domestic labor burden equally for men and women because the sharing of work burdens is set within an over-arching patriarchical structure which values the contributions of men, including men's leisure, more highly than the contributions of women. For example, the presence of children may increase the domestic labor time for women but not for men; living with parents may reduce the domestic labor time for men but not for women.

Age of the respondent is included because of norms associated with respect for the elderly. This may mean that older men are less likely to be involved in domestic labor, although, age may have little bearing on women's domestic labor time. We include the income of the spouse, as a proxy for the level of household well-being, where better-off households may be able to afford more leisure, given that its bargaining effect is controlled for. Finally, we include regional dummy variables to reflect differences among the three counties.

The determinants of weekly hours of domestic labor time are estimated by a Tobit regression and the results are presented in Table 3.6. The first column reports the regression results for all workers with a dummy variable included for the sex of the worker ("1" if the worker is a man). Note that the dummy variable for male workers is negative and significant which indicates that men on average perform less domestic labor after controlling for other socio-economic factors, a result consistent with the descriptive statistics reported in Table 3.4.

For men, financial resources are associated with lower domestic labor time commitments. In the male regression results column, the estimates of the predicted wage and the share of family income variables are both negative and statistically significant. The estimated elasticities indicate that domestic labor time will fall by 0.3 percent with respect to a 1 percent increase in the wage rate, and by 0.56 percent with respect to a 1 percent increase in the share of family income. The predicted market labor hours variable has a negative sign and is statistically significant. For men, market labor and domestic labor time appears to be highly substitutable with a 1 percent increase in market hours resulting in a decline of housework hours by 1.8 percent. In terms of age, older men provide less domestic labor than younger men, given that the age variable is negative and statistically significant. For men, however, the presence of children is not statistically associated with domestic labor time.[22]

---

[21] The presence of children and living with parents or parents-in-law are measured by dummy variables which take the value "1" if the worker has children and lives with his/her parents or parents-in-law.

[22] Bianchi et al. (2000) find, for the US, that the presence of children under 12 increases wives' housework time by more than three times that of their husbands.

Table 3.6 Tobit regressions of the determinants of weekly domestic labor hours[1]

	All workers Marginal Effect	Elasticity	Women Marginal Effect	Elasticity	Men Marginal Effect	Elasticity
Male	-2.578		—		—	
	(-2.12)**					
Predicted wage	-8.761	-0.41	-9.47	-0.28	-4.774	-0.30
	(-3.44)***		(-2.19)**		(-1.64)*	
Share in family income	-9.111	-0.29	-0.205	-0.004	-12.896	-0.56
	(-3.78)***		(-0.05)		(-4.00)***	
Predicted market-work hours	-0.578	-1.74	-0.136	-0.34	-0.512	-1.80
	(-3.45)***		(-0.62)		(-2.24)**	
Spouse's income x100	-0.008		-0.005		-0.026	
	(-1.21)		(-0.61)		(-1.26)	
Number of children	0.724		3.10		-0.285	
	(0.98)		(2.16)**		(-0.35)	
Living with parents	0.804		1.179		0.334	
	(1.30)		(1.04)		(0.48)	
Age	-0.143		-0.024		-0.132	
	(-2.57)***		(-0.25)		(-2.19)**	
Wujin	0.354		-8.068		0.553	
	(0.18)		(-2.48)**		(0.33)	
Yanzhou	-1.811		-3.358		-0.486	
	(-1.85)*		(-1.93)***		(-0.44)	
Constant	77.005		39.620		71.798	
	(6.68)***		(2.64)***		(4.58)***	
χ^2 test for zero slope	217.72		84.48		65.23	
p-value	0.0		0.0		0.0	
Pseudo R^2	0.039		0.037		0.02	
Observations	746		295		451	

Notes: 1. The table presents the estimated marginal effects of the Tobit regressions with t-statistics reported in parentheses; *, **, and *** indicate significance at the 10, 5, and 1 percent levels, respectively.
Source: Calculated from the Survey of TVE workers.

For women, the results concerning the hypothesis that financial resources enable women to reduce their overall domestic work burden are mixed. Notice that the predicted wage and the share of family income variables both have negative signs, but only the predicted wage is statistically significant. As with men, a higher wage rate induces women to substitute market labor for domestic work, with the size of wage elasticity similar to that for men. However, unlike for men, a rise in relative financial contribution has no effect on women's time commitment to domestic labor, at a given wage rate. Moreover, women's market labor time does not have significant effect on their domestic labor time since the predicted market work hours variable is insignificant.[23] For women, unlike for men, the presence of children does increase their work burdens, as indicated by the positive and statistically significant coefficient on the number of children variable. These results together indicate that women's domestic labor burdens do not vary with resources by the same extent as for men and that the substitution of market labor time for domestic labor time is observed only for men, not for women.

4.2.3 Determinants of the Division of Responsibility for Domestic Tasks

Having investigated the determinants of domestic labor time, we now examine the determinants of the division of responsibility for selected domestic tasks using a modified version of the above model. Here, the dependent variable is the division of responsibility for three sets of tasks which were presented in descriptive terms in Table 3.5. Since the dependent variable is defined in a relative manner, we include the share of family income variable to proxy access to financial resources and omit the predicted wage and spouse's income. The variables for education and spouse's education are added to the list of explanatory variables to examine if education fosters value of gender equality within the household. The model is estimated by an ordered probit regression, and the results are presented separately for men and women in Table 3.7; the results for the combined sample of men and women are reported in Appendix 3.1.

For women, the hypothesis that the greater the individual's financial resources, the less likely she is to be responsible for certain domestic tasks is supported for two sets of tasks, namely, the cooking, cleaning, laundry, and the care of elderly and children. Note that for these two dependent variables, the share of family income variable is negative and statistically significant. However, as with the time allocation regression, the number of predicted market labor hours has no significant effect on women's responsibility for all three selected activities. Thus, it appears that it is the actual financial contribution which has the impact on allocation or negotiation of the gendered division of labor, rather than just being involved in market labor. In terms of household composition, living with parents-in-law is associated with a lower probability of responsibility for the domestic tasks of cooking, cleaning, and laundry, as well as tending to plots and livestock, but is not statistically related to care for children and elderly. Education reduces women's responsibility for taking care of private plot and livestock but has no effect on the other two sets of tasks, and spouse's education is not statistically significant for any of three domestic activities.

For men, the share of family income is significant for only one dependent variable, namely, for cooking, cleaning, and laundry. As for the results for women,

---

[23] The result that women's domestic labor time responds to the wage rate but not to market labor time can be explained by the fact that, in our sample, shop-floor production workers tend to work longer hours but earn less than managerial and technical personnel.

the predicted number of market work hours is insignificant for all three dependent variables. We turn now from time and the gendered household division of labor to gendered household decision-making.

Table 3.7 Ordered probit regressions of the division of responsibilities for domestic labor tasks[1]

	Female workers			Male workers		
	Cooking, cleaning etc	Caring elderly/ children	Working plots/ livestock	Cooking, cleaning etc	Caring elderly/ children	Working plots/ livestock
Share in family income	-1.234	-1.295	-0.565	-0.821	0.155	0.074
	(-2.244)**	(-2.234)**	(-0.856)	(-2.091)**	(0.359)	(0.177)
Predicted market work hours	-0.031	-0.022	-0.043	-0.040	-0.035	-0.045
	(-1.069)	(-0.734)	(-1.231)	(-1.281)	(-1.001)	(-1.331)
Education	0.017	-0.019	-0.116	-0.081	0.008	-0.089
	(0.418)	(-0.467)	(-2.175)**	(-3.066)***	(0.258)	(-3.051)***
Spouse's Education	-0.016	-0.040	-0.002	0.034	0.008	0.032
	(-0.406)	(-0.993)	(-0.025)	(1.265)	(0.259)	(1.083)
Age	0.0005	0.013	0.049	-0.007	-0.010	0.003
	(0.045)	(1.017)	(3.599)***	(-0.667)	(-0.934)	(0.241)
Living with Parents/in-laws	-0.308	0.046	-0.327	0.35	0.082	0.014
	(-2.056)**	(0.289)	(-1.774)*	(3.120)***	(-0.654)	(0.119)
Number of Children	0.03	0.128	-0.035	0.116	0.125	0.037
	(0.164)	(0.662)	(-0.150)	(0.938)	(0.894)	(0.277)
Wujin	0.003	0.273	0.434	0.673	0.894	0.356
	(0.006)	(0.637)	(0.89)	(2.867)***	(3.279)***	-1.401
Yanzhou	-0.251	0.125	0.291	-0.007	0.002	-0.232
	(-1.217)	(0.573)	(0.989)	(-0.047)	(0.013)	(-1.416)
Constant	4.648	3.467	3.152	4.351	3.214	3.887
	(2.540)***	(1.840)*	(1.477)	(2.373)***	-1.563	(1.947)*
χ^2 test for zero slops	22.714	11.189	35.153	44.594	24.948	28.701
p-value	0.007	0.263	0	0	0.003	0.001
Scaled R^2	0.079	0.04	0.171	0.097	0.055	0.071
Observations	280	279	196	448	445	397

Note: 1. The table reports the estimates of the Ordered Probit Regressions with t-statistics presented in parentheses; *, **, and *** indicate significance at the 10, 5, and 1 percent levels, respectively.

Source: Calculated from the Survey of TVE workers.

4.3 Household Decision Making

The ability to influence household decisions is viewed as an indicator of status within the household. From the literature we know that while women do have some influence in household decision making, and though their influence may have increased compared to previous generations, men are still the dominant decision makers in the household, which is indicative of women's lower status within households. In analyzing decision-making control as an indicator of women's status, we start by considering the gendered pattern of household decision making, and then examine the determinants in a multivariate manner.

4.3.1 Patterns of Household Decision Making

To investigate the gendered pattern of household decision making, workers were asked to assess how three types of decisions are made in their households, with a "4" indicating by oneself, "3" indicating mostly self in consultation with spouse, "2" indicating self and spouse equally, "1" indicating mostly spouse in consultation with self, and "0" indicating spouse, parents or in-laws alone. Patterns of household decision making are reported using the frequencies and mean scores of the frequency data in Table 3.8.

Table 3.8 Household decision-making control[1]

		Women	Men	t-statistics
		Mean score[2]		
Major purchases		1.98	2.16	-4.57***
		(0.53)	(0.72)	
Children's education		2.01	2.15	-3.91***
		(0.56)	(0.62)	
Own employment		2.82	3.01	-2.94***
		(1.01)	(0.95)	
		Frequency		
Major purchase Choice:				
	0	2.9	3.7	
	1	4.0	2.8	
	2	86.1	72.1	
	3	4.6	16.2	
	4	1.7	5.0	
Observations		301	458	

Notes:
1. Workers assessment of how the following decisions are made in their household with a "4" indicating self, "3" indicating mostly self in consultation with spouse, "2" indicating self and spouse equally, "1" indicating mostly spouse in consultation with self, and "0" indicating spouse, parents, or in-laws alone.
2. Figures in parentheses are standard deviations. The t-statistics test the between-group differences with *** denoting the significance level of 1 percent for a two-tailed test.
Source: Calculated from the Survey of TVE workers.

Men tend to have greater control over household decisions, compared to women. Note that the mean score for decision-making influence in each of the three categories is higher for men than for women. With respect to major purchases, for example, the mean score for men is 2.16 compared to 1.98 for women, a statistically significant difference. This means that men are more likely to view decisions as being made either by themselves, or mostly by themselves with some consultation with their spouse. In contrast, for women the mean score is less than 2, meaning that women are more likely to perceive decisions to be made mostly by their spouse, or in consultation with them. The frequency distribution for major purchases shows this point as well. For example, 21.2 percent of men view decisions about major purchases being made by themselves, or mostly by them in consultation with their spouse (sum of options 3 and 4), compared with 6.3 percent of women.[24]

4.3.2 Determinants of the Patterns of Household Decision Making

Turning now to explanations of the gendered pattern of decision making within households, we assess factors that may affect decision-making control using the model developed above. Here, the dependent variable is the household decision-making variable with respect to the three types of decisions, namely, major purchases, children's education, and own employment. An individual's education relative to his/her spouse's education has been added to the model because relative education levels are perceived to affect one's right or ability to make decisions. Predicted market hours and number of children were insignificant variables in the estimated model of the gendered division of domestic responsibilities, and consequently, these two variables have been excluded from this model. The model is estimated by an ordered probit regression and the results are presented separately for men and women in Table 3.9; the results for the combined sample are presented in Appendix 3.2.

The importance of each determinant of decision-making control differs between men and women and also depends upon the type of decision being made. Starting with men, financial resources and education are both important determinants of male decision-making control. For example, the share of family income variable is positive and significant in the equations explaining decision-making control over major purchases and own employment, whereas education has positive effect on the probability of higher degree of control over all three types of decisions.

For women, surprisingly, the financial resources hypothesis (that an increase in women's resources will enable them greater decision-making control) is not supported by any regression results; note that the share in family income variable is significant but negative in one equation. However, education does give women

---

[24] There are gender differences in the perceptions because this 21.2 percent is considerably greater than the 6.9 percent of women who view decisions about major purchases being made by spouse or parents/in-laws (option zero) and mostly spouse in consultation with self (option one). Although, the men and women in this sample do have partners outside of the sample, so it is not necessary that the views should align themselves.

more control over decisions regarding their children's education. For women, living with parents-in-law reduces their decision-making influence over major purchases and own employment. This supports the idea noted in the literature, that a move to nuclear families is associated with a decline in patriarchical control.

Table 3.9 Ordered probit regressions of household decision-making control[1]

	Women			Men		
	Major Purch.	Children's Educ.	Own Empl.	Major Purch.	Children's Educ.	Own Emp.
Share in family	-0.946	-1.421	-0.017	1.128	0.337	0.700
Income	(-1.587)	(-2.310)**	(-0.034)	(2.816)***	(0.764)	(1.826)*
Education relative	1.033	3.030	0.612	1.393	2.197	1.652
to spouse	(0.963)	(2.756)***	(0.656)	(2.128)**	(3.206)***	(2.544)**
Age	-0.004	0.009	-0.009	-0.003	0.006	-0.004
	(-0.337)	(0.744)	(-1.001)	(-0.438)	(0.902)	(-0.619)
Living with	-0.411	-0.034	-0.274	-0.029	-0.088	-0.004
parents/in-laws	(-2.346)**	(-0.200)	(-2.004)**	(-0.252)	(-0.686)	(-0.039)
Wujin	0.196	0.036	0.117	0.323	0.487	0.125
	(1.016)	(0.188)	(0.770)	(2.106)**	(2.867)***	(0.861)
Yanzhou	-0.104	-0.253	-0.269	0.139	0.571	0.026
	(-0.473)	(-1.081)	(-1.514)	(0.991)	(3.621)***	(0.203)
Constant	2.127	0.829	2.245	0.282	0.166	0.866
	(3.033)***	(1.186)	(3.676)***	(0.648)	(0.353)	(1.988)**
χ^2 test-zero slope	10.644	13.528	9.800	17.691	35.178	12.047
p-value1	0.100	0.035	0.133	0.007	0.00	0.061
Scaled R^2	0.035	0.045	0.032	0.038	0.076	0.026
Observations	301	297	297	456	452	452

Note: 1. The table reports the estimates of the Ordered Probit Regressions with t-statistics presented in parentheses; *, **, and *** indicate significance at the 10, 5, and 1 percent levels, respectively.
Source: Calculated from the Survey of TVE workers.

5 Conclusions

This case study of market labor and women's status draws upon a sample of married men and women who work for wages in the township and village enterprise sector in the rural provinces of Shandong and Jiangsu, China. Women are viewed as having lower status than men based upon the indicators of the greater work burden, greater responsibility for (undervalued) domestic tasks, and lower influence over household decisions. First, women have a greater labor burden than men given their comparable number of hours of market labor and greater amount of domestic labor, and they are more likely to take primary responsibility for domestic work. The gender labor gap of 7.5 hours per week is comparable to other estimates reported in the literature for China. Second, we did not find a statistical relationship between the amount of market labor time and domestic labor time for our sample of women, but a statistically significant relationship for men. Third, while women are not able to substitute market labor time for domestic labor time, access to market work was found to reduce women's domestic labor burdens through a financial avenue. Specifically, the number of hours spent on domestic labor by women is lower for women having access to more highly paid market work, and women with a higher share of family income are less likely to take primary responsibility for major domestic tasks. Therefore, it is not surprising that market work is valued highly by women, in spite of the fact that their participation in the labor market often leads to a longer work day. Women perceive that they have a lower status in the workplace, compared to men, but still indicate that market work is important to them in terms of raising their status within the family, and the earnings which they can contribute to the family.

Women have less control over household decision-making, which is also indicative of their lower status within the household. While we did not find direct evidence to support the hypothesis that financial resources lead to an increase in decision-making control by women, our estimates show that increases in men's income relative to women's income contribute to male decision-making control. The finding that women's earnings are an important determinant of the amount of male domestic labor time, responsibility, and decision-making control suggests that women's earnings are therefore important to their status within the household. The asymmetrical results in decision making between male and female groups may be due to the fact that, in this sample, the employment status of male workers' spouses is more heterogeneous than that of female workers. Hence, the findings from the male sub-sample offers an indicative counterfactual of what would happen to women if they were denied access to waged employment.

In conclusion, the results support the hypothesis that women's access to market work in rural China positively affects their status within households, a hypothesis which has been supported in a variety of other countries. However, participating in the labor market and bringing home a wage do not automatically raise women's status in the household. Social norms and expectations about who should perform domestic tasks, along with the presence of children and living arrangements will all influence women's status. This suggests that understanding the intrahousehold distribution of resources and relative gender status within the household is better served by household bargaining models than by the unitary household models. In terms of policy implications, the broad economic changes and policy reforms ongoing in China are troubling from a gender equity perspective. Specifically, privatization, market reforms, industrial restructuring, and social policies,[25] which result in the disproportionate layoff of female workers, a falling female labor force participation, rising gender wage gap, and increased market work intensity (which compromise women's ability to balance market and domestic work) are likely to reduce women's status within households.

References

Agarwal, B., '"Bargaining" and gender relations: within and beyond the household', *Feminist Economics*, 3, 1 (1997): 1-51.

Alderman, H., Chiappori, P.A., Haddad, L., Hoddinott, J. and Kanbur, R., 'Unitary versus collective models of the household: is it time to shift the burden of proof?', *World Bank Research Observer*, 10 (1995): 1-19.

Bao, X., 'More women wear the pants', *China Daily* (September 10, 2002).

Becker, G.S., *A Treatise on the Family* (Cambridge, USA: Harvard University Press, 1981).

Beijing Review, 'Women's choice: home or work?', 24-26 (April 5, 2001).

Bianchi, S.M., Milkie, M.A., Sayer, L.C. and Robinson, J.P. 'Is anyone doing the housework? Trends in the gender division of labor', *Social Forces*, 79, 1 (2000): 191-228.

Bu, N. and McKeen, C.A., 'Work and family expectations of the future managers and professionals of Canada and China', *Journal of Managerial Psychology*, 15, 8 (2000): 771-794.

Chen, Y., 'Out of the traditional halls of academe: exploring new avenues for research on women' in C.K. Glimartin, G. Hershatter, L. Rofel and T. White (eds), *Engendering China*, (Cambridge, USA and London, UK: Harvard University Press, 1994), pp. 69-79.

Chen, Z. and Woolley, F., 'A Cournot-Nash model of family decision making', *Economic Journal*, 111, (2001): 722-748.

Cheung, W.P. and Tao, C.F. (eds), *Survey on the Social Status of Women in China* (in Chinese) (Beijing: Women's Press, 1993).

China Daily, 'Chinese still stress wives' home role' (March 8, 2002).

Croll, E., *Chinese Women Since Mao* (London, UK: Zed Books, 1983).

———, *Changing Identities of Chinese Women* (Hong Kong: Hong Kong University Press and New Jersey, USA: Zed Books, 1995).

Davis, D. and Harrell, S., *Chinese Families in Post-Mao China* (Berkeley, USA: University of California Press, 1993).

De Brauw, A., Huang, J., Rozelle, S., Zhang, L. and Zhang, Y., 'The evolution of China's rural labor markets during the reforms', *Journal of Comparative Economics*, 30 (2002): 329-353.

---

[25] Wang Xiancai, deputy secretary-general of the Committee of the Chinese People's Political Consultative Conference, Jiangxi Provincial Committee, has been reported as advocating the return of married women to the home in order to care for children (Beijing Review, 2001). He provides a Becker-style argument by stating that women should return home if they cannot earn enough to hire someone to replace their services at home and because men are inferior to women in housekeeping.

Dong, X.Y., Bowles, P. and Ho, S.P.S, 'The Determination of Employee Share Ownership in China's Privatized Rural Industries: Evidence from Jiangsu and Shandong,' *Journal of Comparative Economics*, 30, 2 (2002): 415-437.

Dong, X.Y., MacPhail, F., Bowles, P. and Ho, S.P.S., 'Gender segmentation at work in China's privatized rural industry: some evidence from Shandong and Jiangsu', *World Development*, 32, 6 (2004): 979-998.

Donohoe, M., 'Chinese women losing on equality', *Irish Times* (September 8, 2001).

Elson, D., 'Labor Markets as Gendered Institutions: Equality, Efficiency and Empowerment Issues,' *World Development*, 27, 3 (1999): 611-627.

Folbre, N., 'Hearts and Spades: Paradigms of Households and Economic Development', *World Development*, 14, 2 (1986a): 245-255.

———, 'Cleaning House: New Perspectives on Households and Economic Development', *Journal of Development Economics*, 22 (1986b): 5-40.

Gao, X., 'China's modernization and changes in the social status of rural women', in C.K. Gilmartin, G. Hershatter, L. Rofel and T. White (eds), *Engendering China* (Cambridge, USA and London, UK: Harvard University Press, 1994), pp. 80-100.

Gronau, R., 'Home Production—A Survey', in O. Ashenfelter and R. Layard (eds), *Handbook of Labor Economics*, Volume 1 (Elsevier Science Publishers BV, 1986), pp. 273-302.

Ho, S.P.S., Dong, X., Bowles, P. and MacPhail, F., 'Privatization and enterprise wage structures during transition: evidence from rural China', *Economics of Transition*, 10, 3 (2002): 659-688.

Hoddinott, J. and Haddad, L., 'Does female income share influence household expenditures?', *Oxford Bulletin of Economics and Statistics*, 57, 1 (1995): 77-96.

Hooper, B., ' "Flower vase and housewife": women and consumerism in post-Mao China', in K. Sen and M. Stivens (eds), *Gender and Power in Affluent Asia* (London, UK: Routledge, 1998), pp. 167-194.

Howell, J., 'State enterprise reform and gender: one step backwards for women?', in R. Benewick, M. Blecher and S. Cook (eds), *Asian Politics in Development* (London, UK and Portland, USA: Frank Cass, 2003), pp. 83-108.

Jacka, T., *Women's Work in Rural China* (Cambridge, UK: Cambridge University Press, 1997).

Kandiyoti, D., 'Gender, power and contestation', in C. Jackson and R. Pearson (eds), *Feminist Visions of Development* (London, UK and New York, USA: Routledge, 1998), pp. 135-151.

Katz, E., 'Breaking the myth of harmony: theoretical and methodological guidelines to the study of rural Third World households', *Review of Radical Political Economics*, 23, 3 & 4 (1991): 37-56.

Li, X., 'Gender inequality in China and cultural relativism', in M.C. Nussbaum and J. Glover (eds), *Women, Culture and Development*, (Oxford: Clarendon Press, 1995), pp. 407-425.

Liu, B., 'Chinese women's employment', *Chinese Education & Society*, 33, 2 (2000): 73-94.

Lundberg, S. and Pollak, R.A., 'Separate sphere bargaining and the marriage market', *Journal of Political Economy*, 101, 6 (1993): 988-1010.

Manser, M. and Brown, M., 'Marriage and household decision-making: a bargaining analysis', *International Economic Review*, 21, 1 (1980): 31-44.

Maurer-Fazio, M., Rawski, T. and Zhang, W., Inequality in the rewards for holding up half the sky: gender wage gaps in China's urban labor market, 1984-94', *China Journal*, 41 (1999): 55-88.

McElroy, M., 'The empirical content of Nash-bargained household behavior', *The Journal of Human Resources*, 25, 4 (1990): 559-583.

Phipps, S.A. and Burton, P.S., 'What's mine is yours? The influence of male and female incomes on patterns of household expenditure', *Economica*, 65 (1998): 599-613.

Rofel, L., 'Liberation nostalgia and a yearning for modernity' in C.K. Gilmartin, G. Hershatter, L. Rofel and T. White (eds), *Engendering China* (Cambridge, USA and London, UK: Harvard University Press, 1994), pp. 226-278.

Sen, A.K., 'Gender and cooperative conflicts', in I. Tinker (eds), *Persistent Inequalities* (Oxford, UK: Oxford University Press, 1990), pp. 123-149.

Song, L., 'In search of gender bias in household resource allocation in rural China', *Chinese Economy*, 33, 4 (2000): 69-95.

Stacey, J. *Patriarchy and Socialist Revolution in China* (Berkeley, USA and London, UK: University of California Press, 1983).

Summerfield, G., 'Economic reform and the employment of Chinese women', *Journal of Economic Issues*, 28, 3 (1994): 715-32.

Sun , S.C., 'The power enjoyed by women in daily lives after marriage', in J.C. Sai (eds), *Women's Social Status in Contemporary China* (in Chinese) (Beijing: Beijing University Press, 1995).

Thakur, R., *Rewriting Gender* (London, UK and Atlantic Highlands, USA: Zed Books, 1996).

Duncan, T., 'Intra-household resource allocation', *The Journal of Human Resources*, 24, 4 (1990): 634-664.

UNDP, *The China Human Development Report 1999* (Beijing: China Financial & Economic Publishing House, 1999).

White, Gordon, Howell, J. and Shang, X., *In Search of Civil Society: Market Reform and Social Change in Contemporary China* (Oxford, UK and New York, USA: Oxford University Press and Clarendon Press, 1996).

Whitehead, Ann, ' "I'm hungry Mum": the politics of domestic budgeting', in K. Young, C. Wolkowitz and R. McCullach (eds), *Of Marriage and the Market* (London: Routledge and Kegan Paul, 1981), pp. 93-116.

Wolf, M., *Revolution Postponed* (Stanford, USA: Stanford University Press, 1985).

Xia, W., 'Changes in the position of women in urban families', *Women of China* (October 1989): 11-13.

Yang, J., 'Economic Restructuring and Employment Status of Women in Urban China' (presented at the 3rd Chinese Economists Annual Conference in Shanghai on December 21, 2003).

Yu, S.W.K. and Chau, R.C.M., 'The sexual division of care in Mainland China and Hong Kong', *International Journal of Urban and Regional Research*, 21, 4 (1997): 608-619.

Zhang, W., 'Changing nature of family relations in a Hebei village in China', *Journal of Contemporary Asia*, 32, 2 (2002): 147-170.

Zhou, K.X., 'Women Divided', *Harvard International Review*, 20, 1 (1997): 24-28.

Appendix 3.1 Ordered probit regressions of the division of responsibilities for household tasks-men and women combined[1]

	Cooking, shopping, laundry, etc.		Care of elderly/ children		Tending plots/ livestock	
Male	-1.110	----	-0.807	----	-0.253	----
	(-8.657)***		(-5.899)***		(-1.918)*	
Share in family income	-1.109	-2.577	-0.583	-1.720	-0.289	-0.655
	(-3.597)***	(-10.048)***	(-1.739)*	(-6.272)***	(-0.841)	(-2.290)**
Predicted market work hours	-0.029	-0.037	-0.043	-0.048	-0.052	-0.054
	(-1.197)	(-1.528)	(-1.584)	(-1.797)*	(-1.918)*	(-1.901)*
Education	-0.049	-0.065	-0.015	-0.029	-0.104	-0.108
	(-2.278)**	(-3.065)***	(-0.683)	(-1.263)	(-4.068)***	(-4.220)***
Spouse's education	0.015	0.024	-0.007	0.002	0.028	0.031
	(0.679)	(1.123)	(-0.302)	(0.097)	(1.147)	(1.256)
Age	-0.001	-0.006	0.0005	-0.004	0.020	0.018
	(-0.145)	(-0.847)	(0.064)	(-0.484)	(2.351)**	(2.164)**
Living with parents	0.114	0.114	0.048	0.052	-0.135	-0.130
	(1.297)	(1.322)	(0.499)	(0.543)	(-1.377)	(-1.327)
Number of children	0.034	0.053	0.061	0.089	-0.073	-0.062
	(0.338)	(0.532)	(0.553)	(0.818)	(-0.636)	(-0.539)
Wujin	0.326	0.437	0.677	0.740	0.424	0.458
	(1.300)	(1.773)*	(2.461)**	(2.728)***	(1.471)	(1.592)
Yanzhou	-0.115	-0.182	0.078	0.009	-0.037	-0.069
	(-0.914)	(-1.472)	(0.566)	(0.069)	(-0.242)	(-0.451)
Constant	5.454	5.690	4.833	5.383	4.327	4.514
	(3.641)***	(4.016)***	(3.091)***	(3.493)***	(2.643)**	(2.765)***
χ^2 test for zero slops	243.86	163.836	104.126	67.396	61.171	57.482
p-value	0.00	0.00	0.00	0.00	0.00	0.00
Scaled R^2	0.303	0.210	0.139	0.091	0.100	0.094
Observations	728	728	724	724	593	593

Note: 1. The table reports the estimates of the Ordered Probit Regressions with t-statistics presented in parentheses; *, **, and *** indicate significance at the 10, 5, and 1 percent levels, respectively.

Source: Calculated from the Survey of TVE workers.

Appendix 3.2 Ordered probit regressions of household decision-making for men and women combined[1]

	Major purchases		Children's education		Own employment	
Male	0.275	-----	0.292	-----	0.111	-----
	(2.140)**	(2.194)**	(1.004)			
Share in family	0.413	0.814	-0.343	0.108	0.357	0.532
income	(1.291)	(3.132)***	(-0.988)	(0.385)	(1.216)	(2.251)**
Education relative	1.255	1.299	2.546	2.593	1.445	1.473
to spouse	(2.308)**	(2.392)**	(4.505)***	(4.587)***	(2.776)***	(2.828)***
Age	-0.0005	0.0003	0.008	0.008	-0.004	-0.004
	(-0.093)	(0.060)	(1.306)	(1.436)	(-0.838)	(-0.764)
Living with parents	-0.135	-0.139	-0.067	-0.068	-0.107	-0.108
	(-1.435)	(-1.478)	(-0.667)	(-0.681)	(-1.256)	(-1.268)
Wujin	0.213	0.200	0.252	0.237	0.111	0.105
	(1.842)*	(1.743)*	(2.043)**	(1.931)*	(1.073)	(1.020)
Yanzhou	0.092	0.327	0.298	0.334	-0.046	-0.032
	(0.794)	(1.079)	(2.403)**	(2.725)***	(-0.443)	(-0.313)
Constant	0.786	0.647	0.151	0.152	1.269	1.201
	(2.385)**	(2.004)**	(0.452)	(0.452)	(3.965)***	(3.835)***
χ^2 test for zero slopes	31.065	26.461	48.081	43.231	20.714	19.706
p-value	0.00	0.00	0.00	0.00	0.004	0.003
Scaled R^2	0.041	0.034	0.064	0.057	0.027	0.026
Observations	757	757	749	749	749	749

Note: 1. The table reports the estimates of the Ordered Probit Regressions with t-statistics presented in parentheses; *, **, and *** indicate significance at the 10, 5, and 1 percent levels, respectively.

Source: Calculated from the Survey of TVE workers.

Chapter 4

China's Rural Labor Market Development and its Gender Implications[*]

Scott Rozelle
Linxiu Zhang
Alan de Brauw

1 Introduction

Since the reforms began in China in the late 1970s, the nation has experienced both rapid economic growth and fundamental structural changes to its economy, changes that have been catalyzed by increased employment off the farm. Rural labor markets have grown dramatically over the past twenty years and their emergence has contributed to the rise in rural incomes (Solinger, 1999; West and Zhao, 2000; World Bank, 2001; Parish, Zhe, and Li, 1995; Rozelle, 1996). The rise of rural labor markets, however, is more important than its role of providing rural residents with a means to raise their incomes; labor markets also help drive changes in the structure of the economy and contribute to the nation's modernization (Todaro, 1976; Stark, 1976). According to recent empirical analyses, China's success in modernizing over the past two decades is at least partly attributable to improved rural labor markets (de Brauw et al., 2002; Mohapatra, 2001).

Although scholars recognize the important economic contributions of rural labor market development, they disagree on the role that growing labor markets have played in contributing to the welfare of rural women. Some researchers believe that significant barriers still exist for women in China's rural labor markets. For example, Chan and Senser (1997) and Chan (2001) argue that although women began working more frequently during the 1990s, the process was generally

[*] The paper was originally presented at the International Rice Congress, September 2002 in Beijing. Reprinted from China Economic Review, 2004, Vol. 15, No. 2, page 230-247. L. Zhang, A. De Brauw, and S. Rozelle, "China's Rural Labor Market Development and Its Gender Implications." We acknowledge the financial support of the National Science Foundation (US), the Ford Foundation in Beijing, the USDA National Research Initiative, and China Natural Science Foundation. We acknowledge the able research assistance of Chengfang Liu and Yigang Zhang.

demeaning. Solinger (1999) describes interviews with migrants who, despite having jobs, believe they are disenfranchised and are being treated unfairly. Maurer-Fazio et al. (1999) show that as labor markets have liberalized in the 1990s, discrimination towards women, as measured by the male-female wage gap, has increased. While compelling, their work has largely been confined to urban labor markets. Song and Jiggins (2000) suggest that the adverse impacts of labor market trends spillover into agriculture; when women are being left to tend the fields and have inferior access to off-farm employment, they earn less than men for their on-farm work and have lower welfare.

In contrast, others believe that growing rural labor markets are not only spearheading China's drive towards modernization, they have also created significant new opportunities for women. For example, Rozelle et al. (1999) and Lohmar, Rozelle and Zhao (2001) show that women entered the off-farm sector at higher rates than men between 1988 and 1995. Meng (2000) shows that as rural labor markets have liberalized, women have been earning the same wages as men, all other things equal. Wan (1993) finds that women are actually satisfied with their work and prefer working in the off-farm sector, despite the fact that many of these jobs are far from home and involve working conditions that would be deplored in developed countries. Finally, although no study to our knowledge has studied crop revenues in households in which women do most or all of the farmwork, it seems unlikely that the participation of women in agriculture has had a very large adverse effect on output or incomes. During the 1990s, the cropping sector's productivity has grown rapidly (Jin et al., 2002), which could not have occurred if a large part of the labor force was working inefficiently.

We believe that fundamental disagreements over the effects of China's rural labor market emergence on women's status exist largely because most previous analyses consider only part of the labor market or focus on only part of the country. Few have attempted to quantify certain key issues, such as the degree to which women have had access to off-farm employment or the effect of the participation of women in the on-farm sector. Perhaps because the questions being asked are broad, the current literature seems inconsistent and contradictory.

The overall goal of this paper is to contribute to the ongoing assessment of women's status as China's rural labor markets are emerging. Specifically, we have three objectives. First, we update trends in off-farm labor participation. Specifically, we will attempt to estimate off-farm participation rates in the migrant labor force, focusing on the participation of rural women over the reform era (between 1980 and 2000). Second, we analyze the determinants of participation in the migrant labor market to learn whether, all other factors held constant, women are making gains. Finally, to learn more about the role of women in the on-farm sector, we measure how women's participation affects the efficiency of farming. Our test helps us understand whether or not women's participation in agriculture undermines farm income.

To make our study more manageable, we make several assumptions that narrow the scope of our work. In the rest of this study, we assume, as do Thomas,

Contreras and Frankenberg (1997) and Quisumbing and Malluccio (2000), that increased participation in the off-farm labor market and higher wages for those with off-farm jobs are metrics that are positively correlated with women's welfare. These authors argue that as women take jobs, the income generated is directly attributable to their labor, which increases their decision making power within the household. By the same logic, we assume that if women put all or most of the labor into farming, their welfare will rise (fall) as the farm's efficiency rises (falls). In our multivariate analysis of the determinants of off-farm employment, we focus on migration because it is the most important and fastest growing segment of the off-farm labor force. When we examine the participation of women in agriculture, we restrict our analysis to the effects of women's participation on efficiency, using a supply function approach.

To meet these objectives, the rest of the paper is organized as follows. In the next section, we introduce the data that are used for the analysis, which were collected by the authors in the fall of 2000. The following section describes employment trends between 1981 and 2000, focusing mainly on trends for women. The third section uses multivariate analysis to explain the determinants of migration, and the fourth section examines how the participation of women in agriculture—either as household heads or as field workers—affects the efficiency of crop production. The final section concludes.

2 Data

The data for our study were collected in a randomly selected, nearly nationally representative sample of 60 villages in 6 provinces of rural China (henceforth, the China National Rural Survey—CNRS).[1] To accurately reflect varying income distributions within each province, one county was randomly selected from within each income quintile for the province, as measured by the gross value of industrial output. Two villages were randomly selected within each county. The survey teams used village rosters and our own counts of households to randomly choose twenty households, both those with and without their residency permits (*hukou*) in the village. A total of 1199 households were surveyed.

Several parts of the survey were designed to learn about the household's off-farm labor allocation decisions, including migration decisions. For roughly half of the households surveyed (610 households that were randomly selected from the

---

[1] The provinces are Hebei, Liaoning, Shaanxi, Zhejiang, Hubei, and Sichuan. The data collection effort involved students from the Center for Chinese Agricultural Policy, Renmin University, and China Agricultural University and was led by Loren Brandt of the University of Toronto, Scott Rozelle of the University of California, and Linxiu Zhang of the Center for Chinese Agricultural Policy, Chinese Academy of Sciences. Households were paid 20 *yuan* and given a gift in compensation for the time that they spent with the survey team.

1199, or roughly ten from each village), a twenty-year employment history form was completed for each household member and each child of the household head, even when they were no longer considered "household members." For each year between 1981 and 2000, the questionnaire tracked each individual's participation in off-farm employment, the main type of off-farm work performed, the place of residence while working (within or outside the village), the location of off-farm employment, and whether or not each individual was self-employed or wage earning.[2] The questions were asked for both males and females.

Using the employment history data, we separated off-farm jobs into four types: migrant wage earners (henceforth, migrants); self-employed migrants; local wage earners; and local self employed. Migrants were identified as men or women with off-farm jobs who did not live in the household while working. Local wage earners were individuals that had off-farm employment, were not self-employed, and lived at home while they worked. All respondents that reported being self-employed off the farm were categorized as such. We also asked about the extent of the participation of each member in each year in the household's on-farm activities. A household labor force measure was created by aggregating all individuals in the households above the age 16 who indicated that they were either working in or searching for employment in each year (*size of household labor force*). If a person over 16 indicated they had retired, could not work for health-related reasons, or had full-time enrollment in school, they were not included in the labor force total.

Our data allow us to create other variables over time that can help determine the pattern of shifting off-farm labor over time. Specifically, for each individual in the data set, we know the timing and extent of his/her education (*years of education*), participation in professional or skill-building training (*skill training*) and working experience over the past 20 years (*age*). The survey also collected information on the changing composition of the participation of entire family in the off- farm labor force during this period (a variable we call *average household experience*). As a consequence, we can use our data to create a 20-year retrospective panel that can be used to track employment and some of its key determinants over time.

The CNRS project team also gathered detailed information on household agricultural production. In addition to the plot-specific, farm inputs and outputs, the survey also asked about the characteristics of the plot (e.g., the nature of the plot tenure, its irrigation status, the quality of the soil and the extent to which the

---

[2] Enumerators attempted to ask the employment histories from each individual themselves. If a household member or one of the children of the household head was not present, the respondent (which was almost always the household head or spouse of the household head) answered. Extensive pre-testing found that the data are fairly accurate. In addition, we conducted a practical test to see whether or not a respondent bias problem exists in the employment history part of our data. We replicated the analysis after excluding observations on individuals we did not interview directly, and found that the results of our analysis did not change.

plot was affected by a weather shock in 2000). We also know how much labor each member of the household allocated to on- and off-farm work during the survey year (which we use to create one of our measures of *women-run farms*). Descriptive statistics for selected variables used in the analysis are included in Appendix 4.1.

3 The Evolution of China's Rural Labor Markets

Consistent with previous findings of other national studies of rural off-farm employment, the CNRS data show the off-farm labor force expanded steadily between 1981 and 2000. The data indicate that the proportion of the rural labor force that found some off-farm employment increased from around 16 percent in 1981 to 48 percent by 2000 (Table 4.1). By assuming that neighboring provinces similar to those surveyed have identical rates of off-farm labor participation, we estimate that off-farm rural employment in China rose from less than 40 million in 1981 to more than 200 million farmers in 2000, a growth in off-farm employment of more than 150 million during the reform era. Though this evidence is not conclusive, the large increase in labor flow seems to indicate that China's rural labor markets are functioning well. Although these estimates are based on a relatively small sample, they demonstrate the consistency of our data with much larger national studies by the China National Statistical Bureau (CNSB, 1996) and our own 1995 national village survey.[3]

By disaggregating China's labor trends, our data also demonstrate that labor markets are providing more than just off-farm income to rural residents and are developing in ways consistent with modernization trends (Chenery and Syrquin, 1975). Trends by employment type clearly show that the target destination of workers over the past 20 years has shifted from rural to urban. In 1981 most rural individuals (nearly 85 percent) spent all of the time they allocated to labor farming. Individuals who worked off the farm were almost three times as likely to live at home and work within or close to the village (7 percent were local self-employed; 4.2 percent were local wage earners) than to work outside of the village and live away from home (less than 1 percent were self employed migrants; less than 4

---

[3] Our estimates are also consistent with estimates by the State Statistical Bureau in the late 1980s and mid 1990s and Parish's study (Parish, Zhe and Li, 1995) in the early 1990s. For example, using our data set we estimate that 20 percent of the rural labor force worked off-farm in 1988. This figure nearly agrees with the State Statistical Bureau estimates for that year, 21 percent. In 1993, we estimate that 29 percent of the labor force worked off-farm, which is only three percentage points higher than the best guess made by Parish, Zhe and Li's national study. The CNRS estimates the off-farm employment rate to be 31 percent in 1995, which matches the CNSB estimate of the non-farm labor force (31 percent) and is consistent with our own 1995 community questionnaire-based estimates of rural off-farm employment (34 percent—Rozelle et al., 1999).

percent were migrants). By 2000 almost as many off-farm workers were living away from home (more than 85 percent in cities or suburban villages of major metropolitan areas) as in the village. Migrants composed both the largest and fastest growing component of the rural labor force.

Table 4.1 Labor market participation rates for men and women in rural China, 1981-2000

Employment	1981	1985	1990	1995	2000
Total off-farm employment (percent)	16	18	23	32	48
Of which:					
Men	27	31	38	49	63
Women	4	7	10	18	31

Source: Authors' survey.

The labor movement contours created from the off-farm employment histories of different age cohorts demonstrate one of most striking and consistent characteristics of China's changing employment patterns: the shift towards off-farm employment is dominated by younger workers (Table 4.2). Workers in all age cohort categories participated at similar rates in 1990 (ranging narrowly from 20.5 to 33.6 percent). One decade after the onset of the reforms, there was no clear progression when moving from the oldest to youngest cohorts. By 2000, however, the rise in the off-farm participation rates of younger workers accelerated relative to older ones, and a distinct ranking appeared as one moved from the youngest to the oldest cohort. In 2000 young workers in the 16 to 20 year old cohort participated at rates more than three times (75.8 percent) those of 16 to 20 year olds in 1990 (23.7 percent). Those in the 21 to 25 year old cohort and those in the 26 to 30 year old cohort doubled the off-farm participation rates of their 1990 cohorts. In contrast, older workers, while still increasing their participation rates significantly (by 17 percentage points), worked off the farm at less than half the rate (only 37.6 percent) than those in the 16 to 20 year old cohort.

In the same way that emerging rural labor markets may have numerous effects on the fabric of rural and urban economies, the benefits of participation in labor markets by women vary (World Bank, 2001). By some metrics, such as enrollment in primary and secondary schools, indicators of higher welfare for women rise with development, which implies better labor markets. However, by other indicators (such as the relative number of hours of housework performed by women versus men) there is little improvement. In short, the effect of economic development on women's welfare is complicated and depends on many factors.

Table 4.2 Off-farm labor participation rates by gender for selected age cohorts in rural China, 1990 and 2000

| Age cohorts | Off-farm labor participation rates (percent) | | | | | |
| | 1990 | | | 2000 | | |
	Total	Men	Women	Total	Men	Women
16-20	23.7	29.9	13.1	75.8	74.7	75.6
21-25	33.6	47.3	13.1	67.2	78.8	53.5
26-30	28.8	47.9	8.8	52.5	72.8	33.7
31-35	26.8	44.4	6.8	47.6	70.5	22.5
36-40	20.5	37.3	3.6	43.3	70.0	20.3
41-50	20.8	33.3	5.2	37.6	61.2	18.7

Source: Authors' survey.

Women and Off-farm Employment

According to the CNRS, when considering the rate of off-farm employment among women in rural China, the newly emerging labor markets have begun to have positive effects on women's relative welfare (Table 4.1). Although women have participated at rates far below those of men throughout the entire 20-year sample period, participation rates have risen rapidly since the early 1990s. In the 1980s, consistent with the findings from the national community survey-based study reported in Rozelle et al. (1999), off-farm participation rates of men (more than 25 percent in 1981) far exceeded those of women (less than 5 percent). Moreover, despite low initial levels of involvement in the off-farm sector, women's participation rates grew more slowly than men's rates during the 1980s. In the 1990s, however, the participation rate of women in the off-farm sector increased faster than that of men.

Although women have been entering all employment types, the most striking increases have come in migration (Figure 4.1). Throughout the 1980s, less than 1 percent of women left the farm and worked for a wage as a migrant. Since 1990, however, the rate of growth of the migrant labor force has been higher than any other category of job types for both men and women. By 2000, nearly 7 percent of the female labor force was working as wage-earning migrants. One interpretation of the increase in women's participation in migration is that as labor markets have become more competitive, the scope for managers to exercise discriminatory preferences has declined, therefore opening up new employment opportunities for women. Alternatively, the rise in women's work could have occurred as industries that have a preference for the skills of women have grown.

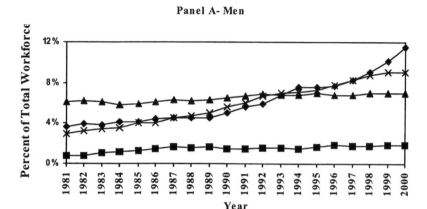

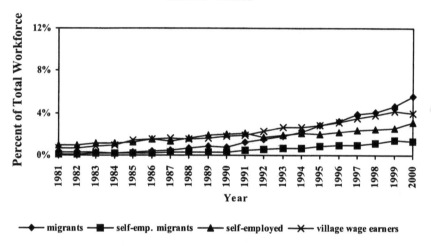

Figure 4.1 Increase in migration by gender, 1981–2000

Perhaps most poignantly, younger women are beginning to specialize by working solely in the off-farm sector. While participation rates among all women are still lower than rates among men (by 32 percentage points—63 percent for men and 31 percent for women) in 2000 (Table 4.1), the gap narrows for younger cohorts and disappears for the youngest cohort (Table 4.2). Both men and women in the 16 to 20 year old age groups have similar off-farm participation rates (about 75 percent). Like men, women in this cohort are increasingly specializing in off-farm labor. Specifically, the majority of young women who work off-farm in 2000 do no work on the farm (59 percent). The shift in the composition of the off-farm labor force towards young migrants who specialize in off-farm work contrasts sharply with the situation in 1990, when most off-farm workers continued to work on the farm on a part time or at least seasonal basis. These findings are consistent with the argument that the emergence of specialized modes of production in different villages across China's geographical landscape has been facilitated by the emergence of labor markets (Mohapatra, 2001).

With older cohorts, however, the gender gap in off-farm employment participation remains and helps explain the observation that women perform a large fraction of household farmwork (Table 4.2). For example, the difference (in percentage points) between male and females widens to 25.3 percent for 21 to 25 year olds; 39.1 percent for 31 to 35 year olds; and 48 percent for 41 to 45 year old.[4] Older men who work off-farm typically also work on farm; however, according to our data women on average during the 1990s accomplish more than 50 percent of the household farm work.[5] In the fifth section of the paper, we will examine the effect on production of having women heavily involved in farming. If women's participation in farming were found to have a negative impact on production, by our initial assumptions it would be considered a negative consequence for women's welfare.

4 Multivariate Analysis: Determinants of Participation in the Migrant Labor Force

To explain the determinants of participation in the migrant labor force among individuals in the sample villages and to examine the increased participation of women after considering multivariate effects, we use a fixed effects conditional logit estimator similar to that developed by McFadden (1974). We assert that in each year, t, an individual, i, from village, v, chooses to participate in migration or not and that this choice maximizes the individual's expected utility, given a vector of individual, household, and community characteristics, X_{ivt}. If we define an indicator variable, y_{ivt}, that is 1 when individual i participates in the migrant labor market and is 0 otherwise, we can estimate the effects of the variables contained in X on the individual's labor market participation decision by estimating:

---

[4] In addition, women in the age categories between 21 and 25 and between 26 and 30 also have a higher probability of not being in the labor force at all. In our entire sample, eight percent of the sample are neither working nor searching for a job; there are more than 10 percent of women between 21 and 30 that fall into this category. However, in almost all cases this is explained by the fact that they have children that are two years old or younger.

[5] Although our data show that women are putting slightly more than half of the total labor hours into farm work, contrary to the statements of those that call attention to the feminization of China's agriculture, de Brauw (2003) finds no evidence that the proportion of hours put into farming by women are rising. Hence, in this paper we refrain from calling the active participation of women in farming "feminization" since this would imply that women are taking on an increasing fraction of the farm work, which they are not. Our data, however, are consistent with an agricultural labor force that is getting older (with more work done by both elderly men and women).

$$\text{Prob}(y_{ivt}=1) = \exp(X_{ivt}\beta) / (1+ \exp(X_{ivt}\beta)) \tag{1}$$
$$\text{Prob}(y_{ivt}=0) = 1 / (1+ \exp(X_{ivt}\beta))$$

where β represents a vector of parameters that corresponds to the effects of the individual and household characteristics on participating in each economic activity.[6]

We use three different approaches to examine the determinants of migration by women during the reform period. For the first two, we specify a dummy variable (*gender*) that is one if an individual is male and zero if female. When we include all observations between 1981 and 2000, we interact the gender indicator variable with an indicator variable for the 1990s (Regression 1 in Table 4.3). Second, we compare the results from Regression 1 with regressions in which we split the sample into data for the 1980s and the 1990s (Regressions 2 and 3 in Table 4.3). From these regressions, we can test for increased participation of women in the labor force in two ways—through the interaction term in Regression 1 and by comparing the magnitudes of the coefficients of the gender variable in Regressions 2 and 3. In Regressions 4 and 5 we use the gender variable to divide the sample into male and female subsamples in order to examine how other factors in the model have affected the participation of men and women during the 1980s and 1990s differently (Table 4.4).

In all of our regression models, we include all individual and household variables, X_{ivt}, that we have over the length of the panel that can help explain participation in the migrant labor force. Based in part on our observations in the previous section, and in part by the labor supply literature, we hypothesize that each person's experience (proxied by age) in year t affects their participation rates. We further hypothesize that human capital measures, including years of education and skill training will positively affect participation rates if labor markets are working relatively efficiently. At the household level, we include two variables, one that controls for the size of the household labor force in year t, and the other that controls for the average amount of off-farm experience that an individual's household members have in year t.[7] Finally, we include a time trend. All variables in all equations are time varying by year for the whole 20 year panel.[8]

---

[6] In using the conditional logit estimator in our empirical work, we add an error term ε_{ivt} and assume it is independently and identically distributed across observations according to the Weibull distribution.

[7] We were somewhat concerned that the "household labor participation experience" variable could be endogenous. In order to address this concern, we dropped the variable from the model and found that the other parameter estimates did not change.

[8] Unfortunately, we only have household-level measures of wealth (proxied by the value of the household's durable goods) and land size that vary over the past 5 years. Because we believed these variables might also affect the individual's decision to migrate, we also ran the basic version of our model with a 5 year panel, including these two explanatory variables. The results are almost identical.

Table 4.3 Conditional fixed effects logit estimators explaining the change in participation of individuals in migration in rural China between the 1980s and 1990s

	Dependent Variable		
Explanatory variables	(Regression 1) Migration	(Regression 2) Migration: Between 1980-1990	(Regression 3) Migration: Between 1990-2000
Age	0.94	0.95	0.92
	(14.96)**	(10.38)**	(30.11)**
Gender	6.12	11.09	3.13
(1=male)	(16.78)**	(19.16)**	(20.73)**
Years of Education	1.10	1.14	1.17
	(7.02)**	(8.40)**	(17.18)**
Skill Training	2.30	2.02	1.53
(1=yes)	(9.25)**	(7.46)**	(7.41)**
Average Household	1.56	1.62	1.16
Experience	(17.55)**	(16.91)**	(15.99)**
Size of Household	1.16	1.29	1.29
Labor Force	(6.86)**	(10.27)**	(17.76)**
Age*	0.99		
90s dummy	(3.15)**		
Gender*	0.57		
90s dummy	(4.81)**		
Education*	1.08		
90s dummy	(5.48)**		
Training*	0.65		
90s dummy	(4.14)**		
Experience*	0.75		
90s dummy	(11.66)**		
Labor Force*	1.13		
90s dummy	(5.43)**		
Time Trend	1.09		
	(11.85)**		
Year Dummies:		Included	Included
N	34,257	12,623	21,631
Likelihood Ratio Index	0.276	0.285	0.267

Notes:
1. * indicates significance at the 10 percentage level.
2. ** indicates significance at the 5 percentage level.
3. Coefficients reported are odds ratios, asymptotic z statistics in parentheses.
4. Odds ratios can be interpreted as the additional probability of an event if there is an additional unit of the explanatory variable, *ceteris paribus*. The *90s dummy* variable is one for all years between 1990 and 2000, and zero otherwise. The odds ratios for the interacted variables should be interpreted as multiplicative. Column (2) only includes data from 1981-1990 and column (3) only includes data from 1991-2000.

China's Rural Economy after WTO

Table 4.4 Conditional fixed effects logit estimators explaining the change in participation of individuals in migration in rural China between the 1980s and 1990s

Explanatory variables	Dependent Variable (Participation in Migration)	
	(Regression 4) Women Only	(Regression 5)
Age	0.89	0.95
	(7.89)**	(12.70)**
Years of Education	1.15	1.11
	(3.30)**	(7.23)**
Skill Training	1.96	2.18
(1=yes)	(2.30)**	(7.95)**
Average Household	1.68	1.61
Experience	(7.76)**	(16.31)**
Size of Household	1.23	1.19
Labor Force	(3.23)**	(7.01)**
Age*	0.97	0.99
90s dummy	(1.78)*	(2.27)**
Education*	1.15	1.03
90s dummy	(3.11)**	(2.18)**
Training*	0.59	0.71
90s dummy	(1.72)*	(2.96)**
Experience*	0.69	0.72
90s dummy	(5.47)**	(11.06)**
Labor Force*	1.09	1.11
90s dummy	(1.40)	(3.62)**
Time Trend	1.18	1.10
	(10.64)**	(3.62)**
N	16,929	16,625
Likelihood Ratio Index	0.201	0.378

Notes:
1. * indicates significance at the 10 percentage level.
2. ** indicates significance at the 5 percentage level.
3. Coefficients reported are odds ratios, asymptotic z statistics in parentheses. Odds ratios can be interpreted as the additional probability of an event if there is an additional unit of the explanatory variable, *ceteris paribus*. The *90s dummy* variable is one for all years between 1990 and 2000, and zero otherwise. The odds ratios for the interacted variables should be interpreted as multiplicative.

In most of our estimations, we use data on 2297 individuals from 610 different households that were employed—in either the on-farm or off-farm sector or both—at some time between 1981 and 2000. For various reasons, the data we use for estimation does not include the full panel of 45,940 observations. First, some individuals enter the labor force during this period and others stop working. Second, we drop one village from the analysis because no migrants left the village for work during the entire sample period. These households could not be included in the migration equation as there was no variation within the village for the left-hand side of equation (1), making the village fixed effect perfectly correlated with the dependent variable for that village. As a result of these limits, we are left with 34,257 observations from 59 villages to explain migration participation in the full model (both men and women) over the whole time period (the 1980s and 1990s).

Results

In almost all respects, the multivariate regression analyses perform well (Tables 4.4 and 4.5). Most of the coefficients of the basic variables in the models have the expected signs and are highly significant. In lieu of reporting the actual coefficient estimates for β in Tables 3 and 4, we report odds ratios, which are $\exp(\beta)$. Odds ratios can be explained more intuitively than raw logit coefficients, as they give the change in probability of migration due to a change in the corresponding right-hand side variable. For example, we find that education increases the individual's participation in off-farm labor markets. For every additional year of education reported, the probability one is in the migrant labor force increases by 10 percent between 1980 and 1990 (or, a person with an additional year of education is 1.10 times more likely to migrate). For interaction terms, odds ratios are interpreted multiplicatively rather than additively (e.g. Wooldridge, 2002). Therefore, an additional year of education has an even larger effect, 19 percent, (1.10*1.08=1.19) on migration between 1990 and 2000. Other coefficients also correspond with our expectations. The coefficient on the age variable implies that the odds of getting a migrant job fall by 6 percent for every year a person ages.

Most importantly, the results clearly demonstrate that the descriptive findings in section 3 hold up to multivariate analysis (Table 4.3). For example, the coefficient on the indicator variable for gender in Regression 1 suggests that male participation in migration during the 1980s (the base period), holding all else constant, was 612 percent (or 6.12 times) higher than female participation. However, by the 1990s, the relative difference was only 57 percent as much (or 0.57*6.12 = 3.48 times; see coefficient on the interaction term in the same regression. When we compare the coefficients on the gender indicator variables in Regressions 2 and 3, we find a similar result. In the 1980s, males were more than 11 times as likely to participate in migration as females. By the 1990s, males were only 3.13 times as likely.[9] Therefore the employment access gap is narrowing considerably over time, though men still participate in migrant labor markets at rates far higher than women.

---

[9] When we use a sample that includes only the final five years of data (with two additional control variables), the difference between males and females falls to 2.79.

Table 4.5 Analysis of the effect of women-headed households on the efficiency of farming, all crops, using village fixed effects

	Dependent variables: ln (gross revenue of all crops)			
	(1)	(2)	(3)	(4)
Household characteristics				
Female-headed	0.120			
	(3.01)***			
Proportion of hours worked on farm by females		0.031		
		(0.75)		
Proportion of female household labor			0.001	
			(2.35)**	
Proportion of female household agricultural labor				0.001
				(1.28)
Asset value	-0.000	-0.000	-0.000	-0.000
	(0.47)	(0.71)	(0.49)	(0.73)
Farm size	-0.001	-0.001	-0.001	-0.001
	(0.54)	(0.59)	(0.52)	(0.57)
Household size	0.015	0.013	0.009	0.013
	(1.95)*	(1.71)*	(1.16)	(1.63)
Household head characteristics				
Age	0.001	0.001	0.001	0.001
	(0.75)	(0.69)	(0.85)	(0.77)
Education (years)	0.004	0.003	0.004	0.003
	(1.08)	(0.97)	(1.09)	(1.00)
Plot characteristics				
Irrigated	0.207	0.204	0.205	0.204
	(7.74)***	(7.61)***	(7.66)***	(7.64)***
High quality soil	0.216	0.221	0.216	0.220
	(8.95)***	(9.13)***	(8.94)***	(9.08)***
Plain	0.147	0.148	0.147	0.151
	(1.24)	(1.25)	(1.24)	(1.28)
Hill	0.097	0.099	0.096	0.101
	(0.84)	(0.85)	(0.83)	(0.87)
Terraced	0.064	0.065	0.059	0.067
	(0.53)	(0.53)	(0.49)	(0.55)
Distance from home	0.005	0.005	0.003	0.004
	(0.44)	(0.41)	(0.27)	(0.38)
Shock from weather, pests, etc.	-0.011	-0.011	-0.011	-0.011
	(17.18)***	(17.19)***	(17.09)***	(17.19)***
Single season	0.576	0.577	0.576	0.576
	(26.66)***	(26.65)***	(26.63)***	(26.64)***
Constant	5.375	5.378	5.337	5.361
	(40.02)***	(39.35)***	(39.08)***	(39.05)***
N	5327	5323	5327	5323
Number of villages	60	60	60	60
R-squared	0.18	0.18	0.18	0.18

Note: 1. Absolute value of t statistics in parentheses. Estimates were corrected for clustering. *, **, and *** indicate significance at 10 percentage, 5 percentage, and 1 percentage, respectively.

When we split the sample into separate regressions for men and women, we find that many of the same factors affect participation in the migrant labor force, although the magnitudes of the impacts differ (Table 4.4).[10] For example, younger women and men both work more as do those with more years of formal education and training. However, the differences between the coefficients in the regressions in women's and men's equations show that both the age and education effects are more pronounced for women. Moreover, these effects are increasing over time. The propensity for younger women with higher levels of education to find a migrant job has risen over time. Such findings support calls by academics and policy makers to increase the education opportunities for young women (Nyberg and Rozelle, 1999).

5 The Participation of Women in Farming and Relative Efficiency

Although the youngest cohort of women, 16 to 20 year olds, have caught up to their male counterparts in access to off-farm employment and are not being discriminated against in any greater degree than before in terms of wage earnings, during the reforms older women have have tended to remain on the farm. When assessing the impact of the reforms on women, one must address questions about whether or not their participation in agriculture has led to lower earnings. Internationally, women-headed households and women-cultivated plots have produced lower yields and revenues (World Bank, 2001). Women are less efficient producers for a variety of reasons (Saito et al., 1994; Quisumbing, 1994). If true in China, then part of the gains that women have gained in the off-farm sector have been offset by the lower incomes that they receive in farming.

In order to answer the question of whether women-headed households are more, less or equally efficient in cropping, we use a fixed-effects regression approach. Specifically, total cropping revenue and enterprise revenue for rice, wheat and maize for each of the household's plots is regressed on the plot, household and village characteristics that are thought to determine plot-specific income.[11] The basic model is:

$$y_{hv} = \alpha + \mu_v + D_{hv}\gamma + X_{hv}\beta + \varepsilon_{hv} \tag{2}$$

where y_{hv} denotes total income per capita or from one of the three specific sources for household h in village v. The variable, X_{hv}, is a vector of plot and household

---

[10] The same patterns appear when using the sample that includes only the last 5 years of data and when the specification includes two additional control variables.

[11] In essence, we loosely follow Yotopoulos and Lau (1973), who examine economic efficiency by examining the profit function. Like Yotopolous and Lau, since we have cross-sectional data, we cannot include prices directly; the prices, which vary by village, are captured by the village dummy variables.

characteristics including the plot irrigation status, is irrigated, its quality, its topography, the distance from the household and the size of the agronomic shock (which vary by plot) and value of the household's assets, the size of the farm, the number of household members, and the age and education of the household head (which vary by household). To control for differences in growing conditions, prices, and other unobservable factors across villages, we also include a village-level fixed effect, μ_v.

In addition to X_{hv}, we include a measure of the level of participation of women in farming, D_{hv}, in order to test whether or not women's participation on the farm affects farm efficiency.[12] Since there is no *a priori* variable that best measures whether a farm is run by women or not, we employ four alternative variables, one in each regression, to attempt to capture the effects of women's management in our model (henceforth, we refer to this variable as the *women-run farms* variable). Specifically, we use an indicator variable that is one if the household head is female and zero otherwise; a variable that measures the proportion of the household's total labor force that is female (measured as the number of people); a variable that measures the proportion of the household's agricultural labor force that is female (also measured as the number of people); and a variable that measures the proportion of agricultural hours of the household worked by females (measured as the number of hours). The coefficient on the women-run farm variable, γ, will provide the test for our hypothesis: holding all other things equal, if $\gamma=0$, then women-run farms are equally efficient in generating farm income when compared to male-run farms; the alternative hypothesis is that women-run farms are less efficient. Since we are interested primarily in whether or not women-run farms are less efficient, we use a one-sided hypothesis test.

Using more than 5000 plot-level observations for the analysis, we find results that are somewhat at odds with the results from other countries in other parts of the world (World Bank, 2001). The coefficients on all four of the women-run farm variables are either insignificant or positive (Table 4.5). According to our data, when all of the other variables in our model are held constant, women-run farms are not less efficient than those of men, implying that women-run farms earn at least as much revenue on their plots as farms run by men. In terms of our hypothesis testing framework, at a 1 percent level of statistical significance, we cannot reject the null hypothesis that women-run farms are equally efficient as men-run ones at generating revenue.

---

[12] Ideally, we would like to be able to include an indicator variable that is 1 when a woman is primarily in charge of the farm and zero otherwise. Unfortunately, from our data it is impossible to tell in which households women make all or most of the important farming decisions. Therefore, we test a number of different variables that could indicate that a farm is run by women (or a farm in which a large fraction of the labor is provided by women), in order to capture several different possible definitions of "women-run farms."

Table 4.6 Analysis of the effect of women-headed households on the efficiency of farming for all crops, rice, wheat and maize, using village fixed effects and controls for ability

	Dependent variables: Total or Enterprise Revenue (in Natural Logs)			
	(1) All crops	(2) Rice	(3) Wheat	(4) Maize
Household characteristics				
Female-headed	0.117	0.068	0.033	0.207
	(2.90)***	(2.68)***	(0.77)	(3.51)***
Asset value	-0.000	0.000	0.000	-0.000
	(0.42)	(1.80)*	(0.43)	(1.04)
Farm size	-0.001	0.001	-0.003	0.000
	(0.54)	(0.80)	(1.82)*	(0.07)
Household size	0.012	0.010	0.004	0.011
	(1.58)	(1.93)*	(0.47)	(1.09)
Household head characteristics				
Age	0.001	0.002	0.002	-0.001
	(0.91)	(2.82)***	(1.74)*	(0.71)
Education (years)	0.004	0.002	0.011	0.015
	(1.18)	(1.01)	(3.01)***	(3.20)***
Mother's education level, head (if female) or spouse of head	0.003	0.003	-0.013	-0.001
	(0.48)	(1.03)	(1.78)*	(0.20)
Plot characteristics				
Irrigated	0.210	-0.015	0.127	0.156
	(7.75)***	(0.62)	(3.22)***	(4.43)***
High quality soil	0.217	0.130	0.129	0.102
	(8.86)***	(8.26)***	(4.47)***	(3.14)***
Plain	0.152	-0.018	0.062	1.255
	(1.28)	(0.33)	(0.43)	(4.26)***
Hill	0.099	-0.015	0.043	1.274
	(0.86)	(0.30)	(0.32)	(4.32)***
Terraced	0.072	-0.045	0.000	1.278
	(0.59)	(0.81)	(0.00)	(4.19)***
Distance from home	0.004	-0.002	0.025	-0.028
	(0.37)	(0.21)	(1.82)*	(1.32)
Shock from weather, pests, etc.	-0.011	-0.008	-0.008	-0.013
	(17.20)***	(13.83)***	(10.36)***	(17.89)***
Single season	0.576	0.257	0.091	-0.086
	(26.37)***	(11.80)***	(1.64)	(2.02)**
Constant	5.367	6.264	5.606	4.972
	(39.59)***	(87.50)***	(35.05)***	(16.40)***
Observations	5220	1630	1009	1083
Number of villages	60	37	43	47
R-squared	0.18	0.22	0.16	0.31

Notes: 1. Absolute value of t statistics in parentheses. Estimates were corrected for clustering. *, **, and *** indicate significance at 10 percentage, 5 percentage, and 1 percentage, respectively.

Hence, according to our findings, although women during the course of rural China's recent development have both taken great responsibilities and provided a large fraction of the labor on the farm, the earnings in these farms have not suffered. The most direct interpretation of this result is, of course, that women are at least as good as at farming as men. However, using the results from Table 4.5, we are unable to reject alternative interpretations. It could be that since female-headed households are frequently, but not always, households in which the husband permanently works outside of the village, these households face fewer capital constraints and therefore are able to produce more. It could also be that farms run by women are not random. Rather, households that have farms by women are households in which the women are particularly capable farmers.

Although "ability" is difficult to control for, in Table 4.6 we run a series of equations for total crop revenue (as in Table 4.5) and for crop-specific revenue (for rice, wheat and maize) which have the same specification as in Table 4.5, except that we add one variable: the education of mother of the household head (if female) or the spouse of the household head. As before, when we add the variable and control for ability, our analysis suggests that cropping revenue earned by women-headed households is not lower than cropping revenue in other households. Our results are robust whether we are explaining total crop revenue or the revenue earned on rice, wheat or maize plots.[13]

6 Summary and Conclusions

In this paper, we have sought to understand the effect of China's labor market development on the welfare of women. To do so, the first part of the paper documents the rapid emergence of China's labor markets during the reform period. Specifically, we show that the rapid rise in employment that began in the 1980s and early 1990s has continued even during the late 1990s, a time when some feared that macroeconomic conditions might keep rural residents on the farm or drive them back to the farm. In our disaggregation of labor market trends, we also show that labor markets are clearly acting in a way consistent with an economy that is in transition from one being dominated by agriculture to one being characterized by the rising presence of other forms of production. Our analysis illustrates that labor markets have allowed migration to become the most important form of off-farm activity and has become increasingly dominated by younger workers who are showing signs of specializing in off-farm work.

Assuming that participation in off-farm labor markets is a sign of increased welfare, our analysis show that because women have had greater access to off-farm

---

[13] We also used an alternative measure of ability (grades of the household head, if female, or spouse of the household head during the final year that the individual was in school). Regardless of the dependent variable, we find that women-run farms are no less efficient than male-run ones.

employment, they have become better off. Although women still lag behind men, access to off-farm jobs has increased more quickly for women than men. By 2000, over 30 percent of women had jobs off the farm, up from only 10 percent in 1990. The brightest outlook, however, is shown to exist for the youngest cohort. In the case of 16-20 year old women, the level of participation is high (more than 75 percent) and equal to that of men.

Although China's rural labor market development has improved the welfare of women according to our criteria, women have not achieved parity with men. Women play an important role in farming in China, both in running the farm as a household head and in allocating labor to agriculture. In the rest of the world when this happens, the revenue produced on the farm has been shown to lower on their farms than those of men. According to our results, however, the efficiency of cropping does not suffer when women run the farm. From this perspective, also, the development of China's rural economy cannot be said to have hurt women. Unfortunately, due to space limitations the source of the higher farming efficiency of women-headed households is not explained in this paper. Further work is needed to pinpoint the sources of these measured gains.

In summary, then, the type of growth that China has been experiencing has led to fast growing labor markets in which women have been able to participate. Policies that facilitate the perpetuation of this growth should be continued (e.g., higher spending on rural education). The government should also take an active role in ensuring that women become even more active in off-farm labor markets so they can close the gaps that still remain and make sure that the gaps do not re-widen in the future.

References

Chan, A., *Worker Under Assault* (Armonk, NY: Sharpe, 2001).

Chan, A. and Senser, R.A., China's Troubled Workers, *Foreign Affairs* 76 (1997): 104–117.

Chenery, H. and Syrquin, M., *Patterns of Development, 1950-1970* (Oxford University Press, London, 1975).

de Brauw, A. (2003), Are Women taking over the Farm in China? Working paper, Williams College, Department of Economics, Williamstown, MA.

de Brauw, A., Huang, J.K., Rozelle, S., Zhang, L.X. and Zhang, Y.G., The Evolution of China's Rural Labor Markets during the Reforms, *Journal of Comparative Economics* 30 (2002): 329-353.

Jin, S.Q., Rozelle, S., Huang, J.K. and Hu, R.F., The Creation and Spread of Technology and Total Factor Productivity in China's Agriculture, *American Journal of Agricultural Economics* 84 (2002): 916-930.

Lohmar, B., Rozelle, S., and Zhao, C.B., The Rise of Rural-to-Rural Labor Markets in China. *Asian Geographer* 20 (2001): 101-123.

Maurer-Fazio, M., Rawski, T. and Zhang, W., Inequality in the Rewards for Holding Up Half the Sky: Gender Wage Gaps in China's Urban Labor Markets, 1988 to 1994, *China Journal* 41 (1999): 55-88.

McFadden, D., Conditional Logit Analysis of qualitative choice behavior, in P. Zambreka (eds), *Frontiers of Econometrics* (New York: Academic Press, 1974).

Meng, X., Institutions and Culture: Women's Economic Position in Mainland China and Taiwan (Working Paper, Department of Economics, Research School of Pacific and Asian Studies, Australian National University, Canberra, Australia, 2000).

Mohapatra, S., The Evolution of Modes of Production and China's Rural Economic Development (Working Paper, Department of Agricultural and Resource Economics, University of California, Davis, CA, 2001).

Neumark, D., Employer's Discriminatory Behavior and the Estimation of Wage Discrimination, *The Journal of Human Resources* 23 (1988): 279-295.

Nyberg, A. and Rozelle, S., *Accelerating Growth in Rural China* (World Bank: Washington, D.C., 1999).

Parish, W., Zhe, X.Y. and Li, F., Nonfarm Work and Marketization of the Chinese Countryside, *China Quarterly* 143 (1995): 697-730.

Quisumbing, A., Improving Women's Agricultural Productivity as Farmers and Workers (Education and Social Policy Department Discussion Paper 37, World Bank, Washington, D.C., 1994).

Quisumbing, A. and Malluccio, J., Intrahousehold Allocation and Gender Relations: New Empirical Evidence from Four Developing Countries (Working Paper, International Food Policy Research Institute, Washington, D.C., 2000).

Rozelle, S., Stagnation Without Equity: Changing Patterns of Income and Inequality in China's Post-Reform Rural Economy, *China Journal* 35 (1996): 63-96.

Rozelle, S., Li, G., Shen, M., Hughart, A. and Giles, J., Leaving China's Farms: Survey Results of New Paths and Remaining Hurdles to Rural Migration, *China Quarterly* 158 (1999): 367-393.

Rozelle, S., Dong, X., Zhang, L. and Mason, A., Gender Wage Gaps in Post-Reform Rural China, *Pacific Economic Review* 7 (2002): 157-179.

Saito, K., Mekonnen, H. and Spurling, D., Raising the Productivity of Women Farmers in Sub-Saharan Africa (Discussion Paper 230, World Bank, Washington, D.C., 1994).

Solinger, D., *Contesting Citizenship in Urban China: Peasant Migrants, the State, and the Logic of the Market* (Berkeley, CA: University of California Press, 1999).

Song, Y. and Jiggins, J., Feminization of Agriculture and Related Issues: two cases study in marginal rural area in China (Paper presented at the European Conference on Agricultural and Rural Development in China, ECARDC VI, January 5 to 7, 2000, Leiden, Holland).

SSB [State Statistical Bureau], *Zhongguo Tongji Nianjian* [China Statistical Yearbook] (Beijing, China: State Statistical Bureau Press, 1990-2000).

Stark, O., Rural to Urban Migration and Some Economic Issues: A Review Utilising Findings of Surveys and Empirical Studies Covering 1965-1975 Period (Working Paper, World Employment Programme Research Series, International Labour Office, Geneva, Switzerland, 1976).

Thomas, D., Contreras, D. and Frankenberg, E., Child Health and Distribution of Household Resources at Marriage (Working Paper, Santa Monica, CA:RAND, 1997).

Todaro, M., *Internal Migration in Developing Countries: A Review of Theory, Evidence, Methodology and Research Priorities* (International Labor Office, Geneva, Switzerland, 1976).

Wan, D., Women in China and Off Farm Employment Decisions, Unpublished Honors Thesis, Department of Economics (Stanford, CA: Stanford University, 1993).

West, L. and Zhao, Y., *Rural Labor Flows in China* (Berkeley, CA: University of California Press, 2000).

World Bank, *Engendering Development, A World Bank Policy Research Report* (World Bank Press: Washington, D.C., 2000).

Wooldridge, J., *Econometric Analysis of Cross Section and Panel Data* (Cambridge, MA: MIT Press, 2002).

Yotopoulos, P. and Lau, L., A Test for Relative Economic Efficiency: Some Further Results, *American Economic Review* 63 (1973): 214-223.

Appendix 4.1 Descriptive statistics for selected variables

Variable	Mean	Standard Deviation
Gender (1=male)	0.490	0.5
Years of Education	6.01	3.66
Male	6.81	3.47
Female	5.23	3.68
Skill Training (1=yes)	0.185	0.389
Male	0.26	0.44
Female	0.11	0.31
Total Land Area, 2000 (mu)	8.91	11.10
Value of Durables, 2000 (*yuan*)	4970	34900
Household Labor Force	3.75	1.94
percentage of female headed households	6.00	—
percentage of households with *female- dominated* in agriculture[1]	12.57	—

Note: 1. "Female-dominated" households here refer to households whose female labors performed more than 75 percentage of hours spending in the agriculture.
Source: Authors' survey.

Chapter 5

Rising Gender Gap in Non-Agricultural Employment in Rural China

Xiaoyun Liu[*]
Terry Sicular
Xian Xin

1 Introduction

In recent decades, the structure of income for rural households in China has changed substantially. In particular, income from non-agricultural pursuits has increased substantially in importance. Most observers believe that this trend will continue. China is land scarce—more than 0.8 billion people live in rural China with less than 0.1 hectare of cultivated land per capita (SSB, 2003)—and has almost no comparative advantage in bulk commodity production, especially of land intensive commodities (Tian, 2000; Lu, 2001). With increased openness to imports of grain and other farm products following China's accession to the WTO, prices and thus the income of farmers will likely decline in major grain producing areas (Huang, 1999; Xin, 2001). Therefore, job opportunities in the non-agricultural sector are vital in sustaining growth for the income of rural households.

Such changes in the structure of rural household income have been associated with shifts in the structure of rural employment. Prior to the reforms, China's labor markets were inflexible and highly segmented, but labor mobility has increased (Sicular and Zhao, 2002). The development of Township and Village Enterprises (TVEs) and the private sector has generated opportunities in non-agricultural employment for rural labor. In recent years, rural workers have shifted out of agriculture and have increasingly participated in non-agricultural employment. Official statistics show that the annual rate of growth in the number of rural workers engaged in non-agricultural employment has averaged at 0.05 percent in the 1990s, rising from 67.140 million in 1985 to 127.07 million in 1995 and 151.65 million in 2000 (China Rural Report, 2003).

These shifts in the composition of rural income and employment have

---

[*] Special thanks are given to Prof. Dong Xiaoyuan, Prof. Zhao Yaohui, Prof. Yao Yang, and anonymous referrers of China Economic Quarterly for their helpful comments on earlier draft. The first author benefited from the training program "Women Economist" held in Peking University funded by the Ford Foundation during the period of 2002-2004.

potentially different implications for men and women. Traditionally, in rural China, women stayed home to care for the family while men worked outside the home, and rural women stayed in the village working in agriculture while men migrated out to find work. Recent evidence suggests that while women now participate in non-agricultural work, they do so less than men (Zhang, 2000). Studies of rural migration find that the probability of migration for women is less than that of men (Zhao, 1997; 2001; Hare, 1999). Such patterns are not necessarily unique to China. Some studies find that rural labor migration also differs by gender in other developing countries (Agesa and Agesa, 1999; Boserup, 1990).

This paper examines the extent of—as well as trends in—gender difference in non-agricultural employment in rural China. Using data from a large-scale survey, we analyze the factors that determine observed gender differences. Many factors that influence labor supply and gender are only one determinant. The low non-agricultural employment of rural women could also result from low human capital or from other social-economic factors. We find that even after controlling for other factors, gender is a significant determinant of the probability of non-agricultural employment. In addition, we examine whether the gender gap has changed over time. We find that the gender gap, in fact, increases between the two years for which we have data—1989 and 1997.

The rest of this paper is organized as follows. Sections 2 and 3 describe microeconomic empirical models and the dataset to be used in this study. Section 4 provides analysis on econometric estimates of probit models, and section 5 offers some conclusions and policy implications.

2 Methodology

The literature on non-agriculture employment in China is relatively large now. Some of the papers examine the determinants of the migration decision, the means of migration, the contributions of migrants to the household income, and the causes as well as consequences of return migration (Zhao, 1997 and 2001; Hare, 1999). Others look more broadly at non-agricultural employment, including local employment by private businesses and TVEs. Gender is typically included in empirical analyses.

Many studies of China's rural employment estimate the probability that individuals participate in various types of work using a logistic or a probit model. Probabilities of employment in various types of work depend on individual, household, and community characteristics.[1] In this paper, we follow this usual approach but modify it to more fully explore gender differences. Specifically, we include interaction terms that allow us to examine the links of male and female non-agricultural employment with individual, household, and community characteristics.

---

[1] For more detailed discussion, please refer to Sicular and Zhao (2002).

The probit model takes the following form, $P (Occup = 1) = F (\beta'x)$, where P is the probability, and the dependent variable *Occup* is a dummy variable.[2] *Occup*=1 means that the individual has non-agricultural employment. F is the standard normal cumulative distribution function. β is the vector of coefficients to be estimated. x is a vector of explanatory variables, and $\beta'x$ is called the probit index.

The interpretation of the probit coefficient β_1 is that each one-unit increase in x_1 leads to an increase of the probit index by β_1 standard deviations. The change in probability for a change in variable x_1 is the height of the normal density multiplied by the coefficient β_1.

According to the theory of labor market, many factors can influence labor market participation. These include individual characteristics, such as human capital, household characteristics—like household size and land—and some community characteristics. Our analysis includes as explanatory variables a range of individual, household, and community characteristics as well as a time dummy.

Individual characteristics include gender, age, education level, and marital status. We expect gender to significantly affect non-agricultural employment. Since some studies have found a nonlinear relationship between age and labor participation, we also include the square of age as an explanatory variable.

In rural areas, farmers in villages usually work in both household and agricultural activities. The demand of housework and household agricultural production may affect participation in a non-agricultural occupation, especially where markets are imperfect, so we include relevant variables. Household size and dependant (the number of household members younger than 12 and older than 70) variables will be used to reflect the demand for housework. The demand for labor in agriculture is captured by the cultivated land of the household. In some studies, land is thought of as the proxy variable for labor surplus, so we also examine this in the model. Having an official cadre in the family has been found to be a factor determining non-agricultural employment, so this variable is included as well. From the theory of labor supply, the income of other household members should influence an individual's labor supply, so the logs of other household members' income are also included as explanatory variables.

Labor market demand in the community or locality is a potential determinant of non-agricultural employment. We use the percentage of village labor working out to represent the local demand for non-agricultural employment. Rural labor is more likely to participate in the non-agricultural sector when the percentage of labor working out in his or her village is high. The presence of TVEs can have an influence on the local employment of rural labor. Therefore, another factor determining non-agricultural employment is whether or not the community has TVEs. Other community factors, such as customs and social norms, may also affect individual choices, and employment behavior can change over time, so we use region and time dummy variables to control the effects of such differences.

---

[2] Employment in non-agricultural household sidelines and self-employment are included here.

Our regression of non-agricultural employment will therefore include the following vector of independent variables:

x = (*Gender, HHsize, Age, Agesq, Edu, Marriage, Old, Child, Land, Cadre, Lnin_others, Workout, Enterpr,* RD, *TD*)
Where
Gender: dummy variable, female=1 and male=0;
Hhsize: household size;
Age : age in years;
Agesq : the square of age;
Edu1- Edu5 : individual education in levels, dummy variables;
Child: number of children younger than 12 years old;
Old: number of household members older than 70;
Marriage: marital status (1=married);
Land: arable land in the household;
Cadre: dummy variable, whether or not is an official cadre, *Cadre*=1 is yes;
Lnin_others: log income of other household members' income;
Workout: percentage of community labor force work out;
Enterpr: dummy variable of whether or not the community has an enterprise;
RD: regional dummy variables;
TD: time dummy variables.

We can use the regression model above to examine the gender difference in non-agricultural employment by testing the null hypothesis of zero coefficients for the gender variable. To examine the development of the gender effect, we put the interaction of the gender and year dummy variables in model 2. According to the regression results of model 2, we can judge whether or not the gender effect changed with time. Moreover, model 1 cannot tell how—or even if—the individual, household, and community characteristics affect men and women differently. This may be important. For example, in rural China, women traditionally take the main role in child-care and the housework, and this may cause differences in the impact of household composition on men's versus women's occupational participation. We, therefore, relax the assumption that the determinants of non-agricultural employment affect men and women equally and include and interaction terms between the gender variable and the individual, household, and community characteristics as follows:

x = (*Gender, Age, Agesq, Edu, Marriage, HHsize, Child, Old, Land, Cadre, Lnin_others, Workout, Enterpr, RD, TD; Gender*Age, Gender*Agesq, Gender*Edu, Gender*Marriage, Gender*HHsize, Gender*Child, Gender*Old, Gender*Land, Gender*Cadre, Gender*lnin_othersinc, Gender*Workout* □ *Gender*Enterpr, Gender*RD, Gender*TD*)

Since there are interaction terms in the model, the change in the probability for a change in any element of variable x is the weighted sum of all partial derivatives. The coefficients of the interaction between the gender dummies and other variables will be significant if the variables to be examined have different effects on male and female non-agricultural occupation.

3 Data

Our analysis uses data from eight provinces in the east, west, and center of China. The data come from the China Health and Nutrition Survey (CHNS). This survey was designed to examine the effects of health, nutrition, family planning policies, and programs implemented by national and local governments in order to understand how the social and economic transformation of Chinese society is affecting the health and nutritional status of its population. The CHNS contains information about household composition, income, employment, education, and other related information. Since our interest is in rural households for our analysis, we use a sub-sample of the CHNS consisting of male and female laborers in rural households. This sub-sample includes nearly 10,000 individuals in the provinces of Guangxi, Guizhou, Henan, Hubei, Hunan, Jiangsu, Liaoning, and Shandong. Data are available for 1989 and 1997.

Table 5.1 gives some descriptive statistics for the sub-sample used in this paper. From 1989 to 1997, the proportion of rural workers who engaged in non-agricultural occupations (that is, the primary or secondary occupation is not farming) increased from 29 to 39 percent. These numbers are higher than the official national data. According to the China Agriculture White Book 2003, 20.8 percent of rural labor was engaged in the non-agricultural sector in 1989 and 29.4 percent in 2002. The official statistics, however, include only those workers whose primary occupation is non-agriculture, while our numbers also include workers whose secondary occupation is non-agriculture. In addition, the provinces covered in the CHNS have less arable land per capita than the national average, and in areas where land is scarcer and labor more abundant, households are more likely to seek non-agricultural employment.[3]

Table 5.1 shows differences between men and women. More men than women have non-agricultural occupations. The non-agricultural employment of men increased from 36 percent in 1989 to 48 percent in 1997, while the non-agricultural employment of women increased from 22 to 29 percent. These numbers reveal an upward trend in rural labor's non-agricultural employment, with a faster increase for men than women. Women's lower participation in non-agricultural work is associated with relatively more hours worked in agriculture. In 1989, the working

---

[3] The average arable land of households in survey area was less than the national average level. In 1997 the national average arable land per capita is 2.07 *mu*, Jiangsu was 1.25 *mu*, Shandong was 1.44 *mu*, Henan was 1.51 *mu*, Hubei was 1.56 *mu*, Hunan was 1.2 *mu*, Guangxi was 1.25 *mu*, and Guizhou was 1.1 *mu* (Rural Statistical Yearbook of China, 1998).

hours of women in agriculture was 2,250 hours and 1,979 hours for men; in 1997, women worked 1,424 hours in agriculture—men 1,232 hours.

Table 5.1 Descriptive statistics for explanatory variables

| | Year 1989 | | | | | | Year 1997 | | | | | | |
| | average | | male | | female | | average | | male | | female | | Notes |
	Mean	Std. Dev.	Mean	Std. Dev.	Mean	Std. Dev.	Mean	Std. Dev.	Mean	Std. Dev.	Mean	Std. Dev.	
non-agri. occupation	0.29	0.45	0.36	0.48	0.22	0.42	0.39	0.49	0.48	0.50	0.29	0.45	Dummy, having non-agri. occupation=1
gender	0.50	0.50	0.00	0.00	1.00	0.00	0.47	0.50	0.00	0.00	1.00	0.00	Dummy, female=1
hhsize	4.94	1.60	4.91	1.59	4.98	1.61	4.62	1.70	4.57	1.74	4.67	1.66	Household size
age	35.04	13.12	35.31	13.19	34.76	13.04	37.47	12.73	37.44	12.79	37.51	12.68	Age of individual
children	0.92	1.00	0.90	0.99	0.95	1.00	0.72	0.85	0.69	0.84	0.74	0.86	Number of children in household
old	0.11	0.34	0.11	0.34	0.11	0.34	0.15	0.40	0.15	0.40	0.14	0.39	Number of old people in household
maritaldumy	0.77	0.42	0.75	0.43	0.79	0.41	0.78	0.42	0.75	0.43	0.81	0.39	Marital status, married=1
officadre	0.04	0.19	0.04	0.19	0.04	0.19	0.08	0.27	0.08	0.27	0.08	0.27	Dummy, is cadre=1
Land	4.81	3.96	4.85	4.12	4.77	3.79	4.93	4.39	4.88	4.27	4.97	4.51	Household arable land area
Eduyr	14.99	8.70	17.35	7.42	12.60	9.23	17.11	8.25	19.05	6.78	14.93	9.15	Individual education year
lnin_others	7.58	1.08	7.53	1.09	7.63	1.07	7.68	1.20	7.60	1.21	7.77	1.19	Log income of other household members
workout	19.76	18.45	19.65	18.34	19.87	18.56	24.83	19.57	24.83	19.68	24.83	19.45	Percentage of workforce worked out of town
enterpr	0.58	0.49	0.58	0.49	0.58	0.49	0.47	0.50	0.48	0.50	0.47	0.50	Dummy, having enterprise in village=1

Of all the workers having non-agricultural occupations, 33 percent are non-skilled manual workers (ordinary laborers, loggers, and so on), 17 percent are service workers (housekeepers, cooks, waiters, door keepers, hairdressers, counter salespeople, launderers, childcare workers, and so on), and 13 percent are skilled workers (foremen, group leaders, craftsmen, and so on).

Table 5.1 also gives information on other characteristics of male and female workers, their households, and their communities. In most regards, these characteristics are fairly similar for men and women, except for education. Rural women workers have four to five fewer years of education than men.

The percentage of the rural labor force working outside the village increased from 20 to 25 percent. Table 5.1 also showed the decreasing number of TVEs. Official statistics generally show that, in the late 1990s, the TVE sector was stagnant. This trend is reflected in the CHNS data, where in 1989, 58 percent of villages had an enterprise, while the proportion was only 47 percent in 1997.

4 Regression Results

Table 5.2 gives the estimated results of the Probit models with and without interaction terms. We begin with a discussion of the models with no interaction terms. Most of the estimated coefficients have the expected signs and significances. The results show that even after controlling the other factors, women are less likely to have non-agricultural employment. The gap in probability of non-agricultural employment between men and women has increased between these two years, and the same results can also be calculated from model 2.

In model 1, all explanatory variables, except the number of elderly, are significant. Human capital is an important determinant of labor market participation. Educational level significantly increases the non-agricultural employment probability. Therefore, women's lower human capital reduced the observed participation of women in non-agricultural employment. Marriage also reduces the probability of non-agricultural employment. These results are consistent with those in other studies, such as Zhao's (1997a) and Hare's (1999). A cadre in the family increases the probability of engaging in non-agricultural occupation. This is also consistent with evidence in other studies (e.g. Parish, Zhe and Li, 1995). The effect of age is non-linear with the maximum age at 36.

Among the household characteristics, the household size increases the probability of non-agricultural employment. This result is a little different from most studies of individual occupation choice in which the household size variable is usually insignificant (Sicular and Zhao, 2002). We think it is because in larger households more labor would be surplus, so the household would try to shift more workers into the non-agricultural sector. The number of children is significant and negatively related to non-agricultural employment. It is natural that if the number of children increases, parents may have to spend more time at home taking care of them. Although the coefficient of the number of elderly is negative, it is insignificant.

We also find that land is negatively associated with non-agricultural employment. This is consistent with Zhao's (1996a) study. Thus, the burden of agricultural work negatively affects non-agricultural employment. Individuals with family members who earn more income are more likely to work in the non-agricultural sector as postulated above.

The community characteristics are found to have a significant effect. The province dummies are significant, which suggests that non-agricultural employment in rural China differs among the provinces. In addition, the probability of non-agricultural employment is higher for villages with a higher ratio of workers working outside the village and for villages that have enterprises.

Table 5.2 Probit regression of non-agricultural employment determinant in rural China

	Model 1		Model 2		Model 3		Notes
	df/dx	p>|z|	df/dx	p>|z|	df/dx	p>|z|	
gender	-0.16	0.00	-0.13	0.00	0.41	0.00	Dummy, Male=0, and female==1
hhsize	0.02	0.00	0.02	0.00	0.01	0.02	Household size
age	0.01	0.00	0.01	0.00	0.03	0.00	Age of individual
agesq	0.00	0.00	0.00	0.00	0.00	0.00	Square of individual age
children	-0.01	0.08	-0.01	0.07	-0.01	0.18	Number of children in household
old	-0.02	0.22	-0.02	0.21	-0.01	0.54	Number of old people in hh
martitaldummy	-0.10	0.00	-0.10	0.00	-0.03	0.31	Marital, not married=0, married=1
officarde	0.12	0.00	0.12	0.00	0.21	0.00	Having cadre=1, otherwise=0
produmy2	0.25	0.00	0.24	0.00	0.21	0.00	Jiangsu Province=1,otherwise=0
produmy3	0.28	0.00	0.28	0.00	0.25	0.00	Shandong Province=1,otherwise=0
produmy4	0.13	0.00	0.13	0.00	0.14	0.00	Henan Province=1,otherwise=0
produmy5	-0.04	0.07	-0.04	0.07	-0.07	0.00	Hubei Province=1,otherwise=0
produmy6	0.07	0.00	0.07	0.00	0.06	0.03	Hunan Province=1,otherwise=0
produmy7	0.09	0.00	0.09	0.00	0.11	0.00	Guangxi Province =1,otherwise=0
land	-0.02	0.00	-0.02	0.00	-0.02	0.00	Household arable land area
edu1	0.06	0.00	0.06	0.00	0.06	0.03	Individual Education level 1
edu2	0.17	0.00	0.17	0.00	0.16	0.00	Individual Education level 2
edu3	0.25	0.00	0.25	0.00	0.23	0.00	Individual Education level 3
edu4	0.55	0.00	0.55	0.00	0.51	0.00	Individual Education level 4
edu5	0.51	0.00	0.52	0.00	0.41	0.01	Individual Education level 5
lnin_others	0.03	0.00	0.03	0.00	0.04	0.00	Log income of other hh members
workout	0.00	0.00	0.00	0.00	0.00	0.00	Percentage of working out of town
enterpr	0.10	0.00	0.10	0.00	0.10	0.00	Having enterprise=1,0 otherwise
year97	-0.00	0.73	0.02	0.18	0.01	0.02	Year 1997=1, otherwise=0
Gender*year97			-0.06	0.01	-0.06	0.02	
Gender*hhsize					0.01	0.20	
Gender*age					-0.03	0.00	
Gender*agesq					0.00	0.00	
Gender*child					-0.01	0.70	
Gender*old					-0.01	0.64	
Gender*mar					-0.16	0.00	
Gender*offica					-0.13	0.00	
Gender*prodummy2					0.02	0.63	
Gender*prodummy3					0.16	0.00	
Gender*prodummy4					-0.06	0.06	
Gender*prodummy5					0.05	0.14	

Gender*produmm6			0.08	0.03
Gender*prodummy7			-0.08	0.01
Gender*land			0.00	0.87
Gender*edu1			-0.03	0.49
Gender*edu2			0.00	0.91
Continue:				
Gender*edu3			0.01	0.80
Gender*edu4			0.11	0.39
Gender*edu5			0.30	0.35
Gender*lnin_others			0.00	0.92
Gender*workout			0.00	0.00
Continue:				
Gender*enterpr			0.00	0.88
Prob > chi^2 =	0.00	0.00	0.00	
Log likelihood =	-4099.6056	-4096.0297	-3999.557	

The regression results of the Probit model, including the interactions of gender and other variables, also appear in Table 5.2. The significance of the interactions of gender and other explanatory variables suggest that the individual, household, and community characteristics have different effects on male and female non-agricultural employment. The change in the probability for change in the gender dummy from male to female is –0.17, indicating that being a female reduces the probability of non-agricultural employment by 17 percent.

One of the interesting results in model 3 is that age affects non-agricultural employment differently for men and women. For men, the effect of age follows an inverse U pattern, but for women, the effect is an upright U. For men, the maximum probability of non-agricultural employment occurs at age 36, but for women, the minimum is at age 37. These results reflect that women younger and older than 37 are more likely to engage in non-agricultural employment.

Marital status affects the probability of non-agricultural employment for men insignificantly. The interaction of the gender and marriage variables, however, is significant and negative, indicating that marriage reduces the probability of non-agricultural employment for women but not for men. Residing in a village that has more labor working outside the village increases the probability of non-agricultural employment significantly for men but only has a little effect on the probability of non-agricultural employment for women.

From the estimation results, we can also conclude that the time dummy variable is significant but has different effects for men and women. In 1997, the probability of non-agricultural employment increased for men but decreased for women, relative to 1989.

An interesting question is whether the impact of gender on non-agricultural employment probabilities differs between richer and poorer households. To address this question, we calculate the male-female difference and predict the probability with the mean value of different income groups. Table 5.3 reports the mean values of the explanatory variables for five different income groups. The results show that the male-female difference in the predict probability increases in higher-income groups. In the low-income group, the male-female difference in the predict probability is 14 percent, while in the high-income group, it is 21 percent.

A possible explanation for this result is that in poor households, all members—whether they are men or women—have to shift to the non-agricultural sector to generate income, while in better-off households, women have less motivation to work outside and are more likely to stay at home working in agriculture. If this explanation is correct, we can conclude that with the development of the rural economy—if rural income increases—the gender gap in non-agricultural employment will also increase.

Table 5.3 Mean value of explanatory variables of different groups

	Group 1 Low 20%	Group 2	Group 3	Group 4	Group 5 High 20%
Gender	0.49	0.49	0.49	0.48	0.47
Hhsize	5.06	4.94	4.72	4.71	4.47
Age	36.42	36.43	36.42	36.03	36.10
Agesq	1491.45	1500.80	1494.94	1470.43	1466.84
children	1.03	0.97	0.78	0.67	0.64
Old	0.13	0.13	0.13	0.14	0.10
martialdummy	0.79	0.78	0.77	0.77	0.76
officarde	0.04	0.04	0.06	0.05	0.09
produmy2	0.06	0.07	0.12	0.19	0.27
produmy3	0.10	0.07	0.09	0.11	0.10
produmy4	0.22	0.17	0.16	0.14	0.10
produmy5	0.15	0.18	0.13	0.14	0.10
produmy6	0.09	0.11	0.12	0.11	0.14
produmy7	0.12	0.15	0.20	0.19	0.20
Land	5.10	4.52	5.02	5.18	4.47
edu1	0.38	0.38	0.37	0.36	0.31
edu2	0.31	0.33	0.37	0.38	0.42
edu3	0.07	0.07	0.08	0.10	0.12
edu4	0.00	0.01	0.01	0.02	0.02
edu5	0.00	0.00	0.00	0.00	0.01
lnin_others	6.38	7.28	7.66	8.07	8.67
workout	19.99	21.15	22.20	23.28	25.78
enterpr	0.39	0.45	0.53	0.59	0.67
year97	0.50	0.50	0.50	0.50	0.50

5 Conclusions and Policy Implications

The empirical estimates discussed above strongly support the conclusion that gender is a significant explanatory variable in determining non-agricultural employment. When others setting in mean value, the male-female difference in the predict probability of engaging non-agricultural occupation is 16 to 17 percent. In other words, being female reduces the probability of non-agricultural employment by 16 to 17 percent.

In this paper, we also found that the probability of women's participation in non-agricultural employment increased less than men between 1989 and 1997, suggesting that the gender gap increased. The comparison of households at different income levels further showed that the gender gap appears to increase with income. Overall, our findings suggest that if the government ignores the gender gap and takes no steps to facilitate female participation in non-agricultural employment, the gender difference will increase.

Education significantly affects the probability of non-agricultural occupations, as other researchers have also pointed out. One reason why women are less likely to work in non-agricultural jobs is because they have lower levels of education. Raising women's educational levels would likely benefit their non-agricultural occupation.

Our analysis revealed the differential impact of certain variables on employment probabilities for men and women. Of interest here are the different impacts of marital status and age. Marriage significantly reduces the probability of non-agricultural employment for women but not for men. Age has an upright U relationship with the probability of non-agricultural employment for women. These findings are consistent with the observation that, during their child-bearing years, married women have to take on the responsibility of caring for the family, which limits their participation in the non-agricultural sector. Young and unmarried women are more likely to engage in non-agricultural occupations.

Social welfare is still not developed in rural China, and households have to take care of their children by themselves, which hinders the ability of parents to work outside the home. If childcare becomes available in the villages, it would liberate more mothers to work in non-agricultural occupations.

References

Agesa, J. and Agesa, R., 'Gender Differences in the Incidence of Rural to Urban Migration: Evidence from Kneya', *The Journal of Development Studies*, Vol. 35 (1999).

Boserup, E., 'Economic Change and the Roles of Women', in I. Tinker (eds), *Persistent Inequality: Women and World Development*, Oxford: Oxford University Press, 1990).

Dong, X., 'Employment and Wage Determination in China's Rural Industry: Investigation Using 1984-1990 Panel Data', *Journal of comparative Economics*, 26 (1998): 485-501.

Hare, D., 'Women's Economic Status in Rural China: Household Contributions to Male-Female Disparities in the Wage-Labor Market', *World Development*, Vol. 27 (1999).

Huang, J.K., Trade Liberalization and China Agriculture, *Agricultural Economics Problems*, 8 (1999).

————, 'The Nature of Distortions to Agricultural Incentives in China and Implications of WTO Accession' (Seminar on WTO Accession, Policy Reform and Poverty Reduction in China, 2002).

Li, S., 'Rural Women: Employment and Income, An Empirical Analysis Based on the Data from Sample Villages', *China Social Science*, 3 (2001).

Lu, F. and Mei, X.F., An Initial Study of the Regional Pattern of the Impact on China's Agricultural (Sector by Its WTO Accession No.4, 2001).

Parish, W.L., Zhe, X. and Li, F., 'Nonfarm work and marketization of the Chinese countryside', *China Quarterly*, 143 (1995): 697-730.

State Statistical Bureau (SSB), *Rural Statistical Yearbook of China* (Beijing: China Statistical Press, 2000).

Sucular, T. and Zhao, Y.H., 'Employment, Earnings and Poverty in Rural China: A Microeconomic Analysis' (Paper Prepared for the Workshop on China's WTO Accession, Beijing, June 28-29, 2002).

Tian, W.M., 'Impacts of Trade Liberalization on China's Feedgrain Market' (paper presented at the symposium *China Agricultural Trade and Policy: Issues, Analysis, and Global Consequences*, San Francisco, California, June 25-26, 1999).

Xin, X., Accession to WTO and its Effects on Livestock Production and Animal Product Market, Ministry of agriculture (Research Report No.20010, 2001).

Zhao, Y., 'Labor Migration and Earnings Differences: Tha Case of Rural China', Economic Development and Cultural Change, 1999.

————, 'Causes and Consequences of Return Migrantion: Recent Evidence from China', JCE, 2001.

————, 'The Role of Migrant Networks in Labor Migration: The Case of China', CEP, 2001.

Part 2
Poverty and Income Inequalities

Chapter 6

The Poverty of Rights and Chinese Farmers' Land Property

Zhaohui Hong

1 Introduction

Generally speaking, human poverty can be attributed to four primary factors: the scarcity of materials, the deficiency of capability, the deprivation of rights, and the lack of motivation (Hong, 2002). The scarcity of materials refers to the lack of basic necessities, such as food and clothing, for human a being's very survival. The deficiency of capability bespeaks the lack of education and professional skills necessary for finding employment. The deprivation of rights is caused by the discrimination and exclusion of social, political, economic, and cultural rights against particular groups. The lack of motivation is reflected in the dependence on social welfare on the part of its recipients who simply do not have any desire to work. Currently, the insufficiency of materials and that of capability can be seen in the experience of Chinese farmers, but the lack of motivation is not yet a serious problem in light of the present stage of China's economic development, which has not generated a dependable welfare system (World Bank, 1992; Jyotsna and Rvallion, 1998, 2000; Riskin, 1994). However, the most serious and yet ignored problem—the poverty of rights—constitutes the most fundamental reason for the overall poverty of Chinese farmers.

The poverty of farmers' rights is evidenced in the following eight areas: their lack of basic civil rights, equal political representation and participation,[1] freedom of movement, social security, equal education opportunities, medical insurance, freedom of demonstration, and the rights to land property. This article focuses on the poverty of farmers' land property rights.

---

[1] For instance, according to Election Law of National People's Congress and its Various Levels, four Chinese farmers are accounted as one representation (25 per cent). See Election Law, regulations 12 and 14, China Election and Governance Website, March 10, 2004 [document online]; available from <www.chinaelections.com>; Internet; accessed 11 May 2004. This 25 per cent of representation is 35 per cent lower than American slaves (60 per cent). See The Constitution of the United States, Article I, Section 2. See George Tindall, America: A Narrative History, vol. 1 (New York: W.W. Norton, 1988), 12.

Farmer's land property rights apply mainly to their rights to land tenure, disposal, and profits. More specifically, the rights to land tenure can be defined as those to use the land according to its functions and features; the rights to land disposal include those of land usage and transfer; and the rights to land profits refer to farmers' natural privilege to obtain profits and interests from their land production, land rent, and land transaction. Therefore, by definition, the poverty of farmers' land property speaks to the exclusion of their rights in all the aforementioned areas.

2 Institutional Factors Contributing to the Poverty of Rights on Chinese Farmers' Land

Since 1949, Chinese farmers have experienced dramatic changes in dealing with their land property. Land reform in the early 1950s ensured farmers' land ownership and made their dream of "land for tiller" come true. However, their land ownership was replaced by collective ownership through political enforcement by the People's Commune after 1958 (She, 1986; Perkins and Ysuf, 1984; Chen, 1994). Deng Xiaoping's reforms in the early 1980s ushered in the Household Responsibility System (HRS), which was designed to return land tenure to rural families but rejected farmers' direct land ownership(Putterman, 1993; Sicular, 1993). Driven by state land eminent domain and private land enclosure, many farmers gradually lost their land tenure and, as a result, became landless by the 1990s (Unger, 2002). Currently, farmers' rights in land property face three main threats: government eminent domain, private land enclosure, and land sale by local village officials.

The main reason for Chinese farmers' lack of land property rights is the fact that farmers' collectives have only a nominal status as the land owner; in reality, the definition of land ownership is highly ambiguous and imprecise. As a direct result, rural collectives are incapable of protecting farmers' basic rights to land tenure, disposal, and profit. According to the *Chinese Constitution, Civil Law, Land Management Regulations,* and *Agricultural Law,* land ownership belongs to the rural collectives,[2] which can be subdivided into village,[3] township, and farmers' collectives composed of two or more economic entities within each

---

[2] Article Ten of the Chinese Constitution stipulates that "except in cases of legally defined state ownership, land in the countryside and urban suburban areas belongs to collectives, so does the land used for housing and that reserved for individual farmers." See *The Constitution of the People's Republic of China* [Zhonghua Renmin Gongheguo Xianfa] (Beijing: Falui Chubanshe, 2002), 36.

[3] Artilce 74 of *the 1987 Civil Law* defines "collective ownership" as "land under collective ownership legally belongs to the rural farmers' collectives." See *Civil Law* [Minfa Tongze] (Beijing: Falui Chubanshe, 1987), 10.

village.[4] However, in actuality, none of these collectives has a clear legal definition. The boundaries of legal land ownership are blurred and compromised. Village committees, which are not economic entities, are nonetheless accorded the right to control a substantial amount of rural land. Consequently, village committees or other privileged groups have numerous opportunities for rent seeking and/or heavy-handed manipulations while farmers themselves have little or no say in the decision-making process. The so-called collective land ownership is actually held in the hands of individual local officials.

The village committee, however, is not a rural collective economic organization. Rather, it is a self-governed community that does not have the legal status as property owner (Kelliher, 1997), which has promoted some scholars to suggest that the economic power of the village committees be taken away. To complicate the matter, other rural collective economic organizations, such as township village enterprises (TVEs), also seem to have *de facto* land ownership because they can occupy land without the permission from farmers' collectives. Local governments in rural areas and village committees often rival against TVEs for land possession (Jia, 1996). Such interlocking and overlapping land ownership has deprived individual farmers' rights in dealing with their own land.

Two seemingly incomprehensible phenomena have appeared due to the ambiguous and multiple land ownership. Individual farmers, who form the farmers' collectives, and who are supposed to be the real landowners, find it impossible to exercise their rights. The farmers' collectives, despite their legal land ownership, do not have any legal representatives' status that enables them to own, manage, and oversee rural land. In other words, the so-called collective land ownership is only nominal at best. Some scholars suggest that the collective land ownership be interpreted as joint ownership by all farmers. Joint ownership, however, is private in essence, which would require constitutional revision of the current legal stipulation regarding the socialist nature of land ownership in China, something that is unlikely to take place any time soon. Clearly, due to legal ambiguity and heavy-handed administrative control, Chinese farmers' rights to land tenure, disposal, and profit have largely been dispossessed. In addition, the unlimited governmental power, ill-defined regulations, and unpredictable policies also affect the capability of farmers' collectives in representing farmers' interests and in protecting land resources. Consequently, rural collectives are bound to fail in their struggle against formidable government organizations.

It is worth noting that although the *Chinese Constitution* accords rural land ownership to farmers' collectives, the constitutional amendment, the *Civil Law*, and *Land Management Law* set up various restrictions to limit farmers' rights to

---

[4] Article 74 of *the 1987 Civil Law* states that "land under collective ownership is operated and managed by rural collective economic organizations such as the village agricultural production cooperatives or village committees.The land that already belongs to and county rural collective economic organizations may be owned by (county) rural collectives." See *Civil Law*, 10.

land property by disallowing any organizations and individuals to buy, sell, transfer, rent, and mortgage their land. Yet, the government has full and unlimited rights to conduct land eminent domain. [5] Furthermore, numerous informal regulations and policies at various levels often play a much more effective and destructive role in dispossessing farmers' land rights.

Given the variety of restrictions, the farmers' collectives, the rightful owners of rural land, have practically nonexistent power. They do not have any tangible rights in land disposal due to restrictions on land sale, rent, transfer, and mortgage. The state, on the other hand, has ultimate control over land disposal because rural collectives cannot transfer their "owned" land unless the state conducts its land eminent domain. Neither do farmers' collectives have a free and independent voice in deciding their profits from land transaction because the compensation from the state's land eminent domain is arbitrarily decided and administratively enforced with total disregard to the fair market value. The state has exclusive power to make non-negotiable decisions on land compensation and land disposal. Needless to say, under these circumstances it is next to impossible for farmers' collectives to use the existing laws and regulations against interventions from various interest groups that encroach upon farmers' rights in a name of the state.

Aside from these problems with the definition and execution of land ownership, farmers' land property rights are also disregarded in other ways. A prevailing misconception is that land ownership and land property rights are one and the same, which seemingly justifies the fact that farmers are automatically disqualified for their basic land rights because of their lack of ownership. In reality, farmers do have land property rights, including those to land tenure, transaction, and profit (Barzel, 1989). The *People's Republic of China's Rural Land Tenure Law,* which became effective 1 March 2003, allows those who have land tenure to "transfer, rent, exchange, or other transaction of their lands."[6] Combined with their rights to land use, disposal, and profit, farmers' land tenure should be defined as a special and substantial land property right. As a matter of fact, the absence of meaningful

---

[5] Article 2 of *the Land Management Law* states "the People's Republic of China implements a socialist public ownership of land, that is, an all people's ownership and working people's collective ownership. No work units or individuals are allowed to forcefully occupy, buy, sell or transfer land in any other illegal form. The state can lawfully acquire land eminent domain from the land under collective ownership for public interests." Article 47 states that "the illegal gains from land sales or other forms of land transfer are to be confiscated. Newly constructed buildings and other infrastructure on the land obtained through land sale or any other forms of land transfer are to be either demolished within a certain time or confiscated; the offenders are to be punished, The personnel in charge are to be administratively punished by his/her work unit or a superior organization." *China Election and Governance Website,* 23 Septmebr 2003 [document online]; available from <www.chinaelections.com>; Internet; accessed 11 May 2004.

[6] See Article 32 of "*The Land Tenure Law of the People's Republic of China,*" *China Election and Governance Website,* 23 Septmeber 2003 [document online]; available from <www.chinaelections.com>; Internet; accessed 11 May 2004.

rights for farmers' collectives makes it necessary for farmers to replace the collectives and exercise their own rights directly and independently. Practically speaking, whoever controls land tenure, disposal, and profit has *de facto* land ownership, not the so-called farmers' collectives that nominally own the land but have no tangible power over any aspects of land control. Presently, the collective land ownership has already been greatly weakened and essentially partitioned.

However, in the midst of both legal land eminent domain and illegal land enclosure, farmers' land rights have been either ruthlessly encroached upon or thoroughly deprived. Not only do farmers find themselves unable to protect their rights to land tenure, they are also too powerless to retain their rights to land disposal and profit. While farmers increasingly deem their right to land tenure as actual land ownership and are doing all they can to defend their livelihood, they are also placed in a rather precarious and powerless condition. Faced with relentless government efforts at land eminent domain and encroachments by other external forces, the most that they can do is conduct passive resistance or quiet sabotage in order to "show their denial of any land ownership other than that by the rural collectives." However, doing so also "makes the protection of their legal rights costly and reduces the value of their land" (Dang, 1997). In the end, the real victims remain the farmers themselves.

In summary, as a result of rural collectives' inability to assert their legal representatives' status as the landowner, farmers' rights to land tenure, disposal, and profit cannot be effectively protected. Moreover, the illegal, unreasonable, and unfair practices of the government and various interest groups in land eminent domain have led to the continuing erosion and deprivation of farmers' land rights, hence, the inevitability of vast rural poverty (Zweig, 1997).

3 The Poverty of Farmers' Rights to Land Tenure

Farmers' rights to land tenure form the core foundation of their overall rights to land property, without which their other rights, such as those to land disposal and profit, are meaningless. Clearly, the availability, amount, and length of farmers' lend tenure have a direct impact on their income and other material benefits. In theory, and according to the law, Chinese farmers have legal rights to land tenure and use, but in actuality their rights have been vastly eroded and compromised (Kung and Liu, 1997).

First of all, rural women are customarily discriminated against. They cannot obtain as much land tenure as their male counterparts, and their contracted land is usually confiscated upon their marriage even if their contract period has not expired (Jacka, 1997; Bossen, 2002). According to the findings of the Research Institute at the All China Federation of Women, more often than not, female farmers cannot obtain tenure of the "responsibility field," deed their land for stock shares and dividends from companies, receive compensation for land eminent domain, or get allocated land for housing, all of which are the essence of the farmers' livelihoods. Four groups of women are especially shortchanged in terms of their rights to lend tenure: unmarried women, those who have only daughters in the family, those who are married into a village from the outside, and those are married from a farming family into nonfarming household. The survey conducted by the Chinese Economic Reforms Institute reveals that 7.2 per cent of the women interviewed currently have no land at all, 45 per cent lost their land share upon marriage, 17 per cent lost land as a result of the government's land eminent domain, and 31 per cent were never allotted land in the first place. Careful comparisons demonstrate that women who lost their land due to marriage were the least protected, followed by those who were separated or divorced and those who were widowed (Wang and Zhi, 2004).

Second, forceful administrative measures were adopted for land adjustment, and the process and procedure of land distribution and reallocation are unfair and untransparent. For example, farmers who work outside their villages often have their land tenure illegally taken away as substitute payment for their loans. Farmers' land tenure is arbitrarily changed to the extent that it is often adjusted every few years and, in the process, some have lost their contract due to the changes in administrative personnel who had been responsible for sealing the contract. It is not uncommon for government agencies to decide either not to renew the contract when its first term expires, or to randomly extend the original contract for 30 years without issuing new certificates for the additional term. As a result, a great number of farmers' land tenure is without any legal guarantee. What is more, farmers often have to deal with a dual system of administrative enforcement. On the one hand, their land may be forcefully taken away in an illicit transfer; on the other hand, they may be forced into compulsory land tenure on the condition that they give up their due rights that come with the tenure.

It is getting more and more common that local governments at various levels fail to protect farmers' land rights, making it impossible for the latter to voice their grievances and obtain justice (Oi, 1989). Some administrative agencies, judicial branches, and village organizations turn a blind eye to cases of blatant rights violation or deliberate delay of settlement. In fact, there are the so-called "five do not do" policies regarding farmers' grievances: local courts do not accept cases involving farmers' complaints about land tenure; rural land management agencies do not accept farmers' requests for refereeing cases of land tenure conflicts; prefecture and county governments do not offer mediation in cases of land tenure conflicts; agricultural administrative agencies do not accept farmers' letters or visits about land tenure disputes; and village-level organizations do not referee or make legal conclusions concerning land tenure cases. Some have deliberately put those cases on hold indefinitely (Xie, 2003).

Last but not least, the current practice of exchanging land for company stocks has also, to some extent, violated farmers' rights to land tenure and use. The basic concept of such a system is to allow farmers to buy shares in a relevant enterprise with their leased land and receive long-term dividends. For instance, in 1996 farmers in Hongsha Village, Sansheng County, Sichuan Province, invested with their land by growing plants and flowers for flower companies. By August 2003, the village purchased stock shares from those companies by sub-leasing its entire 1,100 mu of land. Farmers benefited from the 1,500 *yuan*/mu rental fee every year paid by the various flower companies as well as the dividends from their shares. Those who lease out their land can also work for the flower companies.[7] However, when participating in the cooperative system on land-stock, farmers no longer have any direct land property rights over the crops on the land, for their rights to land use have been transformed into stock shares in the companies. One has to understand that their security based upon the profits from their stock shares is vastly different from that which comes from their direct control of land and crops, because the former is contingent upon the profits of the companies, while the latter rests with the condition of their crops under their control. In other words, the farmers' profits are no longer guaranteed; instead, they are prone to wide fluctuations. If the cooperative system on land-stock does not perform well, farmers will not receive much dividend. Meanwhile, unable to reclaim their land, the farmers have essentially lost their land property rights. Even if the companies perform well, it is not uncommon for a few insiders within the company to exercise monopolistic control over its finance; as a result, farmers' land property rights can also be harmed.

Needless to say, farmers' rights to land tenure and use are critical for their livelihood, and land for their quota of food grain (*kuoliang tian*) is their lifeline without which their very survival is threatened. The land for farmer's responsibility (*zeren tian*) provides them a means to accumulate agriculture capital and maintain a decent life. Once their rights to land tenure and use are divested, widespread rural poverty becomes an inevitability.

4 The Poverty of Farmers' Rights to Land Disposal

The ability of farmers to decide on their land disposal is a significant indicator of their overall land property rights. The current laws, regulations, and practices in China, however, have often resulted in serious violations of farmers' rights to land disposal. To begin, farmers cannot decide on how their land is to be used. According to the existing legal stipulations, "the land that belongs to farmers' collectives is operated and managed by members of collective economic organizations, who are engaged in farming, forestry, husbandry, and fishing productions." Farmers are forbidden from using agricultural land for growing trees and fruits or raising fish. In addition, the 17th Article of *The Land Tenure Law* specifies that farmers have the obligation to "maintaining their land for agricultural

---

[7] "Quicken the Pace of Land Transfer So Farmers Do Not Lose Their Job with Their Land or Their Benefits with Their Work" [Jiahuai tudi liuzhuan, nongmin shidi bu shiye, shidi bu shili], *Sichuang Online*, 23 October 2003 [journal online]; available from <www.scol.com.cn>; Internet; accessed 11 December 2003.

use, not for nonagricultural development."[8] Therefore, farmers' collective land can be used only for crops that may not bring any additional profits regardless of their productivity. Government agencies at various levels can interfere with farmer's decisions as to what kinds of crops can be grown on their land and force farmers to purchase designated production materials or sell their agricultural products to officially selected buyers.

These limitations placed on the farmers' land use have contributed to the prevailing rural poverty. Agricultural profits from farming have shown increasing signs of decline. Regardless of the amount of manpower and materials that farmers invest, profits derived from the land remain marginal, and are unable to meet their needs to make a comfortable living. Forcing farmers to use their land for exclusive agriculture production is tantamount to driving them into poverty. Moreover, along the southeast coastal regions land has become a burden for some farmers for, once getting into other lines of work, they have little time or energy for farming. However, they still have to pay the compulsory land tax. Thus one sees a vicious cycle: the poverty of farmers' rights leads to the paucity of their opportunities, which in turn gives rise to their rising level of overall economic poverty.

Second, current laws and regulations also curb farmers' right to land transfer and limit their opportunities to leave for the cities in search of a better life. Despite the fact that the *Land Tenure Law* allows farmers to conduct land transfer, the ambiguous definition of land ownership makes it practically impossible for them to do so. As stated previously, the ownership of rural land is essentially partitioned by the various farmers' collective economic organizations, and the state has the ultimate control over land disposal. The self-contradictory stipulations in the *Land Tenure Law* do further disservice to farmers. While stating that "in cases where the entire farming households have settled in small towns and cities, their rights to land tenure and legal land transfer are preserved according to their will;" it also announces that "those farming households who have moved to cities and changed to nonagricultural status should return their agricultural and grass land."[9] A direct outcome of these confusing regulations is that farmers are discouraged from leaving the countryside because doing so would mean abandoning their land without any compensation. Farmers who desire to go to the cities are not interested in making any investment in their land because it is highly unlikely they will turn a profit without the ability to transfer their land. Taking the right to land transfer away from farmers who leave for towns and cities is another significant reason for rural poverty. The reality is that once farmers leave their land behind and the possibility to reclaim it, they may soon find themselves becoming the main constituents of the urban poor (Oi, 1999).

---

[8] Article 17 of *The Land Tenure Law of the People's Republic of China*, see *China Election and Governance Web*, 23 September 2003.
[9] See Article 26 of the Land Tenure Law, quoted from *China Election and Governance Web*, 23 September 2003.

Third, the increasingly heated wave of land eminent domain by the state has severely encroached upon farmers' right to land disposal and contributed to their dire economic situation. Since 1990, the land enclosure movement in China has resulted in the loss of land and employment for over 20 million farmers. The annual loss of agricultural land has amounted to more than 10 million mu, and 5 million mu has been forcefully wrestled away from farmers. At the rate of an average loss of 2 mu of land per person over the last 13 years, at least 65 million farmers have seen their land vanished. According to the study conducted by the State Council's Research Institute, between 1987 and 2001, 33.946 million mu has been used for nonagricultural purposes, 70 per cent of which was land taken from farmers. To put it differently, a minimum of 22.76 million mu that had originally been under rural collective ownership now belong to the state. Following the *Guidelines for National Land Usage Plan*, agricultural land used for nonagricultural purposes will exceed 54.5 million mu from 2000 to 2030, which means the number of landless farmers will undergo further dramatic increase (Lin, 2003).

The problem is that the state policy regarding land eminent domain is grossly unfair and unjust. According to legal regulations, the use of farmers' collectives' land for nonagricultural production has to be registered with the county government, which issues proper certificates in acknowledgement of the purported use. In addition, "an agency or individual must follow proper legal procedures in applying to the government for land to be used for nonagricultural developments.[10] In other words, land that belongs to farmers' collectives is acquired by the state first before being transferred again to certain companies or individuals. Essentially the government has control over the use of land that should rightfully belong to farmers' collectives.

It is true that government land eminent domain is a common practice in many countries, but currently in China a wide array of projects, either for building public infrastructure or constructing personal real estate, all invariably lead to land eminent domain through the use of governmental authority. For example, in order to help the Shandong Shenghua Glass Manufacturing Factory acquire land, the local government forced over 100 farming families in Beigu Village in February 2003 (Guli Zheng, Xintaishi) to give up their land on which their very livelihood depended. It has to be pointed out that all these families had a 30-year contract for their land tenure with their local collectives, yet even before all the procedures were completed, a groundbreaking ceremony had taken place! The local police went so far as to dispatch six police cars and arrested and detained those farmers who protested against the blatant violation of their rights for ten days. One official from a local land management office remarked that even though in theory the land eminent domain should not materialize without the consent of every single villager in concern, in reality the stamp of approval of the village committee is all that is

---

[10] See Articles 11 and 47 of the Land Management Law of the People's Republic of China, quoted from *China Election and Governance Web*, 23 September 2003.

needed for the land management office to issue the necessary documents and certificates. This kind of "use-before-purchase" approach is often necessitated by the local government's need to demonstrate their "achievements." Some major government projects frequently used farmers' land illegally to the extent that when the ribbon-cutting ceremony took place, proper documents had to be obtained retroactively (Zhu, 2004).

Fourth, farmers' land property rights have become increasingly victimized by the private land enclosure movement. Currently, incorporating farmers' land into private corporations has become a popular trend, yet the village committees and other rural collective economic organizations often exceed their functions in conducting land tranfer, so much so that farmers do not have any opportunity or rights of negotiating directly with the concerned corporations. There is no doubt that their free will and right to self-determination are violated. In the process of land development, farmers, though the rightful participants, have no actual say in any policy or decision making.

Theoretically, farmers should the have the right to reject any decisions that would result in the erosion of their rights. If adopting a pattern of combining "company, farmers, and base" to organize production and land allocation, then land lease and transfer should be prevented; if entering a contractual relationship over products, then land itself should not be involved; if a short-term land lease is sufficient, then a long-term one should be avoided. In actual practice, however, none of these three principles are observed, and farmers are almost invariably the victims. Even Qi Jingfa, the vice minister of agriculture, admitted that the so-called "company, famers, and base" pattern, which is currently gaining momentum, will turn the farmers into dispensable auxiliary to their land because their product sales are completely controlled by the companies and, consequently, the farmers will lose their right of choice and decision making regarding land use, thus becoming only the "tool of production" for those companies.

In the process of pushing for the corporitization of agriculture, some companies are not really intent upon developing agricultural products; rather, they aim at long-term land control through massive land enclosure. They ally with village leaders and rural economic organizations in forcefully recruiting thousands upon thousands of mu of land from farmers on the pretext of expanding land operations and agricultural developments. The land that is manipulated away from the farmers is then subcontracted to various other enterprises. The fact that farmers have been maneuvered into losing control over their land and that they stand no chance of regaining it has a dire impact on their lives. Additionally, once stock-holding companies become involved in agricultural production, they invariably seek higher productivity at all cost. Glaring disparities between the agricultural companies in economically advanced areas and those in backward regions, as well as unfair comparisons between company-operated agricultural productions and family-oriented ones will ensue. Ultimately, the family-operated agricultural entities, faced with insurmountable odds, will find it hard to survive the onslaught and sink into a deepening poverty.

Fifth, farmers' right to land disposal is frequently violated by local organizations, whose power has greatly expanded in recent years and has given rise to growing corruption. According to Qi Jingfa, by the end of 2000, 98 per cent of villages in China had started a second round of land tenure, with 92 per cent of which confirming a 30-year term. However, within three years, over 5 per cent of the newly contracted land (10 per cent along the east coast) had already been transferred, mortgaged, or sub-leased. It has to be pointed out that the massive scale of land rotation was a result of forceful manipulation, not of farmers' free will; it has provided a hotbed for widespread rural corruption.[11]

A case in point can be seen in Chen Er Township in Li County, Hunan Province, where the farmers were forced to give up over 10,000 mu of their land, to be rented out to Dongting Baiyang Paper Lt. for the cultivation of poplar. The contract signed between the company and the town government was obviously detrimental to the farmers because the town must provide for the company 10,000 *mu* of contiguous land suitable for the growth of poplar at only 128 *yuan*/mu for 20 years, with the company holding the certificate of land operation. To execute the contract, the Chen Er Township government forced all the villages within its jurisdiction to submit a "Commission Agreement on Land Lease Contract," designed to "designate the town people's government to enter into land-lease negotiations with the Hunan Dongting Popolar Paper Lt." on their behalf. This calculateding scheme was followed by large-scale land adjustments in various villages. Each villager was given 0.7-0.9 mu of grain field, while the rest was returned to the village. Each household was required to sign and place their fingerprints on the uniformly printed "Application for Land Transfer." The primary motivation for the Chen Er Township government to help the paper company purchase the farmers' land at such a low price was that the 128 *yuan*/mu rental fee was not to be paid to the farmers; instead, it all went directly to the town and village governments, who would use it to reduce their own debts and deficits, with only a meager amount going to pay the taxes on the farmers' land and vegetable gardens (Liu and Chen, 2003).

It goes without saying that those who have lost their rights to land disposal and other decision-making power are bound to become increasingly plagued by poverty, both in the rural areas and, in the case of those who have left for the cities, in the urban areas as well.

5 The Poverty of Farmers' Rights to Land Profit

The right of farmers to their land profit is another core component of their general land property rights, for land is worthless without cultivators being able to derive income from it. It is commonsense that those who have land tenure and till the land

---

[11] "The Land Tenure Law Promotes Rural Land Encirclement by Big Corporations," <http://www.in.ah.cn>, 10 March 2003.

should be able to derive financial benefits from land disposal and transfer (Carter and Zhong, 1991). However, China's reality is such that farmers are not guaranteed to receive any profit at all from their land, and the real value of the land cannot be realized or even reflected in the process of land circulation.

First of all, farmers have no say in decisions concerning land compensation. The local governments and the village committees have the ultimate authority in determining the amount, time, and duration of the compensation. According to the *Land Management Law*, "No decision regarding land tenure by individuals or entities outside of the farmers' collectives can be made without the consent of two-thirds of the participants at the village conference or two-thirds of the village representatives."[12] In actual practice, however, many local rural collectives decide to transfer their land and lease it to an external entity on a long-term basis without going through any due democratic process. Some even deliberately reveal the secrets of land bidding and its bottom line in order to please the potential purchaser and obtain illegal kickbacks or other kinds of profits (Xie, 2003).

Jeopardizing farmers' interest is also the fact that compensations for their land is almost always below its worth. Even though Article 47 of the *Land Management Law* states that "the compensation for land eminent domain has to include that for the land itself, supplementary expenses for farmers' resettlement, and the replacement value for the crops and other materials attached to the land. It should range from six to ten times the average annual value of production based on the calculation of the previous three years prior to the land acquisition."[13] Yet in Baique Town in Huzhou, Zhejiang Province, the compensation for each mu of the land that farmers had to give up was less than 20,000 *yuan*, equivalent to only 4.2 times the average per capita income of the farmers there in 2001, two to six times less than what the government stipulates. It must also be noted that, in exchange for the far-from-being-adequate compensation, the farmers have permanently lost their collective ownership of the land. The land purchaser, on the other hand, can auction off the land to developers and pocket tens and thousands of *yuan* for a 70-year lease. This form of exploitation of farmers is beyond ruthless (Yang, Shen and Jin, 2003).

Furthermore, the land buyer and farmers' collectives often arbitrarily deduct from the farmers' compensations. As the compensation is commonly rendered to both the farming families and their collectives, in many cases a greatly reduced amount reaches the farmers after much of it gets peeled off by the collectives. This kind of so-called land eminent domain without due compensation to the farmers, with the use of clout of state authority, brings tremendous harm and hardship to the farmers. For instance, the Jinzhou track of Xiangjin Highway Company in Hubei Province gave local farmers 500 *yuan*/mu in settlement fee, amounting to only 10.4 per cent of the legally stipulated minimum compensation of 4,800 *yuan*/mu. The

---

[12] Article 15 of *The Land Management Law of the People's Republic of China*, quoted from *China Election and Governance Web*, 23 September 2003.
[13] Quoted from *China Election and Governance Web*, 23 September 2003.

Shangyu city government in Zhejiang Province pocketed 219 million *yuan* for land transfer, yet farmers received a pitiful 5.91 million *yuan*, 2.7 per cent of the total amount of compensation. Land compensations are, more often than not, subject to layers after layers of embezzlement. Out of the total amount of Xiangjin Highway Company's land compensation, the provincial railroad headquaters deducted 8.37 million *yuan*, the Jinmen city headquaters took 15.02 million *yuan*, the Dongbao District in Jinmen City peeled 1.9 million *yuan*, and the various village and town agencies got a total of 11.92 million *yuan*. In the end, 45 per cent of the total compensation was cut before it even reached the farmers (Yang, Shen and Jin, 2003).

On top of all these forms of exhortation and exploitation, local agencies always go out of their way to minimize the land price in order to attract developers at the expense of farmers; they do so in the name of "improving the investment environment." Governments at various levels force farmers to give up their land at a very low price, regardless of whether the land is to be used for major public projects sponsored by the government or private real estate development solely driven by profits. In the end, the compensation received by farmers is grossly inadequate, much lower than the value of the land or what government agencies would get for subleasing or reselling it. This kind of unjust and unfair exchange is another grave violation of farmers' land property rights. Meanwhile, many district governments have no qualms about sacrificing farmers' interests by artificially reducing the land price or even entering a bidding war in order to make it more appealing to potential investors. Since land can be purchased at an exceedingly low cost in some areas, the transferred land has not been put to good use. The wasted land acquired at the farmers' expense deals another humiliating blow to the increasingly impoverished rural population.

Statistics provided by the Ministry of China's Land Resources reveals that during the first six months of 2002, 73 per cent of the grievances voiced or submitted by farmers concerned unfair land eminent domain and illegal occupation of farm land; 40 per cent of those who felt compelled to visit a higher authority to voice their complaints reported conflicts over land eminent domain, 87 per cent of which were about woefully inadequate compensation. Last year alone, the National Bureau for People's Complaint received as many as 4,116 letters and visitors that reported problems with land eminent domain for the first time, the majority of which revolved around the loss of land and employment, and 41 per cent of which were from the coastal regions such as Zhejiang, Jiangsu, Sichuan, and Guangdong. The quickened pace of urbanization and industrialization has resulted in the increasingly troubling loss of land by the farmers. Both experts on land issues and local farmers believe that the common practice of paying for land with insufficient compensation are responsible for the farmers' double loss of land and jobs, and, with little financial resources, it is impossible for farmers to pursue any meaningful self-employment.[14]

Aside from the unjust policies regarding land eminent domain, the standard for land compensation also lacks uniformity. Chinese farmers traditionally have found it easier to endure poverty than unfair disparity. They are especially disturbed by the fact that farmers in the same area have received different amounts of compensation for their land. Some village organizations frequently apply different standards of compensation for the same project in the same area in order to please different government agencies or corporations, which would in turn provide better returns to officials in these organizations themselves. Clearly, farmers in those areas have had to pay an even bigger price for such unconscionable practices. In 1998, land compensation along the Huzhi Highway in Huzhou, Zhejiang Province, ranged from 4,500 *yuan* to 6,000 *yuan* per mu, whereas the amount for land within the same district went up to 13,500 *yuan*/mu. Worse yet, a small town in Huzhou City, Zhejiang Province, transferred 934 mu of collectively owned land into the hands of the town government in the name of household registration reform, and farmers did not receive one penny of compensation. Cases of such capricious and inconsistent decisions on land compensation have given rise to numerous farmers' visits to higher authorities to voice their grievances, thereby contributing to the escalation of rural conflicts and posing a threat to social stability (Yang, Shen and Jin, 2003).

The value of farmers' land lies in its ability to supply continuous agricultural crops and other materials. If one mu of field is estimated to put out 1,000 *yuan* worth of products, then the real value of this piece of land far exceeds 1,000 *yuan*. Rather, it should be based upon the calculation of an annual worth of 1,000 *yuan* for many years on end, adjusted for inflation. Therefore, taking land away from farmers who have long-term land tenure at grossly reduced costs robs them of not only their anticipated annual profits but also all the future profits that can be derived from the land (Tao, 2003). No doubt the violation of farmers' rights is tantamount to the deprivation of their land property, which again inevitably leads to prevalent rural poverty.

6 The Poverty of Farmers' Land Property Rights and Their Material Poverty

Clearly, deprivation of farmers' rights is directly connected to their economic poverty. The aforementioned poverty of farmers' rights to land tenure, disposal, and profits has created their overall material poverty and deepened the extent and depth of their hardships (Khan and Riskin, 2000; Riskin, 1996; Riskin, Zhao, and Li, 2001).

---

[14] "Investigations of the Situation of Landless and Jobless Farmers," *China Election and Governance Web*, 22 October 2003.

The loss of land first leads to farmers' unemployment. Land eminent domain by the state naturally takes away farmers' land tenure and, consequently, reduces or even eliminates their basic source of income. According to a survey of 42 villages conducted by the city of Huzhou in Zhejiang Province, the land owned by farmers' collectives decreased by 41 per cent between 1992 and 2001, with an average reduction of 0.41 mu per person. During the same time period, among the 11,200 farm laborers who had worked on the land, only 806 were able to find some employment with the help of local governments, constituting 7.2 per cent of all those who have lost their jobs. Besides those who managed to find some type of work on their own, 5,900 remained either jobless or semi-unemployed, making up 53.1 per cent of the original labor force. Farmers who lost their land tenure due to the state land eminent domain are no doubt at a severe disadvantage in the stiff competition on the urban job market due to their limited education and technological know-how. As a result, the disparity between the incomes of the landless and jobless farmers and that of the average regular urban residents is getting progressively wider (Yang, Shen and Jin, 2003). In Pandun Village, Cangshan District, Fuzhou City in Fujian Province, over 700 farmers out of 1,000 have lost their land to land eminent domain. Some try to rent land in neighboring villages; some have become illegal "taxi-drivers" on their motorcycles; others have been on numerous petition trips in an effort to make their hardships known to higher authorities. Ni Shiyan, a villager in Rujiang Village, Mawei District in Fuzhou, remarked: "we are neither farmers nor town's people. We see wide roads and factory buildings in front of us. Yet, we have roads to walk on but no land to live on. Local governments are bent on shortchanging us by buying cheap and selling high, and they have made huge killings by profiting from our land."[15] Nowadays, farmers in Liangshankou, Pantang township (Tongshan County) in Xuzhou City, Jiangsu Province, have on average only 0.04 mu of grain field per person, whereas in 1998, before their land was acquired for the construction of the so-called food city, the villagers had on average 1.3 mu of land per person. Yu Gang had to accept a 15,000 *yuan* payment for his land tenure of more than 3 mu. Even though his family now belongs to the Pantang township, they are still registered as farmers. Rendered landless, they can only survive by finding random work (Wu, 2003).

The loss of both land and work, needless to say, results in drastic decrease of income for farmers. In Xinzhai Village, Yingshou District, Fuyang City in Anhui Province, villagers had an average of more than 1 mu of land before an airport project pushed them off their land. Currently, each villager is left with less than 0.2 mu of land. The 6,500 *yuan*/mu compensation that had been promised by the village officials was changed as soon as their land was occupied. In the end, the compensations, paid in a piecemeal fashion in over 20 small installments, accounted to less than 3,000 *yuan*/mu. Once their land was surrendered, farmers were immediately brushed aside; not one of them received any help in finding new

---

[15] "Investigations of the Situation of Landless and Jobless Farmers."

employment. Zhang Guisheng, a 66-year-old farmer now lives in a small and moldy dwelling with extremely low ceilings, and all he has is a bag of grain worth a few *jin* and a plate of decomposed pickles. Zhang has to survive on three to four *yuan* of income every day by transporting supplies in the nearby city on his rickshaw. The expansion and factory construction projects in Santa Township, Funan County of Anhui Province were completed at the expense of a large amount of high-quality arable land. Farmer Yu Lijun in Tabei Village lost more than 2 mu of his 5 mu of land to the three companies that planed to build freezers for the town. In the beginning, he received 600 *jin* of grain for each mu of his lost land as well as a waiver of land tax. Now that the factory has become bankrupt, the compensations have disappeared even though his land is still being occupied by the company. Yu has tried to register his complaints with various authorities with no results or any sign of a solution.[16]

In the meanwhile, the numerous unfair collections and distributions are also ways of violating farmers' rights and robbing them of their gains. Government sponsored programs such as the "10,000-mu garden land," "home of Chinese vegetables," and various "development zones" have all forced farmers to surrender their land tenure at exceedingly low price. The development of Shanghai's Pudong District provided farmers with 23,000 *yuan* for each mu of their grain field and 28,000 *yuan* for their vegetable field, in addition to 60,000-70,000 *yuan* for the completion of other construction project. However, when transferring the land to developers, the price skyrocketed to 200,000-300,000 *yuan* per mu. Based on the estimates of Mr. Chen Xiwen at the State Council's Research and Development Center, the rural-urban disparity during the age of planned-economy forced farmers to suffer a loss of 600-800 billion *yuan*; whereas the forced land eminent domain during the reform era has cost Chinese farmers a minimum of 2000 billion *yuan* (Chen, 2002).

The deprivation of farmers' land property rights has led to their loss of the very land that they depend upon for their survival. More than simply reducing farmers' income, the loss of land and work as well as the various unfair taxes have driven them to leave their home and join the vast rural exodus into cities, where many of them have become members of the ever increasingly crowd of urban poor (Rozelle, Li, Shen, Hughart, and Giles, 1999; Croll and Huang, 1997; West and Zhao, 2000). A case in point is Zigong City in Sichuan Province. In 1993, the city began its plan of developing a high-tech district, which would occupy 100,000 square kilometers of land. Ten years later, 50 per cent of the land eminent domain has been completed, triggering the involuntary departure of 1,000 farming families in Hongqi Town, where they had lived for generations. On the construction site of the luxurious Blue Eagle Park residential district, Huang Yongnong and several other fellow villagers survive only by picking up trash and making five to six *yuan* a day. Prior to 1995, Huang had 1 mu of land used for growing rice and vegetables, and he did not have to worry about making ends meet. The additional pigs and chickens that he raised,

---

[16] "Investigations of the Situation of Landless and Jobless Farmers."

combined with his income from the land, brought him about 2,000 *yuan* in annual net gain. Since his land has been occupied, Huang has been receiving 80 *yuan* per month as a living subsidy, lower than the 143 *yuan* minimum income for residents in Zigong city. Hongqi Town, located along a rural and urban borderline, was quite well off before the massive land eminent domain started. For example, in Baiguo Village, the 280 villagers had land tenure over 303 mu, used mainly for the production of food and vegetables. Combined with some other supplementary crops, farmers were able to have an average per capita income of 2,000 *yuan* a year. Having been forced off their land since 1995, each farmer has long spent his/her 8,000 *yuan* settlement fee and has had to fend for themselves during the past nine years. To add insult to injury, since 1997 the farmers have been gradually losing the roof over their head as well. Several hundreds of farming families had to sign a relocation contract with the high-tech development district and move into temporary housing. These dwellings are dark, cold, and damp, with leaky roofs above them and muddy roads down below. The landless farmers in Hongqi Town had banked on the promise that they would soon be able to become wage laborers in the new factories, yet years later, on their former home sites, there is no sight of the long-expected factories; instead, rows and rows of commercial apartments have appeared (Xiu, 2003).

Plagued by abject poverty, these landless, jobless, and homeless farmers, beleaguered by arbitrary taxation, have no other form of social security or medical insurance, and their livelihood is in jeopardy (Jyotsna and Ravallion, 1997). It is well known that the social security system for Chinese farmers is way behind that for urban residents, whose own elderly care, medical care, and unemployment benefits are only in their initial stage of getting established and whose coverage is still quite minimal. Farmers have not yet been accepted into even the most rudimentary parameters of social security. Much of the rural population finds it hard to accept the system that depends primarily on farmers' own contribution, supplemented by the collectives and only supported by the government policies. One study shows that only 11.5 per cent of farmers have joined elderly care. Obviously, the landless and jobless farmers have become a new disadvantaged social group in the process of China's urbanization (Yang, Shen and Jin, 2003).

In conclusion, one may think of rights as an abstract concept, but the invisible poverty of rights is the most fundamental cause for economic hardship and the overall condition of poverty. Regrettably, many scholars only scratch the surface when trying to explore causes for the current rural crisis in China, attributing the dire circumstances of farmers to some superficial phenomena, such as the numerous random and ruthless forms of taxation, official corruption, and the weakness of farmers themselves. As a matter of fact, safeguarding farmers' land property rights will help reduce, if not eradicate, rural poverty, and raise the farmers' standard of living and social status as well as level of political participation.

References

Barzel, Y., *Economic Analysis of Property Rights* (New York: Cambridge University Press, 1989).

Blecher, M., 'Inequality and socialism in rural China: a conceptual note,' *World Development*, 13, 1 (1985): 115-121.

Bossen, L., *Chinese Women and Rural Development: Sixty Years of Change in Lu Village, Yunnan* (Lanham, MD: Rowman & Littlefield Publishers, 2002).

Carter, C. and Zhong, F., 'Will market prices enhance Chinese agriculture? A test of regional comparative advantage,' *Western Journal of Agricultural Economics*, 16, 2 (1991): 417-426.

Chen, J., 'On Property Institution of the People's Commune,' *Economic Research*, 7 (1994): 47-53.

Chen, X., 'The Institutional Barriers Have to Be Removed for Farmers to Increase Their Profit' [Nongmin zengshou xu dapo zhidu zhuanai], *China Economic Information Net*, 8 October 2002 (paper online); available from <www1.cei.gov.cn>; accessed 12 December 2002.

Croll, E., and Huang, P., 'Migration for and against agriculture in eight Chinese villages,' *The China Quarterly*, 3 (1997): 128-4.

Dang, G., 'Changes in the authority structure in China's rural society and rural stability' [Zhongguo nongcun shehui quanwei jieguo bianhua yu nongcun wending], *Observation of Rural China* [Zhongguo Nongcun Guancha], 5 (1997): 1-7.

Hong, Z., 'The poverty of social rights: the origin of urban poverty in China and its solutions' (Lun shehui quanli de pinkun: Zhongguo chengshi pinkun wenti de genyuan yu zhili lujing) *Modern China Studies* (Dangdai Zhongguo Yanjiu), 80, 4 (2002): 5-30.

Jacka, T., *Women's Work in Rural China: Change and Continuity in an Era of Reform* (New York: Cambridge University Press, 1997).

Jia, S., 'The overall reform of our rural collective land ownership system,' *Economic Studies*, 12 (1996): 23-36.

Jyotsna, J. and Ravallion, M., 'Are the poor less well insured? Evidence on vulnerability to income risk in rural China,' *Journal of Development Economics*. 58 (1997): 10-23.

———, 'Is transient poverty different? evidence from rural China.' *Journal of Development Studies*, 36 (2000): 82-99.

———, 'Transient poverty in post-reform rural China.' *Journal of Comparative Economics*, 26 (1998): 338-357.

Kelliher, D., 'The Chinese debate over village self-government,' *The China Journal*, 37, 1 (1997): 63-86.

Khan, A. and Riskin, C., *Inequality and Poverty in China in the Age of Globalization* (Oxford: Oxford University Press, 2000).

Kung, J. and Liu S., 'Farmers preferences regarding ownership and land tenure in post-Mao China,' *The China Journal*, 38, 7 (1997): 33-63.

Lin, C., 'Who will care about the fate of farmers? who have lost their land?' [Sui lai guanxin shidi nongmin de mingyun?], *Chinese Economic Times* [Zhongguo jingji shibao], 2 September, 2003.

Liu, J. and Chen, F., 'Strange Things in Linfeng, Hunan: The Linfeng Government Forcefully Reclaims Farm Land to Grow Trees' [Hunan Linfeng guishi], *Xinhua Net*, 19 November 2003.

Oi, J., *State and Peasant in Contemporary China: The Political Economy of Village Government* (Berkeley: University of California Press, 1989).

————, 'The Role of the state in China's transitional economy,' *The China Quarterly,* 12 (1995): 132-149.

————, *Rural China Takes Off: Institutional Foundations of Economic Reform* (Berkeley: University of California Press, 1999).

Perkins, D. and Ysuf, S., *Rural Development in China* (Baltimore: Johns Hopkins University Press, 1984).

Putterman, L. (ed), *Continuity and Change in China's Rural Development: Collective and Reform Eras in Perspective* (New York: Oxford University Press, 1993).

Riskin, C., 'Chinese rural poverty: marginalized or dispersed?' *American Economic Review\,* 84, 2 (1994): 281-284.

————, 'Rural poverty in post-reform China', in R. Garnaut, S. Guo, and G. Ma (eds), *The Third Revolution in the Chinese Countryside* (New York: Cambridge University Press, 1996), pp.245-255.

Riskin, C., Zhao R. and Shi, L., *China's Retreat from Inequality* (New York: M.E. Sharpe, 2001).

Rozelle, S., Guo, L., Shen, M., Hughart, A. and Giles, J., 'Leaving China's farms: survey results of new paths and remaining hurdles to rural migration,' *China Quarterly,* 158, 6 (1999): 367-393.

She, V., *Peasant China in Transition: The Dynamics of Development Towards Socialism, 1949-1956* (Berkeley: University of California Press, 1986).

Sicular, T., 'China's agricultural policy during the reform period,' in Joint Economic Committee of the U.S. Congress (eds), *China's Economic Dilemmas in the 1990's: The Problems of Reforms, Modernization and Independence* (New York: M.E. Sharpe, 1993), pp.340-364.

Tao, P., 'The rights of farmers who have lost their land must be protected' [Shidi nongmin de liyi bixu quebao] *Farmers Daily* [Nongmin Ribao], 23 May, 2003.

Unger, J., *The Transformation of Rural China* (New York: M.E. Sharpe, 2002).

Wang, J. and Zhi, X., 'Protecting Rural Women's Land Rights' [Baozhang nongcun funiu tudi quanli], *China Election and Governance Website,* 15 August 2003 [article online]; available from <www.chinaelections.com>; Internet; accessed 11 May 2004.

West, L. and Zhao, Y., *Rural Labor Flows in China* (Berkeley: University of California Press, 2000).

World Bank, China Strategies for Reducing Poverty in the 1990s, Washington, D.C., 1992.

Wu, Y., 'What to do when farmers lose their land - Jiangsu province's new rural policy: exchanging land for social security' (Nongminshidi zemeban), *China Industrial and Economic News* (Zhongguo chanjing xinwen bao), 14 November, 2003.

Xie, X., 'Vice minister of agriculture: violating farmers' land rights becoming a critical issue' [Nongyebu fubuzhang: Qinghai nongmin tudi quanyi cheng tuchu wenti], *China Youth Daily* [Zhongguo qingnian bao], 21 August, 2003.

Yang, J., Shen, C. and Jin, Z., 'Investigations and Thoughts on the Problem of Landless Farmers' [Dui Shitu nongmin wenti de diaocha yu shikao], *China Election and Governance Web,* 30 October 2003.

Zhu, L., 'Annulling a 30-Year Contract in Three Days: The Sudden Loss of Farmers' Land' [30 nian de hetong 3 tian jiu gei feile: cunmin tudi shui mei jiu mei le], *Xinhua Net,* 3

November 2003 [paper online]; available from <www.xinhua.org>; Internet; accessed 11 March 2004.

Zweig, D., *Freeing China's Farmers: Rural Restructuring in the Reform Era* (New York: M. E. Sharpe, 1997).

Chapter 7

Accounting for Income Inequality in Rural China: A Regression-based Approach[*]

Guanghua Wan

1 Introduction

A resurgence of interest in income distribution in developed, developing, and transition economies is found in literature. Atkinson (2001) notes the doubling back of inequality after an inverted U-pattern in developed countries. Cornia and Popov (2001) investigate rapidly rising inequality in transitional economies. Datt and Ravallion (1992) and Dollar and Kraay (2002) consider the recent controversy over the effects of growth versus redistribution on poverty reduction in the developing world. Traditional approaches to income distribution are mostly descriptive rather than prescriptive. They involve measuring the extent of inequality and speculating on its determinants. Following the work of Shorrocks (1980; 1982), inequality decomposition by income sources requires an identity to express income as the sum of several components. Conversely, inequality decomposition by population subgroups provides rather limited information on the fundamental determinants of inequality, for example, differences in human and physical capital, dependency rates, globalization, and technical change.

Since the early 1970s, economists have used the regression-based approach to inequality decomposition. Unlike its traditional counterparts, this approach allows the contributions of the regression variables to total inequality to be quantified. Although the early work is limited, regarding the number and type of variables that can be considered, recent advances have relaxed this restriction. In theory, regression-based inequality decomposition permits the inclusion of any number or type of variables or even proxies, including social, economic, demographic, and policy factors. The flexibility of this approach, particularly its ability to

[*] This article was originally published in the Journal of Comparative Economics 32(2004): 348-363. It is reprinted here with the permission of the Association for Comparative Economic Studies, which holds the copyright. The author is grateful to Professor Tony Shorrocks for numerous discussions during the preparation of this paper, and to anonymous referees and the editor of this journal for useful comments. All remaining errors are the author's.

accommodate endogeneity of income determination and random errors, makes it attractive to economists and policy-makers. Oaxaca (1973) and Blinder (1973) are the pioneers of this approach; they focus on the difference in mean income between two groups. Other moments of the income-generating process are not considered. Juhn, Murphy, and Pierce (1993) extend this approach so that the decomposition depends on the difference in the entire income distribution between two groups rather than on the difference in mean income only. Bourguignon, Fournier, and Gurgand (2001) relax the requirement of a linear income-generating function imposed by Juhn, Murphy, and Pierce (1993). All these authors focus on explaining differences in income distribution between distinct groups of income recipients; they do not quantify the contributions of specific factors to total inequality. Hence, only a limited number of inequality-related impacts can be identified, although these impacts could be functions of more fundamental determinants. For example, the technique proposed by Bourguignon, Fournier, and Gurgand (2001) can be used to decompose differences in income distribution into only three broad components, namely, price effects, participation effects, and population effects.

In a different strand of literature using semiparametric and nonparametric techniques, DiNardo, Fortin, and Lemieux (1996) and Deaton (1997) describe and compare the entire distribution of the target variable in terms of the density function, rather than attempt to decompose a summary measure of inequality. Although they impose few structural assumptions, the findings are less conclusive than economists and policy makers would prefer, as Morduch and Sicular (2002) argue. Fields and Yoo (2000) and Morduch and Sicular (2002) employ conventional techniques to specify and estimate parametric income-generating functions and derive inequality decompositions based on the estimated regression equations. Their conceptual framework allows for any number of fundamental income determinants but suffers from a number of restrictions. This chapter builds on the work of Fields and Yoo (2000) and Morduch and Sicular (2002); we present a critical evaluation of these papers in section 2.

This chapter is motivated by three issues. First, any regression-based inequality decomposition inevitably involves a constant term and a residual term. These terms give rise to specific problems, which are neglected or not properly addressed in Morduch and Sicular (2002) and Fields and Yoo (2000). Second, the current state of art in regression-based inequality decomposition imposes severe limitations in terms of the functional forms and inequality measures used. Finally, the determinants of regional income inequality in rural China are studied descriptively in the literature, with the exception of Ravallion and Chen (1999).[1] This chapter quantifies the contributions of various determinants to total inequality in rural China and provides a prescriptive analysis. Section 3 proposes a general regression-based framework for inequality decomposition in which the Gini

---

[1] These authors focus on data problems in China and use regression-based decompositions, following Fields and Yoo (2000).

coefficient is used as an example measure of inequality. The proposed method can be applied to any inequality measure, and it imposes few restrictions on the underlying regression model. In Section 4, the root sources of income inequality in rural China are investigated. Section 5 concludes with a summary and policy recommendations.

2 Recent Advances in the Regression-based Approach

Morduch and Sicular (2002), hereafter MS, and Fields and Yoo (2000), hereafter FY, impose specific functional forms on the underlying income-generating function. MS use a standard linear specification while FY employ a semilog regression model. These limitations prevent model selection and possibly introduce errors into the empirical work. Another major limitation of both papers is the inequality measure used. FY consider only the squared coefficient of variation (CV^2). On the other hand, MS require that the inequality measures permit total inequality to be written as a weighted sum of inequalities of factor incomes. Furthermore, MS cannot explain an unusually large proportion of inequality. For their preferred indices of inequality, their decomposition leaves 90.62 and 89.63 percent of inequality in the unexplainable residual term.

Apart from violating the transfer axiom as criticized by MS, FY's technique requires inequality be measured using the log of income. Although not affecting income rankings, this scaling may lead to distortions in the decomposition results. Due to this restriction, a comparison of FY's results with those of other inequality studies is not possible. Moreover, in their "sources of changing contributions" context (p. 148), FY imposes the assumption of orthogonality. Under this assumption, FY's method can be shown to be equivalent to decomposing the R-squared statistic (R^2) from the standard regression model. Consequently, negative or equalizing contributions are ruled out by the method.

In both MS and FY, the contributions of the constant term and the residual term are not derived from the natural rule of decomposition of Shorrocks (1999) or equivalently the before-after approach of Cancian and Reed (1998).[2] Consequently, the residual term and the constant term, which is a uniform addition to or deduction from income from all recipients, may or may not contribute to total inequality depending on the particular inequality measure used. This measure-dependent feature is a deficiency of the MS framework. The framework of FY is also flawed

---

[2] Based on this rule or approach, the effect of a variable on inequality is given by the change in total inequality when the variable is initially included and then removed. See equation (4) for a mathematical representation of this rule.

in this regard as the constant term has no effect on inequality in FY.[3] Podder and Chatterjee (2002) show that a positive (negative) constant will lower (raise) inequality if relative inequality measures such as CV^2 or the Gini index are used.[4] All the measures used by MS and FY are relative inequality measures.

To avoid these problems and restrictions, we develop a general regression-based procedure for decomposing any inequality measure, including the Gini coefficient and Theil's measure. Our approach is consistent with the natural rule of decomposition. It is also flexible enough to be applied to any type of income transformation, for example, the logarithm and Box-Cox transformations. Most importantly, our approach can be used with any parametric specification of the regression model.

3 A New Decomposition Procedure

Let $Y = F(X, U)$ be a regression model in which Y is income or a transformation of original income, X is a vector of income determinants or their proxies, and U is the disturbance term. Assuming the presence of a constant term α in the regression model, Y can be written as:

$$Y = \alpha + \widetilde{Y} + U \tag{1}$$

From equation (1), $\hat{Y} = \alpha + \widetilde{Y}$ is the deterministic part and $\widetilde{Y}$ represents income flows from various determinants. If $F(X, U)$ is linear, $\widetilde{Y} = \Sigma \beta_i X_i = \Sigma Y_i$ where $Y_i = \beta_i X_i$ is the income flow from the ith factor. The model is more general than those of Blinder (1973), Oaxaca (1973), Juhn, Murphy, and Pierce (1993), FY, and MS. In fact, the regression model need not be additive as in equation (1). The additive form is assumed to facilitate the exposition but any linear or nonlinear form could be used.

Total inequality is given by $I(OI)$, where I denotes an inequality measure and OI corresponds to the original income variable so that $OI = Y$ if no transformation is applied to original income. The objective of regression-based decomposition is to attribute $I(OI)$ to the various components of the X vector, the constant α and the residual U. FY apply the variance operator to both sides of the regression and divide both sides by the variance of the dependent variable. This approach was used by Wan (1988) to decompose output variability and by Zhang and Fan (2000)

---

[3] Under the semilog income-generating function of Fields and Yoo (2000), the constant term is not a scalar unless inequality is measured using original income rather than the log of income. Hence, the constant term, if correctly considered, ought to have effect on total inequality.

[4] Fields (2001) and Kolm (1999) discuss the merits of relative versus absolute measures of inequality. Suffice to point out that most inequality studies use relative rather than absolute measures and that the preferred absolute measures include the Kolm index and income range.

to decompose output inequality. In this method, the contribution of the residual term is $(1-R^2)$ and the other terms contribute $\text{Cov}(Y_i, \ln(OI))/\text{Var}(\ln(OI))$. Moreover, the constant term contributes nothing to the inequality of $\ln(OI)$. When the Gini coefficient is applied to equation (1) as in MS, both the residual term and the constant term contribute nothing to overall inequality. In other words, the deterministic part of the model explains the entire income inequality, no matter how poorly fitted the regression model is.

To avoid these problems, we follow the natural rule of decomposition proposed by Shorrocks (1999) and develop a procedure that is not dependent on the inequality measure and not restricted to linear or semilog regression models. To explain our approach, we use the Gini coefficient as a measure of inequality. If the target variable is untransformed income and a linear function is specified, we have:

$$Y = OI = \alpha + \Sigma_i Y_i + U \qquad (2)$$

where $Y_i = \beta_i X_i$ and $\hat{Y} = \alpha + \Sigma_i Y_i$.

Following MS and applying the Gini operator G to both sides of equation (2), we have:

$$G(Y) = 0 + \Sigma_i E(Y_i)/E(Y) C(Y_i) + 0 \qquad (3)$$

where C denotes the concentration index. To allocate total inequality to individual sources, MS use equation (3) so that each source contributes $E(Y_i)/E(Y) C(Y_i)$ to $G(Y)$. The disturbance term plays no role in determining income inequality. Although U is white noise by definition so that it does not alter the shape of the estimated Lorenze curve, U does affect the underlying income density function and thus inequality. The residual term represents unobservable factors or determinants of inequality that are not included in the regression model. The percentage of inequality that is not explained by the model is useful information. Equation (3) also implies that the constant term has no effect on income inequality. However, as a relative inequality measure, the Gini index declines (increases) when a positive (negative) constant is added to every income recipient. Thus, it is inappropriate to use equation (3) for inequality decomposition.

To account for the contribution of the non-included factors or the residual term, we follow the procedure in Shorrocks (1999) and eliminate U from equation (2). Hence, we have

$$Y(U=0) = \hat{Y}$$

and obtain $G(Y|U=0) = G(\hat{Y})$. The contribution of U to $G(Y)$ is defined as:

$$COu = G(Y) - G(\hat{Y}) \qquad (4)$$

In equation (4), the difference between Y and $\hat{Y}$ is due solely to U. As U approaches 0 from above or below, $\hat{Y}$ approaches Y and so does $G(\hat{Y})$ to $G(Y)$. Therefore, it is reasonable to attribute $G(Y) - G(\hat{Y})$ to U.

Since a regression model consists of a deterministic and a stochastic part, the total inequality can be divided into the deterministic part given by $G(\hat{Y})$ and the remaining stochastic part due to U. Hence, the contribution of the residual can be expressed as $G(Y) - G(\hat{Y})$. Despite the fact that the expected values of Y and $\hat{Y}$ are identical, $G(Y)$ and $G(\hat{Y})$ can be respectively written as:

$$G(Y) = \Sigma_i E(Y_i)/E(Y) \; C(Y_i)|_{\text{rank by } Y} \tag{5}$$

$$G(\hat{Y}) = \Sigma_i E(Y_i)/E(Y) \; C(Y_i)|_{\text{rank by } \hat{Y}} \tag{5'}$$

The only difference between (5) and (5') is the ranking of Y_i in calculating $C(Y_i)$.

Having identified the contribution of the residual to total inequality, we turn to the identification of the contribution of the constant term. Applying the Gini operator to equation (1), we obtain:

$$G(Y) = \alpha \,/E(Y) \; C(\alpha) + \Sigma_i E(Y_i)/E(Y) \; C(Y_i)|_{\text{rank by } Y} + 0$$
$$= 0 + \Sigma_i E(Y_i)/E(Y) \; C(Y_i)|_{\text{rank by } Y} + 0 \tag{6}$$

MS use (6) to decompose total inequality. Hence, the constant term makes no contribution. However, $E(Y_i)/E(Y)$ changes for different values of α. In particular, the addition of a positive (negative) constant leads to a decrease (increase) in $E(Y_i)/E(Y)$, because $E(Y)$ becomes larger (smaller) but $E(Y_i)$ is not affected. Therefore, the impact of the constant α is distributed over, or absorbed by, other terms in (6). Our goal is to extract this impact from these terms.

From (4), $G(Y) = G(\hat{Y}) + COu$ so that we focus on $G(\hat{Y})$ and note that $\hat{Y} = \widetilde{Y} + \alpha$. Following Shorrocks (1999), we have:

$$G(\hat{Y}|\alpha = 0) = G(\widetilde{Y}) = \Sigma_i E(Y_i)/E(\widetilde{Y}) \; C(Y_i)|_{\text{rank by } \hat{Y} \text{ or } \widetilde{Y}}. \tag{7}$$

Thus, the contribution of the constant term is defined as:

$$CO_\alpha = G(\hat{Y}) - G(\widetilde{Y}) \tag{8}$$

Clearly, if $\alpha > 0$, $CO_\alpha < 0$, and vice versa. Without α, the individual concentration indices $C(Y_i)$ are weighted by $W_i = E(Y_i)/E(\widetilde{Y})$ in (6). When α is nonzero, the weights become $\widetilde{W}_i = E(Y_i)/E(\widetilde{Y} + \alpha)$. Intuitively, the weights can be adjusted by the difference ($W_i - \widetilde{W}_i$) and the resultant difference in the underlying inequality is attributed to α. Following this reasoning, we have:

$$CO_\alpha = \Sigma_i(W_i - \widetilde{W}_i) \; C(Y_i) = G(\hat{Y}) - G(\widetilde{Y}),$$

which is identical to (8).

In summary, equations (4), (8), and (7) allow one to decompose $G(Y)$ into COu, CO_α, and the contributions of the various terms in the vector X. The percentage contributions are given as:

$$PCu = 100 \, [G(Y) - G(\hat{Y})]/G(Y)$$

$$PC_\alpha = 100 \, [G(\hat{Y}) - G(\widetilde{Y})]/G(Y)$$

$$PC^{\widetilde{Y}} = 100 \, G(\widetilde{Y})/G(Y) = 100/G(Y) \, \Sigma_i E(Y_i)/E(\widetilde{Y}) \; C(Y_i)|_{\text{rank by } \hat{Y} \text{ or } \widetilde{Y}}$$

where $E(Y_i)/E(\widetilde{Y}) \; C(Y_i)|_{\text{rank by } \hat{Y} \text{ or } \widetilde{Y}} = CO_i$ represents the contribution of the i-th variable.

Although these results are obtained by using the Gini index as an inequality measure and a linear income-generating function, this approach can be applied to any measure of inequality and it is not limited to linear regression models. However, the interpretation of the decomposition results may not be straightforward. In general, a contribution is interpreted to measure the effect on total inequality if a particular variable or income source is eliminated. By elimination, it could mean removal or assuming an even distribution of the relevant variable among all income recipients. If inequality increases (decreases), this source or variable makes a negative (positive) contribution and it is inequality-reducing (inequality-increasing).

Using a linear income-generating function and taking the Gini index, we find that the sign of CO_i depends on $E(Y_i)$ and $C(Y_i)$. Since $\tilde{Y}$ is generated from all income determinants, it should be positive. However, $E(Y_i) = \beta_i E(X_i)$ and $C(Y_i) = C(X_i)$. Since $E(X_i) > 0$ for most economic variables, the sign of CO_i depends on β_i and $C(X_i)$. From (2), β_i is the marginal impact of X_i on income not on income inequality; however, $C(X_i)$ takes values between -1 and 1, representing the association between total income Y and the component Y_i or the variable X_i. Put differently, β_i is the partial regression coefficient that measures the impact of X_i on Y controlling for all other factors, whereas $C(X_i)$ captures the correlation between Y and Y_i or X_i without controlling for any factors. For example, a variable such as education level is expected to produce a positive impact on income so that $\beta_i > 0$. However, highly educated people are likely to be in higher income groups so that the correlation between total income and income flows from education should be positive, that is, $C(X_i) > 0$. As a consequence, the contribution of education to total inequality is positive, and thus inequality is increasing. This is equivalent to saying that overall inequality would drop if everyone were to receive the same income flow from education regardless of the education level attained.

Alternatively, a welfare or poverty-relief payment goes to the poor so that it is negatively correlated with total income, that is, $C(X_i) < 0$. Conversely, holding all other variables constant, an increase in the welfare or relief payment to even one recipient will increase the mean of the dependent variable Y. Hence, the marginal impact of this variable on income is positive, that is, $\beta_i > 0$. Consequently, the overall impact is negative and thus inequality-reducing. As another example, the variable of dependency ratio is expected to have a negative marginal impact on household income, that is, $\beta_i < 0$. However, this variable is likely to be inversely correlated with total income so that $C(X_i) < 0$. Therefore, the dependency ratio is expected to be inequality-increasing. In other words, if every household had the same dependency ratio, total inequality would be lower.

4 Sources of Regional Inequality in Rural China

Regional inequality in rural China is increasing over time, which has important social and political implications. Much of the literature focuses on inequality measurements or conventional decompositions, which provide only limited insights into the causes of regional inequality. Therefore, we apply the framework developed in the previous section to identify root sources of regional inequality in rural China. For this purpose, regional or provincial data for 1992 to 1995 are compiled from various issues of Rural Household Survey Statistics, a publication of the National Bureau of Statistics (NBS). With Taiwan excluded, China has 31 provinces or regions, including four autonomous municipal cities. Chongqing is the youngest region in China; before 1997 it was part of Sichuan Province. Therefore, our sample consists of 30 regions. Population data are taken from China Agricultural Yearbook and China Rural Yearbook (NBS, various years). Rural population, instead of agricultural population, is used because the rural survey covers non-urban households. Our analytical results should be robust to the choice of population data given the high correlation between these two series.

In China, more than 50 percent of rural income is from farming activities, and non-farm income come mainly from family businesses. Under these circumstances, inputs other than labor are needed to generate income. Thus, the following variables are considered for inclusion in the underlying income-generating function: per capita disposable income (*OI*), family or household size (*HH*), the dependency ratio (*DEP*), per capita capital input (*K*), the average level of education of household members (*EDU*), per capita possession of cultivable land (*A*), and the proportion of labor force employed in rural industrial enterprises (*TVE*). Family size is incorporated to take account of the income earned from sideline production, which often involves non-laborers. Once household size is included, either labor or the dependency ratio must be excluded. Given the divergence in dependency ratios across regions and its converging trend, we choose to include the dependency ratio. In any case, labor is unlikely to be a significant variable because of its surplus nature in rural China as Wan and Cheng (2001) demonstrate. The inclusion of *TVE* can be justified because of its important impact on regional inequality as Wan (1997 and 2001) and Rozelle (1994) show. All variables in value terms are deflated by rural CPIs.

Given the large number of cross-sectional units relative to the time span, only year dummies are considered. These dummies are intended to capture changes in income attributable to factors such as reform impacts and technical change. However, the effects of dummy variables on income inequality cannot be identified independently. To minimize misspecification errors, we adopt the combined Box-Cox and Box-Tidwell model and write:

$$OI^{(\lambda)} = \alpha + \beta_1 X_1^{(\theta)} (2) + \beta_2 X_2^{(\theta)} + \dots \beta_K X_K^{(\theta)} + \textit{dummy variable terms} + U \qquad (9)$$

In this specification, $OI^{(\lambda)} = \dfrac{OI^\lambda - 1}{\lambda}$ and $X_k^{(\theta)} = \dfrac{X_k^\theta - 1}{\theta}$. As λ approaches 0, the

limit of $\dfrac{OI^\lambda - 1}{\lambda}$ is *Ln OI* from L'Hôpital's rule. Hence, $OI^{(\lambda)} = Ln\ OI$ when $\lambda = 0$

(Judge et al., 1988). The same arguments apply to θ and $X_k^{(\theta)}$. Model (9) encompasses many functional forms, including the semilog income-generating function of FY if $\lambda = 0$ and $\theta = 1$, and the standard linear function of MS if $\lambda = \theta = 1$. If $\lambda = \theta = 0$, a double-log equation is obtained. If λ or θ equals -1, the relevant variable becomes its reciprocal. By allowing λ and θ to take values of 0, 1, and -1, and to be unrestricted, respectively, we obtain 16 different functional forms. In addition, the extended Box-Cox model is estimated with the restriction that $\lambda = \theta$. Hence, a total of 17 models are estimated; see Table 7.1 and related discussions.

In the first round of estimations, all variables are included with year dummies. However, the dummy variables for 1992 and 1994 are not significant in most equations. Therefore, we remove them and reestimate the models. As shown in Table 7.1, the removal did not change the estimated models in any significant way, except the constant term. Therefore, we use the specification with only a dummy for 1993. For the purpose of model selection, we consult the loglikelihood values, and the squared correlation coefficient between predicted and actual *OI* , denoted by r^2, for all the 17 models in Table 7.1.[5]

The column headings in Table 7.1 consist of two parts; the first part indicates the transformation of the dependent variable and the second part indicates the transformation of the independent variables. The symbols λ and θ mean that the transformations are determined by the data. For example, *Ln, Lin,* and *Inv* mean λ or θ equals 0, 1 and -1, respectively. The most flexible model, that is, $(\lambda - \theta)$, produces the largest loglikelihood value. However, the $(Ln - \theta)$ model has similar values for the loglikelihood and r^2, as do the $(\lambda - Lin)$ and the $(Ln - Lin)$ models. Interestingly, the extended Box-Cox model, which imposes the same transformation on both dependent and independent variables so that $\lambda = \theta$, yields the second highest r^2, although its loglikelihood value is relatively small. However, model evaluation and selection will be based on loglikelihood values, not r^2, which is reported for the purpose of indicating goodness of fit.

Since all of the other 16 models are nested with the most flexible model, a standard χ^2 test will be used for model selection. At the 1 percent level of significance, three models, namely $(Ln - \theta)$, $(Ln - Lin)$, and $(\lambda - Lin)$, are accepted. Among these models, the $(Ln - \theta)$ and the $(Ln - Lin)$ models are nested and the χ^2 test rejects the $(Ln - Lin)$ model at the 5 percent significance level. In addition, the $(Ln - Lin)$ and the $(\lambda - Lin)$ models are nested and found to be equivalent by the χ^2 test. Having rejected the $(Ln - Lin)$ model, the $(\lambda - Lin)$ model is rejected by association. In any case, the $(\lambda - Lin)$ model is rejected at the 5 percent level of significance when tested against the most flexible model. Consequently, the $(Ln - \theta)$ income-generating function is chosen for inequality decomposition. Since both the semilog specification of FY and the linear form of MS are rejected, decomposition results using these models will suffer from misspecification errors in addition to the errors generated by the deficiencies in their decomposition frameworks.

---

[5] Table 7.1 also reports the R^2 statistics produced by Shazam. Since the properties of R^2 in the combined Box-Cox and Box-Tidwell model are unknown, we do not use these statistics for model selection.

Table 7.1 Loglikelihood values of alternative models

Model	λ − θ	λ = θ	λ − Ln	λ − Lin	λ − Inv	Ln − θ	Ln − Ln	Ln - Lin	Ln - Inv
With all dummies	-659.507	-666.026	-690.006	-661.748	-703.929	-659.668	-693.774	-662.048	-707.331
Degrees of freedom	108	109	109	109	109	109	110	110	110
R^2	0.786	0.808	0.622	0.775	0.522	0.791	0.631	0.783	0.538
r^2	0.82	0.83	0.604	0.81	0.53	0.808	0.66	0.819	0.5786
1993 dummy only	-659.904	-666.326	-690.291	-662.591	-706.534	-660.017	-694.163	-662.774	-709.611
Degrees of freedom	110	111	111	111	111	111	112	112	112
R^2	0.788	0.810	0.626	0.778	0.511	0.794	0.636	0.784	0.529
r^2	0.819	0.829	0.598	0.810	0.534	0.807	0.654	0.817	0.569

Model	Lin − θ	Lin − Ln	Lin − Lin	Lin - Inv	Inv - θ	Inv - Ln	Inv - Lin	Inv - Inv
With all dummies	-672.05	-718.007	-673.445	-728.493	-665.019	-691.306	-666.031	-704.985
Degrees of freedom	109	110	110	110	109	110	110	110
R^2	0.820	0.612	0.816	0.538	0.748	0.609	0.743	0.51
r^2	0.839	0.642	0.830	0.573	0.767	0.513	0.716	0.464
1993 dummy only	-672.399	-718.642	-673.795	-730.18	-665.876	-691.563	-667.435	-707.768
Degrees of freedom	111	112	112	112	111	112	112	112
R^2	0.822	0.615	0.818	0.534	0.749	0.614	0.742	0.495
r^2	0.838	0.638	0.829	0.561	0.763	0.512	0.691	0.485

Table 7.2 presents the estimation results for the $(Ln - \theta)$ model. The t-statistics in Table 7.2 and the r^2 in Table 7.1 indicate that the model fits the data well. No t-statistic is reported for the θ coefficient because its estimate is obtained by a grid search. However, the hypothesis that $\theta = 0$ can be tested using the χ^2 ratio, which is derived from the loglikelihood values of the $(Ln - \theta)$ and the $(Ln - Ln)$ models. This test indicates that θ is significantly different from zero. In Table 7.2, estimation results for the linear and semilog income generating-functions are also reported. Although most estimates have the same signs and similar t-statistics, the large and negative constant estimate in the linear model indicates its inappropriateness. The coefficient estimates for the semilog specification are smaller than their counterparts in the $(Ln - \theta)$ equation, because the independent variables in the latter are transformed by a power function.

The signs of the coefficient estimates for the $(Ln - \theta)$ model are as expected, including the negative sign for the land variable. Regions with larger land are usually more backward and more heavily involved in farming, compared to land-scarce but more affluent regions, for example, Pearl Delta and Yangtze Delta. Farming has been a loss-making business in China since the late 1980s or early 1990s. Well-known slogans assert that the more one cultivates the greater the loss. Farming loss is attributable to depressed prices for food products, rising prices of inputs, and the imposition of countless fees and levies by various government departments at the local levels. Although these fees and levies may not be linked to the cultivated land area, they can be enforced only on farming families under the administrative control of local governments. Families who move away or who engage in non-farming activities are less subject to the administrative abuse of local governments. As a production factor, land contributes to gross income but not to net income. Therefore, the coefficient for the land variable is expected to be negative when net or disposable income is used as the dependent variable, although it may well be positive in a production function or in a gross income equation. In addition, heterogeneity in land quality and crop composition across regions may contribute to the negative sign on the land coefficient.[6]

The positive coefficient on the family size variable is consistent with expectations because of economies of scale in income generation. In addition, it may indicate the importance of the contributions of school children and the elderly to family businesses, sideline production, and farming. Even that the dependency ratio is included in this model, the impact of family size may also capture effects of an omitted labor input variable. Except for a different intercept for 1993, the income-generating process remains unchanged during the period. Hence, the estimated function can be used to compute inequality decompositions for each year from 1992 to 1995. However, the final model selected is nonlinear in terms of original income, although it is linear in the log of income. To compute inequality

---

[6] Relative to the western regions, the land-scarce eastern regions have high-quality land and produce more value-added crops; hence, they are less likely to suffer losses. We thank one of the referees for making this point.

decompositions for income rather than the log of income, we solve the estimated model for original income. As a consequence, the constant term becomes a scalar so that it does not contribute to inequality. Hence, both the constant and the dummy variable terms can be removed without affecting the decomposition results.

Because the model is nonlinear, the Shapley value approach developed by Shorrocks (1999) is used to identify contributions by individual variables. The contribution of the residual term is obtained according to the procedure outlined in the previous section. Regarding inequality measures, different indices are associated with different social welfare functions that assume different aversions to inequality. In addition, they put different weights on different segments of the underlying Lorenz curve. Therefore, different indices of inequality often produce different measurement results, which may carry over to the inequality decomposition. Hence, decomposition results are likely to depend on the indicator of inequality used. For generality, we consider most of the commonly used measures of inequality in our decompositions. These include the Gini coefficient, the squared coefficient of variation (CV^2), the Atkinson index, Theil-T, and Theil-L.[7]

The decomposition is implemented using a web-based program developed by the World Institute for Development Economics Research of the United Nations University (UNU-WIDER). From the "total" rows of Table 7.3, an increasing trend in inequality is observed. In terms of composition, the percentage contributions are similar across years for any given inequality indicator. As expected, different indicators yield different decomposition outcomes. Nevertheless, the ranking of contributors changes little from one indicator to another or from one year to another. Hence, we interpret the results for 1995 only. All of the variables, except for family size, contribute positively to income inequality in rural China. Factors, which we would expect to contribute negatively to regional inequality, include welfare payments, poverty-alleviation receipts, and both public and private transfers of income. Since we have no observations for these variables, we cannot quantify their contributions to total inequality. However, in rural China, welfare payments are virtually non-existent and poverty alleviation receipts are minimal at the household level. Moreover, private transfers depend on the earning capacity of family members living and working away from home. Thus, affluent regions may

---

[7] Let Z denote the target variable, μ denote the mean of Z, j index observations ($j = 1, 2, ...,$ N), the following formulae are used: Atkinson $= 1 - \prod_j \left(\frac{Z_j}{\mu} \right)^{1/N}$, Theil-L $= \frac{1}{N} \sum_j Ln \frac{\mu}{Z_j}$,

and Theil-T $= \frac{1}{N} \sum_j \frac{Z_j}{\mu} Ln \frac{Z_j}{\mu}$. See Fields (2001) for discussions on these measures.

attract more private transfers so that these may not exert any significant equalizing impact.

Table 7.2 Estimated income generating-functions

Variable	Ln-θ Model		Semilog Model		Linear Model	
	Estimate	t-ratio	Estimate	t-ratio	Estimate	t-ratio
Dependency	-0.0305	-3.864	-0.0109	-4.411	-4.4182	-4.099
Capital	0.0073	6.416	0.0016	6.218	0.5642	5.174
Education	0.3309	8.840	0.2354	9.596	88.8210	8.287
Family Size	0.4696	4.494	0.3069	4.556	127.3600	4.327
Land	-0.0559	-3.639	-0.0437	-4.096	-16.5260	-3.549
TVEs	0.0519	11.460	0.0236	10.840	13.5650	14.290
1993 dummy	-0.0807	-2.483	-0.077	-2.318	-33.766	-2.326
Constant	3.794	13.590	3.530	10.800	-554.710	-3.884
θ	0.720	N.A.				

To explain the equalizing impact of family size, it is noted that poor regions have larger family sizes so that the associated income flows more to the poor than to the rich. Moreover, the concentration index of family size is expected to be negative. When combined with a positive partial coefficient, this variable makes negative contribution to income inequality so that family size is inequality-reducing. However, this equalizing effect will disappear over time because family size is converging in rural China. Consistent with the conventional decomposition results, this study suggests that TVEs are the most significant identifiable contributor to regional inequality. TVEs contribute significantly to economic growth and are more developed in richer areas. Hence, regional inequality would be much lower if the income flow from TVEs were removed or equalized. However, conventional decompositions attribute over 50 percent of total inequality to TVEs in contrast to below 25 and 35 percent as reported in Table 7.3. This difference is attributable to the crudeness of conventional decomposition techniques.[8]

---

[8] Conventional decompositions can be viewed as a special case of regression-based approach with a linear income-generating function; the product of a variable and its coefficient is equal to the income source.

Table 7.3 Decomposition results

	Gini	percent	Atkinson	percent	Theil-L	percent	Theil-T	percent	CV²	percent
1992										
Dependency	0.0246	15.96	0.0061	16.60	0.0063	16.61	0.0067	16.82	0.0153	17.53
Capital	0.0163	10.56	0.0029	7.77	0.0029	7.76	0.0032	8.12	0.0072	8.26
Education	0.0294	19.07	0.0067	18.12	0.0068	18.10	0.0067	16.69	0.0138	15.81
Family Size	-0.0041	-2.68	-0.0066	-17.74	-0.0068	-18.10	-0.0075	-18.82	-0.0187	-21.43
Land	0.0061	3.96	0.0012	3.25	0.0012	3.24	0.0014	3.43	0.0033	3.74
TVEs	0.0457	29.71	0.0130	35.10	0.0132	35.03	0.0148	37.17	0.0353	40.33
Residual	0.0360	23.42	0.0136	36.92	0.0141	37.35	0.0146	36.59	0.0313	35.73
Total	0.1539	100	0.0369	100	0.0376	100	0.0399	100	0.0875	100
1993										
Dependency	0.0237	14.79	0.0059	14.61	0.0060	14.62	0.0064	14.46	0.0143	14.78
Capital	0.0239	14.88	0.0049	12.21	0.0050	12.17	0.0052	11.89	0.0109	11.25
Education	0.0293	18.27	0.0070	17.41	0.0072	17.36	0.0070	15.92	0.0144	14.84
Family Size	-0.0013	-0.78	-0.0059	-14.51	-0.0061	-14.84	-0.0066	-14.98	-0.0161	-16.61
Land	0.0069	4.27	0.0014	3.44	0.0014	3.42	0.0016	3.64	0.0038	3.94
TVEs	0.0471	29.32	0.0134	33.28	0.0137	33.18	0.0152	34.49	0.0353	36.44
Residual	0.0309	19.25	0.0136	33.62	0.0141	34.08	0.0152	34.61	0.0343	35.37
Total	0.1605	100	0.0404	100	0.0412	100	0.0439	100	0.0968	100
1994										
Dependency	0.0250	14.92	0.0073	17.14	0.0075	17.17	0.0081	18.04	0.0189	19.56

Continued:

Capital	0.0234	13.96	0.0056	13.19	0.0057	13.16	0.0062	13.71	0.0139	14.36
Education	0.0342	20.42	0.0087	20.37	0.0088	20.32	0.0086	19.04	0.0173	17.97
Family Size	-0.0015	-0.91	-0.0064	-15.12	-0.0067	-15.48	-0.0075	-16.55	-0.0184	-19.06
Land	0.0058	3.44	0.0013	2.94	0.0013	2.95	0.0014	3.11	0.0033	3.45
TVEs	0.0433	25.86	0.0132	31.06	0.0135	31.01	0.0152	33.67	0.0359	37.25
Residual	0.0373	22.31	0.0129	30.42	0.0134	30.90	0.0131	28.99	0.0255	26.47
Total	0.1674	100	0.0425	100	0.0434	100	0.0450	100	0.0964	100
1995										
Dependency	0.0231	12.82	0.0063	12.77	0.0064	12.76	0.0070	13.59	0.0161	14.97
Capital	0.0316	17.55	0.0075	15.22	0.0076	15.13	0.0081	15.90	0.0179	16.56
Education	0.0288	16.00	0.0069	14.00	0.0070	13.93	0.0069	13.49	0.0143	13.27
Family Size	-0.0030	-1.64	-0.0064	-13.10	-0.0067	-13.34	-0.0073	-14.35	-0.0180	-16.70
Land	0.0053	2.94	0.0009	1.88	0.0009	1.85	0.0011	2.15	0.0028	2.62
TVEs	0.0457	25.38	0.0135	27.45	0.0137	27.27	0.0153	29.94	0.0361	33.50
Residual	0.0485	26.96	0.0205	41.78	0.0213	42.38	0.0201	39.28	0.0386	35.79
Total	0.1800	100	0.0490	100	0.0502	100	0.0511	100	0.1078	100

By 1995, capital ranks as the second largest contributor to regional inequalities, overtaking education. Given that rich regions can afford more capital input, this disequalizing effect is expected. Moreover, the absence of formal capital markets in the less developed areas of rural China is detrimental to capital formation in poor regions. Hence, the contribution of the capital input to regional inequality is likely to continue to increase, unless governments establish rural credit markets to assist poor regions and poor farmers to obtain capital. Education had been ranked as the second largest contributor to regional inequality until 1995. Due to its positive marginal effect and a positive concentration index because better educated people are richer, education is expected to be inequality-increasing. However, investment in education may reduce inequality in the long run, especially in rural China where many families rely on educating their children to escape poverty. Therefore, the government should increase its efforts to provide education to the poor regions.

Land is more equally distributed among households than other factors within individual locations. However, significant disparities exist between regions in terms of land endowment as poor regions have more land. If the marginal impact of land on income is positive, this input variable would help to reduce regional inequality. Unfortunately, due to rural levies, taxes and fees, the marginal impact of land on income is negative so that land is an inequality-increasing factor. In the long run, land could well become an equalizing factor if government taxation and levies were reduced. Overall, our model explains between 73 and 81 percent of the total inequality, when the Gini coefficient is used over the four years. Considering the other three measures over all years, our model explains at least 57 percent of regional inequality in rural China.[9] In terms of the ranking of contributions, all the indicators present a similar picture so that the choice on the inequality indicator is not crucial from a policy-making perspective.

5 Conclusions

This chapter examines regression-based approaches to inequality decomposition in the literature, exposes the flaws, and proposes a more flexible framework that can be used with any inequality indicator and that imposes few restrictions on the specification of the underlying income-generating function. This framework differs from the Shapley value approach developed by Shorrocks (1999), which does not consider explicitly the residual and the constant terms in the underlying income-generation function. We argued that these terms are different from the usual

---

[9] We do not compare our results with those of Ravallion and Chen (1999) because the latter are obtained using the flawed framework of FY. In addition, we use different data in terms of variables and level of aggregation, which renders such a comparison difficult. Nonetheless, more than 76 percent of total inequality is not explained by Ravallion and Chen (1999).

independent variables and deserve special treatment in the decomposition analysis. We apply the proposed framework to an empirical analysis of regional inequality in rural China. The analysis uses a combined Box-Cox and Box-Tidwell model specification, which encompasses many different functional forms. The contributions from a number of variables to regional income inequality in rural China are quantified, and the findings are broadly consistent with expectations.

Our results lead to policy implications that could reduce regional inequality in rural China. First, given the large contribution to regional inequality made by TVEs, governments support promoting TVEs in less developed areas would reduce regional inequality. The Chinese central government is aware of this need but direct government assistance and policy concessions are in short supply. Second, education is the second or third largest contributor to regional inequality, depending on the year. Therefore, China must maintain education provision to the poor. As returns to education increase due to a growing demand for skilled labor, education may become a more important factor in driving regional inequality. How to equalize human capital across regions and households is a major social problem in rural China. Unless proper action is taken, China will experience even higher regional inequality in the long run. Therefore, the government must act quickly to improve the opportunity and the quality of education in the poor areas. Third, by 1995, capital was the second largest contributor to regional inequality. Hence, developing a viable rural credit market is essential for attracting capital input to poor regions. At present, poor households receive little credit, and formal credit markets do not exist in poor areas. Finally, there is an urgent need to convert fees and levies into transparent taxes to make farming a profitable business so that land could become an equalizing rather than disequalizing contributor to regional inequality. In addition, profitable farming is in the interests of the government for food security reasons and beneficial to urban residents interested in a stable food supply.

References

Atkinson, A.B., 'A critique of the transatlantic consensus on rising income inequality', *World Economy* 24 (2001): 433–552.

Blinder, A.S., 'Wage discrimination: Reduced form and structural estimates', *Journal of Human Resources* 8 (1973): 436–455.

Bourguignon, F., Fournier, M. and Gurgand, M., 'Fast development with a stable income distribution: Taiwan, 1979-94', *Review of Income and Wealth* 47 (2001): 139–163.

Cancian, M. and Reed, D., 'Assessing the effects of wives earning on family income inequality', *Review of Economics and Statistics* 80 (1998): 73–79.

Cornia, G.A. and Popov, V., Transition and Institutions: The Experience of Gradual and Late Reformers (Oxford: Oxford University Press, 2001).

Datt, G. and Ravallion, M., 'Growth and redistribution components of changes in poverty measures: A decomposition with application to Brazil and India in the 1980s', *Journal of Development Economics* 38 (1992)2: 75–295.

Deaton, A., The Analysis of Household Surveys Baltimore: Johns Hopkins University Press, 1997).

DiNardo, J., Fortin, N.M. and Lemieux, T., 'Labour market institutions and the distribution of wages, 1973-1992: A semiparametric approach', *Econometrica* 64 (1996): 1001–1044.

Dollar, D. and Kraay, A., 'Growth is good for the poor', *Journal of Economic Growth* 7 (2002): 195–225.

Fields, G.S., Distribution and Development: A New Look at the Developing World (Cambridge, Massachusetts: MIT Press, 2001).

Fields, G.S. and Yoo, G., 'Falling labour income inequality in Korea's economic growth: Patterns and underlying causes', *Review of Income and Wealth* 46 (2000): 139–159.

Judge, G.G., Hill, C.R., Griffiths, W.E., Lutkepohl, H. and Lee, T.C., Introduction to the Theory and Practice of Econometrics (New York: John Wiley, 1988).

Juhn, C., Murphy, K.M. and Pierce, B., 'Wage inequality and the rise in returns to skill', *Journal of Political Economy 101* (1993): 410–442.

Kolm, S.C., The Rational foundations of income inequality measurement, in J. Silber (eds), Handbook of Income Inequality Measurement (Boston/Dordrecht/London: Kluwer Academic Publishers, 1999), pp.19–94.

Morduch, J. and Sicular, T., 'Rethinking inequality decomposition, with evidence from rural China', *The Economic Journal* 112 (2002): 93–106.

NBS (National Bureau of Statistics), various years, China Statistical Yearbook (Beijing: China Statistical Publishing House).

NBS (National Bureau of Statistics), various years, China Agricultural Yearbook (Beijing: China Statistical Publishing House).

Oaxaca, R.L., 'Male-female wage differences in urban labour markets' *International Economic Review* 14 (1973): 693–709.

Podder, N. and Chatterjee, S., 'Sharing the national cake in post reform New Zealand: Income inequality trends in terms of income sources', *Journal of Public Economics* 86 (2002): 1–27.

Ravallion, M. and Chen, S., When economic reform is faster than statistical reform: Measuring and explaining income inequality in rural China, *Oxford Bulletin of Economics and Statistics* 61 (1999): 33–56.

Rozelle, S., 'Rural industrialization and increasing inequality: Emerging patterns in China's reforming economy', *Journal of Comparative Economics* 19 (1994): 362–391.

Shorrocks, A.F., 'The class of additively decomposable inequality measures', *Econometrica* 48 (1980): 613–625.

———, 'Inequality decomposition by factor components', *Econometrica* 50 (1982): 193–211.

———, Decomposition procedures for distributional analysis: A unified framework based on the Shaply value (Unpublished manuscript, Department of Economics, University of Essex).

Wan, G., Factors affecting the variability of foodgrain production in China (Paper presented at the Annual Conference of Australian Agricultural Economics Society, Melbourne, 1997).

———, Decomposing changes in the Gini index by factor components, (unpublished manuscript, Beijing: Centre for China Economic Research, Peking University).

————, 'Changes in regional inequality in rural China: Decomposing the Gini index by income sources', *Australian Journal of Agricultural and Resource Economics* 43 (2001): 361–381.

Wan, G. and Cheng, E., 'Effects of land fragmentation and returns to scale in the Chinese farming sector', *Applied Economics 33* (2001): 183–194.

Zhang, X. Fan, S., Public investment and regional inequality in rural China (Discussion Paper No. 71, Washington: Environment Production and Technology Division, IFPRI, 2000).

Chapter 8

Decomposition of China's Rising Income Inequality: Is the Rural-Urban Income Gap Solely Responsible?

Gene H. Chang[*]

P23 D31 518
P36 P25 015

1 Introduction

China's income distribution inequality has grown rapidly in the past 20 or so years of economic reform, as evidenced by the Gini coefficient of China having risen from a low level of 0.33 in 1980 to 0.46 in 2000 (Chang, 2002). Many scholars (Johnson, 2001; Chang, 2002; Wu and Perloff, 2004) consider that the major factor contributing to the rising national overall income inequality is the great rural-urban income gap, while the income inequalities within rural or urban groups exert only mild influence over the overall inequality. It is an issue of academic curiosity and a policy that aims to find how China's overall income inequality can be decomposed into three components: the intra-group income inequalities within rural residents, within urban residents, and the inter-group income disparity between rural and urban residents.

This chapter reviews the theoretical issues involved in the decomposition of the Chinese income distribution and provide a feasible decomposition by using the coefficient of variation. It demonstrates that the coefficient of variation has several merits over other income distribution measures in decomposition. We then apply this method to the Chinese case. Finally, the results are analyzed, and inferences are drawn.

2 Review of Decomposition of Income Disparity Measures

Commonly used measures for income distribution include the coefficient of variation, the Gini coefficient, a generalized entropy index, and the Atkinson's index (Sen, 1997). When researchers decomposed the overall income inequality in

[*] The author thanks the support from the Chinese Economist Society and Zhejiang University, China for their financial support for this research, and scholars from the US, China, and other countries for their valuable comments in the 2004 Hanzhou International Conference. The author also thanks Xu Ximing for sharing the Chinese data.

China by using these measures, two problems usually emerged. One would be the data problem. To decompose an aggregate measure, researchers generally need detailed household income data, which are not readily available in China. The second problem would be the measures themselves. The measures are supposed to satisfy certain principles—including the Pigou-Dalton Transfer, the Income Scale Independence, and the Principle of Population—to ensure that they would be independent of the population size, income sizes, and the monetary units used. Therefore, a normalized measure can be used to make comparisons across nations or time periods.

When the aggregate measure is decomposed into intra- and inter- group components, the decomposed component measures need to be consistent and reasonable when they are compared with the aggregate measure. A commonly mentioned property is the *Principle of Additive Decomposability*. If it is satisfied, the total inequality is simply the (population and income share weighted) sum of inequality within and between groups.[1]

In fact, there is one more important principle needed for a reasonable decomposable measure. After the decomposition, the intra-group inequality measures and inter-group disparity measures should be *mutually independent*. Let us take the Chinese case as an example. The intra-group indexes measure the disparities within the rural and urban resident groups. The inter-group index measures the rural-urban income disparity. Suppose that there is an increase in the income inequality among rural households only but their mean income remains the same. This change should only increase the rural income inequality index. This change should *not* affect the inter-group index because the rural-urban income gap, measured by the mean incomes of the two groups, did not change.

Furthermore, the measure should satisfy the following conditions in the two terminal cases. In the first case, all rural residents receive the same income μ_r and all urban residents receive the same income μ_u, but $\mu_u > \mu_r$. In this case, the intra-group inequality indexes should vanish to zeros, but the inter-group disparity index should equal the total inequality index. In the second case, both groups have the same mean incomes, so $\mu_u = \mu_r$, but the income distribution within each group is not equal. In this case, the inter-group disparity index should vanish to zero, and the overall inequality index should be fully explained by the summed intra-group inequality indexes.

The above proposed principles are not only reasonable but also necessary. Otherwise, one cannot reasonably decompose and separate the causes of income inequality. Let us call this principle the MEI decomposability. MEI refers to the principle that the intra- and inter- group measures should be *mutually exclusive and*

---

[1] See a discussion of these measures by the World Bank at http://www.worldbank.org/wbp/inequal/methods/measure.htm.

independent of each other. It can be shown that some measures, such as the recently proposed Gini decomposition, violate MEI decomposability.[2]

Among the four measures mentioned above, Atkinson's index is not additively decomposable, and it needs to set up *ex ante* the parameter value for ε, which can be subjective to a researcher's own values and thereby subject to controversy. The generalized entropy index measure is easily decomposable. Wu and Perloff (2004) applied this measure to decompose China's income inequality. Like the Atkinson's, the generalized entropy index also needs to set *ex ante* the parameter values.

The Gini coefficient is probably the most popular measure for income distribution in literature and practice. China sporadically reveals the national overall Gini and intra- group Gini indices for urban and rural residents, even though the data for some years are missing (Chang, 2002). The Gini measure has some advantages. For instance, it takes into account the income difference of every pair of persons. However, it satisfies neither additive nor MEI decomposability. In addition, the broadly suggested decomposition approach requires detailed information about household income that is often unavailable in the Chinese case.[3]

In this chapter, I would like to show that the coefficient of variation serves as a better measure to decompose the Chinese aggregate income inequality. I will show that the coefficient of variation is additively decomposable in its square forms and that it nicely satisfies the IME decomposability. The results after decomposition provide a straightforward interpretation about how the inter-group and intra-group income inequalities—as well as the rural-urban migration—affect the overall income inequality. Using the derived decomposition formula allows the researcher to investigate the Chinese case and draw inferences.

3 Decomposition of Coefficient of Variation

The researcher used the subscript r and u to respectively denote rural and urban variables. x_{ri} is the rural household i's income. x_{ui} is the urban household i's income. When the two groups were merged into the nation's population, the researcher used x_i to denote household i's income. In addition, the following notations give the meaning of the variables:

n_r : The total number of households in rural areas
n_u : The total number of households in urban areas
n: The total households in China, i.e., $n = n_r + n_u$
p_r : Percentage of the national households living in rural areas, i.e., $p_r = n_r / n$

---

[2] Dagum C. attempts to decompose Gini in his several papers. His work was summarized and discussed by Mussard, Seyte and Terraza (2003). Yet the "Between-Group Gini" violates the MEI decomposability. It is discussed by a mimeo by the author.
[3] An alternative decomposition of the Gini coefficient, which could be used for the available Chinese data, is discussed in a mimeo by the author.

p_u : Percentage of the national households living in urban areas, i.e., $p_u = n_u / n$

μ_r : Mean income of rural households

μ_u : Mean income of urban households

μ : Mean income of households of the entire nation

The researcher first decomposed the variance of the income of the entire nation. The coefficient variation is a concept that normalizes the variance to a unit and scale free measure. The entire variance is:

$$\mathrm{var}(x_i) = \frac{1}{n} \sum_{i=1}^{n} (x_i - \mu)^2$$

$$= \frac{1}{n} \left(\sum_{i=1}^{n_r + n_u} x_i^2 - n \, \mu^2 \right)$$

$$= \frac{1}{n} \sum_{i=1}^{n_r} x_{ri}^2 - \frac{1}{n} \sum_{i=1}^{n_u} x_{ui}^2 - \mu^2$$

$$= \frac{p_r}{n_r} \sum_{i=1}^{n_r} x_{ri}^2 - \frac{p_u}{n_u} \sum_{i=1}^{n_u} x_{ui}^2 - \mu^2$$

$$= p_r \left(\frac{1}{n_r} \sum_{i=1}^{n_r} x_{ri}^2 - \mu_r^2 \right) - p_u \left(\frac{1}{n_u} \sum_{i=1}^{n_u} x_{ui}^2 - \mu_u^2 \right) + (p_r \mu_r^2 + p_u \mu_u^2 - \mu^2)$$

$$= p_r \, \mathrm{var}(x_r) + p_u \, \mathrm{var}(x_u) + \mathrm{var}(\mu_r, \mu_u)$$

Hence, the variance of the entire nation's household income is decomposed into three parts. The first term of the above equation is the intra-rural group income inequality, with its share of the national population p_r as the weight. The second term is the intra-urban group income inequality with its national population share p_u as the weight. The last term is the inter-group income inequality between the average rural income and average urban income. This last term has a straightforward interpretation. It means that if all rural households n_r receive the same income of μ_r and all urban households n_u receive the same income of μ_u, then the variance of recipients' income should be $(p_r \mu_r^2 + p_u \mu_u^2 - \mu^2)$, as shown below:

$$\mathrm{var}(\mu_r, \mu_u) = \frac{1}{n} \left(\sum_{i=1}^{n_r} \mu_{ri}^2 + \sum_{i=1}^{n_u} \mu_{ui}^2 - n\mu^2 \right)$$

$$= \frac{n_r}{n} \mu_r^2 + \frac{n_u}{n} \mu_u^2 - \mu^2$$

$$= p_r \mu_r^2 + p_u \mu_u^2 - \mu^2$$

From the above expression, we can see that this inter-group variance is independent of the intra-group variances. It is only affected by the rural or urban mean incomes rather than their intra-group variances. A further check of the two terminal cases can easily verify that it satisfies the MEI decomposability.

To transform the above equation from variances to coefficients of variation (cv), we note that $cv = \dfrac{\sqrt{\text{variance}}}{\text{mean}}$. Let $cv(x)$, $cv(x_r)$, and $cv(x_u)$ stand for the coefficients of variation for the national, rural, and urban household incomes, respectively. We then have the decomposition for the national aggregate coefficient variation as follows:

$$[cv(x)]^2 = p_r(\frac{\mu_r}{\mu})^2[cv(x_r)]^2 + p_u(\frac{\mu_u}{\mu})^2[cv(x_u)]^2 + [cv(\mu_r,\mu_u)]^2$$

The data for calculating the variances are available in the published Chinese data. China provides the mean incomes of rural residents and urban residents (derived from very large survey samples consisting about 66,000 respondents in rural areas and 40,000 urban respondents). For income distribution, it provides data grouped by income intervals. The problem with this data is that the income interval sizes are not consistent for all survey years. To avoid this problem, the researcher chose those years in which data have more consistent definitions.

Table 8.1 lists the population shares of rural and urban residents in China from 1990 to 2002, as well as the mean incomes of the respective groups. Table 8.2 shows the estimated variances and coefficient variations of intra- and inter-groups. In addition, for the comparison purpose, the last column lists the ratio of the urban mean income to the rural mean income.

Table 8.2 suggests that during the past 14 years, the main driving force for the increase in the aggregate income inequality is the rural-urban income gap or the urban income inequality. The change in income inequality among rural residents was moderate, and, in fact, was reduced somewhat during the same period. Another finding is that the aggregate income inequality has grown rapidly since 2000, and the intra-urban inequality emerges as the most significant factor for this increase. These findings differ from the conclusions drawn in Chang's 2002 paper and Wu and Perloff's 2004 paper. Chang (2002) used the earlier data and concluded that the rural-urban income gap was the major reason for aggregate income inequality. Wu and Perloff (2004) concluded that the increases in inequality within rural and urban residents and the growing rural-urban gap are equally responsible for the overall increase. Evidence displayed in Table 8.2 dismisses the income inequality within rural residents as a causal factor but suggests that the other two factors are responsible, with the intra-urban inequality becoming increasingly significant for the overall increase.

Table 8.1 Population shares and per capita annual income

Year	Population share		Annual per capita income		
	Rural (%)	Urban (%)	Nation (*yuan*)	rural (*yuan*)	Urban (*yuan*)
1990	74%	26%	907	686	1523
1995	71%	29%	2,365	1,578	4,288
1996	70%	30%	2,816	1,926	4,845
1997	68%	32%	3,079	2,090	5,189
1998	67%	33%	3,261	2,162	5,458
1999	65%	35%	3,490	2,210	5,889
2000	64%	36%	3,725	2,253	6,317
2001	62%	38%	4,076	2,366	6,907
2002	61%	39%	4,704	2,476	8,177

Table 8.2 Income inequality and its decomposition

Year	Estimated Variance				Estimated Coefficient of Variation				Urban-Rural Ratio
	National	Rural	Urban	Rural-Urban	National	Rural	Urban	Rural-Urban	
1990	329,330	172,598	251,146	135,987	0.63	0.61	0.33	0.41	2.22
1995	3,129,541	1,129,580	2,803,779	1,513,774	0.75	0.67	0.39	0.52	2.72
1997	4,637,676	1,533,177	4,725,360	2,085,873	0.70	0.59	0.42	0.47	2.48
1998	5,337,862	1,595,756	5,574,282	2,415,268	0.71	0.58	0.43	0.48	2.52
1999	6,604,028	1,686,381	7,000,858	3,069,272	0.74	0.59	0.45	0.50	2.66
2000	8,226,306	1,855,453	8,913,972	3,814,257	0.77	0.60	0.47	0.52	2.80
2001	11,000,000	1,978,280	11,861,201	4,840,485	0.80	0.59	0.50	0.54	2.92
2002	18,000,000	2,066,342	23,799,262	7,740,583	0.91	0.58	0.60	0.59	3.30

4 Concluding Remarks

The income inequality in China has widened during the reform period—at the same time as the per capita income has increased rapidly. Many previous studies consider the rising rural-income gap being mainly responsible for China's overall income inequality. This chapter examines popular income distribution measures and suggests using the coefficient of variation, which possesses more desirable properties than other measures to decompose the Chinese overall income inequality.

By using more data, this study finds that the overall income inequality in China has grown rapidly, especially since 2000. The main reasons for the recent widening inequality are the intra-urban resident inequality and the rural-urban income disparity—the former of which is becoming increasingly significant. On the other hand, the income inequality within the rural resident group has not risen during recent years and was not a factor contributing to the overall inequality increase.

In addition, the rural-urban migration has contributed to the overall inequality increase. As the urban population share in the nation p_u increases, the influence (represented by the weight) of the urban income inequality on the national aggregate becomes increasingly critical. The rural migrants in cities are often paid very low wages that urban residents would not accept. This is another reason for the increase in the intra-urban income inequality.

It is desirable for a society to share gains from economic growth with more residents in the nation, which is why many development economists are studying policies for equitable growth. The suggested decomposition method by this chapter as well as its application may help us to better understand the nature of China's income inequality and to search for better, more effective policies.

References

Chang, G.H., 'The Cause and Cure of China's Widening Income Disparity', *China Economic Review*, Vol. 13 (2002): 335-340.

Dagum, C., 'Inequality Measures between Income Distribution with Applications', *Econometrica*, 48, 7 (1980): 1791-1803.

Johnson, D.G., presentation at Beijing University, China, April, 2001. The international data cited by Johnson were from publications of International Labor Organization.

Mussard, S., Seyte, F. and Terraza, M., 'Decomposition of Gini and Genralized Entropy Inequality Measures', *Economics Bulletin* (January 27, 2003).

Sen, A., *On Economic Inequality* (Oxford: Oxford University Press, 1997).

Wu, X. and Perloff, J.M., 'China's Income Distribution over Time, Reasons for Rising Inequality' (working paper, Ontario: University of Guelph, and Berkeley: University of California, respectively, 2004).

Chapter 9

Economic Openness, Local Governance and Rural Economy

Ding Lu

1 Introduction

Over the past decade, China has witnessed a rising trend of urban-rural income disparity in its economy. This phenomenon, together with the aggravation of income disparity across regions and households, has caused great concerns among policy-makers and researchers. At his first meeting with the media after becoming the premier of China in March 2003, Wen Jiabao listed the "agriculture being lagging behind and peasants' income being stagnant" and the "growing development disparity between urban and rural areas and between the east and west regions" as two of the five top issues on the agenda of his government.[1]

In the literature about China's urban-rural disparity, most studies attribute the problem to either government policies or institutional barriers that have retarded rural development and the income of peasants. For instance, Johnson (2000) summarized three major policy areas that have adversely affected rural incomes: the restrictions on rural to urban migration, the less accessibility of education in rural areas, and the urban-biased allocation of investment and credit. Based on findings of inter-sector gaps in labor productivity, Yang and Zhou (1999) and Lu (2002) pointed out that barriers to inter-sector reallocation of labor, particularly in the form of the Household Registration (*hukou*) System, might have caused much of the income disparity between urban and rural residents. Yang (1999) observed the "urban-biased policy mix" in terms of subsidies, investments, and banking credits that favor urban areas to be a major contributor to the rising urban-rural disparity after the mid-1980s.

These observations shed light on the sources of China's rising urban-rural disparity in the 1990s. Recent policy changes in China have to some extent, however, made some of these observed sources of disparity increasingly less important in analyzing urban-rural income gaps. One important change has been the reforms in the Household Registration (*hukou*) System. The System, established in the late 1950s, confines people, especially those in the rural areas, to

---

[1] "China's New Premier's Meeting with Correspondents", Xinhuanet.com, March 18, 2003.

the place of their birth and has been a major institutional barrier to labor mobility.[2] In China's Tenth Five-year Plan of National Economic and Social Development (2001-05), it was explicitly stated that the institutions segregating the urban and rural areas should be broken up and that the Household Registration System should be reformed to allow orderly flows of population between urban and rural areas. It also called for abandonment of unreasonable restrictions on rural workers' entry into the urban labor market.[3]

A major reform was launched in October 2001 when the *hukou* system was officially relaxed to allow rural people the freedom to relocate to more than 20,000 cities and towns nationwide.[4] Since 2001, led by Shijiazhuang in Hebei province and Jinan in Shangdong province, dozens of large cities, including some provincial capitals, have substantially relaxed *hukou* restrictions on rural people's right to work and live permanently in those large cities. In December 2001, Guangdong became the first province that abandoned the registration divide between rural and urban households. In May 2003, Jiangsu province made even more comprehensive reforms to adopt a new *hukou* system free of discrimination against rural people.[5] In 2003, China's State Council terminated the *Act of Compulsory Deportation*, which had allowed the police to arrest and deport people who did not have legal permit to live and work in the cities.[6] An *Act of Household Registration* is being drafted to found the legal basis for a nationwide household registration system that will treat all citizens equally and ensure their freedom of migration.[7]

As for the urban-biased policies, the Tenth Five-year Plan of National Economic and Social Development (2001-05) emphasizes that agriculture should be given foremost priority in national economic development in order to ensure a sustained and steady growth of the agricultural sector and the fast growth of peasants' income.[8] Starting in 2003, the government gradually phased out the taxes on special agricultural products. In his report to the National People's Congress in

---

[2] For a more detailed discussion on the *Hukou* system, see Chan and Zhang (1999).

[3] *Guidelines for the Tenth Five-year Plan of National Economic and Social Development of the People's Republic of China (2001-05)*, approved by the Ninth People's National Congress at its fourth assembly, March 15, 2001.

[4] 'Hukou System Relaxation', Straits Times (Singapore), October 10, 2001; 'Household registration reform in 20,000 cities and towns', *Beijing Qingnianbao (Beijing Youth News)*, August 28, 2001.

[5] The unstoppable reforms of the household registration system, *Fazhi Ribao (Rule of Law Daily)*, June 16, 2003.

[6] 'The Sunzhi Gang incident and reform of household registration system', www.rdyj.com.cn/2003/rdqk-12-10.html.

[7] 'The Act of Household Registration to break up the urban-rural divide', *Shangwu Zhoukan (Business Watch)*, April 2, 2004, www.businesswatch.com.cn.

[8] *Guidelines for the Tenth Five-year Plan of National Economic and Social Development of the People's Republic of China (2001-05)*, approved by the Ninth People's National Congress at its fourth assembly, March 15, 2001.

March 2004, Premier Wen announced a five-year plan to phase out taxes on all agricultural products. Noting a 20 percent increase of the central government's expense on agriculture in 2003, he called on the governments at all levels to increase their budget to support agriculture.[9]

Contrary to these policy changes in favor of rural people, there have been some apparently not so favorable developments. A major event is China's accession to the World Trade Organization in 2001, which has further opened up the domestic market to foreign agricultural goods. The impact of a more open agricultural product market on the welfare of farmers and rural residents remains to be assessed.

A widely reported drag on rural residents' disposable income growth has been the extra burden of local fees and levies imposed on the rural residents. Unlike in urban areas, where most of the public goods are funded by state or local government budget, rural residents below the township level are levied to finance their basic medical care, public schools, township- and village-level administrations, and other local community public facilities. The extra-budgetary nature of these levies makes rural residents vulnerable to the abuse of administrative power by local officials. Despite a reform that was officially announced in 1999 to streamline hundreds of rural fees and levies into a few taxes in a period of three to five years, so far the progress has been limited, and these fees and levies are still heavy and discretionary in many rural areas (Lin, 2002 and CASS, 2004).

It is therefore interesting to use more recent data to evaluate the effects of fiscal support and market openness on urban-rural disparity. Factors other than the education gap and productivity variance should also be investigated. In particular, the local government's administrative efficiency may be crucial to the successful implementation of the state policy to lift peasants' income and boost agricultural growth. In this chapter, we use the provincial 1998 to 2002 data to empirically evaluate the effectiveness of government fiscal support to the agricultural sector on closing the income gap between the urban and rural residents. We also want to check whether market openness has aggravated or ameliorated the urban-rural disparity. Meanwhile, we try to find out the relationship between the quality of local governance and the income gap between urban and rural households.

The second section explains the data and methodology. The empirical results are presented in the third section. The last section summarizes the findings and discusses their institutional basis and policy implications.

---

[9] Wen Jiabao, 'Government Report to the Second Assembly of the Tenth National People's Congress', *People's Daily* (Beijing), March 6, 2004.

2 Data and Methodology

In this research, we use the official survey data of urban-rural household consumption ratios to gauge urban-rural income disparity.[10] As shown in Figure 9.1, the nationwide household consumption ratio displays an upward trend since the mid-1980s. The trend, however, became less obvious in more recent years.

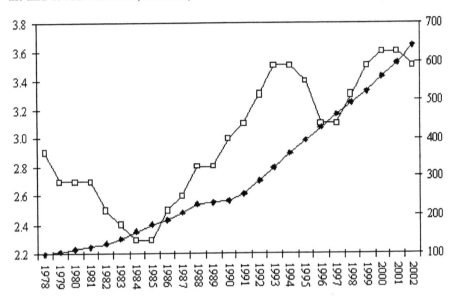

—□— Household Consumption Ratio —◆— Per Capita GDP

Source: China Statistical Yearbook, various years.

Figure 9.1 Urban-rural household consumption ratio vs. per capita GDP (1978=100)

To evaluate the effects of fiscal support and market openness on urban-rural disparity, we must first control a major determinant on inequality—that is, the level of development. According to Williamson (1965), the hypothesis by Kuznets (1955) of the relationship between per capita income growth and income disparity is applicable to the scenario of regional income disparity. Lu (2002) observes that Chinese provinces with higher per capita income in the 1990s tend to have more equal urban-rural consumption levels. Based on these studies, we include the per capita income in our model as a factor that might influence the urban-rural disparity and expect the relationship to be of a non-linear quadratic type.

---

[10] The survey data on household incomes are less indicative for standard-of-living disparity between the urban and rural residents as some of the reported rural household income may include agricultural capital costs.

As for the measurement of fiscal support to agricultural and rural development, in every provincial government's budget sheet, there are three expenditure items: "supporting agriculture production," "comprehensive agricultural development," and "agriculture, forestry, water conservancy, meteorology." These items reflect the scale of such fiscal support and can be used as proxies for it. Some other items, such as "supporting underdeveloped areas" and "developing land and sea area," may also influence agricultural and rural development. We, however, do not use them because their relationship of fiscal support to rural development is less certain. On the one hand, the size of underdeveloped areas, where per capita income falls below the official poverty line, may vary from province to province. In some richer provinces, there are no such areas at all. The expense on "developing land and sea area," on the other hand, may be associated with projects not related to agriculture or rural development.

It only makes sense to compare these proxies of fiscal support across provincial economies on a common basis. One possibility is to compare their weights in the provincial government's total expense. However, due to different economic structures across regions, a low weight of these items in total budget may not necessarily imply a low level of fiscal support if the share of agriculture in the economy or the share of rural people in the population is also small. To make these proxies inter-regionally comparable, we divide the sum of them by the added-value of the primary industry (agricultural and mining sectors) in GDP accounts.

Market openness affects rural household income mainly through the imports of foreign agricultural products. Lacking the provincial data of agricultural imports, we use import/GDP ratio as a proxy for market openness. In the literature, there is little consensus on the likely impact of market openness on urban-rural income disparity. According to a forecast by Deutsche Bank (2001), China's accession to WTO would reduce its wheat and other grain production by 2.77 and 1.68 percent, respectively, from the baseline by 2006. Li and Zhai (2000) estimate that the WTO accession package would increase the disposable income of urban households by 4.86 percent while reducing that of rural households by 1.5 percent from the baseline. Wei and Wu (2002) point out, however, that urban-rural income inequality tends to decline in response to an increase in market openness, based on the empirical evidence they collected from China's regional 1988 to 1993 data.

A variable related to market openness is the level of price subsidies provided by the government. Being a former centrally-planned economy, China has come a long way to transform itself into a market-based economy, yet there still remain the legacies of the pre-reform economic system. The one most relevant to rural household welfare is the government's price subsidies for various goods and services. Due to concerns over the negative impact of market openness on Chinese farmers, the issue of subsidies to the agricultural sector was one of the toughest in the process of negotiations for China's WTO accession. While China sought farm subsidies equivalent to 10 percent of the value of national agricultural production, many WTO members wanted it to be contained at the 5 percent level permissible to industrialized countries. The final deal was 8.5 percent (WTO, 2001). In China's provincial budget data, the price subsidies include those meant for non-agricultural products as well. It therefore reflects the overall government role to intervene the market. We use the ratio of price subsidies to the provincial government budget as a proxy for such intervention.

Given the extra-budgetary nature of the rural fees and levies collected by the local authorities, the efficiency of local governance may play a crucial role in determining the success of the state policy to contain the gap of urban-rural disparity. Lin, Tao and Liu (2003) describe the many "unfunded mandates from the center" in China's bureaucracy as follows:

> ... since higher-level government needs local governments to implement the policies, but does not provide sufficient funding, and since there is an information asymmetry in regulation enforcement between the two (i.e., the higher-level government cannot perfectly monitor the implementation of regulations), local governments may easily expand local bureaucracy and engage in rent-seeking in the name of implementing the higher-level government regulations. Given that local government expansion encourages rent seeking, crowds out private investment, reduces farmer consumption, they will aggravate rural tax burdens and lower rural income growth. (Lin, Tao and Liu, 2003, p. 18)

The severity of the problem nevertheless varies across regions. We use two proxies to gauge the quality of local governance. One is per bureaucrat administration cost, which partially measures the severity of bureaucratic rent-seeking. The other is the relative size of bureaucracy to the total employment, which reflects the degree of bureaucracy expansion.[11] To make the per bureaucrat administration cost more comparable across regions, we divide it by per capita income to adjust for regional variance in living costs.

As for the relative size of bureaucracy, it may be influenced by the level of development and the population size. More developed regions may be more efficient in general and thus have a relatively smaller size of bureaucracy, and regions with larger population may need a relatively smaller size of bureaucracy thanks to economies of scales in administration. In this empirical exercise, we estimate the excessive bureaucracy size by controlling these factors (see Appendix).

Table 9.1 provides summary a of statistics for the panel data of these proxies in the 1998 to 2002 period. The mean values of both per capita income and urban-rural household consumption ratio kept rising over the five years. As the average import/GDP ratio increased, the average price subsidy ratio dropped, indicating the growing market openness in most provinces. Meanwhile, the mean values of both agricultural support and administrative cost substantially increased. Only the

---

[11] The size of an average township government expanded from 20-30 staffs to over 200 in 2000 (Yep, 2002). The bureaucrats-population ratio increased from 1:400 in early 1950s to 1:28 by 2003 ("How many people support a bureaucrat?" *Boxun News*, November 8, 2003.

average government size (or its excessive-size estimate) does not show a clear trend.

Table 9.1 Summary of statistics

	Urban-rural household consumption ratio				Per capita GDP (at the 1998 price)			
	Mean	Max	Min	STDEV	Mean	Max	Min	STDEV
1998	2.89	4.43	1.80	0.71	7139	25193	2301	4675
1999	3.03	4.85	1.79	0.77	7635	30143	2422	5632
2000	3.10	4.92	1.77	0.76	8520	34228	2637	6477
2001	3.18	4.80	1.86	0.69	9260	36943	2861	7064
2002	3.45	8.87	1.90	1.25	10343	40737	3160	7896
	Imports over GDP				Price subsidies over fiscal budget			
	Mean	Max	Min	STDEV	Mean	Max	Min	STDEV
1998	10.2%	57.7%	1.5%	13.5%	4.9%	9.0%	2.1%	1.9%
1999	11.1%	63.2%	1.7%	15.2%	4.4%	11.4%	1.4%	2.4%
2000	13.2%	70.3%	2.3%	18.2%	3.9%	15.1%	1.4%	3.0%
2001	13.2%	65.4%	1.4%	17.6%	3.5%	14.7%	0.9%	2.9%
2002	13.9%	74.8%	1.8%	18.9%	2.5%	11.2%	0.5%	2.4%
	Agricultural support over primary industry value-added				Per bureaucrat administration cost over per capita GDP			
	Mean	Max	Min	STDEV	Mean	Max	Min	STDEV
1998	5.3%	15.8%	2.1%	3.4%	1.25	4.15	0.26	0.77
1999	5.9%	16.8%	2.1%	3.8%	1.31	4.27	0.27	0.81
2000	6.7%	18.4%	2.3%	4.5%	1.38	4.07	0.38	0.81
2001	8.0%	21.4%	2.4%	5.5%	1.62	4.48	0.43	0.93
2002	9.0%	24.0%	2.6%	6.0%	1.81	5.18	0.50	1.05
	Government size (bureaucrat staff over total employed population)				Excessive government size (the part of the size unexplained by population and per capita GDP)			
	Mean	Max	Min	STDEV	Mean	Max	Min	STDEV
1998	2.04%	4.58%	1.09%	0.79%	0.44%	2.18%	-0.19%	0.44%
1999	2.14%	4.84%	1.20%	0.85%	-0.28%	0.25%	-0.77%	0.29%
2000	2.15%	4.64%	1.21%	0.85%	0.18%	0.65%	-0.60%	0.40%
2001	2.13%	4.83%	1.11%	0.87%	-0.53%	0.33%	-1.23%	0.47%
2002	2.04%	4.58%	1.09%	0.79%	0.19%	1.91%	-0.62%	0.86%

Source: Complied from *China Statistical Yearbook*, 1999-2003.

The basic model (1) describes the hypothetical relationship between the urban-rural household consumption ratio (HHCR) and the rest of the proxies:

$$HHCR_{it} = a + b_1 Y_{it} + b_2 Y_{it}^2 + b_3 (ImpRatio)_{it} + b_4 (PriceSub)_{it}$$
$$+ b_5 (AgrSuppt)_{it} + b_6 (AdminCost)_{it} + b_7 (GovtSize)_{it} + u_i + e_{it} \qquad (1)$$

where u_i represents a random effect that is varying over cross section units and invariant over time for a given cross section unit and e_{it} is residual:

$$e_{it} = \rho\, e_{i,t-1} + z_{it}$$

where $|\rho| < 1$ and z_{it} is independent and identically distributed with zero mean and variance. The Hausman test has been conducted to determine whether a fixed-effect regression model with a within estimator or a random-effect model with a GLS estimator should be applied for the regression. Table 9.2 gives the variable definitions and their expected signs.

Table 9.2 Variable definition and expected impact on urban-rural disparity

Variable	Expected sign for b	Intuition/Reason
Y = per capita GDP	+	Kuznets-Williamson
Y^2	−	
ImpRatio = Import/GDP	+	Li and Zhai (2000)
PriceSub = Price subsidies/Fiscal Expenditure	−	WTO (2001)
AgrSuppt = Fiscal Support to Agriculture/Primary Industry Value-added	−	Wen's policy
AdminCost = Per bureaucrat Admin Cost / Per capita GDP	+	Lin, Tao and Liu (2003)
GovtSize = Government Staff/Total Employment	+	
ExGovtSize = part of GovtSize unexplained by population size and per capita GDP	+	Used alternatively with GovtSize

3 The Results

Table 9.3 displays the regression-estimated results for model (1). According to the results, evidence for the Kuznets-Williamson effect may exist but appears to be very weak for the period under study. This is not surprising because such an effect may take a longer length of time to realize. The insignificance in coefficients of

ImprtRatio and PriceSub does not provide support to the claim that greater market openness is associated with worse urban-rural disparity. The insignificant coefficient of GovtSize (or excessive government size) apparently suggests an insignificant correlation between a larger size of bureaucracy and the contemporary level of urban-rural disparity. When we use "excessive government size" defined in Table 9.1 and Appendix 9.1 to replace the Govtsize, all the coefficient signs remain the same while the coefficient of excessive government size becomes even less significant.

Table 9.3 Impact on contemporary urban-rural disparity

Dependent	HHCR		HHCR	
	Coefficient	z-statistics	Coefficient	z-statistics
Y	4.84E-06	0.11	4.12E-06	0.09
Y^2	-8.69E-10	-0.93	-7.49E-10	-0.79
ImpRatio	0.2675	0.32	0.1825	0.22
PriceSub	2.4177	0.80	2.0301	0.68
AgrSuppt	5.1120	2.16 ****	4.4001	2.05 ****
AdminCost	0.6439	5.33 *****	0.6528	5.30 *****
GovtSize	-7.4347	-0.68	*-0.1273*	*-0.14*
Constant	1.9147	4.37	1.8177	4.19
R-square				
-- within		0.2374		0.2401
-- between		0.6060		0.5973
-- overall		0.5191		0.5129
Wald chi2(8)		79.5		78.5
Prob > chi^2		0.0000		0.0000
ρ		0.3122		0.3324
Modified Bhargava et al. Durbin-Watson		1.3756		1.3351
Baltagi-Wu LBI		2.0399		2.0148
No of observations		155		155
Model		GLS-random effect		GLS-random effect

Notes:
1. The number in italics refers to excessive government size defined in App.9.1.
2. Significance level: ***** 99%; **** 95%, *** 90%, ** 80%, * 70%.

The two significant coefficients found in the exercise are those of AgrSupprt and AdminCost. The highly significant (at 99% level) and positive coefficient of AdminCost suggests that less efficient local governance does relate to greater urban-rural disparity. The coefficient of AgrSupprt is significant at 95 percent level, and its positive sign indicates a positive co-relationship between AgrSupprt and urban-rural disparity, which sounds puzzling. Two competing explanations may solve this puzzle. One possible explanation is simply that provinces with higher urban-rural disparity ratios tend to allocate more fiscal supports to agriculture out of concerns over rural underdevelopment.

Another possible explanation to this co-relationship may be derived from the link between "unfunded mandates" and bureaucracy expansion, discussed in Lin, Tao and Liu (2003). The hypothesis is that such a relationship may even exist in the context of state policy to support agricultural development. When the central government implements such a policy, the mandate is often not fully funded and needs cooperation from the local governments to raise more funds. Thanks to the asymmetric information in the bureaucratic hierarchy, it is easy for the local officials to expand local bureaucracy and engage in rent-seeking in the name of implementing the policy to support agriculture.

To test this hypothetical explanation, we run regressions to check whether the growth of fiscal support to agriculture has been more associated with urban-rural disparity, the existing level of support, or the bureaucracy expansion and administrative cost increase. The results are shown in Table 9.4.

As demonstrated by these results, the change of fiscal support to agriculture (ΔAgrsuppt) is significantly and positively related to the existing level of such support (at significance level over 99 percent) and the bureaucracy size or relative administrative cost (at significance level over 95 percent). It is, however, negatively related to urban-rural disparity with a significance level of more than 90 or 95 percent.

These results suggest that regions with higher urban-rural disparity were getting smaller increases in fiscal support to agriculture. Therefore, we can reject the first explanation that increases in fiscal support to agriculture were driven by concerns over urban-rural disparity and rural underdevelopment. These results also show that the fiscal support to agriculture has its own momentum of growth and is closely associated with bureaucracy expansion or administrative cost increase.

To further investigate the dynamics of urban-rural disparity, we regress the changes in urban-rural disparity (ΔHHCR) on its contemporary level (HHCR) and the differences or growth rates of other exogenous variables. Results are recorded in Table 9.5.

The first model differs from the second and third models by including the variable of changes in fiscal support (ΔAgrSuppt) but excluding three variables of per capita income growth (ΔY/Y), the changes in administrative cost (ΔAdminCost) and government size (ΔGovtSize). This differential in modeling is based on the results of Table 9.4 to avoid the multicollinearity problem since ΔAgrSuppt is significantly correlated to these three variables.

In all three models estimated in Table 9.5, HHCR exhibits highly significant positive correlations with its changes, suggesting that regions with higher urban-rural disparity tended to experience larger increase (or slower reduction) in such disparity during the years under study. Meanwhile, the change in price subsidies (ΔPriceSub) appears to be a variable that has some moderately significant (at around the 80 percent level) impact on containing the rise of disparity. In the third regression model, where the GovtSize variable is adjusted for population and level of development, increase of administrative cost becomes associated with deteriorating disparity at a moderate level of significance over 70 percent. The impact of rising market openness in terms of import ratio is again insignificant as in the case of the contemporary HHCR-model.

Table 9.4 Factors that affect growth of fiscal support to agriculture

Dependent	Δ Agrsuppt			Δ Agrsuppt		
	Coefficient	t-statistics		Coefficient	t-statistics	
Agrsuppt	0.2685	5.55	*****	0.2268	4.62	*****
HHCR	-0.0027	-1.67	***	-0.0043	-2.64	*****
ΔY/Y	-0.0417	-2.10	****	-0.0448	-2.27	****
Δ Govtsize	1.0886	2.13	****			
Δ AdminCost				0.0113	1.95	****
Constant	0.0015			0.0075		
R-square						
-- within		0.2809			0.2778	
-- between		0.7114			0.6640	
-- overall		0.4877			0.4685	
F(4,89)		8.69			8.56	
Prob > F		0.0000			0.0000	
ρ		-0.1011			-0.0721	
Modified Bhargava et al. Durbin-Watson		2.1623			2.1248	
Baltagi-Wu LBI		2.5956			2.5752	
No of observations		124			124	
Model	Fixed-effects (within) regression			Fixed-effects (within) regression		

Note: 1. Significance level: ***** 99%; **** 95%, *** 90%, ** 80%, * 70%.

4 Concluding Remarks

Using panel data of China's provincial economies in the 1998 to 2002 period, this chapter examines the factors that have affected urban-rural disparity. The study reveals a divergent trend across regions in the development of urban-rural disparity. It also shows that: (a) evidence that trade openness has worsened urban-rural disparity has been weak; (b) inefficiency of local governance, especially in terms of administrative cost, is positively correlated with urban-rural disparity and perhaps its growth; (c) increase of fiscal support to agriculture has less to do with the need to curb rising urban-rural disparity than with the excessive growth of bureaucracy size or administrative cost; and (d) price subsidies may have a role in containing urban-rural disparity but its significance is moderate.

Table 9.5 Changes in urban–rural disparity

Dependent	ΔHHCR		ΔHHCR		ΔHHCR	
	Coefficient	t-statistics	Coefficient	t-statistics	Coefficient	t-statistics
HHCR	1.0062	17.34 *****	0.9817	15.71 *****	0.9856	16.50 *****
ΔImpRatio	0.8627	0.97	0.6401	0.69	0.6042	0.64
ΔPriceSub	-3.5212	-1.30 **	-3.3081	-1.20 **	-3.4032	-1.24 *
ΔAgrSuppt	0.8132	0.23				
ΔY/Y			0.5037	0.41	0.6241	0.52
ΔAdminCost			0.2090	0.85	0.2529	1.11 *
ΔGovtSize			-7.3431	-0.34	*.04792*	*0.12*
Constant	-2.2903		-2.2256		-2.2893	
R-square						
-- within		0.8464		0.8511		0.8501
-- between		0.2904		0.2858		0.2873
-- overall		0.3853		0.3899		0.3869
F		79.89		53.36		52.94
Prob > F		0.0000		0.0000		0.0000
ρ		0.2852		0.3064		0.2921
Modified Bhargava et al. Durbin-Watson		1.6056		1.6458		1.6765
Baltagi-Wu LBI		2.4037		2.4305		2.4510
No of observations		93		93		93
Regression type	Fixed-effects (within)		Fixed-effects (within)		Fixed-effects (within)	

Notes:

1. The number in italics refers to changes in excessive government size defined in App.9.1.

2. Significance level: ***** 99%; **** 95%, *** 90%, ** 80%, * 70%.

These results are useful in understanding the institutional basis of the urban-rural disparity issue. In particular, it is interesting to learn from the results that the increase in fiscal support to agricultural development was unlikely to have been driven by concerns over rural underdevelopment but rather has its own momentum of growth and is closely associated with the expansion of bureaucracy and the rise in administrative cost. This observation implies that the relationship between "unfunded mandates" and bureaucracic expansion discussed in Lin, Tao and Liu (2003) also works in political economics of implementing the central government's policy to support agricultural development. The finding of the correlation between high administrative cost and urban-rural disparity also indicates the substantial role of bureaucratic rent-seeking in dragging the growth of rural household income.

The policy implications of these results are straightforward. Since fiscal support may not work well in curbing urban-rural disparity with the risk of being manipulated by local officials' rent-seeking, public policy to promote rural development should place emphasis elsewhere. Bureaucracic expansion and rising administrative costs are the symptoms of poor governance and rampant rent-seeking. Policy makers should therefore promote institutional reforms to improve the quality of local governance, especially by improving accountability of bureaucrats to the local rural population. Meanwhile, further opening up the domestic market to international trade should be pursued for its overall benefits to the economy. The fear of its possible worsening impact on urban-rural disparity is largely unfounded.

A major innovation of this chapter is its novelty in measuring the quality of local governance and linking it to the urban-rural disparity issue. The empirical findings are useful for evaluating recent-year public policies toward rural development and urban-rural equality. In particular, the results revealed in the chapter provide empirical evidence for the hypothetical link between "unfunded mandates" (in the context of agricultural support) and the expansion of bureaucracy. This chapter thereby attests the role of bureaucratic rent seeking in causing rural poverty, which is well discussed in the literature.

Several limits of this study are worth mentioning here. First, the panel data analysis is not able to explicitly reveal the causality of changes. Second, the limited size of the data restricts the degree of freedom to include some important explaining variables, such as education gaps between urban and rural residents. Finally, more layers of study are desirable to examine the determinants of the quality of local governance. These limits will inspire future studies on the topic.

References

Chan, K.W. and Zhang, L., 'The Hukou System and Rural - Urban Migration in China: Processes and Changes', *China Quarterly*, 160 (1999): 818-855.

China Academy of Social Sciences (CASS), *Report on Urban-Rural Income Inequality* (Beijing: CASS, 2004).

Deutsche Bank, *Quantifying the Impact of China's WTO Entry* (London: Deutsche Bank, 2001).

Johnson, D.G., 'Reducing the urban-rural income disparity. Office of Agricultural Economics Research' (The University of Chicago, Paper No.00-07, 2000).

Kuznets, S., 'Economic growth and income inequality', *American Economic Review* (Nashville) 45 (1) (1955): 1-28.

Li, S. and Zhai, F., The Impact of Accession to WTO on China's Economy (Working paper, Beijing: Development Research Centre, 2000).

Lin, J.Y., Tao, R. and Liu, M., Decentralization and Local Governance in the Context of China's Transition (CCAP working paper 03-E3, 2003).

Lin, S., 'Too many fees and too many charges: China streamlines its fiscal system', in J. Wong and D. Lu (eds), *China's Economy into the New Century: Structural Issues and Problems*, Singapore: World Scientific, 2002), pp.175-192.

Lu, D., 'Rural–urban income disparity: impact of growth, allocative efficiency, and local growth welfare', *China Economic Review* 13 (2002): 419–429.

Ray, Y., *Maintaining Stability in Rural China: Challenges and Responses* (Center for Northeastern Asian Policy Studies, the Brookings Institution, 2002).

Wei, S. and Wu, Y., 'Globalization and Inequality Without Differences in Data Definition, Legal System and Other Institutions' (NBER working paper No.8611, 2002).

Williamson, J.G., 'Regional inequality and the process of national development', *Economic Development and Cultural Change* 13 (1965): 3-45.

World Trade Organization, *Working Party Report on China's Accession to WTO* (Geneva: World Trade Organization, 2001).

Yang, D.T., 'Urban-based policies and rising income inequality in China', *The American Economic Review* (Nashville) 89 (2) (1999): 306-310.

Yang, D.T. and Zhou, H., 'Rural-Urban Disparity and Sectoral Labour Allocation in China', *Journal of Development Studies* 35(3) (1999): 105-133.

Zhao, X.B. and Tong, S.P., 'Unequal economic development in China: Spatial disparities and regional policy reconsideration, 1985-1995', *Regional Studies* (Cambridge) 34 (6) (2000): 549-561.

Appendix

The relative size of government (Government Staff/Total Employment) may be influenced by the level of development and the size of the population. More developed regions may be more efficient in general and therefore have a relatively smaller size of bureaucracy, while regions with larger populations may need a relatively smaller size of bureaucracy thanks to economies of scales in administration. In Appendix 9.1, we control these factors by regressing the relative size of government on population and per capita income. The residuals thus generated are used as a proxy for excessive bureaucracy size.

Appendix 9.1 Deriving the excessive government size

Dependent	GovtSize Coefficient	t-statistics	
Population	-0.0017	-1.85	***
Y	-6.69e-07	-3.76	*****
Constant	0.0440	2.61	
R-square			
-- within		0.1941	
-- between		0.4157	
-- overall		0.4041	
F(2,91)		10.96	
Prob > F		0.0001	
ρ		0.5422	
Modified Bhargava et al. Durbin-Watson		1.1397	
Baltagi-Wu LBI		2.0207	
No of observations		93	
Fixed-effects (within) regression			

Note: 1. Significance level: ***** 99%; *** 90%.

Part 3
Rural-Urban Migration

Chapter 10

Characteristics of Rural-Urban Migrants: The Case of Tianjin, China

Zhigang Lu
Shunfeng Song

1 Introduction

The tremendous abundance of labor in rural areas is one of the most perplexing issues currently facing the policymakers in the People's Republic of China. The central and municipal authorities fear that large-scale labor movement out of rural China will have politically and socially destabilizing effects on the cities and towns to which they migrate. Due to the pressing nature of the problems caused by such large migratory flows, much of the current government policy in China is directed at reducing these flows, using any available means. On one hand, the *hukou* system and other restrictive policies toward rural-urban migrants influence the efficiency of human capital in China's economy. On the other hand, it raises the discrimination issues against migrants. Migrant groups often have poor working and living conditions. They receive lower income and less social welfare.

In China's rural areas, the number of surplus laborers amounted to 130 million in 2002 (Economic Information Daily, April 16, 2003). Many left the countryside to find jobs in cities and towns. In 2003, the population of migrant laborers reached 98.2 million. More and more rural laborers transfer to non-agricultural industries in cities. By early 2004, migrant laborers took 57.6 percent of the jobs in the second industry and accounted for 52.6, 68.2, and 79.8 percent of the workforce in wholesales, retails and restaurant, manufacturing, and construction, respectively. Undoubtedly, migrant laborers are becoming an important component of China's industrialization.

The mobility of laborers from agricultural to non-agricultural industries has contributed to an increase of average income for rural people as migrant workers send a significant portion of their income back home. At the same time, migrant workers have made a great contribution to the urban economy by complementing cities' labor forces and providing low-cost work.

However, migrant laborers have suffered from discrimination and injustices in many aspects, including employment opportunity, government policies, income level, and social welfare. Most migrant workers engage in dangerous, dirty, tiring, or low paid jobs that city residents usually don't want to do. In many places, rural migrants are viewed as inferior people who are associated with poor images.

This chapter has two purposes. First, in sections 2 and 3, the chapter discusses the driving forces and barriers of rural-urban migration. Second, in section 4, the chapter examines the characteristics of rural migrants based on a survey conducted in Tianjin, China. Tianjin is one of the four municipalities that are directly controlled by the central government (Beijing, Shanghai, and Chongqing are the other three). The city governs 13 districts and five counties with a population of 10.07 million (NBSC, 2003); it is representative of large Chinese cities that are facing a flood of rural migrants.

In a survey conducted in the fourth quarter of 2003, we distributed 2,000 questionnaires and received 1,600 back. Among the returned forms, 455 (28.4 percent) were completed by migrant workers and 1,145 (71.6 percent) by urban workers who were permanent Tianjin residents. Using the survey data, we try to understand the social and economic characteristics of rural-urban migration in China. To improve rural migrants' welfare and to better protect them from economic and social discrimination, it is important to understand their current situation and primary concerns.

2 Driving Forces behind Rural-Urban Migration

According to Chan (2001), the number of registered *hukou* migrants remained between 16 and 20 million in the 1980s and 1990s. The number of non-*hukou* migrants, however, increased dramatically in the early 1980s and mid-1990s, reaching 100 million in 1997. The 2000 population census data show 144.39 million rural residents moved into cities and towns (*chengzhen*), which was 11.6 percent of the total population in 2000 (NBSC, 2002).

The massive rural-urban migration since 1980 can be broadly attributed to the following factors: huge surplus of rural labor unleashed by the decollectivization program since 1978, rapid industrialization, widening income and consumption disparities between rural and urban residents, heavy taxation on the agricultural sector, and other historical and social and cultural issues.

Before the economic reform, rural people were discouraged to engage in non-agricultural production. Rural laborers were restricted from moving to urban areas by tight controls of *hukou* registration, employment opportunities, and rationings of grain and other products. With the introduction of the Rural Household Responsibility System and the rural decollectivization in 1978, it became essential to transform the surplus rural laborers from agricultural to nonagricultural sectors. Despite the practice of Family Planning Policy, the rural population increased by 40 percent to 807.39 million from 1978 to 2002, according to the fifth population census.

During the same period, China's economic strategy promoted relatively capital-intensive, heavy industrialization to the detriment of more labor-intensive agriculture. In particular, the extensive use of machinery, herbicide chemicals, and other agricultural technologies have greatly liberated the rural labor force, improved production efficiency, and freed farmers' time.

With the rapid expansion of China's rural labor force, improvement in production efficiency, and the continuing reduction of cultivated land, a larger portion of rural laborers has become underemployed or excessive, relative to the available agricultural resources. Zhang (1994) calculated that in the early 1980s there were about 70 million surplus rural laborers, which was 18 percent of the entire rural labor force. The surplus grew into about 130 million ten years later, or 28 percent of the total rural labor force. Banister and Taylor (1989) estimated that the surplus labor force constituted about 40 percent of rural employment in farming, or 25 percent of all rural laborers in the 1980s.

The widening rural-urban disparities are another factor of the increasing rural-urban migration. Urban residents' income and consumption levels are much higher than those of their rural counterparts. They also enjoy various state-subsidized welfares on food supply, education, employment, medical services, and so on. In 1978, the annual per capita disposable income for urban residents was 343 *yuan*, 2.6 times that for rural peasants, which was 134 *yuan*. In 2001, the urban-to-rural income ratio increased to 2.9:1, with 6,860 *yuan* for urbanites and 2,366 *yuan* for rural peasants. As for consumption, in 1978 the per capita consumption of urban residents was 405 *yuan*, 2.9 times that for rural peasants (138 *yuan*). In 1999, the consumption gap ratio rose to 3.5:1, with 6,796 *yuan* for urbanites and 1,927 *yuan* for rural residents, demonstrating widening income and consumption disparities between urban and rural residents in China (NBSC, various years, 1994-2003).

The heavy tax burden on farmers also drives rural residents to migrate. Although the central government emphasized the importance of alleviating the burden on farmers, local authorities have always had their ways to counterplot the central government's policies. Based on their interests, local governments concoct various pretexts to apportion different charges on farmers.

Heavy levies mainly include three taxations, three surcharges, and five fees. The three taxations include: agricultural tax, agriculture special product tax, and slaughter tax. The three surcharges are mutual funds, provident funds, and village management fees. The five fees include: the education fee, the planned-parenthood fee, the planned-foster fee, the military training fee, and the village road development fee. In addition, local governments also aggregated the burden on farmers by charging some other fees for projects, such as building model schools, roads, and water conservancy.

According to Zhang (2004), local governments tax a significant portion of farmers' income. In 1995, per capita tax payment was 138.6 *yuan*, with an incidence rate of 12.5 percent. This number increased to 162.6 *yuan* in 1996, 187 *yuan* in 1997, and 202.9 *yuan* in 1998, all with an increase higher than 10 percent (of per capita annual income). Even worse, the agricultural taxation is regressive.

For example, in 1996, the tax rate was 16.7 percent for rural families with an annual income between 400 and 500 *yuan*. This rate decreased to 8.7 percent for those with income of 800-1,000 *yuan* and 2.8 percent with income of 2,500-5,000 (Zhang, 2004). The high tax not only burdens lower farmers' income but also discourages them from investing in agricultural production, pushing them to migrate to cities.

Table 10.1 Reasons for rural-urban migration (responses are not mutually exclusive. Total number of respondents is 455)

Reasons	Number Responded (person)	Percent age (percent)
Higher income in cities	187	41.1
Better opportunities in cities	203	44.6
Better quality of life in cities	143	31.4
Burden of taxes and fees	117	25.7
Better education	170	37.3
Better education for children	123	27.0
Loss of land in the countryside	98	21.5
Other	41	9.0

Source: Survey conducted by the authors in Tianjin, 2003.

In developed economies, off-farm labor mobility is typically viewed as being a function of relative wages in the farm and non-farm sectors. In China, the off-farm job-seeking decision is similar to the decision in other countries even though China's institutional factors, which were built into the system to keep the agricultural population on farms, have complicated this decision (Zhao, 1999). Table 10.1 lists major reasons why rural laborers wanted to migrate to the city of Tianjin. Our survey data, described in more detail later, show that rural people migrate to Tianjin to seek higher income, better opportunities, a better quality of life, and a better education for themselves and their children. Interestingly, more than 20 percent of migrants in the survey migrated because of loss of land in the countryside, probably to the rapid industrialization and urbanization.

3 Barriers of Rural-Urban Migration

Several institutional and social barriers have made the rural-urban migration difficult. First, the Household Registration System (also known as the *hukou* system), which was established in 1951 and formalized in 1958, was "the Great Wall" between the cities and the countryside within China. For a long time, it was a rural-urban divide that kept peasants away from cities. Before 1978, one's urban *hukou* status was the ticket to many benefits, such as food rations, housing, employment, and healthcare. People had to obtain permission from both places of origin and destination if they wished to relocate. The household registration system greatly reduced rural-urban migration and labor mobility across cities.

Since the mid-1980s, with the economic reforms on the urban sector, several factors have made household registration less important. For example, enterprises enjoy a greater flexibility in hiring and firing employees, and urban *hukou* is not required for many jobs. Rationing no longer exists because people can essentially buy anything in the market. Survival in cities depends more on money than on one's *hukou* status. Also, housing has been commercialized and separated from employment and urban residence. The erosion of the household registration system has greatly facilitated rural-urban migration.

However, a set of regulations was instituted by the Ministry of Labor (MOL) in early 1995. It requires that, to be considered a legal temporary resident in a city, every migrant must obtain three certificates and one card: an identification certificate that is issued by the police department of the originating county and is usually valid for ten years, a temporary resident certificate that is issued by the police department of the destination city and must be renewed each year, an employment certificate that is issued by the labor bureau of the originating county to certify that person's employment eligibility, and an employment card that is issued by the labor bureau of the destination city to show proof of employment in the city.

In Beijing, for example, the cost of a temporary resident certificate, an employment certificate, and an employment card is 198, 200-400, and 50 *yuan*, respectively. In addition to the above three certificates and one card, some local governments require migrants to present other certificates to work or stay in the cities, such as a training certificate, a health certificate, or a fire control certificate, which all cost money. In Tianjin, our survey results show that rural migrants pay an average of 120 *yuan* in administrative fees per year.

A second barrier of rural-urban migration relates to the social welfare provisions in cities. The above mentioned *hukou* system also created a dichotomy in social welfare provisions between rural and urban people. The permanent residents of cities enjoy various social welfare, subsidies, insurance, and other government supports, especially the unemployed, disabled, elderly, and low-income people.

Migrant workers, however, have no chance to receive the same social welfare and government supports that permanent urban citizens do as long as their *hukou* status is "agricultural," no matter how long they have lived and worked in cities. Because of the lack of social welfare support, migrants face a greater risk to migrate, and many have to rely on their relatives and friends when they run into economic difficulties. In many cities, because migrants' children are not allowed to enter public schools without paying a much higher fee, migrants have to set up schools by themselves in order to have their children educated.

A third barrier comes from the prejudice of city dwellers toward rural migrants. In recent years, big cities in China have all seen a sharp increase of crimes, and many people blame rural migrants for the increase. Undoubtedly, some migrants commit such crimes as robbery and murder and are engaged in drugs and prostitution, but this is not the whole picture. Migrants contribute to the urban development by creating jobs, taking jobs that urban residents don't want to take, and providing low-cost labor. It is unfair to characterize rural migrants as ignorant outsiders who crowded cities with dirt, disorder, and crimes. It is also unfair to claim that migrants are the main source of deteriorating urban employment, environment, safety, and transportation.

Finally, rural workers face disadvantages in finding jobs in cities when they compete with their urban counterparts. Historically, every urban resident was entitled to a job and that job was an "iron bowl." Providing jobs and keeping employees were two responsibilities of state-owned enterprises (SOEs).

Following the economic reform, SOEs started to pay more attention to efficiency, and many began laying off redundant workers. With an excess of urban laborers and limited job offerings, migrant workers are naturally taken as a threat to urban workers' employment, or reemployment, and as a result, are discriminated against. In cities, many SOEs and some private enterprises still require job applicants to hold urban *hukou*, thus giving a preference to urban workers. Furthermore, SOEs require employees to have higher education or more work experience. Most rural migrants, however, only graduated from high school at most and have less non-farm working experience, suggesting that their chance of being hired is very remote.

4 Characteristics of Rural-Urban Migrants: the Case of Tianjin

The data used in this study came from a survey conducted in Tianjin from October to December 2003. Questions were asked to both urban residents and rural migrants on employment, demographics, residential status, income, and so on. Specific questions were asked to migrants about their household composition, place of origin, income sent back to hometowns, life in Tianjin, and future migration decisions.

The survey was conducted in 30 different companies, covering ten different occupations. Overall, 455 migrants and 1,145 city workers completed the survey. We define migrant workers as those who live and work in Tianjin but do not have Tianjin urban *hukou*. Based on the survey data, this section summarizes economic and social-demographic characteristics of rural migrants and compares them with those of urban labors.

Unless otherwise mentioned, tables and figures are calculated and constructed with sample sizes of 455 for rural migrants and 1,145 for city workers. In comparisons, we don't report the P-values if the differences are obvious.

4.1 *Economic Characteristics*

We discuss economic characteristics of migrant workers regarding their employment, income, welfare conditions, and education. Figure 10.1 lists the occupation choices of rural migrants in the sample.

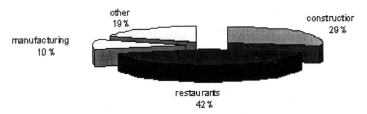

Figure 10.1 Occupation type of migrant workers

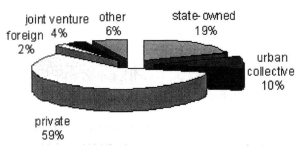

Figure 10.2 Ownership of migrant's workplace

Of the 455 migrants, 42 percent work in restaurants and 29 percent in construction, leaving less than 30 percent for all other sectors. This finding reflects Xie's (2000) concept of self-isolated careers, arguing that many migrants voluntarily engage in low-class jobs with lower pays and thus form a concentration in those kinds of careers. Without urban *hukou*, migrant workers have to avoid direct competition with urban workers. Consequently, they tend to engage in hard-labor occupations or in such industries that use unskilled laborers, such as construction, restaurants, manufacturing, retail, mining, domestic service, and waste collection.

Table 10.2 compares migrant workers with urban workers in regard to their occupation status. We observe that rural migrants are more likely than urban residents to work as security guards, or as unskilled workers in general, whereas urban residents are more likely to work as managers and technicians/professionals.

The survey suggests that rural laborers tend to work in privately owned companies. Figure 10.2 shows 59 percent of migrant laborers work in private companies and only 19 percent in state-owned enterprises. In China, most state-owned and urban-collective companies still require their employees to have urban *hukou*, which puts migrants in a disadvantaged position when competing for SOE jobs. Foreign-owned companies or joint ventures tend to hire people with certain skills. Migrants, however, are less educated (Table 10.3) and less trained. In the sample, 57 percent of the migrant workers, compared with 53 percent of urban workers, claimed that they started out on their current jobs without any training. Rural *hukou* and less education/training make finding jobs in foreign-owned companies or joint ventures incredibly difficult for migrant workers.

Table 10.2 Comparison of occupation status (percent)

	Manager	Clerk	Guard	Sales person	Driver	Professional/ technician	Unskilled worker	Other
Migrant worker	3.9	38.2	10	1.5	1.1	5.7	11.9	26.6
Urban worker	13.2	38.8	4.3	3.8	3.1	14.6	4.9	17.4

Table 10.3 shows that migrant workers are far less educated than city workers. In the survey, 73.6 percent of migrant workers have an education of middle school or less, while the number is only 21.1 percent for urban workers. Urban workers are much better educated. In the sample, about half (50.3 percent) of all urban workers graduated from vocational schools and colleges, compared with only 12.5 percent for migrant workers.

In China, rural migrants are also called "floating people." This implies that many migrants do not have permanent residences or jobs in cities. They "float" between cities and shift between jobs. In our survey, 38.7 percent of migrant workers have been employed more than once in the same city, or in other cities, before their current jobs. More than half (52.7 percent) of migrant workers have worked in their current workplaces for less than one year. On average, the migrant workers in our sample have worked in their current workplaces for 2.17 years. Table 10.4 shows that most migrant workers are employed with either no contract (53.4 percent) or a one-year contract (15.9 percent). In contrast, more than half (51.4 percent) of city workers are hired with either a permanent employment status or a minimum three-year contract. Only 14.4 percent of the city workers worked without a contract.

Table 10.3 Education levels of migrant and urban workers (percent)

	Below elementary	Elementary school	Middle school	High school	Vocational school	College or above
Migrant worker	5.7	10.3	57.6	13.8	9.0	3.5
Urban worker	2.7	1.5	16.9	28.4	25.8	24.5

Table 10.4 Comparison of employment contracts (percent)

Contract type	Permanent	Longer than 3 years	Between 1-3 years	In a year	Temporary (no contract)	Other
Migrant worker	7.3	5.3	10.8	15.9	53.4	6.7
Urban worker	31.8	19.6	17.2	9.4	14.4	7.6

For many families in rural China, a household's income largely depends on the earnings of family members who work outside the home. Remitting money home is a popular way for migrants to support their families. In our survey, 59.3 percent of migrant workers send money regularly to their families in the countryside. On average, the migrant workers in our sample send 236.2 *yuan* per month to their families, which is 31 percent of their monthly income. It is worth mentioning that more than half of migrant workers in our sample (54.1 percent) regularly go home to work on the farm during the planting and harvesting seasons.

Table 10.5 compares employment channels between rural and urban workers. Interestingly, our survey suggests that migrant workers seldom ask the government to help them find jobs even though they pay various administrative fees to the government. In the sample, only 1.5 percent of migrant workers had directly asked the government for help in finding jobs, contrasting with 20 percent of urban workers. Less than half of rural workers (44 per cent) found jobs through friends and relatives, while only 20.9 percent of urban workers sought such kind of help, indicating that migrants are more dependent on friend and relative networks than are urban workers during a job search. Relatively, migrant laborers tend to seek help more from government-sponsored employment agencies. For both migrant and urban workers, a significant portion of each group found jobs on their own.

Table 10.5 Comparison of employment channels (percent)

	Self	Employment agencies	Friends or relatives	Government	Other
Migrant worker	37.4	12.1	44	1.5	5
Urban worker	43.5	5.9	20.9	20	9.7

Income disparities between rural migrants and permanent urban residents are evident in our sample. The survey results show an average monthly income of 762 *yuan* for migrant workers and 1,468 *yuan* for urban workers. Table 10.6 presents the income levels of the two groups in six categories. About 66 percent of migrants have an income of less than 800 *yuan* per month in comparison to 27 percent for urban workers. Only 5 percent of migrants make more than 1,500 *yuan* per month, while a third of urban workers make that same amount. The picture looks worse if work hours are considered. On average, migrants in the sample work 64 hours per week, while urban workers only work 46 hours per week. Measured by hourly rate, urban workers are paid 2.7 times as much as migrant workers on average.

Table 10.6 Income distribution of rural migrants and urban residents

Category	Migrant Workers (percent)	Urban Workers (percent)
<500 *yuan*	19	6
500-799 *yuan*	47	21
800-1000 *yuan*	16	14
1000-1200 *yuan*	10	13
1200-1500 *yuan*	3	14
>1500 *yuan*	5	32

Table 10.7 compares the welfare conditions between migrants and non-migrants. Clearly, migrant workers receive far less social protection than urban workers. Our survey data suggest that only 14.3, 8.6, and 7.3 percent of migrants have medical, retirement, and unemployment insurance, respectively. These proportions are much higher for urban workers, 68.2, 63.8, and 51.8 per cent, respectively. Such disparities reflect a wide coverage gap between migrant and urban workers in China's social protection system and suggest that most rural migrants are still left out of the welfare system. Table 10.7 also shows that migrants are less satisfied with their salary than their urban counterparts are (P-value=0.01). This could suggest that migrant workers are discriminated against in the labor market or that their wage expectations are too high.

Table 10.7 Welfare condition comparison (percent)

	Subsidiary houses	Medical insurance	Retirement insurance	Unemployment insurance	Satisfaction of salary
Migrant worker	21.2	14.3	8.6	7.3	45.9
Urban worker	25.7	68.2	63.8	51.8	54.2

If employees lose their jobs, whom can they turn to for support? Table 10.8 shows migrant workers are more "self-supporting" than urban labors. They often get by with the support of their families, relatives, or friends. Urban residents expect the government to help them more, and they also rely more on their own savings, probably because they have more savings.

Table 10.8 Comparison of unemployment supports (percent)

	Government support	Family support	Own savings	Support from relatives and friends	Loans from banks
Migrant worker	13.8	58.9	15.2	8.1	4.0
Urban worker	31.2	37.3	23.1	4.0	4.5

Table 10.9 reports what migrant and urban workers will do when they face unemployment. Not surprisingly, rural migrants are much more mobile and flexible than city workers. More than 30 percent of migrant workers would return to their place of origin (the countryside) after losing their jobs, while only 8.3 percent of city workers would go back to their original cities. About 23 percent of migrants will look for jobs in other cities, but less than 11 percent of city workers are willing to do that. On the contrary, most urban workers want to stay in the same city to find new jobs (62.8 percent), whereas only 36.3 percent of migrant workers will. These findings suggest that a strong "flowing pattern" exists for rural migrants.

Table 10.9 Comparison of actions facing unemployment (percent)

	Back to original places	Find jobs in other cities	Find new jobs in same city	Other
Migrant worker	30.8	22.9	36.3	10.1
Urban worker	8.3	10.8	62.8	18.1

4.2 Socio-demographic Characteristics

Figure 10.3 presents the age distribution of rural migrants. Most migrant workers (69 per cent) are younger than 25, and less than 10 percent are older than 40. The sample mean is 25.3. Figure 10.4 shows the marital status of the migrants. More than 70 percent of migrant workers are single. These findings suggest that young and single individuals have smaller moving costs and thus are more able to migrate.

Figures 10.5 and 10.6 report the places of origin and *hukou* status of rural migrants in Tianjin. Distance seems to have an inverse effect on migration. In the sample, about a quarter of migrants (27 percent) were "local farmers" in adjacent districts or towns of Tianjin, 46 percent came from adjacent provinces such as Hubei and Shandong, and 27 percent migrated from other places. Half of the rural migrants have no Tianjin *hukou*, regardless of whether they are urban or rural. Among those who have, about a quarter (26 per cent) hold temporary Tianjin urban *hukou*.

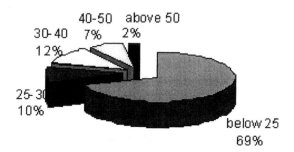

Figure 10.3 Age distribution of migrant workers

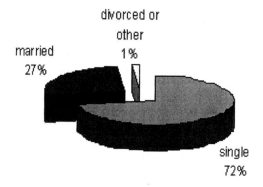

Figure 10.4 Marital status of migrant workers

Our survey suggests that female migrants are disadvantaged when finding a job and receiving pay. First, much fewer migrant women are hired in Tianjin. Out of the 455 rural migrants, 32 percent were female and 68 percent were male. Second, female migrants have more restrictions in their job search.

The sample data showed that female migrants are more likely to work in services and light manufacturing industries. Third, female migrants face more age discrimination. In our sample, female workers were four years younger on average than male workers, with an average age of 22.7 and 26.6, respectively. Fourth, female workers make less money. On average, the monthly per capita earning was 671 *yuan* for females but 805 *yuan* for males.

While this chapter does not attempt to discuss all factors of gender inequality, we believe that some cultural and institutional barriers could explain why women have more difficulty in finding jobs and in receiving fair pay. For example, both information on jobs and social connections are less available to rural women. Rural women still take care of most of the household responsibilities and thus do not have the same opportunities to explore as much as rural men do. Also, rural women receive less education than their male counterparts. In addition, job recruiting advertisements are frequently gender-specific by stating "men only" or requiring female applicants to be young and good-looking. Relative to rural male migrants, rural women have less advantage in competing in the urban labor market because they are less able to perform physical work and less educated for technical jobs.

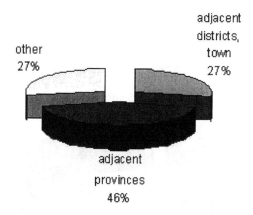

Figure 10.5 Origins of migrants

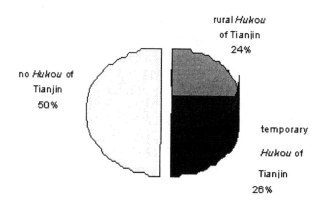

Figure 10.6 Hukou status of rural migrants

Institutionally, rural female migrants face more obstacles to stay in cities. For instance, due to the lack of social protection to rural migrants, employers are less willing to hire female rural workers for such reasons as maternity leave and childcare. Until 1998, a child inherited his or her mother's *hukou*, which means that a child born in a city to a female migrant couldn't have urban *hukou*, regardless of the father's *hukou* status. This implied that female migrants were second-class migrants.

How do rural migrants think of their new lives in the city? In our survey, 70 percent of rural migrants considered life in the city to be safe. Still, an alarming 18 percent said they have been crime victims in the city. About 39 percent of the migrants expressed their fear of falling victim to crimes, such as fraud, robbery, and pocket lifting. Figure 10.7 shows how satisfied migrants are with their lives in the city. Twice as many migrants feel some level of satisfaction (31 per cent) as those who feel some level of dissatisfaction (15 per cent). Most migrants (54 per cent) were neutral.

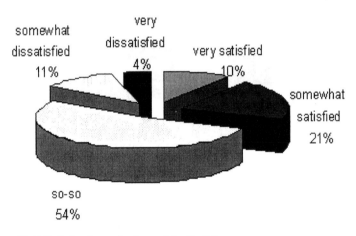

Figure 10.7 Satisfaction of migrants' city life

Figure 10.8 presents how migrants perceive the discrimination they have experienced in various aspects. The two most common discriminations both came from the labor market: 28 percent of the responds said they are mostly discriminated against in their workplace, and 20 percent said they are discriminated against when they apply for a job. Eighteen percent felt that they are discriminated against by the urban society in general, 9 percent felt discriminated against by the government welfare provisions, 7 percent from children education, and 4 percent when purchasing a house.

Finally in our survey, we asked rural migrants what would be their main reason if they decided to go back to their homelands. Figure 10.9 reports our findings. Thirty one percent considered their families in the countryside, 18 percent listed low wages, and 17 percent listed difficulty in finding a job. Thirteen percent thought they would return home because of the bad quality of life in the city; 12 percent attributed discrimination in the city as their reason to go back to the countryside.

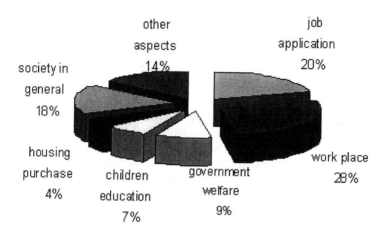

Figure 10.8 Perception of discrimination by migrants

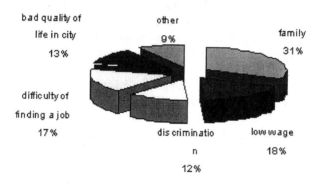

Figure 10.9 Reasons of going back to countryside

5 Conclusions

Over the past two decades, China has witnessed a massive rural-urban migration. As a result, many rural workers have found new jobs and homes in the cities. This chapter has discussed the driving forces and barriers of rural-urban migration, arguing that migration is attributed to pulling forces in the cities, such as a higher income, better opportunities, a better quality of life, and a better education for themselves and their children. It is also attributed to pushing forces in the countryside, such as poor living conditions, an increasing surplus of labor, a loss of land, and a heavy tax burden.

Several institutional and social barriers, however, have made rural-urban migration difficult. First, because of the *hukou* system, rural migrants are subjected to paying myriad fees for working and living in the cities. Second, due to the lack of social protection and government support, rural migrants face a greater risk when living in the cities. They have to rely on themselves, their families, or their friends when they run into economic difficulties; they also have to pay higher fees to have their kids educated in city schools or even build schools for their children themselves. Third, the prejudice of city residents makes many rural migrants feel unsafe and discriminated against. Finally, because most rural workers are less-educated and many enterprises still require urban *hukou* status, rural migrants are at a disadvantage when competing for jobs against their urban counterparts.

This chapter has examined the characteristics of rural migrants. Based on a survey conducted in Tianjin in 2003, we have derived the following conclusions on migrant workers: 1) Because of no urban *hukou* status, they mostly engage in physical-labor occupations and non-technical jobs. 2) Private enterprises are the primary working destinations for migrant workers. 3) Most of them started their current jobs without job-related training experience. 4) Their employment is unstable, and few of them are hired with permanent employment status or contracts of longer than three years. 5) They are more dependent on themselves in seeking employment opportunities. 6) They are far less educated than urban workers. 7) They work an average of 18 hours longer per week than their urban counterparts yet receive a much lower pay. Their average monthly income is only 52 percent that of urban workers. Their average hourly wage rate is only 37 percent that of their urban counterparts. 8) Few of them enjoy social welfare benefits. Our survey data show that only 14.3, 8.6, and 7.3 percent of migrant workers have medical, retirement, and unemployment insurance, respectively. 9) They are more self-reliant than city workers when they lose their jobs. 10) They have a much higher mobility than city workers when unemployment does occur. 11) Young, single, and male rural laborers are more likely to migrate than female rural laborers. 12) Distance has a negative effect on migration, and thus, most migrants in Tianjin come from adjacent areas and provinces. 13) Most of them consider life in the city to be safe and feel satisfied with their new urban lives, even though a good portion of them have been victims of urban crimes and are not happy with their current situations. 14) Migrants feel discriminated against in cities, especially in their workplaces and when applying for a job. A significant portion of them feel discriminated against by urban society in general. 15) More than 30 percent of migrants would consider their families in the countryside to be the main reason for them to return home. Low wages, the difficulty of finding jobs, and a bad quality of life in the city are also reasons for going back to the countryside.

Comprehensive policies are urgently needed to help rural migrants. Further reforms on the household registration system, the employment system, the education system, and the social protection system will help migrant workers fit into the urban environment more quickly and smoothly. Restrictions on migration are not economically efficient or socially just.

References

Banister, J. and Taylor, J.R., 'China: Surplus Labour and Migration', *Asia-Pacific Population Journal*, 4(4) (1989): 1-18.

Chan, K.W., 'Recent Migration in China: Patterns, Trends and Politics', *Asian Perspective*, 25(4) (2001): 127-153.

Economic Information Daily (2003, April 16).

Hong, Z., 'Mitigating Farmers' Burden and Protecting Their Rights', in B. Liu, Z. Zhang, and G. Huo (eds), *China Farming Countryside and Peasantry Issue Report* (Beijing: China Development Press, 2004), pp.401-425.

National Bureau of Statistics of China (NBSC), Tabulation on the 2000 Population Census of The People's Republic of China (Beijing: China Statistical Press, 2002).

————,China Statistical Yearbook, various issues (Beijing: China statistics press, 1994-2003).

Xie, J.Y., Rural-Urban Migration and Economic Development in Current China (in Chinese) (Beijing: China's Population Press, 2000).

Zhang, C., Studies on China's Rural Population (in Chinese) (Beijing: China's Population Press, 1994), p.138.

Zhao, Y., 'Leaving the Countryside: Rural-to-Urban Migration Decisions in China,' *American Economic Review* 89 (1999): 281-286.

Chapter 11

Choices between Different Off-farm Employment Sub-Categories: An Empirical Analysis for Jiangxi Province, China

P25 013

018 015

P23 P32

Xiaoping Shi
Nico Heerink
Futian Qu

1 Introduction

Raising the income of farmers in rural China is receiving increased attention from policymakers. More than 20 years of economic reform—opening China up to foreign trade—have led to high economic growth rates, while unfortunately widening the rural-urban income gap as well. Considering the prevailing scarcity of arable land in rural China—the average-sized land holding being about 0.5 *ha* per household—much of the income growth for rural households must come from off-farm employment.

In fact, the growth of rural township and village enterprises (TVEs) as well as private enterprises (PEs) has been a major driving force in economic growth and the increase in household income in rural China. However, it has also contributed to the increasing income inequalities among different regions of China—largely the coastal provinces—where TVEs and PEs are predominant with a lack of off-farm employment opportunities. Therefore, an important question facing China's policymakers today is what measures must be taken to help rural households increase their off-farm income-earning opportunities.

Empirical studies show that social networks, income gaps, land constraints, and household compositions are important factors that determine whether or not a household participates in non-farm activities (Du, 2000; Zhao, 2001a; Zhu, 2002). These factors, however, may differ depending on the sub-category of off-farm activity. For instance, social networks are very important for rural-to-urban migration (Zhao, 2001a), while connections to local policymakers are important for rural villagers seeking local non-farm work (Cook, 1999; Yao, 1999). Consequently, obtaining a better understanding of the influential factors of participation decisions in different off-farm activities, such as self-employment, local employment, migration, as well as their relative importance may contribute to better policies that raise and diversify rural household incomes and improve risk management. Therefore, this chapter's objective is to examine which factors compel participation in various types of off-farm activities in China.

The rest of this chapter is organized as follows. Section 2 briefly reviews the available theories on participation determinants in off-farm activities. Section 3 describes the research selection area and the data set used in this study. Section 4 examines the relative importance of the four off-farm employment types in the research area as well as the income earned in each. Model choice and estimation results for the participation in off-farm employment are discussed in Section 5. This chapter then concludes by summarizing the major conclusions and suggesting a few policy implications in Section 6.

2 Theoretical Considerations

The participation of rural households in off-farm activity supplements and diversifies their income, increasing their welfare and reducing the risks of agricultural production, and an increase in the off-farm labor supply may reflect an *ex post* response to a shocked realization (Kochar, 1999). It may also suggest an *ex ante* decision based on the need for alternative sources of income in a risky environment (Barrett and Reardon, 2000; Rose, 2001). An empirical study by Giles (2002) shows that off-farm activities have been used as a means of smoothing shocks in rural China's agricultural production.[1] Therefore, participation in off-farm activities may be more important for farm households with credit, or liquidity, constraints than for other households. This is because participation in off-farm activities may enable farm households to invest in farms by purchasing or renting equipment, financing initial investments, and investing in skills training (De Brauw et al., 2002).

Whether or not to partake in off-farm activities is a choice that members of rural households make in a particular environment based on their own resources, the local institutions that shape their consumption and farm production, as well as other factors. Everything influential, however, can be classified as either "push" or "pull" factors.

The large urban-rural income gap is a major "pull" factor (Todaro, 1969; Zhong, 2003). Another "pull" factor may be the preference to work outside the farm or live a more colorful life in the city (Wu et al., 2003). In China's case, however, discrimination against rural workers in urban areas—including low or delayed payments, high school fees, lack of social security, and so on—is a significantly negative "pull" factor.

"Push" factors that drive rural laborers to seek off-farm employment include: land constraints; farm production risks; and rural market failures, such as

---

[1] The data used in this study come from annual village surveys held in 44 villages of Shanxi, Jiangsu, Anhui and Henan provinces, covering roughly 3,100 households during 1986–1997.

imperfect—or missing—insurance as well as consumption and credit markets. They force rural laborers to find other sources of income or ways to loosen these constraints (Rozelle et al., 1999; Reardon et al., 2001; de Brauw et al., 2003). In a perfect market environment, the rewards for working on-farm and working off-farm are equal. Farm households would reallocate their time to off-farm work until the marginal return of labor in off-farm activities equals that of farm production. However, low-income economies are generally characterized by abundant labor resources in agricultural production and persistent market imperfections (Cook, 1999). If a farming household faces imperfections in the agricultural labor market, working off-farm may affect leisure and labor input in farm production. If a household faces imperfections in the non-farm labor market, labor may not be as diverse as desired.

Imperfections in the agricultural labor market occur when hired workers are imperfect substitutes for those within the family—when the husband and wife in a household cannot be efficiently replaced by other workers, or when there are high transaction costs in monitoring hired laborers. In poor rural areas, one family member's decision of whether or not to engage in off-farm labor affects the decisions of the rest of the family (Du, 1999). The imperfections of the agricultural labor market imply that a household's production decisions cannot be separated from those of consumption. Therefore, both farm and family considerations influence the household as well as the individual in the decision to engage in off-farm employment.

Non-farm labor markets are segmented and characterized by entry barriers. As a result, access to off-farm employment is difficult for specific groups of farming households. In particular, those with the most difficulty are poor (Reardon, 1997) or have fewer social (*Guanxi*) or political connections (Cook, 1998; Kung, 1999; Yao, 1999; Zhao, 2001b; Zhang and Li, 2001; Gilles, 2002;).

The absence of local TVEs and PEs may limit local employment opportunities. Geographic location is an especially important factor in the local development of small enterprises. In China, areas that are close to large cities or the coast have more-developed local enterprise sectors. Their labor markets are more developed, especially where PEs dominate, like in the Zhejiang province (Kung and Lee, 2001). Poor infrastructure may restrain the movement of labor across regions because of the high costs involved in migration (Somwaru et al., 2001)

Institutional barriers may also prevent farm households from participating in off-farm labor. Examples include: the household registration system (*Hukou*), which constrains the movement of labor in China; the insecure rural land property rights, which make farmers reluctant to leave their farms; and the grain production quota system, which—until recently—required farmers to fulfill their obligations before they could engage in off-farm employment (Kung and Liu, 1997; Liu et al., 1998; Rozelle et al., 1999; Lohmar et al., 2000; Brandt et al., 2002; Gale, 2002; Kung, 2002).

The development of agricultural land markets may affect off-farm labor participation as well. In China, farming households may loose their land-use rights if they do not either cultivate their land or rent it to other households. In some areas, however, land rental markets are absent, and farmers may choose not to engage in off-farm employment so that they do not loose their land rights.

Off-farm employment studies pay particular attention to the role of individual characteristics—one's education level, gender, and age, for example—in gaining access to off-farm employment (Du, 1999; Du, 2000; Kung and Lee, 2001; Zhang et al., 2002;). There has been less emphasis on the characteristics and decision-making of farming households. The theory of New Economics of Labor Migration (NELM) emphasizes that the decisions of migrants make up the decisions of a migrant's household (Stark, 1991; Taylor and Martin, 2001). It stresses that the decision to migrate is an important way for rural households to overcome credit and insurance constraints via remittance flows and income diversification, respectively.

The theories on off-farm labor participation above regard off-farm employment as an entirety. The factors driving participation in it, however, vary among the different off-farm activity sub-categories.

Former migrants who return to their village—and the social networks they bring with them—are very important to their neighbors who are considering migration and looking for employment in a city (Zhao, 2001b). In China, a significant kind of migration is seasonal, a so-called "circular migration," making the cost of travel an important consideration when contemplating it (Hare, 1999; Zhao, 2001a).

The presence of children in the household may act as a bottleneck for migration and is more compatible with self-employment or agricultural labor within the same village. When elderly family members also live in the household, however, they traditionally handle a large part of the childcare and thereby facilitate the pursuit of off-farm employment for the parents.

Until recently, local officials played a critical role in allocating employment because most TVEs were collectively owned. Therefore, political connections were vital to rural workers hoping to enter the non-agricultural work force at local TVEs (Yao, 1999). In regard to PEs, any local non-farm opportunities are primarily allocated by way of market mechanisms—meaning that one's social capital and political connections would be negligible (Kung and Lee, 2001).

The initial asset status of farm households is important when starting a small business not only in case any credit markets are missing but also for financing the start-up costs involved in accessing off-farm employment. Self-employment also requires managerial skills that are needed to run a business.

Because particular skills are needed for certain jobs, off-farm employment opportunities are limited, and strong competition exists among households, those households with better education and human capital are more likely to enter the non-agricultural work force (Du, 1999; Kung and Lee, 2001; Zhang et al., 2002;). The role of human capital in agricultural off-farm employment, however, is most likely limited.

In this study, a detailed empirical analysis will be made of the factors determining participation in different kinds of off-farm employment. In China, empirical studies of off-farm employment have thus far somewhat neglected to explain the differences in participation among the different sub-categories of off-farm activities. An exception is the study by de Brauw et al. (2002), which used data collected from 610 rural households across sixty different villages in six provinces (Hebei, Liaoning, Shaanxi, Zhejiang, and Sichuan). With this data, they examined the determinants of engaging in self-employment, local employment, and migration. Although their results indicate important differences among the three—especially between self-employment and the other two—they do not attempt to explain any of them.[2]

In our study, however, we more closely analyze the relative importance of self-employment, local wage-employment, and migration for households in terms of time spent and income earned. In addition, close attention is paid to the factors driving the individual participation in these sub-categories. We further distinguish local wage-employment into both agricultural and non-agricultural because the skills required for either are fundamentally different.

3 Area Selection and Data Description

This chapter uses data collected through a survey of farm households in the Jiangxi province for a research project on economic policy reforms, agricultural incentives, and soil degradation in Southeast China.[3] Jiangxi province is located in this region of China, bordering Fujian, Guangdong, Zhejiang, Hunan, Hubei and Anhui provinces. It represents about 1.8 percent of China's geographic area and 3.5 percent of its population. In Jiangxi province, agricultural production dominates the local economy. Agriculture was 21.9 percent of the 2002 GDP—6.5 percent higher than the average level of the whole country. Its 2002 GDP per capita equaled 5,829 *yuan*, or $705—71 percent of the national average (Statistical Yearbook of China, 2003).

Detailed data collection of off-farm employment, household, and individual characteristics, among other relevant variables, in 2000 was conducted in three villages in Jiangxi province in August 2000 and the beginning of 2001. The villages were selected using a series of criteria, which included the economic development level, market access, and geographical conditions, after consulting local researchers and policymakers in addition to making several site visits. The three villages are considered to be representative of the diverse rural conditions that can be found in Northeast Jiangxi province and in a much larger hilly area with rice-based production systems in southeast China (Kuiper et al., 2001). The three villages selected are Banqiao: in Yujiang County, Shangzhu in Guixi Cityl; and Gangyan in

---

[2] Their results show that education and household assets (land, durables) affect migration and local off-farm employment, but do not affect self-employment. Moreover, the (negative) impact of age is much smaller for self-employment.

[3] The research is a joint project of Nanjing Agricultural University, Wageningen University and the Institute of Social Studies, The Hague, financed by the Netherlands Ministry of Development Cooperation (SAIL program) and the EU (INCO program).

Yanshan County. The approximate location of the three villages is shown in Figure 11.1.

Banqiao is located in a hilly area. Farmers cultivate rice on terraced lowland and cash crops—particularly peanuts and fruit trees—on sloping land. Banqiao is located near a major national road, the prefecture capital, and a peanut wholesale market. The quality of the roads connecting its hamlets, however, is poor.

Shangzhu is located in a mountainous area with poor transportation infrastructure. All the hamlets in Shangzhu are located in the mountains with only footpaths connecting most of them. Rice is cultivated in terraces in the valleys and lower mountain ranges. The main cash crops are bamboo and bamboo shoots.

Figure 11.1 Location of the three sample counties

Gangyan is a very large village in terms of population and is located in a plains area. Rice fields are the most important crop, while vegetables are the main cash crop. Gangyan is very close to the county capital and an old, national road. The quality of the roads connecting the hamlets is good. Table 11.1 offers a brief description for each of the three villages.[4]

About 23 percent of the households were interviewed in each village, totaling 331 interviewed households: 54 in Banqiao; 109 in Shangzhu; and 168 in Gangyan. Each household was randomly selected and interviewed twice in August 2000 as well as the beginning of 2001. Collected data includes: the amount of labor time

---

[4] More information about the villages can be found in the village selection report (Kuiper et al., 2001).

spent on both agricultural and off-farm activities; agricultural versus non-agricultural income; demographic characteristics; land endowments; land renting, and assets, among other things.

Table 11.1 Description of the three villages

		Banqiao	Shangzhu	Gangyan
Location	Prefecture	Yingtan	Yingtan	Shangrao
	County	Yujiang	Guixi	Yanshan
	Township	Honghu	Tangwan	Wang-er
	Distance to market (km)[5]	10	remote	20
	Road quality	Poor	Very bad	Good
Population	Persons	900	2028	3200
	Households	220	472	730
	Hamlets	4	16	7
Land	Farmland/capita (mu)	1.89	1.36	1.21
	Paddyland/capita (mu)	1.37	0.16	1.18
	Dryland/capita (mu)	0.56	0.20	0.03
	Upland/total land	60-70%	97%	'plain'
Agricultural production	Main crops	Rice, peanuts, fruit trees	Rice, bamboo, bamboo shoots	Rice, vegetables
	Irrigation condition	Irrigated	Rain-fed or irrigated with conserved water	Irrigated

Source: Kuiper et al. (2001).

4 Off-farm Activities Participation in the Research Areas

In the household survey, local agricultural employment, local non-agricultural employment, self-employment and (temporary) migration inside China are distinguished as the main types of off-farm activities. Local agricultural employment consists of crops harvesting, rice transplanting, bamboo shoots digging, etc. Local non-agricultural employment comprises wood (bamboo) processing, house building, teaching, etc. Self-employment includes shop-keeping, small handcraft making and selling, transportation, etc. We define household members working off-farm and not living together with other household members as migrants. Most migrants (89 percent) work outside their counties and even their provinces (81 percent), but they are still considered as household members because they still keep close contacts with the other household members living inside the village and usually send income back.

Of all the surveyed households, 82 percent had at least one member participating

---

[5] Distance refers to the hamlet where the village committee office is located; for other hamlets the distance is usually larger, particularly in Shangzhu.

in off-farm employment in the year 2000, as can be seen from Table 11.2. In Gangyan village, the participation rate was as high as 90 percent. In Banqiao and Shangzhu, it was 72 and 74 percent, respectively. Thirty percent of the households in the three villages had one member involved in off-farm employment, whereas 53 percent had two or more such members.

The involvement in different sub-categories of off-farm activities in 2000 is summarized in Table 11.2. Agricultural off-farm employment is more important in Shangzhu (with 19 percent of the household involved), the remote village, than in the other two villages. Around 24 percent of the households in the three villages have members who participated in local non-agricultural employment. Only 13 percent of the households were involved in self-employment activities in the three villages.

Table 11.2 Percentages of households with members involved in different types of off-farm activities in the three villages, 2000

	Banqiao	Shangzhu	Gangyan	Total
Agricultural employment	6	19	11	13
Non-agricultural employment	19	18	30	24
Self-employment	15	9	15	13
Migration	54	57	74	65
Total off-farm employment	74	72	90	82

Source: Calculated from the 2000 survey data.

Migration is the most important type of off-farm employment, with 65 percent of the households involved in it. There are important differences between the three villages in the participation in migration. In Gangyan village, 74 percent of the households were involved in migration in 2000, whereas in Banqiao this was only 54 percent, and in Shangzhu 57 percent. Non-agricultural employment was the second most important type of off-farm employment with 24 percent of all interviewed households participating in it. Again, participation was highest in the village of Gangyan—30 percent. Out of the households involved in migration in 2000, 35 percent had one member who migrated, 22 percent two members who migrated, and 7 percent three or more such members.

The average amount of time households had spent on off-farm activities, and the average income earned through off-farm activities are presented in Table 11.3. On average, households had spent more time on migration than any other type of off-farm activity. A limited amount of time is spent on agricultural employment. For Shangzhu, the remote village, the time spent on agricultural employment is much greater than the other two villages. Households in Banqiao village spent about 50 percent more time on self-employment than households in the other two villages. This is probably due to the easy access to product markets in this village. For the other types of off-farm employment, there are only small differences between villages in the average time that household spent on them. Within the villages, however, there are large differences amongst households in regard to the amount of time spent on each type of off-farm activity.

Table 11.3 Average hours spent and income obtained from off-farm activities per participating household

Activity	Banqiao	Shangzhu	Gangyan	Average
Agricultural employment ($n=42$)				
Time spent (hours)	32.0	333	98.3	211
Income (*Yuan*)	66.7	992	337	645
Wage rate (*Yuan*)[6]	2.08	2.76	3.26	2.93
Non-farm local employment ($n=80$)				
Time spent (hours)	1243	1472	1384	1389
Income (*Yuan*)	2999	2514	3111	2916
Wage rate (*Yuan*)	2.41	2.36	2.48	2.44
Self-employment ($n=44$)				
Time spent (hours)	3356	2366	2196	2446
Income (*Yuan*)	6038	2503	2495	2851
Return per hour (*Yuan*)	1.19	1.87	2.88	2.46
Migration ($n=215$)				
Time spent (hours)	3287	3421	3360	3368
Remittances (*Yuan*)	1859	1472	2918	2340
Remittances per hour (*Yuan*)	0.39	0.41	0.89	0.68
All off-farm activities ($n=246$)				
Time spent (hours)	2489	2664	2732	2678
Total income (*Yuan*)	4014	2977	4469	3995
Income per hour (*Yuan*)	0.71	1.06	1.48	1.26
Percentage of time in total (%)	38	41	40	40
Percentage of income in total (%)	37	49	46	46

Source: Calculated from the 2000 survey data.

Hourly income for all four types of off-farm employment are highest in Gangyan, the village with the highest participation rate in off-farm employment. For migration and self-employment in particular, income is much more for households in Gangyan than anywhere else. Rather surprisingly, the average wage rate for agricultural employment in the three villages is higher than hourly income from the other three

---

[6] Hourly wages and incomes per hour are calculated from household data. The results will differ from those obtained by dividing wages (incomes) by time spent on an activity at the village level when the wage rate (income per hour) and the time spent on an activity are correlated (see e.g. Heerink 1994: section 2.2.6).

types of off-farm employment. This type of employment is mainly carried out during peak seasons and is rather intensive. Moreover, in some cases it refers to the simultaneous renting out of oxen and labor. Therefore, the wage rate of agricultural employment also includes the rent for oxen in these cases. Average income from migration is lower than that of the other three types of off-farm employment. This income refers only to the remittances sent to the household members in the village and thereby excludes consumed or saved earnings sent from home by the migrant.

Although hourly income from off-farm employment is highest in the village of Gangyan, the share of income obtained from off-farm activities is highest in Shangzhu. The reason for this is that agricultural income in Shangzhu, the remote village, is significantly less than that of Gangyan or Banqiao.[7] As a result, off-farm income contributes 49 percent of the income for Shangshu households involved in off-farm employment, 46 percent in Gangyan, and only 37 percent in Banqiao.

5 Econometric Model Specification and Estimation

5.1 Model Specification

The model that will be used for the regression analyses explains participation decisions through an individual's characteristics, the available resources of the individual's household, and local factors. To examine whether individual characteristics, household resources, and local factors perform the same across different types of off-farm activities, we will estimate the model separately for each of the four types of off-farm activities distinguished in the survey.

We use a multinomial logit model to examine off-farm activities participation of individual household members. The model is specified as:

$$Y_i = c_i + c_{1i}X_1 + c_{2i}X_2 + c_{3i}X_3 + c_{4i}X_4 + c_{5i}X_5 + \varepsilon_i,$$

where
Y_i = polychotomous variable representing participation of an individual in off-farm activity type i
X_1 = (column vector of) demographic and human capital characteristics of the individual;
X_2 = (column vector of) household resources;
X_3 = (column vector of) social capital resources of a household;
X_4 = (column vector of) local institutions;
X_5 = (column vector of) village characteristics;
$c_{0i}, c_{1i}, c_{2i}, c_{3i}, c_{4i}, c_{5i}$ = (row vectors of) coefficients to be estimated;
ε_i = error term with standard properties

---

[7] Incomes per capita are 1,720 *yuan* in Banqiao, 1,042 *yuan* in Shangzhu, and 1,854 *yuan* in Gangyan respectively for the households in our sample.

The dependent variable is a polychotomous variable that equals 0 if a labor force member does not participate in off-farm employment, 1 for agricultural employment, 2 for non-agricultural employment, 3 for self-employment, and 4 for migration. Each set of explanatory variables may consist of one or more variables. Only "push" factors are included in the model. No information is available on "pull" factors in our data set. Table 11.4 gives an overview of the definitions and sample statistics of the variables that are used in the regressions.

Table 11.4 Variable definitions and sample statistics

	Independent variables	Variable definitions	Mean	S. D.	Min.	Max.
X_1	Age	Age	37.2	13.4	17	66
	Education	Number of schooling years	5.02	2.99	0	16
	Gender	Gender of individual member (1= male)	0.52	0.50	0	1
X_2	Children	Number of children (aged 0-7) in household	0.26	0.50	0	3
	Elderly	Number of elderly (aged 65+) in household	0.21	0.46	0	2
	Labor	Number of laborers in household	3.45	1.29	1	11
	Irrigated	Contracted irrigated land area (in mu)	5.60	2.12	1	15
	Dryland	Contracted dry land area (in mu)	0.47	0.63	0	5
	Forest	Contracted forest land area (in mu)	1.45	2.78	0	15
	Durables	Current value of total durables (in *Yuan*)	1451.1	2060.2	-642.8	16762.5
X_3	Social	Social capital dummy variable (1= link outside province)	0.56	0.50	0	1
X_4	Renting	Land rent dummy variable (1= household rents out land)	0.09	0.29	0	1
X_5	Banqiao	Village dummy variable (1= Banqiao)	-	-	0	1
	Gangyan	Village dummy variable (1= Gangyan)	-	-	0	1

Table 11.5 gives the expected sign of each explanatory variable for each equation. Five demographic and human capital variables are distinguished. The first variable listed in the table is the age of the individual. Younger individuals are more likely to be involved in migration because they often do not have their own family to care for. Older people are more likely to be involved in local off-farm employment, which can more easily be combined with living in the village. Moreover, they are likely to have more experience and contacts that are relevant to find local off-farm jobs. The squared term is added to the equation to account for nonlinearities in the impact of age. Education can play a role in obtaining job information. Moreover, people with higher education are usually more productive and thereby have better opportunities to find off-farm employment—except for agricultural employment, where education generally plays a minor role) . Given the age and education level of an individual, males are more likely to be involved in off-farm employment than females due to women's unequal access to the off-farm workforce and the traditional role of women

in a family. Gender—measured by a dummy variable that equals 1 for males—is therefore expected to have a positive impact.

Table 11.5 Expected signs for explanatory variables in the models

Independent variables		Expected signs			
		Agricultural employment	Non-farm employment	Self-employment	Migration
X_1	Age	+	+	+	-
	Age^2	-/+	-/+	-/+	-/+
	Education	-/+	+	+	+
	Gender	+	+	+	+
X_2	Children	-/+	-/+	-/+	-/+
	Elderly	-/+	-/+	-/+	-/+
	Labor	+	+	+	+
	Irrigated	-	-	-	-
	Dryland	-	-	-/+	-/+
	Forest	-	-	-/+	-/+
	Durables	-	-/+	-/+	-/+
X_3	Social	-	-	-	+
X_4	Renting	+	+	+	+
X_5	Banqiao	-	+	+	+
	Gangyan	-	+	+	+

Participation in off-farm employment depends on the characteristics of not only the individual in question but probably that individual's household as well. The number of dependents—children and elderly—in a household can have mixed effects on off-farm participation. Typically, more dependents in a household require more income to satisfy their food and other needs. On the other hand, more dependents also mean that more time is needed to take care of them, making less time available for other household members to work off-farm. Elderly people, however, may take care of the young children in a family, which provides the parents with the opportunity to work either on-farm or off-farm. Individuals who are 16 to 65 years old, healthy, and either working or searching for employment are defined as labor force members. A large number of labor force members within a household is expected to increase the likelihood for each of them to work off-farm, considering the limited opportunities for expanding farm production.

A large area of irrigated land contracted by a household from the village group or committee is expected to reduce the need for working off-farm. The same holds for forests and dry land, which are mostly used for growing cash crops and bamboo. These cash income sources can be important for either financing migration that may be very costly in the initial stage or starting a private business. The net impact of dry land and forests on migration and self-employment can therefore be negative—reduced land scarcity—as well as positive—increased cash availability.

The last household characteristic included in the model is the current value of total durables of a household. According to the theoretical framework presented in Section 2, poor households are more eager to find ways of obtaining extra income, while rich households can finance their migration more easily. Besides, asset-rich households have more opportunities for starting their own business as well as gaining access to local non-farm employment. Therefore, we expect a negative impact of asset position on off-farm agricultural employment—the poverty effect—whereas the impact on migration, self-employment, and local non-agricultural employment is indeterminate.

Personal relationships (*guangxi*) and other types of social capital may play an important role in obtaining, like off-farm employment in China. It is not easy to measure, however. In our data set we have only limited information that can be used for that purpose. To measure social capital for individuals, we define a dummy variable that equals 1 if other household members are working outside the province, or when other relatives who live outside the province send moneyld. It is different from the definition used by Zhao (2001b), who measured social capital as the number of earlier migrants from a village. Because our observations come from three villages only, we cannot apply a similar definition. Instead, our definition focuses on kinship relations at the household level, which are quite relevant for rural China. Relatives and friends play important roles in assisting finding a job for other individuals, including transferring job information to migrants, providing temporary accommodations, food, and so on (Zhao, 2000; Meng, 2000; Murphy, 2000; Cook, 1998). Unfortunately no data are available in our data set on connections to local policymakers, which may play a role in gaining access to local wage employment (Yao, 1999; Cook, 1999).

Local institutions such as land markets may affect incentives for off-farm employment. Renting out land, defined as a dummy variable in our model, is expected to facilitate off-farm employment, especially migration. Having the land cultivated is a very important precondition for households who intend to migrate because they may lose the use rights of contracted land that is not cultivated from the village committee. Moreover, the renting out of land reduces the amount available for on-farm production and increases the cash available for initial migration and self-employment.

Finally, two dummy variables for Banqiao and Gangyan village are added to the model to control for unobserved factors that systematically differ between the three villages. For example, poor access to information and high transportation costs in Shangzhu, the remote village, are likely to reduce the possibilities for migration and local off-farm employment for its inhabitants.

5.2 Estimation Results

Estimation results for participation decisions in the four types of off-farm activities are presented in Table 11.6. To examine the effect of distinguishing between different types of off-farm employment, regression results for off-farm employment as a whole are presented in the last column for comparison. The estimated equations perform satisfactory in terms of goodness of fit. We will first discuss the results for each of the four types of off-farm employment and then compare the conclusions with those for off-farm employment as a whole.

First, the results for demographic and human capital characteristics show that age has a significant impact on the first two employment types. For agricultural employment and local non-farm employment, age has a positive sign while the lifecycle effects (age square) are all negative. These results are consistent with those of Zhang et al. (2002) and Kung and Lee (2001). They mean that, up to a certain age, older individuals are more likely to work in these two types of off-farm employment than younger persons. The age at which off-farm employment participation is at its maximum (the 'turning point') is 39 years for agricultural employment and 35 years for local non-agricultural employment. The coefficient for age in the equation for migration is negative, as expected, but surprisingly it does not differ significantly from zero. Probably this is caused by the high correlation between age and the squared age term. The latter variable also has a negative—but not statistically significant—coefficient.

Education is found to have a significant positive effect on migration—as is commonly found in migration studies—but education does not affect self-employment and local wage employment. For self-employment, this finding is consistent with the results obtained by de Brauw et al. (2002) in an 'almost nationally representative sample in six provinces,' but for local wage employment, a positive impact of education was found in their study. Our results suggest that the role of education in gaining access to local off-farm employment is probably less important in our, relatively poor, research area than in more developed areas in China. For agricultural off-farm employment we find a negative impact of education, indicating that low-educated people who want to work off-farm tend to opt for this type of off-farm employment.

Table 11.6 Regression results of individual participation in four different types of off-farm activities (multinomial logistic regression) and in total off-farm employment (probit analysis)

	Agricultural employment		Non-agricultural employment		Self-employment		Migration		Off-farm participation	
			Dependent variable: individual off-farm activities participation							
	Coef.	z	Coef.	z	Coef.	z	Coef.	z	Coef.	z
No. of Observations			1003						1003	
Demographic and human capital characteristics										
Age	0.47***	3.07	0.21**	2.22	0.14	1.34	-0.06	-1.20	-0.04*	-1.86
Age²	-0.006***	-3.30	-0.003**	-2.48	-0.002	-1.59	-0.000	-0.70	-0.000	-0.01
Education	-0.16*	-1.80	0.08	1.25	0.07	0.95	0.14***	3.94	0.08***	4.45
Gender	2.94***	4.98	1.95***	4.78	1.43***	3.17	1.08***	5.93	0.65***	6.86
Household resources										
Children	0.20	0.51	-0.41	-1.11	-0.39	-0.94	-0.40**	-2.41	-0.27***	-2.94
Elderly	0.47	1.30	-0.04	-0.09	0.03	0.07	0.40**	2.11	0.13	1.32
Labor	-0.40	-1.97	-0.10	-0.62	0.10	0.54	0.15*	1.92	0.08*	1.93
Irrigated	0.08	0.76	-0.13	-1.42	-0.13	-1.16	-0.08*	-1.79	-0.05**	-1.58
Dryland	0.43	1.54	-0.37	-0.97	0.07	0.24	0.07	0.46	0.05	0.58
Forest	-0.02	-0.21	-0.29**	-2.19	-0.02	-0.26	0.01	0.21	-0.02	-0.88
ln(Durables)	-0.26*	-1.76	0.04	0.49	0.03	0.24	-0.02	-0.47	0.02	0.70
Social capital										
Social	0.27	0.48	-0.10	-0.27	-0.04	-0.08	-0.16	-0.80	-0.10	-0.95
Local institutions										
Renting	0.62	0.65	-0.88	-0.83	-0.42	-0.40	1.22***	4.04	0.50***	3.10
Village dummies										
Banqiao	-1.17	-1.61	-0.92	-1.50	0.25	0.40	-0.30	-0.92	-0.17	-1.01
Gangyan	-0.51	-1.07	0.14	0.33	0.12	0.51	0.61***	3.01	0.33**	2.83
Constant	-10.7***	-3.27	-5.70**	-2.85	-5.80**	-2.52	0.40	0.41	0.26	0.53
LR chi²			504.3***						326.5***	
Pseudo R²			0.24						0.24	

Notes: 1. * Denotes statistically significant at 10% level; 2. ** Denotes statistically significant at 5% level; 3. *** Denotes statistically significant at 1% level.

The gender dummy variable has a significant and positive impact for all four types of off-farm employment, showing that males have a higher likelihood to participate in off-farm employment than females. This is consistent with many studies indicating that women take major responsibility in taking care of children and household affairs in rural China (Kung and Lee, 2001; Zhang et al., 2002; Zhao, 2001a). The estimated coefficients for agricultural and local non-agricultural employment in our regression analyses are two to three times larger than that of migration. Hence, the bias against women is much larger in local employment than in migration.

Household characteristics also have some significant effects on the off-farm participation decisions of individuals. The number of young children has a statistically significant negative impact on migration. Because the presence of young children in a household is difficult to combine with non-local work, it limits migration but not the other types of off-farm employment. Another interesting finding is that the presence of older people in a household stimulates migration but not the other types of off-farm employment. In many Chinese families, children are now raised to a large extent by their grandparents because both parents would have full-time jobs. The results indicate that the presence of grandparents makes it easier to find off-farm employment through migration.

The number of laborers in a household has a significantly positive impact on migration and a significantly negative impact on agricultural off-farm employment. Rural households need a certain minimum input of labor in on-farm agricultural activities in order to cultivate the (little) land they do have and harvest the crops. Local wage employment and self-employment can relatively easy be combined with such agricultural activities, but not migration. An increase in a household's labor force size frees more members from such agricultural activities and allows them to search for off-farm employment in other provinces. The negative impact of the labor force size on off-farm agricultural employment suggests that some of these migrating household members were previously involved in off-farm agricultural activities.

Different types of contracted land may play different roles for a household. They are treated as not only production factors but sources of cash and credit as well. Irrigated land mainly produces rice, while dry land and forests produce cash crops and wood products. The regression results indicate that households with a relatively large area of irrigated land are less likely to be involved in migration but not in the other three types of off-farm employment. Land scarcity, therefore, seems to play an important role in migration decisions.

The sizes of dry land and forests do not have a statistically significant impact on the four types of non-farm employment, except for the negative impact of forests on non-agricultural employment. This finding suggests that increased land availability dampens the "push" effects from increased cash availability and improved access to credit—even exceeding the "push" effect in the case of forests and non-agricultural employment.

Household wealth is found to have a significantly negative impact on agricultural employment. This result thereby confirms the finding of Rozelle et al. (1999) that poor households are eager to find alternative sources of income. In our research area, however, poor households can only access agricultural employment, not any of the other three types of off-farm employment.

The network variable is not significant for all four types of off-farm employment. As discussed above, it is defined as a dummy variable that equals 1 if other household members are working outside the province, or if other relatives who live outside the province send money to the household. On the one hand, the presence of kinship relationships at the household level is expected to stimulate migration, but on the other hand, when one or more household members are already involved in migration—or when relatives send money to the household—the need for other household members to search off-farm employment lessens. These results are consistent with those of Kung and Lee (2001) who found that social networks do not assist in obtaining non-farm employment because non-farm employment is primarily allocated by means of market mechanisms.

The renting out of land has a significantly positive impact on migration. Households involved in renting agricultural land to other households seem to opt for the type of off-farm employment that cannot be combined with working on the farm and that reduces household food consumption. The impact on the other three types of off-farm employment does not differ significantly from zero.

As discussed in Section 4, households in the village of Shangzhu—the remote village—rely more on agricultural off-farm employment than households in the other two villages, whereas households in Gangyan—the plains-area village—are more involved in migration than the households in the two other villages.

The estimated coefficients for the village-level dummy variables in the agricultural employment equation are insignificant for both Banqiao and Gangyan. This means that the difference in agricultural employment between Shangzhu and the other two villages is largely explained from differences between these villages in the factors specified in the model. Differences in village-specific factors—market access, economic development, geography—do not have a significant effect. In the migration equation, however, the estimated coefficient for the Gangyan dummy variable is positive and significantly different from zero. This implies that village-level factors seem to contribute positively to the relatively high migration rate in Gangyan village in addition to the other factors specified in the model.

For reasons of comparison, the results of a probit analysis for participation in off-farm employment as a whole are shown in the last column of Table 11.6. They confirm that education, male gender, labor force size, the renting out of land, and village-level factors for Gangyan have a significant positive impact on off-farm employment, while the presence of children and the size of irrigated land have a significantly negative effect.

Such an aggregate analysis, however, misses some valuable insights that can be gained from a disaggregated analysis, such as the much larger gender bias for the two types of local wage employment and the finding that education and the renting out of land stimulate only migration and not the other types of non-farm employment, while the presence of children in a household constrains only migration.

Moreover, the results of the aggregate analysis suggest that the presence of elderly people in a household does not affect off-farm employment decisions and that age is negatively related to off-farm employment even at young ages. Therefore, the results show that empirical analyses of the factors that drive participation in off-farm employment can provide a more adequate and far richer picture when a distinction is made between relevant sub-categories of off-farm employment.

6 Conclusions

In this chapter, we analyzed the differences between four sub-categories of off-farm employment—agricultural employment, local non-agricultural employment, self-employment, and migration—in three villages within the Jiangxi province. Migration is the most important type of off-farm employment in these villages in terms of participation rates and time spent on it, but the contribution of migrant remittances to household income is smaller than the income earned from self-employment or local non-farm employment (Tables 11.2 and 11.3). Agricultural employment is a minor activity both in terms of time spent on it and its contribution to household income.

Our empirical analysis of the factors driving the participation in each of the four types of off-farm employment (Table 11.6) reveals that the presence of young children in a household restrains any participation in migration but not in the other types of off-farm employment, where working and child care can more easily be combined. The presence of elderly people in a household stimulates migration because elderly people frequently take care of small children in Chinese society. Education has a positive impact on migration only. Hence, education plays a negligible role in gaining access to local off-farm employment in our research area. We further find that the difference between males and females in access to off-farm employment is much larger for both agricultural employment and local non-agricultural employment than it is for migration.

Households with few assets are more involved in agricultural employment probably because poor households are more eager to find additional income sources but do not have access to the other types of off-farm employment. When farmers are able to rent their land out to other farmers, they tend to opt for migration. Land scarce farmers who cannot rent their land to others opt for local wage employment or self-employment in order not to run the risk of losing their land rights.

Given the prevalence of surplus labor in rural areas and the high land scarcity, improving off-farm employment opportunities will be an important way to increase the income of rural households, particularly in poor areas in west China and other parts.

The Chinese government recognizes that the population increase in Shanghai, Beijing, and other mega-cities in China is approaching its limits and realizes that as many future off-farm income-earning opportunities for rural households should be created within each region or province. In other words, local wage employment and self-employment will be stimulated more in the near future. Such a policy should not only focus on creating new employment opportunities in regions where out-migration is predominant, but take individual preferences for the different types of off-farm employment into account as well.

The results of our regressions analyses indicate that demographic factors play an important role in this respect. The trend towards smaller rural families with fewer young children—resulting from China's population policy—as well as the gradual aging of China's population both stimulate migration to other provinces. We further find that the gender bias in local wage employment is much larger than in migration and that education only stimulates migration. Policies to promote rural off-farm employment in relatively poor regions, such as our research area, should thereby focus on creating more employment opportunities for females and educated people in order to reduce the incentives for migration to other provinces.

Land distribution policy may also play a role in this respect. Households with fewer land resources participate more in migration or local non-agricultural employment. The question may therefore be raised as to whether the distribution of land use rights should continue to be based on household—and/or labor force—sizes. A land distribution policy that would take into account a household's comparative advantage in agricultural production or off-farm income-earning opportunities may be more efficient and contribute to equity as well. Reduced land availability will stimulate households with a comparative advantage in off-farm employment to exploit these advantages and reduce their agricultural activities. In areas with sufficient local off-farm employment opportunities for women and educated people, such households are likely to opt for local employment opportunities and not migration.

References

Barrett, C. and Reardon, T., 'Asset, Activity, and Income Diversification Among African Agriculturalists: Some Practical Issues' (Working Paper of Food and Agricultural Organization of the United Nations (FAO), No. ESA/02-05, 2000).

Brandt, L., Huang, J., Li, G. and Rozelle, S., 'Land Rights in China: Facts Fictions and Issues', *China Journal*, Vol. 47 (2002): 67-97.

Cook, S., 'Work, Wealth and Power in Agriculture: Do Political Connections Affect Returns to Household Labor', in A.G. Walder (eds), *Zouping in Transition: The Process of Reform in Rural North China* (Cambridge, Mass: Harvard University Press 1998).

———, 'Surplus Labour and Productivity in Chinese Agriculture: Evidence from Household Survey Data', *The Journal of Development Studies*, Vol. 35(3) (1999): 16-44.

De Brauw, A., Huang, J., Rozelle, S., Zhang, L. and Zhang, Y., 'The Evolution of China's Rural Labor Markets during the Reforms', *Journal of Comparative Economics*, Vol. 30(2) (2002): 329-353.

De Brauw, A., Taylor, J. E. and Rozelle, S., 'Migration and Source Communities: A New

Economics of Migration Perspective From China', *Economic Development and cultural Change,* Vol. 52(1) (2003): 75-101.

Du, Y,. 'Study on Factors Influencing Farm Household Participation in Off-farm Activities in Poor Rural Area', *Agricultural Technical Economics* (in Chinese), No. 4 (1999): 32-36.

————, 'Impact of Shadow Price of Labor on Labor hourly Supply', *China Rural Survey* (in Chinese), No. 5 (2000): 36-42.

Gale, F., 'How Many Nonfarm Jobs in Rural China? Evidence From China's Agricultural Census' (Paper presented at WCC conference U.S. and China, 2002).

Giles, J., 'Off-farm Labor Markets and Household Risk-coping' (Paper presented at WCC conference U.S. and China, Washington. D.C., April 2002).

Hare, D., '"Push" versus "Pull" Factors in Migration Outflows and Returns: Determinants of Migration Status and Spell Duration among China's Rural Population', *The Journal of Development Studies*, Vol. 35(3) (1999): 45-72.

Heerink, N., 'Population Growth, Income Distribution, and Economic Development – Theory, Methodology, and Empirical Results' (Berlin, New York: Springer-Verlag, 1994).

Kochar, A., 'Smoothing Consumption by Smoothing Income: Hours-of-Work Responses to Idiosyncratic Agricultural Shocks in Rural India', *Review of Economics and Statistics*, Vol. 81(1) (1999): 50-61.

Kuiper, M., Heerink, N., Tan, S., Ren, Q. and Shi, X., Report of Village Selection for the Three Village Survey (Department of Development Economics, Wageningen University, The Netherlands, 2001).

Kung, J.K., 'The Evolution of Property Rights in Village Enterprises: The Case of Wuxi County', in Oi, J.C. and A.G. Walder (eds), *Property Rights and Economic Reform in China* (Stanford, CA: Stanford Univ. Press, 1999).

————, 'Off-farm Labor Markets and the Emergence of Land Rental Markets in Rural China', *Journal of Comparative Economics*, Vol., 30(2) (2002): 395-414.

Kung, J.K.S. and Lee, Y., 'So What If There Is Income Inequality: The Distributive Consequences of Nonfarm Employment in Rural China', *Economic Development and Culture Change*, Vol. 50(1) (2001): 19-46.

Kung, J. and Liu, S., 'Farmer's Preferences Regarding Ownership and Land Tenure in Post-Mao China: Unexpected Evidence from Eight Countries', *The China Journal*, No. 38 (1997): 33-63.

Liu, S., Carter, M. and Yao, Y., 'Dimensions and Diversity of Property Rights in Rural China: Dilemmas on the Road to Further Reform', *World Development*, Vol. 26 (1998): 1789-1806.

Lohmar, B., Carter, C. and Rozelle, S., 'Grain Quota Policies and Household Labor Allocation in China' (Paper presented at the Annual Meetings of the American Agricultural Economics Association, Chicago, Illinois, July 31- August 3, 2000).

Meng, X., *Labor Market Reform in China* (Cambridge: Cambridge University Press, 2000).

Murphy, R., 'Migration and Inter-household Inequality: Observation from Wenzi County, Jiangxi', *The China Quarterly*, Vol. 164 (2000): 965-982.

Reardon, T., 'Using Evidence of Household Income Diversification to Inform Study of the Rural No-farm Labor Market in African', *World Development*, Vol. 25(5) (1997): 735-748.

Reardon, T., Julio, B. and Escobar, G, 'Rural Nonfarm Employment and Incomes in Latin American: Overview and Policy Implications', *World Development*, Vol. 29(3) (2001): 395-409.

Rose, E., 'Ex Ante and Ex Post Labor Supply Response to Risk in a Low-Income Area', *Journal of Development Economics*, Vol. 64(2) (2001): 371-88.

Rozelle, S., Taylor, J. E. and de Brauw, A., 'Migration, Remittances, and Productivity in China', *American Economic Review*, Vol. 89(2) (1999): 287-291.

Somwaru, A., Diao, X., Gale, F. and Tuan, F., 'China's Employment and Rural Migration' (selected paper, American Agricultural Economics Association Meeting, Chicago, Illinois, August 5-8 2001).

Stark, O., *The Migration of Labor* (Cambridge, MA: Blackwell, 1991).

Taylor, J. E. and Martin, P. L., 'Human Capital: Migration and Rural Population Change', in G Rausser and B. Gardner (eds), *Handbook of Agricultural Economics* (New York: Elsevier, 2001).

Todaro, M., 'A Model of Labor Migration and Urban Unemployment in Less Developed Countries', *The American Economic Review*, Vol. 59(1) (1969): 138-148.

Wu, X., Qi, M. and Feng, X., 'Rural Migrants Flow Mechanisms', *China Population Science* (in Chinese), No. 6 (2003).

Yao, Y., 'Rural Industry and Labor Market Integration in Eastern China', *Journal of Development Economics*, Vol. 59 (1999): 463-496.

Zhang, L., Huang, J. and Rozelle, S., 'Employment, Emerging Labor Markets, and the Role of Education in Rural China', *China Economic Review*, Vol. 13 (2002): 313-328.

Zhang, X. and Li, G, 'Does Guanxi Matter in Non-farm Employment' (EPTD Discussion Paper No. 74, Wahington, D.C.: International Food Policy Research Institute, 2001).

Zhao, S., 'Organizational Characteristics of Rural Labor Mobility in China', in L. A. West and Y. Zhao (eds), *Rural Labor Flows in China* (Berkeley: Institute of East Asian Studies, University of California, 2000).

Zhao, Y., 'Causes and Consequences of Return Migration: Recent Evidence from China' (Working Paper of China Center for Economic Research, Beijing University, 2001a).

————, 'The Role of Migrant Networks In labor Migration: The Case of China' (Paper presented at the International Conference on Urbanization in China, Xiamen, June 2001b).

Zhong, Z., 'Migration, Labor Market Flexibility, and Wage Determination in China-A Review' (Working paper of China Center for Economic Research, Beijing University 2003).

Zhu, N., 'The Impact of Income Gap on Migration Decisions in China', *China Economic Review*, Vol. 13 (2002): 213-230.

[2004]

Chapter 12

Urban-Rural Hukou Differentials in China's Labor Relations

Xianguo Yao[*]
Puqing Lai

1 Introduction

In the past two decades, China's economic reform has gained tremendous achievements, and its GDP has kept an annual growth rate of 9 percent. Numerous enterprises, especially non-state-owned enterprises, are emerging in coastal areas, and enormous labor forces are employed in various enterprises. Up to 2002, there were more than 8 millions industrial and service enterprises in China, which had employed about 364 million employees (National Statistic Bureau, 2002). The labor relations between employers and employees are becoming increasingly important and, at the same time, are experiencing some radical changes.

For example, the previous labor relations under the planned system have changed to market-oriented labor relations. Some studies (Guest, 1998; Hill *et al*, 2000) indicate that labor relations in China are converting to those of western industrial countries in many aspects, such as inequalities in labor-capital negotiation, job instability, incompleteness of labor contracts, and so on.

A case study (Cooke, 2002) on two privatized enterprises also shows that the ownership change in the state-owned enterprises (SOEs) has brought negative results to workers and the gulf between emerging management practices and the interests of workers is rapidly widening.

Furthermore, the urban-rural dual structure in Chinese economy makes the labor relations between employers and employees more complex and diversified. In China's labor market, there are not only various enterprises with different ownerships, but also two types of workers with different identities. According to a sociological research, the employment of rural workers is restricted within informal sectors and plagued with various labor relation problems (Li and Zhuang, 2002).

[*] The authors gratefully acknowledge the financial support of the National Natural Science Foundation of China (No. 70233003). They thank Prof. Zhang Junsen, Prof. Li Shi, and Dr. Li Hongbin for their comments and suggestions. The paper has been published in Economic Research Journal, Issue 7, 2004, in Chinese, and this is the revised version.

It can be found very often that in the same enterprise, two types of workers are treated differently just because of their *hukou* status. For example, the heavier, dirtier, and shabbier jobs are always assigned to workers with rural *hukou*, and those rural workers have no security in their positions. They can be dismissed at any moment. Furthermore, urban workers have social welfare, more or less, but their rural counterparts have almost nothing. However, those kinds of unequal treatment are not resulted from productivity-related differences among workers but mostly from their *hukou* differences.

Unfortunately, until now, most studies on labor relation disparities between urban and rural workers in China are basically qualitative, and the empirical studies, if anything, are limited to wage gaps and occupational segregation. Meng and Zhang (2001) adopted the survey data of Shanghai to analyze the extent of the wage gaps and occupational segregation between rural migrant workers and urban resident workers, and they found significant differences in wage and occupational attainment.

Another study (Cai et al., 2002) reveals that most wage gaps between rural and urban workers cannot be explained by productivity-related differences, implying that urban workers are favorably treated while their rural counterparts are discriminated against. However, economic welfare in employment lies not only in wage earnings and occupational attainment but also in other factors such as working conditions, job stability, and other non-wage welfares, which should be considered together if researchers expect to better understand the welfare differences between two groups. Otherwise, the real economic welfare differences would undoubtedly be underestimated.

This chapter will adopt new empirical data to analyze urban-rural *hukou* disparities in several labor relation factors. Our strategy is to incorporate the Social Pension Insurance (SPI), Social Medical Insurance (SMI), Social Unemployment Insurance (SPI), the rate of signing labor contracts, union membership, and so on into the usual wage disparity analysis. In this way, we can get a complete picture of the wage and non-wage disparities.

The chapter is organized as follows: in Section 2, we will present the data and outline the method of Blinder-Oaxaca decomposition. Section 3 presents the empirical results. Section 4 summarizes the findings and discusses their possible policy implications.

2 Data and Method

The data sets used here come from two surveys. The first is the Zhejiang Enterprises Survey (ZE), and the second is the Rural Floating Labor Force Survey (RFLF). The former is conducted by HongKong Chinese University and the College of Economics at Zhejiang University in late 2003, and the latter by the College of Economics at Zhejiang University in early 2004.

The questionnaires, both containing workers' individual information and enterprises' labor relations, are quite similar. The ZE survey samples come mainly from large- and medium-sized enterprises. The RFLF survey supplements the ZE survey by including employees from small-sized enterprises and informal sectors. Thus, the surveys provide a good foundation to analyze labor relations.

The ZE survey covers nine counties in Zhejiang province, 311 enterprises, and 568 employees who were randomly sampled from 79 enterprises. Among the 568 employees, 359 have urban *hukou* and the remaining 209 do not. The sample size of the RFLF survey is 319, among which 71 are workers with urban *hukou*, and the rest 248 are rural workers. In each survey, workers' basic individual information, family background, employment and income, and enterprises' labor relation factors (e.g. the pension, medical, and unemployment insurances, labor contract, union membership, training, promotion, and job-hopping intention) are provided.

Table 12.1 presents information on wage, working hours, social insurances, and other labor-related factors of the urban and rural workers in Zhejiang province. A notable gap exists between urban and rural workers.

Table 12.1 Labor relation status of urban and rural workers in Zhejiang, 2003

	Urban Workers		Rural Workers		Difference
	Mean	SD	Mean	SD	
Monthly wage	1,213.21	713.73	981.78	530.77	231.43
Weekly working hours	48.34	10.63	57.10	14.88	-8.76
Months of training	6.27	10.27	3.18	5.77	3.09
Dummy variables					
Pension insurance	0.81	0.40	0.39	0.49	0.42
Medical insurance	0.65	0.48	0.24	0.43	0.41
Unemployment insurance	0.52	0.50	0.08	0.28	0.44
Labor contracts	0.73	0.44	0.54	0.50	0.19
Union membership	0.55	0.50	0.17	0.37	0.38

First, rural workers work longer hours but earn less money. On average, rural workers work nearly nine hours more than their urban counterparts every week, but their average monthly income is 19 percent lower. And the hourly wage of rural workers is 30 percent less than that of urban workers.

Second, the urban-rural gaps of the three basic social insurances are even wider than that of wage. The percentage of the rural workers having SPI, SMI, and SUI are only 39, 24, and 8 percent, respectively. Gaps in the participating rates of the three social insurances between urban and rural workers are 42, 41, and 44 percentage points, respectively.

In addition, 73 percent of urban workers but only 54 percent of rural workers have signed formal labor contracts. Only 17 percent of rural workers join labor unions and the gap between the two groups amounts to 38 percentage points.

The urban-rural disparities in China's labor relations may be due to two factors. The first is the differences in individual productivity-related characteristics and the characteristics of enterprises. In China, a country that is undergoing transition, the enterprise characteristics, such as ownership and employment scale could be very important in the determination of labor relations. The second is non-productivity-related characteristics, such as race, gender, or in our case, *hukou* status, which also could affect the labor relation status. If equally productive individuals, even within the same enterprise, are treated differently simply because of their *hukou* status, that can be defined as discrimination.

Table 12.2 presents information on the individual characteristics of the two groups. As expected, urban workers are more educated. On average, they have 3.57 more years of schooling than rural workers. They are slightly older than rural workers and have 4.52 years longer of working experiences. By gender, about 65.7 percent of urban workers and 69.1 percent of rural workers are men.

Table 12.2 Summary statistics of human capital and enterprise characteristics

Continuous variables	Urban workers		Rural workers		Difference in mean
	Mean	SD	Mean	SD	
Age	32.99	9.85	30.95	8.72	2.04
Years of schooling	12.76	2.39	9.19	2.19	3.57
Experience	12.63	10.19	8.11	7.03	4.52
Employment scale	514.28	595.70	327.20	543.61	187.08
Dummy variables		percent	percent	Difference in percent	
Male		65.7	69.1	-3.4	
State-owned Enterprise		42.6	25.8	16.8	
Private enterprise		46.5	47.7	-1.2	
Foreign-invested enterprise		7.9	11.8	-3.9	
Individual enterprise		3.0	14.7	-11.7	

The statistics also show that 25.8 percent of rural workers and 42.6 percent of urban workers are employed by SOEs, while 14.7 percent of the rural workers and only 3 percent of the urban workers are employed by individual enterprises. Generally speaking, SOEs have more regular, more formal labor relations than individual enterprises, and the proportions of urban and rural workers working in private and foreign-invested enterprises are similar to this.

The above description of individual characteristics and the characteristics of enterprises does not provide a clear picture of how the differences in personal and enterprise features affect wage and non-wage welfares. Even if such information were clear, it would still be difficult to identify to what extent the differences in labor relation factors can be attributed to the differences in their individual and enterprise characteristics.

Blinder (1973) and Oaxaca (1973) developed similar decomposition approaches to decompose the wage disparities into components caused by two factors: a difference in productivity, and an "unexplained" component that is often referred to as discrimination. The Blinder-Oaxaca approach has been widely used in earning discrimination analyses. And this chapter will also adopt it to analyze the urban-rural disparities in major labor relation factors. The Blinder-Oaxaca decomposition of the wage disparity can be written as:

$$\bar{Y}^H - \bar{Y}^L = (\hat{\beta}_0^H - \hat{\beta}_0^L) + (\bar{X}^H - \bar{X}^L)\hat{\beta}^H + \bar{X}^L(\hat{\beta}^H - \hat{\beta}^L) \tag{1}$$

Here, Y is the level form or logarithm form of wage, X is independent variable vector, a bar over a variable denotes the mean value, and $\hat{\beta}$ are OLS estimated parameters from the wage equation. The superscripts— H and L —denote high and low wage group. On the right hand side of the equation, the second item is attributable to different human capital or other productive characteristics, while the first as well as the third items are the unexplained wage disparities due to differences in intercepts and coefficients, which is often attributed to discrimination.

After a customary decomposition of wage disparities, this chapter will extend the Blinder-Oaxaca approach to analyze the urban-rural differences in social insurance participation, labor contract, and union membership. Unlike the wage variable, these non-wage variables are binary variables. Thus we will use linear probability model (LPM) to estimate the non-wage equation. The model is given as:

$$P(y = 1 \mid x) = \beta_0 + X\beta + u \tag{2}$$

Here P(Y=1) is the probability of individuals participating in social insurances, signing a labor contract, and joining a trade union. X is an independent variable, in our case, including education, experience, on-job training, gender, labor contract, union membership, employment scale, enterprise's ownership, and so on. The Blinder-Oaxaca approach requires the estimation of LPM equations for urban and rural workers separately and then subtract one group's estimation results from the other group's results; finally we get (3):

$$\bar{P}^u - \bar{P}^r = (\hat{\beta}_0^u - \hat{\beta}_0^r) + (\bar{X}^u - \bar{X}^r)\hat{\beta}^u + \bar{X}^r(\hat{\beta}^u - \hat{\beta}^r) \tag{3}$$

Here P denotes the probabilities of workers' having social insurances, having written labor contract or participating union. The superscripts—u and r—denote urban and rural workers, respectively. On the right hand side of the equation, the second item is attributable to different individual and enterprise's characteristics, and the first and the third items are unexplained differences due to *hukou* discrimination in labor relations.

It is worth nothing that the predicted probabilities of LPM may be over one or below zero, which may cause difficulties in decomposing the urban-rural differences. Fortunately, because the Blinder-Oaxaca approach only uses the mean values of independent variables to differential decomposition, that defect of LPM will not affect the final decomposed results.

3 Empirical Results and Discussion

3.1 Wage Determination

Wage is one of the key factors in labor relations, and the following empirical evidence will answer the question of whether there is wage discrimination between urban and rural workers. Based on the Mincer human capital earning equation, we add gender and on-job training as human capital explanatory variables, and labor contract, union membership, employment scale, and enterprise's ownership as enterprise characteristics explanatory variables.

Table 12.3 provides the results from the wage equation estimation of urban and rural workers. White's (1980) heteroscedasticity-robust standard errors were used to calculate t values. The results indicate that the return to education of urban and rural workers is 8.6 percent and 4.2 percent, respectively. This is a conspicuous gap between the two groups, which may have resulted from discriminations in human capital investments. Krueger (1963) argues that in a society, the dominant groups, in our case, the urban workers, possess more power to affect public decision-making in educational investments and cause educational inequality between urban and rural workers.

A recent study (Wang, 2003) confirms that the basic educational investments in rural area are far lower than that of urban area. For the rural population, an immediate consequence of the investment deficiency is the inferiority of educational quality, which may lead to future wage disparities between the two groups.

Work experience has a positive, but not statistically significant, impact on wage compensations for both groups. Gender is also an important factor of wage determination. In our sample male workers earn about 20 percent more than female workers, which might be an evidence of gender discrimination consistent with other studies (Liu, Meng and Zhang, 2000; Wei, 2004).

Unlike other wage determination studies in China's labor market, this chapter, for the first time, adds two dummy variables—labor contract and union membership, and the findings are very interesting. For rural workers, whether signing labor contracts or being a union member has little impact on their wage, while for urban workers both variables are economically and statistically significant.

Holding other factors constant, signing labor contracts enables urban workers to get a 27 percent wage rise. However, union membership has an unexpectedly negative impact. It is inconsistent with traditional union theory and might be related with the particular role of China's union, which we shall discuss later.

Table 12.3 Wage equation estimation results of urban and rural workers (OLS)

| | Urban workers | | Rural workers | |
	Coeff.	T-Ratio	Coeff.	T-Ratio
Years of schooling	0.086	6.34	0.042	3.38
Experience	0.011	1.19	0.022	1.77
Experience^2	-0.000	-0.12	-0.001	-1.74
On-job training	0.026	0.38	0.078	1.54
Dummy for male	0.186	3.72	0.201	3.65
Dummy for labor contract	0.270	4.56	0.068	1.21
Dummy for union membership	-0.123	-1.86	0.001	0.01
Log(employment scale)	-0.040	-1.49	0.013	0.60
Dummy for private enterprise	-0.351	-3.34	-0.001	-0.01
Dummy for foreign enterprise	-0.137	-0.89	0.113	0.85
Dummy for individual enterprise	0.169	0.54	0.053	0.37
Constant	0.713	2.77	0.542	2.49
Observation		291		330
R^2		0.286		0.119

In addition, the model has also taken into consideration whether different ownerships affect the wage level. The estimated results indicate that urban workers in SOEs (the control group) earn more money than those in private enterprises. For rural workers, there is no obvious wage gap between enterprises with different ownership, which implies that rural workers might have to face more fierce competition in the labor market than urban workers.

3.2 Social Insurances

It is an obligation for enterprises to provide social insurance, which is also an important part of labor relations. China's social welfare insurance systems was established in the 1990s, and the State Council of China has issued a series of policy documents, such as Trial Procedures for Childbirth Insurance for Enterprise Employees (1994), Trial Procedures for Industrial Injury Insurance for Enterprise Employees (1996), Decision on Establishing a Uniform Basic Pension Insurance System for Enterprise Employees (1997), Decision on Establishing a Basic Medical Insurance System for Urban Employees (1998), and Regulations on Unemployment Insurance (1999).

According to relevant policies, rural workers are also included in social insurance systems, and enterprises have obligations to provide all kinds of insurances for them. However, due to the regional segregation of China's current social insurance systems and the feeble bargaining power of rural workers on labor market, the social insurance discriminations against rural workers still exist. This chapter selects the representative SPI, SMI, and SUI to analyze the urban-rural differences in social insurances.

Table 12.4 presents the LPM estimation results of SPI, SMI, and SUI. For urban workers, one more year of schooling increases the SPI, SMI and SUI participating rates by 3.3, 3.7, and 3.6 percent, respectively, but for rural workers, education has little impact on SMI and SUI. It may be connected with the institutional segment in the urban-rural dual labor market, in which whether workers could enjoy social insurances or not depends basically on the workers' *hukou* status. Holding human capital variables and enterprise characteristics constant, gender has no economical and statistical significance to the three social insurance participation, implying there is wage discrimination but no social insurance discrimination against female workers.

Unlike wage determination, the model indicates that labor contracts and union membership are important to urban and rural workers' social insurances participation. On average, urban workers writing labor contracts would bring an increase of over 20 percent in the social insurances participation as well as over 10 percent in the union memberships. For rural workers, the marginal effects of labor contracts on SPI and SMI are about 0.13 and 0.16, and union membership has a significant impact only on SPI (about 0.14). What's more, both variables are not closely related to SUI for rural workers. The findings imply that labor contracts and labor unions are more important for urban workers than rural workers with regard to social insurances participation.

For urban workers, there is little difference among SOEs, private, and foreign-invested enterprises in SPI and SMI. However, rural workers are better treated in private and foreign-invested enterprises than in SOEs, probably because most rural workers in SOEs are temporary workers who are treated differently from the formal workers. In enterprises of individual ownership, both urban and rural workers are treated the worst, which is also consistent with the observable reality and can be explained intuitively.

3.3 Labor Contracts and Union Membership

China started to try out a labor contract system in mid-1980s and promoted it in the 1990s. According to the *Labor Law of the People's Republic of China* (1994), employers and employees should sign written labor contracts, with or without fixed periods. Now in China's labor market labor contracts have gradually become a legal proof of formal labor relations and an important channel for workers to guard their interests. In our sample, the rates of signing labor contracts among urban and rural workers are 73 and 54 percent, respectively. Compared with other labor relation factors, the urban-rural difference in labor contracts is relatively small.

According to official statistics, there are more than 120 million union members in China, including workers, teachers, officers, soldiers, and nearly 1 million grass roots unions. However, union's real influence in labor relation affairs may be negligible. Some researchers (White, 1996; Cooke, 2002) argue that China's unions only had limited impact on employees' welfare because of its institutional dependence. However, the study shows that union membership has a positive impact on social insurances. So it is noticeable that whether an urban-rural gap in union membership does exist and to what extent the difference in the union membership can be attributed to *hukou* discrimination.

Table 12.5 reports the LPM estimated results of labor contracts and union memberships for urban and rural workers. For urban workers, human capital variables such as years of schooling, experience, and training have positively significant impacts on labor contracts. For rural workers, the marginal utility of education on labor contracts is 4.7 percent, but the effects of experience and training are not significant.

Our findings reveal that the employment scale has economical and statistical significance in labor contracts for both urban and rural workers. The larger the enterprise's employment scale is, the better it handles labor contracts. In addition, workers in SOEs and foreign-invested enterprises have higher rates of signing labor contracts than those in private and individual enterprises, and in the four types of enterprises, the individual enterprise is the most unwarranted one.

With regard to the union memberships of workers, the results indicate that one more year of education boosts the participating rate of union membership by 3.8 percent for urban workers and by 1.9 percent for rural workers. The marginal utility of experience is 4.6 percent for the urban workers, but it's not significant for rural workers. Like social insurances, there is no conspicuous difference between male and female workers in labor contracts and union membership, suggesting gender discrimination on China's labor market lies mainly in wage determination, rather than other labor rights. The enterprises' characteristics also have considerable impact on the participating rate of union membership. The marginal utility of employment scale on union membership is about 10 and 4 percent for urban and rural workers, respectively. For enterprises with different ownerships, workers in SOEs have the highest probabilities in union participation, while workers in foreign-invested enterprises the lowest.

3.4 The Decomposition of Urban-rural Hukou Discriminations in Labor Relations

Based on the above estimation results of major factors in labor relations, the chapter adopts the Blinder-Oaxaca approach to differentiate the urban-rural disparities in labor relations. Table 12.6 decomposes wage, three social insurances, labor contracts, and union membership disparities into the explained and unexplained components in terms of proportions. As for the urban-rural wage gaps, the results reveal that about 70 percent is explained and 30 percent unexplained, suggesting a substantial level of wage discrimination against rural workers.

Table 12.4 Estimation results of the social insurances involvement for urban and rural workers (LPM)

	Social Pension insurance (SPI)				Social medical insurance (SMI)				Social unemployment insurance (SUI)			
	Urban workers		Rural workers		Urban workers		Rural workers		Urban workers		Rural workers	
	Coeff.	T-Ratio	Coeff.	T-Ratio	Coeff.	T-Ratio	Coeff.	T-Ratio	Coeff.	T-Ratio	Coeff.	T-Ratio
Years of schooling	0.033	3.02	0.027	2.14	0.037	3.03	0.011	0.99	0.036	3.21	0.011	1.65
Experience	0.010	1.34	0.043	3.75	0.018	2.04	0.012	1.07	-0.008	-0.82	-0.001	-0.06
Experience^2	-0.000	-0.12	-0.001	-2.55	-0.000	-0.92	-0.000	-0.52	0.001	2.41	0.000	0.32
On-job training	0.022	0.39	0.134	2.42	0.066	1.06	0.129	2.56	0.027	0.44	0.044	1.52
Dummy for male	-0.028	-0.64	-0.081	-1.44	0.013	0.25	-0.052	-0.96	0.013	0.24	-0.022	-0.65
Dummy for labor contract	0.184	2.88	0.130	2.22	0.210	3.02	0.159	3.07	0.246	3.68	0.005	0.15
Dummy for union membership	0.051	0.93	0.139	1.78	0.136	2.11	0.114	1.42	0.245	3.64	0.073	1.21
Log(employment scale)	0.009	0.41	0.047	2.28	0.018	0.81	0.008	0.39	0.025	1.09	-0.001	-0.08
Dummy for private enterprise	0.050	0.64	0.292	4.21	-0.045	-0.55	-0.177	-1.51	0.070	0.72	0.116	3.29
Dummy for foreign enterprise	0.022	0.17	0.278	2.74	-0.010	-0.07	-0.247	-1.86	0.037	0.24	0.061	1.51
Dummy for individual enterprise	-0.508	-4.11	0.191	2.12	-0.213	-1.19	-0.264	-2.09	-0.007	-0.05	0.054	1.04
Constant	-0.000	-0.00	-0.733	-4.20	-0.344	-1.51	0.038	0.20	-0.550	-2.45	-0.155	-1.20
Observation.	312		267		315		268		315		268	
R^2	0.220		0.282		0.216		0.161		0.280		0.062	

Table 12.5 Estimation results of labor contracts and union membership for urban and rural workers (LPM)

	Labor contracts				Union membership			
	Urban workers		Rural workers		Urban workers		Rural workers	
	Coeff.	T-Ratio	Coeff.	T-Ratio	Coeff.	T-Ratio	Coeff.	T-Ratio
Years of schooling	0.020	1.79	0.047	4.83	0.038	3.29	0.019	2.18
Experience	0.017	1.94	-0.016	-1.67	0.046	5.65	0.001	0.13
Experience^2	-0.000	-1.43	0.001	1.99	-0.001	-3.25	0.000	1.03
On-job training	0.072	1.41	0.070	1.36	0.049	1.06	0.038	0.98
Dummy for male	0.127	2.19	-0.021	-0.43	0.074	1.34	0.084	2.42
Log(employment scale)	0.052	2.69	0.053	2.63	0.098	4.65	0.040	2.71
Dummy for private enterprise	-0.126	-1.81	0.043	0.47	-0.094	-1.05	-0.108	-1.34
Dummy for foreign enterprise	0.043	0.44	0.169	1.58	-0.249	-2.00	-0.146	-1.51
Dummy for individual enterprise	-0.516	-3.51	-0.140	-1.14	-0.175	-1.33	-0.071	-0.82
Constant	0.030	0.15	-0.131	-0.76	-0.849	-3.92	-0.238	-1.81
Observation.	344		388		344		359	
R^2	0.125		0.147		0.336		0.131	

Table 12.6 The Blinder-Oaxaca decomposition of the urban-rural disparities in major labor relation factors

	Wage	SPI	SMI	SUI	Labor contracts	Union membership
Total diff	0.351 (100 percent)	0.439 (100 percent)	0.435 (100 percent)	0.451 (100 percent)	0.169 (100 percent)	0.390 (100 percent)
Explained	0.246 (70 percent)	0.301 (69 percent)	0.321 (74 percent)	0.357 (79 percent)	0.201 (119 percent)	0.318 (81 percent)
Unexplained	0.105 (30 percent)	0.138 (31 percent)	0.114 (26 percent)	0.094 (21 percent)	-0.032(-19 percent)	0.072 (19 percent)

Table 12.6 shows that the statistic differences in social insurances between urban and rural workers, on average, reach nearly 45 percentage points and exceed the wage gaps by nearly 10 points. Holding human capital and enterprises' characteristics constant, the unexplained parts of the SPI, SMI, and SUI disparities still amount to 31, 26 and 21 percent, respectively, indicating the social insurances' discrimination against rural workers are marginally lower than that of wage discrimination, though it is by no means unimportant. If only taking the wage gaps into consideration, researchers would underestimate the real discriminations between the two groups.

It is interesting to note that as for signing labor contracts, there's no clear evidence of urban-rural discrimination. Both urban-workers-weighted and rural-workers-weighted decompositions show that most urban-rural differences in signing labor contracts can be attributed to workers' human capital and enterprises' characteristics. Why? It probably has something to do with the way of signing labor contracts in Chinese enterprises.

Employers are always in a privileged position in the contract-signing process, and they decide whether they would sign labor contracts with their staff. It can be easily found that in some enterprises, especially medium- and small-sized ones, either all employees have labor contracts or no one does. Therefore, the signing of labor contracts depends mainly on enterprises' employment scale, ownership, management practices, and pressures from the local government, rather than workers' *hukou* status.

Finally, 81 percent of the urban-rural disparities in union membership can be attributed to human capital and enterprises characteristics, and the remaining 19 percent can be viewed as discrimination. It suggests that though the *Law of Union* grants all workers the right to organize and join labor unions freely. The *hukou* system causes a gap in union membership between urban and rural workers.

4 Conclusions

It is well known that abnormal welfare differences would bring about economical inefficiencies and severe social problems. In China's labor market, the urban-rural disparities are highly complicated and diversified.

There are not only wage disparities but also disparities in professions, social insurances, working conditions, labor contracts, union memberships, and so on. In this chapter, we attempt to provide, for the first time, an extensive set of evidence on urban-rural disparities in major labor relation factors through analyzing Zhejiang's enterprises and rural workers' survey data. Compared with other investigations on urban-rural disparities in China, this chapter extends from wage disparities analysis to disparities in SPI, SMI, SUI, labor contracts, and union membership.

Our findings reveal that there are considerable gaps between urban and rural workers in three social insurances, among which about 20 to 30 percent can be viewed as discrimination. It is also found that the number of rural workers participating in labor unions is extremely small, and nearly one-fifth of the disparities in union membership cannot be explained.

All these facts indicate that the real discriminations of rural workers are far greater than the discrimination in wage only. If simply considering the wage factor, we would underestimate the real welfare disparities between the two groups as well as the discrimination against rural workers.

In addition, other variables such as labor contracts and union memberships are added to the wage equation and the social insurances equation. The results are very interesting. It is found that labor contracts are helpful for wage rises while union memberships are not. However, both variables have substantially positive impacts on the three social insurances (SPI, SMI, and SUI). It suggests the role of China's labor unions is ambiguous, and their functions are still hindered by the traditional institutions.

References

Blinder, A., 'Wage discrimination: reduced form and structural estimations', *Journal of Human Resources*, 8 (1973): 436-455.

Cooke, F.L., 'Ownership Change and Reshaping of Employment Relations in China: a Study of Two Manufacturing Companies', *the Journal of Industrial Relations,* 44 (2002): 19-39.

Cotton, J., 'On the Decomposition of Wage Differentials', *Review of Economics and Statistics,* 70 (1988): 236-243.

Fang, C., Yang, D. and Wang, M., The Political Economics of Labor Mobility (Shanghai People Press, 2002).

Frenkel, J. and Sorash, K., 'Logics of Action, Globalization, and Changing Employment Relations in China, India, Malaysia, and the Philippines', *Industrial and Labor Relations Review,* 55 (2002): 387-412.

Guest, D., 'Is the Psychological Contract Worth Taking Seriously', *The Journal of Organizational Behavior*, 19 (1998): 649-664.

Hill, S., McGovern, P., Mills, C., Smeaton, D. and White, M. Why Study Contract? Labor contracts, Psychological Contracts and the Changing Nature of Work (Presented to ESRC Conference, London School of Economics, 2000).

Li, Q. and Zhuang, T., 'The Rural Laborers and the Informal Employment in Cities', *Sociology Research*, 6 (2002).

Liu, P., Meng, X. and Zhang, J., 'Sectoral Gender Wage Differentials and Discrimination in the Transitional Chinese Economy', *Journal of Population Economics*, 13 (2000): 331-352.

Krueger, A., 'The Economics of Discrimination', *Journal of Political Economy* (1963): 481-486.

Oaxaca, R., 'Male-female wage differentials in urban labor markets', *International Economic Review*, 14 (1973): 693-709.

Wang, D., 'China's Rural Compulsory Education: Current Situation, Problems and Policy Alternatives', *Chinese Agriculture economic review*, 1 (2003): 356-373.

Wei, Z. 'The Impact of Health in Non-farming Employment and wage determination', *Economic Research,* 2 (2004).

White, H., 'A Heteroskedasticity-consistent Covariance Matrix Estimator and a Direct Test for Heteroskedasticity', *Econometica* 48 (1980): 817- 838.
Zhang, J. and Zhao, Y., Economic Return to Schooling in Urban China, 1988-1999 (Working Paper, 2002).

Chapter 13

Human Capital, Rural Industrialization and China's Labor Market in the 1990s

Yuyu Chen
Chunbing Xing

P23 O15
P25 O18
J24 R23

1 Introduction

Increasing the income of rural residents and accelerating rural industrialization are among the priorities of the Chinese government.[1] Human capital, especially education, plays an important role in this process. The premise, however, is that the labor market functions well; to be specific, human capital should be awarded in the market, which in turn may serve as an incentive to promote the accumulation of human capital. In this article, we investigate the role played by education in rural industrialization and evaluate China's rural labor market in the 1990s by estimating the return to education.

While in Psacharopoulos's (1994) survey the average return to education is about 10 percent in the world—and 9.6 percent in Asia, existing research indicates that the return to education in rural China is extremely low, approximately between 0 and 6 percent.[2] The low return to education contradicts the facts. First, although the average amount of schooling for the Chinese labor force has increased tremendously, it is still low compared with those in developed countries. The overall secondary school enrollment rate in 1995 was only 67 percent in China, yet it was 97 percent in the United States. Second, the enthusiasm of investing in human capital is high in China with education ranked third in a rural household's total expenditures (7.81 percent) in 1995,[3] just below food (58.62 percent) and housing (13.91 percent).

Previous research has at least two possible weaknesses. One is how most researchers based their estimation on the sample of wage earners but didn't pay

---

[1] Between 1996 and 2001, the average growth rate of per capita income was only 3.8 percent for rural residents but 6.7 percent for urban residents. Meanwhile, the proportion of wage income in the total rural income rose from 22.5 percent in 1995 to 32.6 percent in 2001 (Statistics Yearbook of China, 2002).

[2] De Brauw, Huang, Rozelle, Zhang and Zhang's (2002) research support this conclusion. Meng (1996) and Parish, Zhe and Li (1995) find no significant effect of education on wages.

[3] Statistics Yearbook of China, 2002, p.385.

enough attention to the role of education in a dual economy—education can bring return by increasing the probability of being employed by the modern sector—and the other is even if we focus on the return to education for wage-earners, researchers have confined their efforts on the effect of education on the wage level, leaving the compensation mechanism within the wage sector almost untouched. This chapter aims to complement this field of research by paying more attention to these two shortfalls.

Using the data from the China Health and Nutrition Survey (CHNS), we estimate the role of education in wage determination and in increasing the probability of being a wage earner. Furthermore, we discuss the wage mechanism within the wage sector using information on both piece rate and time wage pay. We estimate the wage return to education by estimating the wage equation for wage-earners. As wage-earners are only a fraction of the whole rural labor force, we use Heckman's two-stage model to cope with sample selection. The estimated return rate is about 0 to 5 percent and insignificant, and we find no significant sample selection.

Using the Probit model, we find that the probability of being employed by the wage sector increases by 1.5 to 3.2 percent significantly with one more year of schooling. What does this mean for the rural labor force? To answer this question, we estimate the role of wage income in determining the per capita income of rural households. The results indicate that, with someone being a wage-earner, the household's per capita income increases by about 50 percent. That is, one more year of schooling will increase one's income by 5 to 7 percent by increasing the probability of employment by the wage sector. This is one of the main contributions made in this article.

Another contribution we made is that we explore the wage mechanism within the wage sector. The data from the 1989 wave indicate that whether the respondents received a piece rate pay or a time wage is closely related to their education level, with the less educated more likely to receive piece rate pay. Furthermore, while the wage return to education reaches 7.5 percent for incentive workers (those with piece rate pay), it remains low for non-incentive workers (those with time wage). The result also indicates that the average time wage level is about 20 percent higher—although not significant—than that of piece rate pay. Hence, merely estimating a wage equation, while paying no attention to wage mechanisms, may underestimate the role of education in the labor market. We also find that the less educated suffer a higher risk of unemployment and have a less healthy working pattern with long hours even on weekends.

All of the above results indicate that education improves the well-being of laborers several ways in China's rural labor market. The return to education, at least, can be reduced to two forms: wage return and job opportunity return. However, the low wage return rate may indicate that the wage mechanism within the wage sector lacks incentive for the well-educated to use their skills and knowledge efficiently, and we saw no improvement in this respect during the 1990s.

We give a brief literature review in Section 2. Section 3 is model specification, and the main results regarding wage return to education and job opportunity return to education are presented in Section 4. Section 5 examines the wage mechanism, and we conclude the chapter with Section 6.

2 Literature Review

The relationship between human capital and both income and economic growth are well-documented.[4] At the micro level, existing research indicates that education provides laborers with knowledge, making them more skillful and thus more productive. This can be reflected in the wage level, with the more well-educated receiving more income (Schultz, 1961). However, this relationship is complicated by the well-known ability bias (Becker, 1993; Card, 1999), especially when we use an econometric model to estimate it. Broadly speaking, researchers try to cope with this problem in three ways: using the institutional variation of the education system as instrumental variables, using family background to control ability bias or as instrumental variables, and using information of twins or siblings to differentiate the ability bias.

Card (1999) gives a comprehensive survey of this research, and the return rate for developed countries is approximately around 5 to 10 percent.[5] For developing countries, Duflo's (2001) research—after controlling the omitting variable problem—indicates that the return rate for Indonesia is about 6 to 10 percent. All these researches draw a clear picture that the better educated receive more income. Is it the same case in China? If not, is there something wrong with our labor market?

Scholars have no consensus on the role of the rural labor market in the process of rural industrialization. One group of economists evaluates the labor market by examining the return to education. Meng's (1996; 2000) research indicates that the rural labor market didn't perform well because human capital was not compensated in the wage income, which is determined mainly by non-market factors. Zhang, Huang, and Rozelle (2002) find that labor markets have improved in the sense that rural workers have been increasingly rewarded for their education both in terms of access to off-farm jobs as well as higher wages. Unfortunately, their data are confined to Jiangsu, a relatively well-developed province in China, and thus not representative of the country as a whole. In addition, even though they implicitly assume off-farm jobs make rural residents better off, they make no further effort to explore to what extent off-farm jobs have increased labor income. Wei (2004) found

---

[4] Researches of Barro (1991) and others indicate that education has positive effect on economic growth. More recent researches also indicate that education play an important role in the reduction of poverty (Besley and Burgess, 2003).

[5] Most researches indicate that controlling family background or using siblings and twins' data reduce the effect of education on wages, and the effect increases when using institutional characteristics of education system as instruments (see Card, 1999). We controlled family background in this paper.

that, taking sample selection into consideration, the return to education is still low. He didn't investigate how education increases off-farm job access.

Duality is the main characteristic of LDCs, with income levels differing significantly between regions and sectors (Lewis, 1954; Basu, 1997). Under this regime, education level may be associated with labor migration between regions and/or sectors (even among sub-sectors within the wage sector), so the wage differentials may serve as the return to education. Why differentials remain and what role education plays in labor migration require further research.[6] This article provides no explanation but evidence for these issues, and it points out that the return of education may be severely underestimated and misleading if we ignore the basic characteristics of a developing economy.

3 Model Specification

We construct a wage equation within the wage sector and a migration model to examine returns on education both in terms of higher wages and off-farm job access.[7]

3.1 Wage Return to Education

3.1.1 Wage Equation

As mentioned earlier, education makes laborers more skillful and productive, and thus improves wages. Based on Mincer (1974), we have:

$$\ln(wage) = a + \beta_1 S + \gamma X + u_1 \tag{1}$$

S is years of schooling; vector X includes experience,[8] experience-squared, marital status, family background, province dummies, and indicators of village cadre and town administrative staff. Because the ownership of the work units varies greatly, we controlled the ownership dummies (see Appendix 13.1 for descriptive figures).

3.1.2 Wage Equation with Sample Selection

Sample selection may be severe because only a small fraction of laborers is employed in the wage sector (for more rigorous discussion, see Wooldridge, 2001). We use Heckman's (1979) two-stage model to estimate the wage equation.

---

[6] Those interested in this can refer to Lewis (1954), Harris and Todaro (1970), Stiglitz (1974), and Leibenstein (1957).

[7] *Migration* in this article refers to rural residents finding jobs in wage sector.

[8] Experience=age-years of schooling-6.

$$wd = 1[a + \beta_2 S + \lambda X' + u_2 > 0] \tag{2}$$

The equation above is a function that indicates whether or not a respondent has wage income (wd=1 indicates wage earner; otherwise, wd=0).

Assuming (i) *wd*, S, and X' can always be observed and *ln(wage)* can only be observed when *wd*=1, (ii) the expectations of (u_1, u_2) are zero and independent from S, X, and X', (iii) $u_2 \sim N(0,1)$, and (iv) $E(u_1 | u_2) = \eta_1 u_2$, we have:

$$E(\ln(wage) | S, X, wd = 1) = a + \beta_1 S + \gamma X + \eta_1 m(a + \beta_2 S + \lambda X') \tag{3}$$

with $m(.) \equiv \phi(.)/\Phi(.)$. We estimate $m(a + \beta_2 S + \lambda X')$ using the Probit model first and then put it back into (3) and run OLS. If the coefficient of $m(a + \beta_2 S + \lambda X')$ is significant, sample selection does matter; if not, the results of (1) and (3) should be consistent.

3.2 Return to Education in Terms of Wage-job Access

To fully estimate the return to education, we must recognize two facts. First, wage income increases the income level of rural households; and second, education increases the access to wage-jobs.

3.2.1 Migration Decision Function for Rural Labor

We estimate the role of education in labor migration using the Probit model. The dependent variable is whether the respondent is employed in the wage sector. We assume that the respondent makes a decision according to a latent function:

$$y^* = a + \beta_2 S + \lambda X' + u_2 \tag{4}$$

y^* is the unobservable latent variable, upon which the respondent makes a decision. S is the years of schooling. We predict β_2 to be positive because education improves productivity, makes the labor force more able to process information and adapt to new environments, and may also serve as a signal in the labor market. $X's$ control other variables, including personal characteristics, demographic information,[9] and head of house information (the head of the household's education is inclusive to control the unobservable, such as ability). In equation (4), u_2 is the error term, and we assume that it is normally distributed. Therefore, we have:

---

[9] Some other researches (Zhang et al. (2002) for example) also controlled the number of children and elders who need care. We don't control them because what we concern is male labor, upon whom these factors have no effect on their decision making.

$$wd = \begin{cases} 1 & y^* > 0 \\ 0 & y^* \le 0 \end{cases} \text{ and,} \tag{5}$$

$$P(wd = 1 \mid S, X') = P(u_2 > -a - \beta_2 S - \lambda X') = \Phi(a + \beta_2 S + \lambda X') \tag{6}$$

Hence, one more year of schooling is associated with increased probability of being employed by the wage sector:

$$\Delta P(wd = 1 \mid S, X') \approx \phi(\tilde{a} + \tilde{\beta}_2 \cdot S + \tilde{\lambda} \cdot X')\tilde{\beta}_2 \tag{7}$$

3.2.2 The Influence of Wage Income on Household Income

Although, by using the Probit model, we can estimate the increased probability of job access associated with more education, the return rate in monetary terms is still unknown. The latter relies heavily on the extent to which wage income increases one's income. Unfortunately, we have no such data on the individual level, but we have household level income data and can examine the influence of wage income on household per capita income. The model specification is as follows:

$$\ln pc = \alpha + \beta_3 wd + \theta_1 Y + \varepsilon \tag{8}$$

We predict the coefficient of wd— β_3 —is positive. Vector Y controls other variables, including the area of land, number of persons contributing to household income, family size, sex ratio, education, and the experience of sons and household head. wd is a function of education. For convenience, we use the Linear Probability Model.[10]

$$wd = a' + \gamma_0 S + \gamma_1 X' + u_2' \tag{9}$$

So one more year of schooling is associated with the increased probability of being employed: $\gamma_0 (\gamma_0 \approx \phi(\tilde{a} + \tilde{\beta}_2 \cdot S + \tilde{\lambda} \cdot X')\tilde{\beta}_2)$. Put (9) into (8), and we have:

$$\ln pc = \overline{\alpha} + \beta_3 \gamma_0 S + \beta_3 \gamma_1 X' + \theta_1 Y + (\beta_3 u_2' + \varepsilon)$$

where $\overline{\alpha} = \alpha + \beta_3 \alpha'$ \hfill (10)

---

[10] We also estimate the effect of education on migration using LPM, the results of which are similar to those of Probit and thus are not reported.

One more year of schooling is associated with the $\beta_3 \gamma_0$ increase of per capita income. Furthermore, we can calculate the increase of an individual's income. One thing that must be noted is that education enters equation (5) in two ways: one directly affects the laborer's productivity, and the other increases the probability of being employed.

3.3 Background and Data

The data came from the China Health and Nutrition Survey (CHNS), which was conducted by an international team of researchers whose backgrounds include: nutrition, public health, economics, sociology, Chinese studies, and demography. The CHNS contains valuable information about education and income,[11] though its main concern is health and nutrition. The survey has been conducted four times, once in 1989, in 1991, in 1993, and in 1997. The sample includes more than 3,000 households and 16,000 individuals. Because males and females have different roles in the rural labor market, we focus on male laborers between the ages of 16 and 65.[12]

We calculate the hourly wage by using the monthly wage and the number of working hours per month. The 1989 survey has incentive worker information, while the 1991, 1993, and 1997 surveys have none. Using the 1989 data, we further explore the issue of wage mechanism within the wage sector in section 5.1. There is no direct education measure in terms of years of schooling in the survey (except in 1993), so we calculate using the existing data. We also split the data into two sets, which contain the information of household heads and that of sons separately, merging them again by household ID. The sample size reduces greatly after these manipulations.

Panel A in Table 13.1 indicates that during the period between 1991 and 1997, the education level of the male labor force increased 11.45 percent from 6.68 years in 1991 to 7.44 years in 1997. Meanwhile, the wage level increased correspondingly—from 133.7 *yuan* per month in 1991 to 176.4 *yuan* per month in 1993 and 208.0 *yuan* per month in 1997. Panel B is about the sons, whose education level is higher than their household head, which is 7.43, 7.68 and 8.39 years of schooling in 1991, 1993, and 1997, respectively.

Several facts must be mentioned. First, the term *rural area* is in a broad sense, which includes townships and county seats.[13] Second, as shown in Appendix 13.2, about 82 percent of respondents live with their families, indicating that most rural laborers migrate within the rural area (internal migration in contrast to rural-urban migration). Our results will provide evidence mainly for internal migration, but the

---

[11] The income data are the income that respondents received one year prior to the survey year. We follow the survey year however.

[12] We didn't limit our sample according to this constraint when estimating wage equation, but the results are similar because very few wage earners are beyond this age range.

[13] See Wei (2004) for detailed description.

data also show that young laborers stay outside longer than prior generations. This may indicate that external migration plays a more and more important role.

Third, although education level and wage level show an increasing trend, the share of wage-earners in the whole labor force decreased slightly from 1993 to 1997. This may have something to do with the whole economic situation. The statistics in Appendix 13.4 indicates that the participation rate among wage-earners differs greatly; those who work less than 9 months a year, account for 20 to 30 percent. We discuss the relationship between participation rates and education levels in Section 5.

Table 13.1 Summary statistics

		A: Full Sample			B: Restricted Sample (sons of house head)		
		1991	1993	1997	1991	1993	1997
Schooling	N	2,618	2,617	2,790	676	702	838
	Mean	6.68	6.76	7.44	7.44	7.68	8.39
	S.E.	(3.46)	(3.38)	(3.30)	(2.80)	(2.75)	(2.63)
Wage earner	N	2,622	2,634	2,800	678	707	843
	Mean	27.8	28.4	27.7	22.7	27.0	26.1
	S.E.	(44.8)	(45.1)	(44.7)	(41.9)	(44.4)	(43.9)
Monthly Wage	N	950	981	1,183	234	290	449
	Mean	133	176	207	124	158	198
	S.E.	(91)	(153)	(189)	(87)	(103)	(129)
Hourly wage	N	933	922	1,125	231	264	417
	Mean	0.81	0.97	1.21	0.66	0.81	1.14
	S.E.	(1.28)	(1.12)	(1.27)	(0.5)	(0.56)	(1.02)

Notes: 1. Wages of year 1991 and 1993 are adjusted using the price index provided by the survey, and the 1997 wages used rural CPI from SSB (1988□100) for adjustment. Standard errors are in parentheses.

4 Results

4.1 Wage Determination within Wage Sector

4.1.1 Wage Equation

Panel A of Table 13.2 reports the estimated equation without family background. The coefficients of education in 1991, 1993, and 1997 are -0.006, 0.0003, and 0.010, respectively, which are rounded to zero and considered to be insignificant. In contrast to the insignificance of education, the coefficients of experience in 1991 and 1993 are 0.022 and 0.032, respectively—both significantly positive. In addition, the coefficient in 1997 is 0.013 and thus insignificant.

We also control unobserved variables, such as ability, by controlling family background.[14] The results are reported in Table 13.2. The effect of education on wages remains insignificant. The coefficients in 1991 and 1997 turn out to be reduced (-0.021 and -0.019, respectively), and the coefficient in 1993 is 0.025, which is slightly higher. It should be noted that the standard errors also become large. We exclude control variables, such as province dummies, ownership dummies of work units, and marital status to test the robustness of our specification. While the R-square decreases greatly, the coefficients change little, indicating that the results are, in fact, robust.

4.1.2 Heckman's Two-step Model

Table 13.2 reports the results of Heckman's (1979) model (the Probit part will be reported in Section 4.2). We control human capital, marital status, household characteristics, and region dummies in the Probit part. Using the two-stage procedure, we get the coefficients of education -0.005, 0.040, and 0.022 in 1991, 1993, and 1997, respectively. Columns (1), (3), and (5) of panel C report the results with the education of household heads excluded. The coefficients are reduced, except in 1997. Although the coefficients of education increase—especially in 1993 and 1997—in Heckman's two-stage model, the standard errors also increase and the coefficients remain insignificant.

In 1991 and 1993, the coefficients of *lmbda*, the inverse Mills ratio, are insignificant, which indicates that the selection bias might not be a serious problem. Although it is significant in 1997, the education coefficient remains insignificant. This result is different from that of Zhang et al.'s (2002), which finds that in 1996, one more year of schooling is associated with a 5 to 9 percent increase of wages. This may be caused by the sample they used, which covers only about three villages in Jiangsu, a relatively well-developed province.

The results in this section show that education is not rewarded in the rural wage sector, almost replicating the results of Meng's (1996; 2000) and other researchers yet are still far away from Psacharopoulos's (1994) and Card's (1999). This may be caused by several possibilities: the labor market didn't function well; the rural wage sector is an unskilled, intensive sector, requiring only a minimal education level; or education does have return but in other forms, which will be discussed in Section 5.

---

[14] The education level of house head and their children is positively correlated. One more year of schooling of house head is associated with 0.228 (0.028), 0.226 (0.028), and 0.190 (0.025) more years of schooling of their children (results are not reported to save space, standard errors in parenthesis).These results are similar to those in Card (1999, p. 1823).

Table 13.2 Wage equation of 1991, 1993 and 1997

| | Dependent Variable=log(wage) | | | | | |
| | 1991 | | 1993 | | 1997 | |
	(1)	(2)	(3)	(4)	(5)	(6)
	A		Family background exclusive			
Schooling	-0.006		0.000		0.010	
	(0.009)		(0.010)		(0.010)	
N	678		678		633	
Adj. R^2	0.1678		0.1592		0.0919	
	B		Family background inclusive			
Schooling	-0.018	-0.021	0.026	0.025	-0.012	-0.019
	(0.022)	(0.031)	(0.021)	(0.029)	(0.018)	(0.025)
N	152	126	176	164	178	162
Adj. R^2	0.0107	0.0994	0.0173	0.091	-0.0117	0.079
	C		Heckman two-step model			
Schooling	0.006	-0.005	0.050	0.040	0.014	0.022
	(0.029)	(0.039)	(0.048)	(0.050)	(0.037)	(0.039)
lambda	-0.007	0.032	-0.082	-0.087	-0. 384**	-0.391**
	(0.118)	(0.149)	(0.195)	(0.220)	(0.191)	(0.195)
N	572	555	518	512	448	447
Censored	469	469	425	425	400	400
Wald Chi^2	63.6[25]	158.43[36]	61.21[22]	321.45[30]	47.80[26]	47.46[32]

Notes:
1. Experience, province dummies, ownership dummies, marital status, and indicators for village leader and administrative staff are controlled in Panel A's regressions. Constants are suppressed.
2. Experience and education level of house head are controlled in Panel B. Column (2), (4), and (6) also control province dummies, ownership dummies, marital status, and experience of house head. Constants are suppressed.
3. Only wage equations are reported in Panel C. Experience, province dummies, and ownership dummies are controlled. Column (2), (4), and (6) also control indicators for village leader and administrative staff, marital status, and house head's education and experience. The coefficients of Lambda reflect whether or not the selection bias is significant.
4. ***, **, and * indicate significance at the 1, 5, and 10 percent level, respectively. Standard errors in ( ) and Freedom in [ ].

Table 13.3 Labor migration model

	Dependent Variable=Wage Earner Dummy					
	1991		1993		1997	
	(1)	(2)	(3)	(4)	(5)	(6)
Schooling	0.021***	0.022***	0.033***	0.032***	0.020***	0.018**
	(0.007)	(0.007)	(0.009)	(0.009)	(0.007)	(0.007)
Experience	0.025***	0.027***	-0.007	-0.002	0.010	0.010
	(0.009)	(0.009)	(0.009)	(0.009)	(0.007)	(0.007)
Experience2×100	-0.090***	-0.085**	0.012	0.006	-0.030	-0.027
	(0.034)	(0.033)	(0.023)	(0.023)	(0.024)	(0.023)
Marital status	0.027	-0.011	-0.033	-0.043	-0.039	-0.040
	(0.046)	(0.045)	(0.055)	(0.056)	(0.034)	(0.032)
Number of income contributing members	0.006	0.001	-0.028**	-0.034***		
	(0.010)	(0.010)	(0.012)	(0.012)		
Land	-0.022***	-0.012**	-0.001	-0.001	-0.012***	-0.014***
	(0.005)	(0.005)	(0.002)	(0.002)	(0.003)	(0.004)
Wage earner (hd)		0.381***		0.298***		0.239***
		(0.072)		(0.065)		(0.069)
Schooling (hd)		-0.011**		0.006		-0.004
		(0.005)		(0.005)		(0.004)
Village leader (hd)		-0.039		0.028		0.124
		(0.048)		(0.106)		(0.117)
Administrative Staff (hd)		0.189		-0.157*		
		(0.184)		(0.021)		
Obs.	599	590	545	540	559	532
Pseudo R^2	0.1658	0.2597	0.1408	0.1985	0.1164	0.1811

Notes:

1. We use command *dprobit* in STATA to estimate the model.
2. We control house heads' information in column (ii), (iv), and (vi) to test robustness. We also control province dummies.
3. *hd* refers to house heads' information.
4. ***, **, and * indicate significance at the 1, 5, and 10 percent level, respectively. Standard errors in ( ).

4.2 Return to Education in Terms of Wage-job Opportunity

4.2.1 The Effect of Education on Labor Migration

Education may be rewarded by an increased employment probability in the wage sector, which provides a higher income than does the non-wage sector. We estimate the effect of education on rural labor migration using the Probit model. The dependent variable is whether or not the respondent has a wage income (wd=1 if so, and wd=0 otherwise).

The estimated effect of education on labor migration is significant, with the coefficients being 2.2, 3.2, and 1.5 percent in 1991, 1993, and 1997, respectively. No trend of increasing importance is observed. In contrast, experience is not significant, except in 1991.

We also control other variables. Marriage has a negative yet insignificant effect on labor migration. The number of household members contributing to household income has no significant effect in 1991, but the effect turns significantly positive in 1993. The effects of land area are consistently negative—in 1991, 1993, and 1997—and significant, except in 1993. This can also be contributed to an increased reservation wage level. The characteristics of household heads have a significant effect on labor migration. If the head of household is also a wage-earner, then the probability for that person to become employed increases 20 percent. The estimated effects of household heads' education and administrative status are not significant.

Even after we drop the head of household information, the estimated effects of education on labor migration change little, indicating that our results are robust.

4.2.2 Effect of Wage Income on Household's Per Capita Income

Wage income greatly increases the per capita income level as reported in Table 13.4. In 1991 and 1993, wage income increased the per capita income by 56 and 47 percent, respectively. No data are available for 1997. However, Meng (2000) finds that the gap between farm and off-farm work deepened during the 1990s. Therefore, we can believe that wage income significantly increased per capita income in the 1990s.

The land area, number of contributing members, family size, sex ratio, and region are controlled. Per capita income decreases by 1 to 2 percent with the increase of land size (insignificant in 1991 but significant in 1993). The number of contributing members has a negative effect, which can be explained by the association between the number of contributing members and family size. Females contribute less than males, and the estimated effect of sex ratio turns out to be negative.

Education can also improve the productivity of farm laborers and the self-employed; it also has externality. To single out the effect of education on labor migration, we control education in the regression. In 1991 and 1993, the education of both the household heads and their sons has a significant effect on household per capita income, with the coefficient being 2.5 to 2.8 percent (significant) and 1.7 to 2.3 percent (insignificant), respectively. Once we control more variables, the R-square increases, but the estimated effects of wage income change little.

Table 13.4 The effect of wage income on household per capita income

	Dependent Variable=log(Per Capita Income)					
	1991			1993		
	(1)	(2)	(3)	(4)	(5)	(6)
Wage earner	0.589***	0.579***	0.559***	0.556***	0.510***	0.471***
	(0.080)	(0.090)	(0.095)	(0.079)	(0.091)	(0.092)
Wage earner (hd)	0.457***	0.412***	0.352***	0.563***	0.330***	0.245**
	(0.088)	(0.100)	(0.106)	(0.088)	(0.105)	(0.109)
Land		-0.016*	-0.013		-0.010**	-0.011***
		(0.009)	(0.010)		(0.004)	(0.004)
Number of income		-0.031	-0.036		-0.111**	-0.122**
contributing members		(0.029)	(0.030)		(0.046)	(0.048)
Family size		-0.022	-0.031		0.065	0.067
		(0.032)	(0.032)		(0.043)	(0.045)
Sex ratio		0.125	-0.037		-0.074	-0.020
		(0.220)	(0.225)		(0.243)	(0.250)
Schooling			0.028**			0.023
			(0.014)			(0.017)
Experience			0.040***			-0.011
			(0.015)			(0.017)
Experience2×100			-0.156***			0.035
			(0.041)			(0.043)
Schooling (hd)			0.025*			0.017
			(0.013)			(0.015)
Experience (hd)			-0.031			0.046
			(0.026)			(0.033)
Experience^2×100 (hd)			0.032			-0.058
			(0.028)			(0.035)
Province	no	yes	yes	no	yes	yes
N	672	607	563	704	544	511
Adj. R^2	0.1887	0.1851	0.2195	0.1701	0.1617	0.1907

Note: 1. ***, **, and * indicate significance at the 1, 5, and 10 percent level, respectively. Standard errors in ( )

4.2.3 Return to Education in Terms of Wage Job Access

Using the results from 4.2.1 and 4.2.2, we can roughly calculate the return to education in terms of increased wage-job access.

Table 13.5 Return to education in terms of increased wage-job opportunity

year	$\beta_0(1)$	$\gamma_0(2)$	$\beta_0*\gamma_0(3)$	Family size(4)	Return rate(5)
1991	0.559	0.022	0.012	4.347	0.054
1993	0.471	0.032	0.015	4.507	0.068

$\beta_0*\gamma_0$ in Table 13.5 is what we want: one more year of schooling is associated with a $\beta_0*\gamma_0$ increase of per capita income, and this increase is through labor migration. Remember, what we need is the individual return rate, and we have no sign of perfect income-sharing within the household.[15] Therefore, we calculate the individual return next by using $\beta_0*\gamma_0$ times the average family size, which is shown in column (4) in Table 13.5. As shown in column (5), the return rates in 1991 and 1993 are 5.4 and 6.8 percent, respectively. We must admit that the calculation is rough and based on strong assumptions. However, the results are meaningful for us to understand the role of education in the Chinese rural labor market.

5 Further Discussions

5.1 Time Rate vs. Piece Rate Wages

In the above analysis, we use the hour wage to examine the return to education, and the underlying assumption is that wages reflect productivity and compensations, which is probably not true in China during the period under investigation. In addition to wages, workers receive subsidies, bonuses, and in-kind compensation, which is common in China, especially for those in state-owned enterprises (SOEs). This probably is not the case, however, for incentive workers. Piece wages should be more accurate measurements of worker productivity. The 1989 survey asks respondents whether they are paid a time rate or a piece rate, thus providing valuable information for the evaluation of wage mechanisms within the wage sector. The estimated model is as follows:

$$\ln(wage) = a + \beta_1 sch + \beta_2 sch * time_d + \beta_3 time_d + X\gamma + u \qquad (11)$$

$time_d$ is a dummy with $time_d = 1$ when a worker receives a time wage and

---

[15] Those interested in this can refer to Kochar (2000).

$time_d = 0$ when a worker receives a piece rate pay. β_1 is the return rate for incentive workers, and $\beta_1 + \beta_2$ is for non-incentive workers.

Columns (1), (2), and (3) of Table 13.6 report the results. The overall effect of education on hourly wages in 1989 is about 0.032. After we add the time rate dummy to the model, the estimated effect of education on wages increases to 0.075. This indicates that education can improve wages for workers.

Table 13.6 Wage mechanism within wage sector: 1989

	Dependent Variable= Log(wage)			Dependent Variable= Time Wage Dummy
	(1)	(2)	(3)	(4)
Schooling	0.032***	0.051**	0.075*	0.036***
	(0.013)	(0.022)	(0.044)	(0.007)
Experience	0.028	0.028	0.028	-0.010
	(0.012)	(0.012)	(0.012)	(0.006)
Experience2×100	-0.040	-0.040	-0.041	0.029
	(0.025)	(0.025)	(0.025)	(0.013)
Schooling× $time_d$		-0.018	-0.044	
		(0.017)	(0.044)	
$time_d$			0.222	
			(0.348)	
N	334	334	334	345
Adj. (Psudo) R^2	0.149	0.149	0.148	0.226

Notes:
1. The dependent variable of column (1)–(3) is log(hour wage). We run OLS regression and control experience, sex, marital status, ownership of work unit, and province dummies, with constant suppressed;
2. Column (4) is a Probit model. The dependent variable is non-incentive worker indicators.
3. Experience, experience-squared, marital status, and province dummies are controlled.
4. ***, **, and * indicate significance at the 1, 5, and 10 percent level, respectively. Standard errors in ( )

As for non-incentive workers, the estimated effect of education is at about 3.1 percent, much lower than that of piece rate wages, but on average, time rate wages are about 22.2 percent higher than piece rate wages (even if it is not significant).

Column (4) is a Probit model, which indicates that one more year of schooling is associated with a higher probability (3.6 percent higher) of receiving time rate wages (see Appendix 13.3 for descriptive figures). Therefore, time rate wages can be regarded as an advantage for workers. The difference between piece rate and time rate wages may serve as the return if increased education helps workers migrate to the time rate wage sector.

Now we can answer the question at the end of subsection 4.1. The fact that the return rate of piece rate wages (for those less educated) is higher than that of time rate wages may indicate that the low return rate of education is not caused by the structure of the rural economy but by the wage mechanism of the rural labor market. Thus, even if we don't take into account the return to education in terms of wage-job access, we cannot conclude that education is not compensated.

5.2 Other Forms of Return to Education

Even if better-educated laborers do not receive higher wages, they may have more decent positions, with more leisure time and less risk of unemployment. We discuss this matter briefly in this subsection.

Table 13.7 The relationship between working time and education level

	(1) Dependent Variable= Working Months per Year			(2) Dependent Variable= Working Days Per Week			(3) Dependent Variable= Working Hours Per Day		
	1991	1993	1997	1991	1993	1997	1991	1993	1997
Schooling	0.132***	0.045	0.091***	0.031**	-0.01	-0. 037**	-0.004	-0.028	0. 004
	(0.036)	(0.043)	(0.031)	(0.015)	(0.016)	(0.017)	(0.024)	(0.044)	(0. 042)
Experience	0.024	0.099***	0.019	-0.013	0.017	-0.006	-0.014	-0.001	-0.020
	(0.027)	(0.029)	(0.022)	(0.011)	(0.011)	(0.012)	(0.017)	(0.030)	(0.027)
Experience2×100	0.050	-0.111	-0.004	0.031	-0.029	0.009	0.019	-0.006	0.030
	(0.053)	(0.054)	(0.042)	(0.021)	(0.020)	(0.022)	(0.033)	(0.056)	(0.051)
N	728	742	680	731	732	683	730	731	681
Adj. R^2	0.211	0.207	0.109	0.065	0.046	0.113	0.03	0.032	0.026

Notes:
1. Column (1), (2), and (3) are the results of OLS regression, with the dependent variable being working months per year, working days per week, and working hours per day, respectively.
2. Province dummies and ownership dummies are controlled, and constant are suppressed.
3. ***, **, and * indicate significance at the 1, 5, and 10 percent level, respectively. Standard errors in ( ).

Our data indicate that between 1991 and 1997, about 20 percent of wage-earners are working less than 9 months per year (see Appendix 13.4). In Table 13.7, column (1)–with the years 1991, 1993, and 1997—shows that one more year of schooling is associated with 0.13, 0.04, and 0.09 more work per month and about 1.3, 0.4, and 1.0 percent of the total working months, respectively. In column (2), more schooling is associated with fewer working days per week (except in 1991); in column (3), the estimated effect of education on the number of working hours per day is negative, except in 1997. Hence, the working pattern of the well-educated laborers may be different than that of less-educated ones. Zhang et al. (2002) also find that more education is associated with more working days per year. However, one should keep in mind that the estimated standard errors are large when compared to the magnitude of the coefficients, making our conclusions weak.

The effect of education on the labor participation rate may be related to the macroeconomic environment. The effects of education on the number of working months are significant in 1991 and 1997 but insignificant in 1993. The Chinese economy experienced considerable fluctuations between 1991 and 1997: the growth rates of the GDP fluctuated from 4.2 percent in 1990 to 14.1 percent in 1992 and then to 9.8 percent in 1996. The significant effect of education is associated with a more adverse economic environment. We guess that education can protect workers from the risk of unemployment.

6 Conclusions

Human capital is crucial for economic development. By examining the return to education, we evaluate the labor market in the 1990s—an important period of rural industrialization and economic transition—from central planning to market orientation. Between 1991 and 1996, the amount of schooling seems to have no effect on wage level—even after taking the sample selection problem into consideration.

Another important form of return to education may lie in the increased opportunity of being a wage-earner, given the fact that wage income increases the per capita income of rural households significantly. Using the data of per capita income, we find that wage income may increase per capita income by 56 and 47 percent in 1991 and 1993, respectively, and that one more year of schooling increases the probability of being a wage-earner by 1.2 and 1.5 percent in 1991 and 1993, respectively, as well. This is equivalent to a return of 5 to 7 percent income increase to education for an individual.

Using the 1989 data, we shed some light on the issue of wage mechanisms within the wage sector. The less educated laborers are more likely to earn piece rate wages. The return rate of education is about 7.5 percent for incentive workers and 3 percent for non-incentive workers, but the average level of time rate wages is higher than that of piece rate wages. Thus the low rate of wage return to education may not have been caused by the structure of rural economy but by the inefficient wage mechanism within the wage sector, which promotes the accumulation of human capital but does not provide any incentive for workers to efficiently develop their talents and/or skills, especially when workers are paid by the hour.

In addition, more education is associated with decent jobs that offer healthy work patterns; it also may protect workers from the risk of unemployment. Both benefits comprise an important part of the return to education.

References

Barro, R.J., 'Economic Growth in a Cross Section of Countries', *Q.J.E.*, 106(2) (1991): 403-407.

Becker, G. S., *Human Capital: A theoretical and empirical analysis with special reference to education* (3rd ed) (Chicago and London: The University of Chicago Press, 1993).

Benhabib, J. and Spiegel, M.M., 'The Role of Human Capital in Economic Development: Evidence from Aggregate Cross Country Data', *Journal of Monetary Economics*, 34(2) (1994): 143-174.

Besley, T. and Burgess, R., 'Halving Global Poverty' (*Working Paper*, 2003).

Card, D., 'Causal Effects of Education on Earnings', in O. Ashenfelter and D. Card (eds), *Handbook of Labor Economics* (Elsevier, 1999).

Chen, Y., Xing, C., 'Rural Modernization and the Role of Education in Rural Labor Market', (*Working Paper*, Peking University, 2004).

De Brauw, A., Huang, J., Rozelle, S., Zhang, L. and Zhang, Y., 'The evolution of China's rural labor markets during the reforms: rapid, accelerating, transforming', *Journal of Comparative Economics*, 30(2) (June 2002): 329-353.

Duflo, E., 'Schooling and Labor Market Consequences of School Construction in Indonesia: Evidence from an Unusual Policy Experiment', *A.E.R*, 2000, 91(4) (2000): 795-813.

Harris, J.R. and Todaro, M.P., 'Migration, unemployment and development: A two-sector analysis', *A.E.R.* 60 (1970): 126-142.

Heckman, J.J., 'Sample selection bias as a specification error', *Econometrica*, 47 (1979): 153-161

Kochar, A., 'Parental benefits from intergenerational coresidence: empirical evidence from rural Pakistan' *J.P.E.* 108(6) (2000): 1184-1209

Leibenstein, H., 'Underemployment in backward economies.' *J.P.E.* 65 (1957): 91-103

Lewis, W.A., 'Economic development with unlimited supplies of labor', *Manchester school*, 28 (1954): 139-191

Meng, X., 'An examination of wage determination in China's rural industrial sector', *Applied Economics*, 28(1) (1996): 715-724.

———, *Labor Market Reform in China* (Cambridge University Press, 2000).

Parish, W.L., Zhe, X. and Li, F., 'Nonfarm work and marketization of the Chinese countryside', *China Quarterly*, 143 (1995): 697-730.

Psacharopoulos, G., 'Returns to investment in education: a global up-date', *World Development*, 22 (1994): 1325–1343.

Romer, P., 'Endogenous Technological Change', *J.P.E.*, Pt. 2, 99(5) (1990): S71-S102.

Schultz, T.W., 'Investment in human capital' *A.E.R.* (1961): 1-17.

Schultz, T.P., 'Notes on the Estimation of Migration Decision Functions', in R.H. Sabot (eds), *Migration and the Labor Market in Developing Countries* (Colorado: Westview

Press/Boulder, 1982.

Stiglitz, J.E., 'alternative theories of wage determination and unemployment in LDCs: The labor turnover model', *Q.J.E* (1974): 194-227.

The World Bank, *Higher education in developing countries: peril and promise* (Washington D. C., 2000).

Wooldridge,J.M., *Econometric Analysis of Cross Section and Panel Data* (Cambridge, Massachusetts: The MIT Press, 2001).

Zhang, L., Huang, J. and Rozelle, S., 'Employment, emerging labor market, and the role of education in rural China', *China Economic Review* 13 (2002): 313-328.

Wei, Z. 'The Role of Health on Off-farm Employment and Wage Decision', *Economic Research Journal (in Chinese)* (2004): 64-74.

Appendix 13.1 Ownership of work unit

Ownership	1991		1993		1997	
	Persons	percent	Persons	percent	Persons	percent
State-owned enterprises	324	33.79	319	32.22	394	33.62
Small collective enterprises	222	23.15	253	25.56	230	19.62
Large collective enterprises	108	11.26	138	13.94	124	10.58
Private	259	27.01	161	16.26	243	20.73
Family contract [1]	□	□	96	9.7	130	11.09
Joint venture [2]	8	0.83	□	□	13	1.11
Others	35	3.65	18	1.82	25	2.13
Unknown	3	0.31	5	0.51	13	1.11
Total	959	100	990	100	1172	100

Notes:

1: Family contract data are not available in 1991.
2: Joint venture is included in the item of *private* in 1993.

Appendix 13.2 Months living away from family

Months Living Outside	1991				1993			
	Total		Son		Total		Son	
	Persons	percent	Persons	percent	Persons	percent	Persons	percent
<=0	768	81.79	181	79.04	764	81.97	208	73.5
<=3	823	87.65	192	83.85	790	84.76	212	74.92
<=6	857	91.27	201	87.78	824	88.41	230	81.28
<=12	939	100	229	100	932	100	283	100

Appendix 13.3 Piece rate pay, time wage, and education level

Education level	Non-incentive (persons)	Incentive (persons)	Incentive (percent)
Below primary	61	22	26.5
Lower middle school	132	6	4.3
Upper middle school and above	85	2	2.3
Total	278	69	19.9

Appendix 13.4 Working months of wage earners per year

Working months	1991				1993				1997			
	Tolal		Son		Tolal		Son		Tolal		Son	
	Persons	percent	Persons	percent	Persons	percent	Persons	percent	Persons	percent	Persons	percent
<=3	60	6.35	25	10.82	73	7.49	34	11.71	42	3.62	28	6.42
<=6	122	12.9	42	18.17	137	14.06	61	21.02	104	8.97	53	12.14
<=9	185	19.56	51	22.06	195	20.01	83	28.6	178	15.35	82	18.78
<=12	945	100	231	100	975	100	290	100	1,160	100	437	100

Chapter 14

Economic Conditions and Urbanization: Comparing Five Chinese Provinces[*]

Aimin Chen

1 Introduction

China's income disparity has widened along with its rapid economic development. Among the sectors, the urban-rural income disparity—measured by the ratio of urban per capita disposable income to rural per capita net income—has increased from 2.57 in 1978 to 3.11 in 2002.[1] This has made solving the "Three Agricultural Problems" a top priority for the government in order to sustain China's development.

Regionally, China's eastern as well as coastal provinces and municipalities have developed at a faster pace than its interior counterparts, leading to a severe disparity. As shown in Table 14.1, the top ten provinces and municipalities with the highest per capita GDP are mostly from the eastern and coastal regions, and those below the top ten are mostly from the hinterland region. Moreover, the severity of disparity is alarming. The highest per capita GDP in Shanghai, among the 31 units listed, is 9.65 times that of the lowest level in Guizhou. Furthermore, the income gap between the region and rest of China has widened over time (Chen, 2005).

The regional income disparity correlates very negatively with the extent of the urban-rural income disparity. Provinces and municipalities with the highest per capita GDP, such as Jiangsu, Zhejiang, Liaoning, Shanghai, Beijing, and Tianjin, have a lower urban-rural income disparity, indicated by the lower multiples of urban to rural incomes (Table 14.1). Meanwhile, the regional disparity correlates

---

[*] Many of the observations and thoughts in this article originated from two research fieldtrips on China's urbanization. The author and seven other economists of the Chinese Economists Society (CES) made the first fieldtrip June and July of 2001 in cities of southern and northern Fujian Province. The second trip took place June 18-July 7 in eight cities of Jiangsu Province (June 18–22), Zhejiang Province(June 23–26), Hainan Province (June 27–July 2), and Inner Mongolia Autonomous Region (July 3–July 9). Durng the trips, delegates visited factories, farms, country markets, urban construction projects and sites, etc. and held interviews and conferences with local officials, experts, and academicians.
[1] *China Statistical Yearbook 20*02, p. 320, 2003, p. 344, and the author's calculation.

positively with the extent of urbanization and industrialization as indicated by the high levels of urbanized population and non-agricultural employment (Table 14.1).

Table 14.1 Income and development disparity among China's provinces (2000)

	GDP Per Capita (*yuan*)		Ratio of Urban to Rural Incomes			Population Residing in Cities and Towns (%)		Non-Agricultural Employment (%)
China	7039	China	2.79		China	36.22	China	50.0
Shanghai	27187	Tibet	4.84	1	Shanghai	88.34	Beijing	88.3
Beijing	17936	Yunnan	4.28	2	Beijing	77.54	Shanghai	86.9
Tianjin	16377	Guizhou	3.73	3	Tianjin	71.99	Tianjin	80.1
Zhejiang	12906	Xinjiang	3.60	4	Guangdng	55.00	Liaoning	62.3
Jiangsu	11539	Shaanxi	3.55	5	Liaoning	54.24	Zhejiang	62.2
Fujian	11293	Qinghai	3.47	6	Heilngjng	51.54	Guangdng	58.9
Guangdng	11180	Gansu	3.44	7	Jilin	49.68	Jiangsu	57.8
Liaoning	11017	Chngqing	3.32	8	Zhejiang	48.67	Shanxi	53.3
Shandong	9409	Guangxi	3.13	9	Inner Mng	42.68	Fujian	53.1
Heilngjng	8818	Sichuan	3.10	10	Fujian	41.57	Hubei	52.0
Hubei	7757	Ningxia	2.85	11	Jiangsu	41.49	Hebei	51.2
Hebei	7545	Hunan	2.83	12	Hubei	40.22	Heilngjng	50.5
Xinjiang	7087	Anhui	2.74	13	Hainan	40.11	Jilin	49.8
Jilin	6675	Guangdng	2.67	14	Shandong	38.00	Jiangxi	48.1
Hainan	6587	Inner Mng	2.51	15	Shanxi	34.91	Shandong	46.9
Inner Mng.	5896	Shanxi	2.48	16	Qinghai	34.76	Inner Mng	45.5
Hunan	5732	Hainan	2.46	17	Xinjiang	33.82	Shaanxi	44.3
Henan	5550	Shandong	2.44	18	Chngqng	33.09	Chngqng	43.5
Chngqing	5143	Hubei	2.43	19	Ningxia	32.43	Xinjiang	42.3
Qinghai	5088	Henan	2.40	20	Shaanxi	32.26	Ningxia	42.2
Anhui	5075	Jiangxi	2.39	21	Hunan	29.75	Sichuan	40.4
Shanxi	4985	Jilin	2.38	22	Guangxi	28.15	Gansu	40.3
Jiangxi	4838	Fujian	2.30	23	Anhui	27.81	Anhui	40.2
Sichuan	4814	Heilngjng	2.29	24	Jiangxi	27.67	Hunan	39.2
Ningxia	4725	Hebei	2.28	25	Sichuan	26.69	Qinghai	39.1
Shaanxi	4607	Liaoning	2.27	26	Hebei	26.08	Hainan	39.7
Yunnan	4559	Beijing	2.25	27	Gansu	24.01	Guangxi	37.8
Guangxi	4500	Tianjin	2.25	28	Guizhou	23.87	Henan	35.9
Tibet	4483	Zhejiang	2.18	29	Yunnan	23.36	Guizhou	32.7
Gansu	3838	Shanghai	2.09	30	Henan	23.20	Tibet	26.2
Guizhou	2818	Jiangsu	1.89	31	Tibet	18.93	Yunnan	26.1

Sources: Chen, *Modern China*, January 2006

Urbanization can thereby contribute to reducing both the urban-rural income disparity and regional disparities. The effects of urbanization on the urban-rural income disparity are apparent in two ways: (1) farmers will leave their low-paying agricultural jobs and enjoy the fruits of industrialization with their urban counterparts, reducing the gap between them through the process of urbanization; and (2) cross-sectional evidence that provinces with higher levels of urbanization and industrialization have higher per capita GDP and lower urban-rural disparity clearly indicates that urbanization is key. By the same logic, urbanization serves to bridge the gap among regions on top of geographical, institutional, and policy factors that contribute to China's regional disparity.

In this article, the author examines in a greater detail economic development and conditions as well as urbanization in the provinces of Jiangsu, Zhejiang, Hainan, Fujian, and the autonomous region of Inner Mongolia. (For simplicity, we will refer to them as the "five provinces.") The key variables to be examined include: economic scale; natural conditions; openness; the development of private enterprises (POEs); the reform of state enterprises (SOEs); and the situation of urbanization. The analysis will focus on the relationship between urbanization and the other variables. The author intends to show that the five provinces differ in their extent and mode of urbanization as a result of different stages of development and economic conditions.

This research differs from previously existing research on China's urbanization in that it combines statistical analysis with fieldtrip observations of the five provinces. The choice of the five provinces was by design to include provinces of different economic conditions as well as the availability and ease at which connections and contacts can be made and trips arranged.

The author first uses a relative ranking approach to compare the different economic conditions of the provinces and then examines the dynamic development of each province between 1988 and 2000. These data are then supplemented by fieldtrip observations and information gathered during interviews and conferences with local officials, interviewees, and academicians. While our data and field observations are inadequate for a regression analysis, they provide clear indications of variations within the natural and economic conditions among the provinces. The fieldtrips afforded us additional explanations and insights that cannot be obtained from statistical data or regressions. In that sense, this research offers a unique approach and valuable insight for a better understanding of China's urbanization.

The remainder of this chapter is organized as follows. Section 2 compares the economic and natural conditions of the five provinces based on 2000 data. Section 3 compares the development of the provinces dynamically using data starting in 1988 when the Hainan province was first established and ending in 2001. Section 4 analyzes the situation as well as the features of urbanization in the five provinces, and Section 5 concludes this chapter.

2 Natural and Economic Conditions and Characteristics

The analysis of this section is based on data presented in Tables 14.2 to 14.6—with Table 14.2 reporting the relative rank of the Jiangsu province among the thirty-one provincial-level economic units in the nation, Table 14.3 the Zhejiang province, Table 14.4 Inner Mongolia, Table 14.5 the Hainan province, and Table 14.6 the Fujian province. Tables 14.7 to 14.11 report the development of the provinces between 1988 and 2000—in the same order—measured in several key variables.

The statistics quoted in the analysis are from Tables 14.2 to 14.6, unless otherwise specified. We first compare the scale features of the provinces, seeing that Hainan is the smallest unit among the five. In fact, Hainan is one of the smallest provincial economies in the country as indicated by its 28th rank among the 31 units as measured either by population or GDP size. Meanwhile, Jiangsu is a large province—with second place in GDP size after Guangdong and fifth in population size. In terms of land resources, however, Inner Mongolia ranks the highest among the five units with a per capita-managed arable land size of 7.37 *mu* (1 *mu* equaling 1/15 *ha*), 3.72 times the national average of 1.98 *mu*. Among the five, Fujian is the scarcest in land, with a per capita level of 0.8 *mu*, and then there is Zhejiang at 0.84 *mu*, Hainan at 1.01 *mu*, and Jiangsu at 1.21 *mu*. In other words, except for Inner Mongolia, the four other provinces are relatively land-scarce economies with lower than average land endowment (see Tables 14.7 to 14.11).

In terms of economic development, Jiangsu, Zhejiang, and Fujian among the five that are above national average per capita GDP of 7,078 *yuan* (see Table 14.1), while Hainan and Inner Mongolia are below national average with Inner Mongolia being the lowest of the five. If economic efficiency can be measured by per capita GDP, then Zhejiang has the highest efficiency because it has the highest GDP per capita among all provinces, only next to the three provincial municipalities of Beijing, Tianjin, and Shanghai where populations are mostly urban (see Table 14.1).

Considering the openness factor, it can be categorized as manufacturing-oriented and tourism-oriented openness. The former is measured by the variables of joint venture firms, foreign direct investment, and foreign trade, suggesting economic development and an investment environment. Meanwhile, the latter, by revenues from international tourism, suggests more appropriately natural, geographical, cultural, and historical conditions. We will see that Jiangsu and Zhejiang belong to the former, and Hainan belongs to the latter, while Fujian has features of both.

Fujian, Zhejiang, and Jiangsu are among the highest rankings in the number of joint venture firms per 10,000 people as well as in gross value produced by joint venture firms as a ratio to GDP). These values for the three provinces are above national average—with Zhejiang slightly lower in the gross value produced. With policies that favor the coastal areas in attracting foreign investment, geography and local conditions each play a role.

Table 14.2 Relative development of Jiangsu Province (2000)

Variables (Unit)	Ranking (Provincial Value) (National Value)	Variables	Ranking (Provincial Value) National (Value)	Variables	Ranking (Provincial Value) (Natioanl Value)
Population (10,000)	5 (7438) (126583)	% of Tertiary Sector Employment	16 (28.1) (27.5)	State-owned Enterprises (SOE) per Million Population	23 (34.3) (42.3)
GDP (100 Million)	2 (8582) (89113)	Ratio of Foreign Trade to GDP	6 (0.436) (0.436)	SOE Profits per 10,000 *yuan* GDP	15 (1.29) (2.73)
Per Capita GDP (*Yuan*)	5 (11539.03) (7039)	FDI as Ratio to GDP	4 (0.061) (0.037)	Average Employment per SOE	12 (1610.8) (1472.8)
% of Population Residing in Cities and Towns	11 (41.49) (36.22)	No. of Joint Venture Firms to Per Million Population	7 (42.48) (22.47)	Agricultural Support and R&D as Ratio GDP[1]	23 (0.015) (NA)
% of Non-Agricultural Employment	7 (57.8) (50)	Ratio of Gross Value Produced by Joint Venture Firms to Million *yuan* GDP	6 (0.34) (0.26)	Outlays on Science and Rechnology as Ratio to GDP	24 (0.0015) (NA)
Ratio of Urban to Rural Per Capita Income	31 (1.89) (2.787)	Foreign Tourism Revenues as Ratio to GDP	14 (0.0069) (NA)	Education Outlays as Ratio to GDP	28 (0.0137) (NA)
% of Primary Sector Employment	25 (42.2) (50)	Private Enterprises per Million Population	6 (2339.3) (1392)	Employment in Science and Technology per 10,000 People	15 (12.93) (12.61)
% of Secondary Sector Employment	4 (29.7) (22.5)	Private Firm Employment per 10,000 People	4 (315) (190.12)	Employment in Edcation per 10,000 People	21 (168.87) (161.01)

Notes: 1. Provincial government outlays on agricutltural support and R&D as a ratio to GDP are higher for provinces with a greater agricutltural sector. We have made adjustment to control for such potential structural bias by doing the following: Adjusted Ratio = Unadjusted Ratio – Adjustment Factor × Unadjusted Ratio; Adjustment factor = (Provincial Primary Sector as Ratio to GDP – National Primary Sector as Ratio to GDP)/National Primary Sector as Ratio to GDP.

Sources: Author's calculation from China Statistical Yearbook (Zhongguo tongji nianjian, 2001).

Table 14.3 Relative development of Zhejiang Province (2000)

Variables	Ranking (Provincial Value)	Variables	Ranking (Provincial Value)	Variables	Ranking (Provincial Value)
Population (10,000)	10 (4677)	% of Tertiary Sector Employment	7 (31.3)	State-owned Enterprises (SOE) per Million Population	28 (30.32)
GDP (100 Million)	4 (6036.34)	Ratio of Foreign Trade to GDP	7 (0.38)	SOE Profits per 10,000 *yuan* GDP	17 (1.224)
Per Capita GDP (*Yuan*)	4 (12906.4)	FDI as Ratio to GDP	10 (0.022)	Average Employment per SOE	20 (1387.2)
% of Population Residing in Cities and Towns	8 (48.67)	No. of Joint Venture Firms to Per Million Population	6 (45.26)	Agricultural Support and R&D as Ratio GDP[1]	27 (0.123)
% of Non-Agricultural Employment	5 (62.2)	Ratio of Gross Value Produced by Joint Venture Firms to Million *yuan* GDP	7 (0.20)	Outlays on Science and Rechnology as Ratio to GDP	14 (0.002)
Ratio of Urban to Rural Per Capita Income	29 (2.18)	Foreign Tourism Revenues as Ratio to GDP	13 (0.0070)	Education Outlays as Ratio to GDP	29 (0.013)
% of Primary Sector Employment	27 (37.8)	Private Enterprises per Million Population	3 (3827.2)	Employment in Science and Technology per 10,000 People	20 (9.998)
% of Secondary Sector Employment	3 (30.9)	Private Firm Employment per 10,000 People	2 (642.5)	Employment in Edcation per 10,000 People	25 (149.6)

Notes: 1. Provincial government outlays on agricutltural support and R&D as a ratio to GDP are higher for provinces with a greater agricutltural sector. We have made adjustment to control for such potential structural bias by doing the following: Adjusted Ratio= Unadjusted Ratio – Adjustment Factor× Unadjusted Ratio; Adjustment factor = (Provincial Primary Sector as Ratio to GDP – National Primary Sector as Ratio to GDP)/National Primary Sector as Ratio to GDP.
Sources: Author's calculation from China Statistical Yearbook (Zhongguo tongji nianjian, 2001).

China's Rural Economy after WTO

Table 14.4 Relative development of Inner Mongolia (2000)

Variables	Ranking (Provincial Value)	Variables	Ranking (Provincial Value)	Variables	Ranking (Provincial Value)
Population (10,000)	23 (2376)	% of Tertiary Sector Employment	10 (29.1)	State-owned Enterprises (SOE) per Million Population	26 (31.86)
GDP (100 Million)	24 (1401.01)	Ratio of Foreign Trade to GDP	11 (0.153)	SOE Profits per 10,000 yuan GDP	23 (0.815)
Per Capita GDP (*Yuan*)	16 (5896.5)	FDI as Ratio to GDP	24 (0.008)	Average Employment per SOE	1 (2606.3)
% of Population Residing in Cities and Towns	9 (42.68)	No. of Joint Venture Firms to Per Million Population	21 (3.79)	Agricultural Support and R&D as Ratio GDP[1]	6 (0.065)
% of Non-Agricultural Employment	16 (45.5)	Ratio of Gross Value Produced by Joint Venture Firms to Million *yuan* GDP	15 (0.072)	Outlays on Science and Rechnology as Ratio to GDP	15 (0.002)
Ratio of Urban to Rural Per Capita Income	15 (2.512)	Foreign Tourism Revenues as Ratio to GDP	11 (0.0074)	Education Outlays as Ratio to GDP	13 (0.021)
% of Primary Sector Employment	16 (54.5)	Private Enterprises per Million Population	15 (1136.4)	Employment in Science and Technology per 10,000 People	9 (16.7)
% of Secondary Sector Employment	16 (16.5)	Private Firm Employment per 10,000 People	14 (174.24)	Employment in Edcation per 10,000 People	6 (262.6)

Notes: 1. Provincial government outlays on agricutltural support and R&D as a ratio to GDP are higher for provinces with a greater agricutltural sector. We have made adjustment to control for such potential structural bias by doing the following: Adjusted Ratio = Unadjusted Ratio – Adjustment Factor × Unadjusted Ratio; Adjustment factor = (Provincial Primary Sector as Ratio to GDP – National Primary Sector as Ratio to GDP)/National Primary Sector as Ratio to GDP.
Sources: Author's calculation from China Statistical Yearbook (Zhongguo tongji nianjian, 2001).

Table 14.5 Relative development of Hainan Province (2000)

Variables	Ranking (Provincial Value)	Variables	Ranking (Provincial Value)	Variables	Ranking (Provincial Value)
Population (10,000)	28 (787)	% of Tertiary Sector Employment	11 (29.1)	State-owned Enterprises (SOE) per Million Population	11 (50.953)
GDP (100 Million)	28 (518.47)	Ratio of Foreign Trade to GDP	10 (0.204)	SOE Profits per 10,000 *yuan* GDP	26 (0.698)
Per Capita GDP (*Yuan*)	15 (6587.93)	FDI as Ratio to GDP	3 (0.068)	Average Employment per SOE	10 (1630.9)
% of Population Residing in Cities and Towns	13 (40.11)	No. of Joint Venture Firms to Per Million Population	10 (12.45)	Agricultural Support and R&D as Ratio GDP[1]	4 (0.082)
% of Non-Agricultural Employment	26 (38.7)	Ratio of Gross Value Produced by Joint Venture Firms to Million *yuan* GDP	13 (0.077)	Outlays on Science and Rechnology as Ratio to GDP	30 (0.001)
Ratio of Urban to Rural Per Capita Income	17 (2.456)	Foreign Tourism Revenues as Ratio to GDP	6 (0.017)	Education Outlays as Ratio to GDP	17 (0.019)
% of Primary Sector Employment	6 (61.3)	Private Enterprises per Million Population	5 (2541.3)	Employment in Science and Technology per 10,000 People	17 (11.99)
% of Secondary Sector Employment	28 (9.6)	Private Firm Employment per 10,000 People	8 (236.34)	Employment in Edcation per 10,000 People	14 (188.79)

Notes: 1. Provincial government outlays on agricutltural support and R&D as a ratio to GDP are higher for provinces with a greater agricutltural sector. We have made adjustment to control for such potential structural bias by doing the following: Adjusted Ratio = Unadjusted Ratio − Adjustment Factor × Unadjusted Ratio; Adjustment factor = (Provincial Primary Sector as Ratio to GDP − National Primary Sector as Ratio to GDP)/National Primary Sector as Ratio to GDP.

Sources: Author's calculation from China Statistical Yearbook (Zhongguo tongji nianjian, 2001).

Table 14.6 Relative development of Fujian Province (2000)

Variables	Ranking (Provincial Value)	Variables	Ranking (Provincial Value)	Variables	Ranking (Provincial Value)
Population (10,000)	18 (3471)	% of Tertiary Sector Employment	12 (28.6)	State-owned Enterprises (SOE) per Million Population	18 (39.38)
GDP (100 Million)	11 (3920.07)	Ratio of Foreign Trade to GDP	5 (0.444)	SOE Profits per 10,000 *yuan* GDP	20 (1.079)
Per Capita GDP (*Yuan*)	6 (11293.8)	FDI as Ratio to GDP	2 (0.072)	Average Employment per SOE	23 (1220.2)
% of Population Residing in Cities and Towns	10 (41.57)	No. of Joint Venture Firms to Per Million Population	4 (77.53)	Agricultural Support and R&D as Ratio GDP[1]	17 (0.025)
% of Non-Agricultural Employment	9 (53.1)	Ratio of Gross Value Produced by Joint Venture Firms to Million *yuan* GDP	5 (0.41)	Outlays on Science and Rechnology as Ratio to GDP	17 (0.0021)
Ratio of Urban to Rural Per Capita Income	23 (2.301)	Foreign Tourism Revenues as Ratio to GDP	5 (0.019)	Education Outlays as Ratio to GDP	20 (0.016)
% of Primary Sector Employment	23 (46.9)	Private Enterprises per Million Population	11 (1411.7)	Employment in Science and Technology per 10,000 People	22 (9.64)
% of Secondary Sector Employment	9 (24.5)	Private Firm Employment per 10,000 People	12 (195.91)	Employment in Edcation per 10,000 People	9 (226.48)

Notes: 1. Provincial government outlays on agricutltural support and R&D as a ratio to GDP are higher for provinces with a greater agricutltural sector. We have made adjustment to control for such potential structural bias by doing the following: Adjusted Ratio = Unadjusted Ratio – Adjustment Factor × Unadjusted Ratio; Adjustment factor = (Provincial Primary Sector as Ratio to GDP – National Primary Sector as Ratio to GDP)/National Primary Sector as Ratio to GDP.
Sources: Author's calculation from China Statistical Yearbook (Zhongguo tongji nianjian, 2001).

Table 14.7 Economic development in Jiangsu Province since 1988 (National Values in Parentheses)

Variables	1988	1990	1992	1994	1996	1998	2000
Population (10,000)	6438	6767	6911	7021	7110	7182	7438
Per Capita GDP	1516	1689	2858	5785	8447	10021	11773
(*yuan*)	(1355)	(1634)	(2287)	(3923)	(5576)	(6307)	(7078)
GDP (100 million)	969.22	314.39	1971.6	4057.39	6004.21	7199.95	8582.73
Of which:	31.5	30.4	19.97	16.6	16.1	14.1	12
Primary Sector (%)	(25.7)	(27.1)	(21.8)	(20.2)	(20.4)	(18.6)	(15.9)
Secondary Sector (%)	57.3	59.2	56.77	53.9	51.2	50.6	51.7
	(44.1)	(41.6)	(43.9)	(47.9)	(49.5)	(49.3)	(50.9)
Tertiary Sector (%)	11.2	10.4	23.26	29.5	32.7	35.3	36.3
	(30.2)	(31.3)	(34.3)	(31.9)	(30.1)	(32.1)	(33.2)
Ratio of Urban	NA	NA	NA	NA	NA	NA	41.49
Population							(36.22)
Employment by	NA	NA	NA	NA	41.6	42.8	42.2
Primary Sector					(50.5)	(49.8)	(50)
By Secondary Sector	NA	NA	NA	NA	33.3	30.4	29.7
					(23.5)	(23.5)	(22.5)
By Tertiary Sector	NA	NA	NA	NA	25.2	26.8	28.1
					(26)	(26.7)	(27.5)
Average Salary	1796	2129	2800	4974	6603	8256	10299
	NA	(2140)	(2711)	(4538)	(6210)	(7479)	(9371)
Growth Rate of		0.18	0.32	0.77	0.33	0.25	0.25
Average Salary		(0.27)	(0.67)	(0.67)	(0.37)	(0.20)	(0.25)
Per Capita Managed	1.41	1.38	NA	1.32	1.26	1.25	1.21
Crop Land (mu)	(2.06)`	(2.1)		(2.18)	(2.3)	(2.06)	(1.98)
Ratio of FDI to GDP	0.009	0.033	0.061	0.076	0.071	0.076	0.062
	(0.018)	(0.015)	(0.035)	(0.060)	(0.052)	(0.049)	(0.038)
Growth of FDI		0.21	10.78	1.57	0.38	0.27	-0.03
(Multiples)		(0.09)	(2.24)	(2.01)	(0.24)	(0.08)	(-0.10)
Urban Per Capita	NA	NA	2138	3779	5186	6018	6800
Disposable Income			(2026)	(3496)	(4838)	(5424)	(6279)
Rural Per Capita Net	797	884	1061	1832	2457	3377	3595
Income	(545)	(630)	(784)	(1221)	(1578)	(2162)	(2253)
Multiples of Urban to			2.016	2.063	2.111	1.782	1.892
Rural Per Capita			(2.585)	(2.863)	(3.067)	(2.509)	(2.787)
Income							

Notes: GDP measures for provinces did not start until 1992 and were proxied by national income figures.

Sources: *China Statistical Yearbook*, 1989–2001 and the author's calculations.

China's Rural Economy after WTO

Table 14.8 Economic development in Zhejiang Province since 1988 (National Values in Parentheses)

Variables	1988	1990	1992	1994	1996	1998	2000
Population (10,000)	4170	4168	4236	4294	4343	4456	4677
Per Capita GDP (*yuan*)	1541[a]	1727[a]	2850	6149	9455	11247	13451
	(1355)	(1634)	(2287)	(3923)	(5576)	(6307)	(7078)
GDP (100 million)	638.69	836.81	1220.6	2666.8	4146.0	4987.5	6036.3
Of which:	30	30.4	21.52	16.6	14.7	12.7	11
Primary Sector (%)	(25.7)	(27.1)	(21.8)	(20.2)	(20.4)	(18.6)	(15.9)
Secondary Sector	54.8	56.2	53.53	52.1	53.1	54.3	52.7
	(44.1)	(41.6)	(43.9)	(47.9)	(49.5)	(49.3)	(50.9)
Tertiary Sector	15.2	13.4	24.95	31.1	32.2	33	36.3
	(30.2)	(31.3)	(34.3)	(31.9)	(30.1)	(32.1)	(33.2)
Ratio of Urban Population	NA	NA	NA	NA	NA	NA	48.67
							(36.22)
Employment by Primary Sector	NA	NA	NA	NA	41.9	41.8	37.8
					(50.5)	(49.8)	(50)
By Secondary Sector	NA	NA	NA	NA	31.4	29.6	30.9
					(23.5)	(23.5)	(22.5)
By Tertiary Sector	NA	NA	NA	NA	26.7	28.6	31.3
					(26)	(26.7)	(27.5)
Average Salry	1841	2220	2884	5597	7413	9759	13076
	NA	(2140)	(2711)	(4538)	(6210)	(7479)	(9371)
Growth Rate of Average Salary		0.21	0.30	0.94	0.32	0.32	0.34
		(0.27)	(0.67)	(0.37)	(0.20)	(0.25)	
Per Capita Managed Crop Land	0.9	0.91	NA	0.98	0.94	0.90	0.84
(mu)	(2.06)`	(2.1)		(2.18)	(2.3)	(2.06)	(1.98)
Ratio of FDI to GDP	0.004	0.005	0.016	0.035	0.030	0.022	0.022
	(0.018)	(0.02)	(0.035)	(0.060)	(0.052)	(0.049)	(0.038)
Growth Rate of FDI (Multiples)		0.64	3.95	3.778	0.329	-0.133	0.22
		(0.09)	(2.24)	(2.01)	(0.24)	(0.08)	(-0.10)
Urban Per Capita Disposable	NA	NA	2619	5066	6956	7837	9279
Income			(2026)	(3496)	(4838)	(5424)	(6279)
Rural Per Capita Net Income	902	1045	1359	2225	2966	3815	4254
	(545)	(630)	(784)	(1221)	(1578)	(2162)	(2253)
Multiples of Urban to Rural			1.927	2.277	2.345	2.054	2.181
Inocme			(2.585)	(2.863)	(3.067)	(2.509)	(2.787)

Notes: GDP measures for provinces did not start until 1992 and were proxied by national income figures.

Sources: *China Statistical Yearbook*, 1989–2001 and the author's calculations.

Table 14.9 Economic development in Inner Mongolia Province since 1988 (National Values in Parentheses)

Variables	1988	1990	1992	1994	1996	1998	2000
Population (10,000)	2094	2163	2207	2260	2307	2345	2376
Per Capita GDP (*yuan*)	921[a]	1080[a]	1744	3013	4259	5068	5872
	(1355)	(1634)	(2287)	(3923)	(5576)	(6307)	(7078)
GDP (100 million)	191.57	286.62	378.62	681.92	984.78	1192.29	1401.01
Of which:	45.8	46.6	15.96	30.6	31.8	28.7	25
Primary Sector (%)	(25.7)	(27.1)	(21.8)	(20.2)	(20.4)	(18.6)	(15.9)
Secondary Sector	40.4	40.8	55.65	38.4	39.3	40.2	39.7
	(44.1)	(41.6)	(43.9)	(47.9)	(49.5)	(49.3)	(50.9)
Tertiary Sector	13.8	12.4	28.39	31.0	28.9	31.1	35.3
	(30.2)	(31.3)	(34.3)	(31.9)	(30.1)	(32.1)	(33.2)
Ratio of Urban Population	NA	NA	NA	NA	NA	NA	42.68
							(36.22)
Employment by Primary	NA	NA	NA	NA	52.4	53.9	54.5
Sector					(50.5)	(49.8)	(50)
By Secondary Sector	NA	NA	NA	NA	21.5	17.8	16.5
					(23.5)	(23.5)	(22.5)
By Tertiary Sector	NA	NA	NA	NA	26.1	28.2	29.1
					(26)	(26.7)	(27.5)
Average Salary	1548	1846	2339	36758	4716	5792	6974
	NA	(2140)	(2711)	(4538)	(6210)	(7479)	(9371)
Growth Rate of Average		0.19	0.27	0.57	0.28	0.23	0.20
Salary			(0.27)	(0.67)	(0.37)	(0.20)	(0.25)
Per Capita Managed Crop	6.53	6.76	NA	7.77	10.17	6.89	7.37
Land (mu)	(2.06)`	(2.1)		(2.18)	(2.3)	(2.06)	(1.98)
Ratio of FDI to GDP	0.0014	0.003	0.001	0.005	0.006	0.0063	0.0062
	(0.02)	(0.015)	(0.035)	(0.060)	(0.052)	(0.049)	(0.038)
Growth Rate of FDI		2.16	-0.51	6.71	0.79	0.264	0.164
(Multiples)		(0.09)	(2.24)	(2.01)	(0.24)	(0.08)	(-0.10)
Per Capita Urban Disposable	NA	NA	1495	2498	3431	4353	5129
Income			(2026)	(3496)	(4838)	(5424)	(6279)
Per Capita Rural Net Income	450	607	672	970	1208	1981	2038
	(545)	(630)	(784)	(1221)	(1578)	(2162)	(2253)
Multiples of Urban to Rural			2.224	2.576	2.840	2.197	2.516
Income			(2.585)	(2.863)	(3.067)	(2.509)	(2.787)

Notes: GDP measures for provinces did not start until 1992 and were proxied by national income figures.

Sources: *China Statistical Yearbook*, 1989–2001 and the author's calculations.

Table 14.10 Economic development in Hainan Province since 1988 (National Values in Parentheses)

Variables	1988	1990	1992	1994	1996	1998	2000
Population (10,000)	628	663	686	711	734	753	787
Per Capita GDP (*yuan*)[a]	999[b]	1193[b]	2126	4820	5500	6022	6894
	(1355)	(1634)	(2287)	(3923)	(5576)	(6307)	(7078)
GDP (100 million)	62.09	95.01	141.68	330.95	389.53	438.93	518.48
Of which:	62.4	60	38.21	32.5	36.8	37.4	37.9
Primary Sector (%)	(25.7)	(27.1)	(21.8)	(20.2)	(20.4)	(18.6)	(15.9)
Secondary Sector	22.5	26.7	27.06	25.3	20.9	20.6	19.8
	(44.1)	(41.6)	(43.9)	(47.9)	(49.5)	(49.3)	(50.9)
Tertiary Sector	15.1	13.3	34.73	42.2	42.3	42	42.3
	(30.2)	(31.3)	(34.3)	(31.9)	(30.1)	(32.1)	(33.2)
Ratio of Urban Population	NA	NA	NA	NA	NA	NA	40.11
							(36.22)
Employment by Primary	NA	NA	NA	NA	60.2	61.6	61.3
Sector					(50.5)	(49.8)	(50)
By Secondary Sector	NA	NA	NA	NA	11.8	10.2	9.6
					(23.5)	(23.5)	(22.5)
By Tertiary Sector	NA	NA	NA	NA	28.1	28.2	29.1
					(26)	(26.7)	(27.5)
Average Salary	1416	1982	2720	4488	5476	6248	7408
	NA	(2140)	(2711)	(4538)	(6210)	(7479)	(9371)
Growth Rate of Average		0.40	0.37	0.65	0.22	0.14	0.19
Salary		(0.27)	(0.67)	(0.37)	(0.20)	(0.25)
Per Capita Managed Crop	1.21	1.17	NA	1.91	1.35	1.32	1.01
Land (mu)	(2.06)`	(2.1)		(2.18)	(2.3)	(2.06)	(1.98)
Ratio of FDI to GDP	0.15	0.09	0.26	0.23	0.17	0.13	0.07
Growth Rate of FDI		-0.10	3.39	1.03	-0.14	-0.09	-0.40
(Multiples)		(0.09)	(2.24)	(2.01)	(0.24)	(0.08)	(-0.10)
Per Capita Urban	NA	NA	2318	3920	4926	4852	5358
Disposable Income			(2026)	(3496)	(4838)	(5424)	(6279)
Per Capita Rural Net	566	653	842	1304	1519	2018	2182
Income	(545)	(630)	(784)	(1221)	(1578)	(2162)	(2253)
Multiples of Urban to			2.751	3.006	3.242	2.404	2.456
Rural Income			(2.585)	(2.863)	(3.067)	(2.509)	(2.787)

Notes: GDP measures for provinces did not start until 1992 and were proxied by national income figures.

Sources: *China Statistical Yearbook*, 1989–2001 and the author's calculations.

Table 14.11 Economic development in Fujian Province since 1988 (National Values in Parentheses)

Variables	1988	1990	1992	1994	1996	1998	2000
Population (10,000)	2845	3037	3116	3181	3261	3299	3471
Per Capita GDP (*yuan*)	1090[a]	1313	2264	5386	8136	10369	11601
	(1355)	(1634)	(2287)	(3923)	(5576)	(6307)	(7078)
GDP (100 million)	307.59	465.84	694.7	1685.3	2606.9	3330.2	3920.1
Of which:	38.6	38.4	28.49	22.1	21.5	18.3	16.3
Primary Sector (%)	(25.7)	(27.1)	(21.8)	(20.2)	(20.4)	(18.6)	(15.9)
Secondary Sector	46.8	46.4	41.97	43.9	41.8	43.4	43.7
	(44.1)	(41.6)	(43.9)	(47.9)	(49.5)	(49.3)	(50.9)
Tertiary Sector	14.6	15.1	29.54	34	36.7	38.3	40
	(30.2)	(31.3)	(34.3)	(31.9)	(30.1)	(32.1)	(33.2)
Ratio of Urban Population	NA	NA	NA	NA	NA	NA	41.57
							(36.22)
Employment by Primary	NA	NA	NA	NA	49.5	48.6	46.9
Sector					(50.5)	(49.8)	(50)
By Secondary Sector	NA	NA	NA	NA	24	20.4	24.5
					(23.5)	(23.5)	(22.5)
By Tertiary Sector	NA	NA	NA	NA	26.5	31.1	28.6
					(26)	(26.7)	(27.5)
Average Salary	1647	2162	2777	4889	6684	8531	10584
	NA	(2140)	(2711)	(4538)	(6210)	(7479)	(9371)
Growth Rate of Average		0.31	0.28	0.76	0.37	0.28	0.24
Salary			(0.27)	(0.67)	(0.37)	(0.20)	(0.25)
Per Capita Managed Crop	0.95	0.95	NA	1.07	0.82	0.84	0.8
Land (mu)	(2.06)`	(2.1)		(2.18)	(2.3)	(2.06)	(1.98)
Ratio of FDI to GDP	0.035	0.051	0.169	0.181	0.129	0.104	0.091
	(0.018)	(0.015)	(0.035)	(0.060)	(0.052)	(0.049)	(0.038)
Growth Rate of FDI		0.47	2.29	0.075	-0.29	-0.193	-0.124
(Multiples)		(0.09)	(2.24)	(2.01)	(0.24)	(0.08)	(-0.10)
Per Capita Urban	NA	NA	2283	3672	5172	6485	7432
Disposable Income			(2026)	(3496)	(4838)	(5424)	(6279)
Per Capita Rural Net	613	764	9841	1577	2048	2946	3230
Income	(545)	(630)	(784)	(1221)	(1578)	(2162)	(2253)
Multiples of Urban to			2.319	2.327	2.525	2.201	2.300
Rural Income			(2.585)	(2.863)	(3.067)	(2.509)	(2.787)

Notes: GDP measures for provinces did not start until 1992 and were proxied by national income figures.

Sources: *China Statistical Yearbook*, 1989–2001 and the author's calculations.

In terms of relative ranking, the Hainan province is in tenth place in terms of the number of joint venture firms it has, but its size of 12.45 firms per million people is well below the national average of 22.47. Moreover, while Hainan's industrial value produced by joint venture firms—as a ratio to GDP—is ranked thirteenth, its size is barely one-third of the national average, suggesting that the distribution of joint venture activities is severely skewed toward the few leading coastal provinces, like Jiangsu, Zhejiang, and Fujian. For Inner Mongolia, it is not surprising that its joint venture firms as well as the value produced by these firms are both below the national average in their ranking and size measures. This could be attributed to Inner Mongolia's high transportation costs, cold weather, and low level of economic development that are detrimental in attracting foreign firms and their investment.

Considering the variable of foreign direct investment (FDI) as a ratio to GDP, Fujian, Jiangsu, and Hainan all ranked among the highest. Zhejiang is tenth but is lower than national average in size. Inner Mongolia has the scarcest FDI, ranking 24th with a size measure that is 16 percent of the national average. The indicator of foreign trade—the sum of export and import values as a ratio to GDP—suggests a similar pattern. Among the five, Fijian, Jiangsu, and Zhejiang are ranked among the highest, even though Zhejiang is slightly lower than the national average in terms of size. Hainan and Inner Mongolia also have above-average rankings but are much lower than the average value in size.

The above shows that Jiangsu and Fujian are indisputably most open in terms of joint ventures, foreign direct investment, and foreign trade activities by both their ranking and size measures. Zhejiang comes next, followed by Hainan, while Inner Mongolia is the least open and most in need of foreign investment. One important feature worth emphasizing is that no matter measured by joint venture, FDI, or foreign trade activities, provinces with a relative ranking about the national average have considerably lower-than-average levels measured in size, suggesting that these economic activities are concentrated disproportionally in a few coastal cities, such as Guangdong, Fujian, Jiangsu, Zhejiang, and the provincial municipalities except Chongqing. Moreover, the openness associates closely with the extent of economic development, as suggested in this study by the cases of Fujian, Jiangsu, and Zhejiang provinces. We will show later that openness also correlates with the extent of urbanization and the development of private enterprises.

If we consider tourism-oriented openness, Fujian and Hainan stand out among not only the five provinces, but also nationwide, whereas the advantages of Zhejiang and Jiangsu seem to have disappeared.[2] We can therefore conclude that Jiangsu and Zhejiang are more of manufacturing-oriented open economies, and Hainan is a tourism-oriented open economy, whereas Fujian possesses the advantages of both. It must be pointed out that tourism-oriented openness is entirely based on the ratio of foreign tourism revenue to GDP. This ratio can be

---

[2] For details, see Table 14.1 in Chen and Song (2003).

very high for small economies although the size of tourism industry may be small. This is why Tibet has a much higher ranking in this measure than Zhejiang (*ibid*).

The speed at which private enterprises develop and state enterprises withdraw suggest the extent of a local economy's reform. Two variables—the number of private enterprises per million people and the employment in private enterprises per 10 thousand people—are used here to measure the development of private enterprises. With the exception of Inner Mongolia, Zhejiang, Jiangsu, Hainan, and Fujian have performed better than the national average in these two measures—led by Zhejiang with its number of private enterprises ranked second and its private employment third in the nation. This is quite consistent with the widely observed, more rapid development of the east coast, especially the Township-Village Enterprises (TVEs) in Zhejiang and Jiangsu.

Our fieldtrip interviews and conferences informed us that one distinctive difference between the TVEs in Jiangsu and Zhejiang is that TVEs in Jiangsu were predominately collective-owned, whereas those in Zhejiang were private-owned. Zhejiang has been known to have effectively fostered the development of private enterprises. Our statistics support this perception.

As shown in Tables 14.2 and 14.3, Zhejiang has 3,827 private enterprises per million people, ranked third in the nation, while Jiangsu has 2,339 and is ranked sixth in the nation. The former is 1.64 times that of the latter. Moreover, in Zhejiang, 644 out of ten thousand people are employed in private enterprises, coming in second in the nation next to Shanghai, while Jiangsu has 315 people employed in the private enterprises and is ranked fourth in the nation. In other words, more than twice as many people out of every ten thousand in Zhejiang are employed in private enterprise than in Jiangsu. Clearly, there are more private businesses, creating more employment opportunities, in Zhejiang than in Jiangsu. Private-owned TVEs are the most important source of these private businesses.

The well-known "Wenzhou and Taizhou Model (wentai moshi)" has been characterized by its private ownership of TVEs. In Taizhou, a medium-sized city in Zhejiang Province, 98 percent of the gross value of industrial output has been produced by private businesses.[3] Our data and analysis here have provided an indirect support to the nature of private ownership of Zhejiang's TVEs. Correspondingly, we will see below that Zhejiang has the least state enterprises.

In terms of the number of state enterprises as a ratio to population, Hainan is the only one among the five with a higher-than-average number of state enterprises. Zhejiang has the least, followed by Inner Mongolia, Jiangsu, and Fujian, respectively. Hainan's above-average number results primarily from its small population and the fact that it has many state farms, which are unique to Hainan and categorized as state enterprises. During our interviews, local officials emphasized that Hainan did not have a severe state enterprise problem if not for the state farms. In fact, none of the five has been as severely burdened by state enterprises as in the cities, such as Chongqing, Wuhan, and Shenyang.

---

[3] For details, see Hong and Song (2003).

3 Some Dynamic Developments

The above analysis is based on 2000 data. Below, we will analyze some dynamic developments of the provinces since 1988—when Hainan was first established as a province—based on the information in Tables 14.7 to 14.11. Our analysis based on the time series data will provide more information in order to shed light on the economic situations and developments within each province that the 2000 data were unable to fully illuminate alone.

3.1 Sectoral Structural Development

In examining the sectoral structural changes in the provinces, we looked at the variables of three sectors as shares of GDP across the provinces (across Tables 14.7 to 14.11) and observed the following characteristics: (1) in all five provinces, the shares of the manufacturing sector's GDP in 2000 were lower than in 1988, while nationwide, it has slightly increased; (2) the primary sector's shares of GDP have all decreased at a faster pace than it has nationwide; and (3) the tertiary sector's shares of GDP have all grown at a faster rate than the national average. Hence, it is obvious that the sectoral structure of the five provinces has been changing more rapidly than the trend nationwide. Fujian, Inner Mongolia, and Hainan, however, still have higher than the national average of the primary sector's share of GDP and lower than the national average of the manufacturing sector's shares.

Among the five, Zhejiang and Jiangsu stand out with their manufacturing sectors, while Fujian and especially Hainan are in the tertiary sector, and Inner Mongolia takes the middle place. Hainan has nearly the lowest share of the manufacturing sector in the nation. This pattern is consistent with the stylized fact that Zhejiang and Jiangsu are the nation's manufacturing bases, while Hainan's supporting industries are tourism and specialty-agriculture. Fujian and Inner Mongolia also have better-than-average tourism resources as previously mentioned.

One characteristic worth emphasizing is that while the primary sector's shares in GDP of the five provinces have been decreasing, the shares of employment in the sector have been relatively stable—even rising. Two underlying factors may be at work. First, if we assume the data are reliable, the concurrence of the primary sector's falling share in GDP and its stable, or rising, share in employment suggests that many laborers in the primary sector have close to zero marginal productivity. In other words, there exists a large redundant labor force in the agricultural sector that needs to flow elsewhere, and all five provinces are faced with the challenging task of creating non-farm jobs. Second, the data may be inaccurate to have included non-farm laborers or half-time farmers as farm laborers. This is caused by the simultaneous existence of China's unprecedented migration of rural workers into the cities and the traditional household registration system in which many non-farmers by occupation have continued to be counted as farmers because of their rural *hukou*, or household registration, status that cannot be changed easily. In the Zhejiang and Jiangsu provinces, for example, many former farmers, who are now employed in non-farm jobs, have leased their land to farmers from inland provinces, but they are still counted as farmers.[4] China, therefore, must not only generate many non-farm jobs rapidly, but enhance the accuracy of the population's statistical accounting as well.

3.2 Urban-Rural Income Disparity

The income disparity is measured by the ratio of urban per capita disposable income to rural per capita net income. Jiangsu province has the lowest ratio— 1.892—in the nation among all provincial economies (see Tables 14.1 and 14.7). Zhejiang has the third lowest ratio, followed by Fujian, Hainan, and Inner Mongolia, respectively. Dynamically, Jiangsu's ratio had declined from 2.016 in 1992 to 1.892, while Zhejiang had increased from 1.927 to 2.181 during the same period. Since Zhejiang's disparity situation is the third lowest in the nation, the increase over that time span remains unexplainable by either casual observations of its prosperity or the statistical indications of good development that were discussed earlier. Fujian's ratio shows a slight declining trend, but Hainan's decline is quite obvious—from 2.751 in 1992 to 2.455 in 2000, a decline from more than the nation's average to less than that since 1998. Inner Mongolia takes the same upward trend as the nation, rising from 2.22 in 1992 to 2.516 in 2000, even though the disparity level has always been below the nation's average.

Provincial disparities are a result of different economic conditions and development amongst the provinces. The small disparities in Zhejiang and Jiangsu obviously arise from industrialization and urbanization, like the development of township village enterprises (TVEs). Meanwhile, Fujian's below-average disparity can be explained by its rich geographic and natural conditions that had led the development of southern Fujian to be ahead of most regional economies in the nation. On the other hand, Hainan's lower ratio did not result from a faster development of the provincial economy but rather the urban per capita income that grew at a much slower pace than the national average (see Table 14.10). The poor growth of urban income, in turn, can be attributed to the inclusion of low-paid workers at state-owned farms into the urban population and the burst of real estate bubbles in the early-1990s.[5] For Inner Mongolia, its above-average rural-urban disparity can be explained primarily by its above-average ratio of urban population.

3.3 The Openness of the Economies

Dynamically, Jiangsu province not only scored better than the national average with a FDI measured in volume (as a ratio of FDI to GDP), but had been growing faster than the national average as well. FDI in Zhejiang grew faster than the

---

[4] Conference notes, with officials of the city of Zhangjia Gang. June 18, 2002.
[5] For detail, see Chen (2003a).

national average, but it trails not only Jiangsu, but also the national average in volume. A similar trend is shown in Inner Mongolia. Meanwhile, Fujian and Hainan provinces have shown an opposite trend, growing at a slower pace—since 1992 and 1994, respectively—than the national average despite hosting more FDI measured in volume. These statistics suggest a few facts: (1) unlike Jiangsu's economy that has greatly benefited from FDI, Zhejiang's leading development is boosted primarily by the growth of domestic private businesses; (2) Fujian and Hainan are more open because of their geographic conditions, both being coastal and sub-tropical provinces as well as special economic zones that have led to both foreign tourism and FDI, but their advantages are gradually fading as other regional economies have sped up in improving their environment for foreign tourism and FDI; and (3) Inner Mongolia seems to be most in need of FDI, owing to its inland geographic conditions and high transportation costs, but the growth rate of FDI is above-average because of its very low starting point.

4 Urbanization: Level, Model, and Characteristics

4.1 The Current Level of Development

Measured by the ratio of population residing in urban areas, above-average levels of urbanization were found in all five provinces in 2000—higher than the national level of 36.22 percent (Table 14.1). Of the five, Zhejiang ranks the highest with a ratio of 48.67 percent, followed by Jiangsu, Fujian, Inner Mongolia, and Hainan. While Inner Mongolia has a statistically higher ratio of urban population than either Jiangsu or Fujian, it included many state forest workers that hold urban household registration. Also with potential to discount is Hainan's urban population ratio of 40.11 percent because it consists of a large number of state-owned farm workers.

During the planning years, China's northernmost province of Heilongjiang and southernmost province of Hainan had stationed most of China's state-owned farms in order to open vast uncultivated land in the north and plant rubber trees, producing rubber products in the south. State employees and their families were entitled to the distribution of commodity grains from the government as well as the status of the urban population, which was a privilege. Meanwhile, they have been counted as part of the agricultural labor force because of their profession. Hainan province has 290,000 such farmers with urban population status.[6] If these people are excluded from the calculation, Hainan's urban population ratio should be 36.43 percent[7] instead of the 40.11 percent as shown in Table 14.1. Therefore, the statistical ratios of urbanization for Zhejiang, Jiangsu, and Fujian are less

---

[6] Conference notes, Hainan Research Institute on Reform and Development, June 28, 2002.

[7] Author's calculation based on Hainan's total population in 2000 of 7.87 million and urban population of about 3.16 million with the state farm employees included.

discountable. In fact, these three provinces may have underestimated their urbanization ratios because more farmers who hold an agricultural population status have left their land to work in non-farm jobs in the cities, their peripheries, and local TVEs. This is one of the factors contributing to their less than the national average urban-rural income disparity, as mentioned above.

4.2 Diverse Models of Urbanization

Diverse economic conditions of the provinces have led to their different models of urbanization. China's urbanization takes primarily two forms. One is through migrating surplus rural labor to urban areas in conjunction with developing medium and large cities, and the other is thorough industrializing towns and townships in addition to developing small cities.

In turn, there have been primarily two ways by which China industrializes its towns and townships—one being through the growth of township-village enterprises (TVEs), which has effectively turned towns into cities and villages into towns and urban subdivisions. Another—more recent—development has been to urbanize China's countryside locally by concentrating non-agricultural enterprises into industrial parks within city suburbs, specializing and deeply processing agricultural products in close proximity to agriculture productions—thereby establishing new villages by moving villagers into new subdivisions of urban style.

Zhejiang and Jiangsu provinces are well known for their development of TVEs. The model of urbanization thorough localized industrialization is best illustrated here where towns have been so well developed that many are larger than small or even medium cities elsewhere. Shengze in Jiangsu province, for example, is a case of a town on the path to becoming a small city. The town has a population of about 160,000 and more than 1,000 industrial firms of which 970 are private-owned. In-migrants comprise about 75 percent of workers on the floor. The town affords more than 400 restaurants and 15 hotels, and the rural per capita income is 6,800 *yuan*, much higher than the national average of 2,253 *yuan* in 2000 (Chen, 2003). The township government proudly attributes the success to the development of TVEs in every village during the 1980s.[8]

Yonglian Town—formerly Yonglian Village—within the Jiangsu province, is an example of villages turning into towns. With 1.31 million tons of steel production and 2.2 billion *yuan* in revenue, Yonglian is entitled the First Steel Village of China. The enterprise, Yonglian Steels Group, developed from a 20-ton cement production with a twenty thousand-*yuan* investment in 1979. The town, which is still interchangeably called Yonglian Village, currently affords one hospital, one clinic, two market places, and many enterprises. Farmers can enjoy

---

[8] Conference notes, Shengze Township government, June 21, 2002.

70 percent free medical care at the town's own hospital and are reluctant to work at a rate of 30 *yuan* per day.[9]

In contrast, Fanglin Village of Zhejiang province has remained a village. It is an example of a poor rural village being turned into a village richer than an urban subdivision. Populated with 266 households and 472 laborers, the village affords the Fanglin Industrial Group with many subsidiaries, markets, and enterprises with controlling shares. The success of these enterprises has brought to the village a per capita income of 10,433 *yuan*, 228 houses of about 3,000 sq ft—priced at 12,000 *yuan*—and most impressively, a free nursing home center to house the village's elderly. The quality and amenities of the village's housing and nursing home center are of first rate even by western standards.[10] Needless to say, this is not the typical picture of China's villages, but it is nonetheless a real case of how successfully industrialization of rural villages can enrich the lives of Chinese farmers. The success of the industrial enterprises, meanwhile, owes much to the location of the village being within the close proximity of market places, roadways, and more relatively industrialized cities.

Pinghu City of Zhejiang province, meanwhile, serves as an example of the more recent model of moving industry to the peripheries of the cities to urbanize local rural areas. In Pinghu City, industrial parks extend to connect the city with peripheral rural areas, enabling redundant farmers in the agricultural sector to work in non-agricultural enterprises. Farmers from surrounding rural areas comprise 99 percent of the employment at the Mozhihua Corporation Ltd. (in Pinghu City), for example, a leading textile firm with shares publicly traded in China (*China Small City Series III*, CCTV, May 3, 2002).

The government has run pilot projects in selected towns. More successful examples are seen in richer parts of the country, such as Pinghu City of Zhejiang province, Longgang Town of Zhejiang Province, Zhongshan City of Guangdong province, and Jiaomei Town and Maxiang Town of Fujian Province. These examples and experimental locales serve as models for the future development of China's large number of towns and old communes.

It must be pointed out, of course, that even in Jiangsu and Zhejiang, the examples of Yonglian Town and Fangling village are not typical. Nonetheless, no one would argue against the success of TVEs in these two provinces that has brought upon susequent rural industrialization. The places that we visited had shown no sign of farmers having difficulties in leaving their farms to begin non-farm jobs. The rural enterprises have instead been employing rural migrants from inland provinces, contributing to the urbanization and industrialization of relatively poorer areas.

Moreover, we have observed that the dividing line between urban and rural areas has become indistinct, that villages are becoming towns and expanding

---

[9] Interview notes, Mr. Wu Dongcai, CEO of Yonglian Steel Group and Head of Yonglian Village, June 19, 2002.
[10] Interview notes, Fanglin Village, June 25, 2002.

toward the cities, and that to remain a farmer or to become an industrial worker has become largely a choice of profession. This is how urbanization becomes realized through rural industrialization.

Pinghu City of Zhejiang province, on the other hand, serves as a typical example of how cities expand to urbanize rural areas on their peripheries. The industrial parks have expanded toward the rural areas and provided many non-farm jobs to the indignant farmers. In regard to the Mozhihua Textile Corporation, a well-known company publicly listed in China, for example, 99 percent of its employees were farmers in the periphery rural villages (CCTV4, 5/3/02).

As a result of successful rural industrialization, the urbanization in Jiangsu and Zhejiang provinces has now shifted to urban modernization and the formation of large metropolitan areas. Being at a more advanced stage of urbanization with greater economic capacity than other areas, cities here have not only the necessity but also the financial capability to emphasize modernization, city beautification, and long-run sustainable growth.

While Jiangsu and Zhejiang have both taken the path of urbanization through rural industrialization, differences exist between the two provinces in terms of their specific methods for developing TVEs. In Zhejiang, TVE development has been driven primarily by private initiatives enterprises, whereas in Jiangsu, public initiative through the development of TVEs with collective ownership has prevailed. This explains why Zhejiang is a forerunner of developing private enterprises among not only the five provinces in our fieldtrip study, but all the provinces in China as well.

Compared to Jiangsu and Zhejiang, Fujian province is also located on China's southeast coast and more open, but it differs from the two in its mode of urbanization. Not only has Fujian not had as advanced TVEs, its economic development has also been adversely affected because of its sensitive location nearest to Taiwan, which is only across the Taiwan Strait from Fujian. This has given the province a late start in its development and made the development more or less depend on the degree of tension between the two sides of the Strait.

Fujian's urbanization characterizes strong disparity within the province. Simply put, southern Fujian is considerably more urbanized than northern Fujian. Southern Fujian shares similar characteristics of urbanization with Zhejiang and Jiangsu. The city of Xiamen has not only attracted considerable FDI and foreign enterprises as a special economic zone, but also become a desirable tourist attraction because of its coastal line and natural conditions. The cities of Quanzhou and Zhangzhou, meanwhile, are the most famous hosts of Taiwanese kinship investment. Urbanization in the southern towns of Maxiang and Jiaomei is of a similar pattern as Shengze of Jiangsu and Longgang of Zhejiang. These towns have been urbanized through rural industrialization and have absorbed many migrants from inland provinces.

In northern Fujian, however, urbanization is much less advanced. In Wuyi city, for example, urban per capita income in 2000 was 6,049.2 *yuan*, and rural per capita income was 2,944.8 *yuan*. The two towns of Xingcun and Wuyi also have less than the 1999 provincial average rural per capita income of 3,230 *yuan* (Chen, 2006). In fact, as stated above, the towns were so poor that they were unable to satisfy the requirement of having "one major street, one residential subdivision, and one public green land (or lawn) of at least three acres" to become small cities.[11]

Urbanization in Fujian, therefore, requires not only the development of the large metropolitan areas of the "Golden Triangle," such as Xiamen, Quanzhou, and Zhangzhou, but more importantly, solving the "Three Agricultural Problems" in northern Fujian as in most other Chinese provinces. Because of the mountainous, inland conditions and historical development of northern Fujian—both of which are falling behind its southern counterpart—its urbanization cannot and should not follow the same pattern as Zhejiang, Jiangsu, or southern Fujian. Instead of urbanizing through rural industrialization and expanding industrial parks on the peripheries of large cities, it seems more efficient for northern Fujian cities to encourage their poor farmers to migrate to southern Fujian cities for non-farm employment. This view is shared by local government officials who stated during our interview that "Rather than building roads to rural houses, it is more sensible to welcome rural residents to settle in the cities "and that "Leaving farmers behind in the countryside will only cause more trees to be cut, grass pulled, more children born, more land occupied, and more food consumed."

While Fujian's urbanization differs somewhat from that of Zhejiang and Jiangsu, Inner Mongolia and Hainan's differ distinctively. Inner Mongolia is the third largest provincial-level unit measured by land size, next to Tibet and Xinjiang. Its average arable land is 3.72 times larger than the national average and is naturally the highest among the five units in our study. Moreover, the autonomous region—especially its eastern part—has vast grasslands and unpolluted skies, specialty animal husbandry, as well as rich ethnic cultures. However, its inland location, poor transportation, and long winters have made production costs much higher than in most provinces. Moreover, the economy has been historically dominated by state enterprises. As a result, except for its higher per capita arable land and tourism average, the economic development of Inner Mongolia is mediocre at best (see Table 14.6) and is the worst among the five provinces.

During the field study, we have observed the distinct differences between Inner Mongolia and the other four units beyond the ethnic and cultural aspects—in the mode and extent of economic development. Whether it is in the municipality of Hailaer or Manzhouli, there are fewer high-rise buildings, fewer cars, fewer roads, fewer hotels, fewer foreigners or other non-Mongolians, and fewer residential sub-divisions and city construction projects. It is quite obvious, then, that the cities here are much less developed and urbanized, making the urbanization task—and thus its mode—different from the other four provinces.

---

[11] For details of the comparison between Southern and Northern Fujian cities, see Chen (2006).

Inner Mongolia is relatively more land abundant but less labor abundant. The focal problem of its urbanization, therefore, is not how to let farmers settle in the cities. Dealing with the "Three Agriculture Problems" in Inner Mongolia is rather how to industrialize the agriculture sector, enriching the scientific contents of—and enhancing the value added to—its agriculture products, which would thereby raise the income of farmers. The Tianbao Green Food Products Production Base (Tianbao luse shipin chanye jidi) that we visited has taken an important step toward such development. Moreover, urbanization in Inner Mongolia must face the challenge of retiring cultivation to preserve forest and soil. Its industrialization and modernization of agriculture must not occur at the expense of ecology. This is why animal husbandry in Inner Mongolia is experimenting with domestic and housed feeding in order to raise the added value and protect the environment. The eastern part of the autonomous region has been less industrialized and decertified, which makes it possible for the province to develop urban tourism based on its unspoiled natural environment.

The development of Inner Mongolia must not only overcome the unfriendly natural environment of long-lasting winter conditions and poor transportation, but also attract large amounts of capital investment. Capital investment is essential to industrializing its agriculture, reforming its state enterprises, improving education, drawing in talent, and improving its transportation as well as other infrastructure. Relatively speaking, Inner Mongolia is most lacking in its funding and capital when compared to other provinces. To attract capital and talent, including foreign capital, a more open economy with expanded foreign trade—especially boarder trade with Russia and other central Asian countries—and tourism is of critical importance. Meanwhile, developing tourism within Inner Mongolia must place more emphasis on its unique attraction of ethnic culture.

As a special economic zone located in southernmost China, Hainan's tropical and sub-tropical weather as well as its island geographic condition are its most distinctive tourism resources in China. Meanwhile, compared to the four other provinces, Hainan has a relatively small manufacturing sector. In fact, its manufacturing sector ranks 28th among a total 31 units in the nation, leaving the specialty agriculture and tourism to be the supporting industries of Hainan's economy.

As a small island economy, urbanization in Hainan also differs distinctively from the other provinces. It cannot absorb rural surplus labor through expanding manufacturing sector but rather must rely on developing specialty agriculture and agricultural tourism. Meanwhile, much of Hainan's agriculture surplus labor results from its state farms that were formed during the planning years. In other words, reforming its state farms is also a way of dealing with Hainan's surplus agricultural labor problem. [12]

Urbanization in Hainan takes the form of migrating the rural population to medium or large cities and promoting the development of the latter. Its

---

[12] For more detailed discussion about Hainan's state farms, please see Chen (2003a).

urbanization also utilizes Hainan's special geographic, economic and natural conditions, paying special attention to the scale and ecological effects. More specifically, the northern and southern areas are the leading forces in the urbanization, the eastern and western areas play a supplementary role, and the central area is to be relieved of poverty in the process.

Geographically, the island of Hainan features a mountainous central area that flattens gradually as it expands to the sides where major highways and transportation facilities are located. Historical and natural conditions have facilitated the development of the coastal plains where eight of Hainan's total nine municipalities can be found. In the north is the provincial capital of Haikou City and in the south is Sanya City, the Hawaii of the Orient. Haikou and Sanya are the two largest cities, forming the two economic centers of the province. In the west, there exists Hainan's largest chemical industry, and in the east is the province's light industry base. Meanwhile, only one city—the smallest of all nine throughout the province, consisting of 106,000 people in 2000 (*Statistical Yearbook of Hainan*, 2001, p. 352)—is located in central Hainan where the cost of development is high, resulting from the mountainous geographical conditions, poor transportation, and a backward economic background.

As a result, urbanization and industrialization of the province are led by the coastal plains, featuring the cities of Haikou in the north and Sanya in the south in addition to the industrial areas in the east and west. In the development of Hainan's Tenth Five-Year Plan, the province planned to promote the development of large cities and limit that of small ones, reflecting the "scale feature" of its urbanization. Furthermore, its urbanization also follows the principle of the "three no's," which is "no devastation to the resources, no pollution to the environment, and no replicated construction."

The model of urbanization in Hainan suggests not only practicality and feasibility, but also a correction to the stereotype that over-emphasizes the development of small cities and towns. The three aspects of Hainan's urbanization are also coherent and complementary to each other. Through the development of coastal plains and poverty relieving the central area, Hainan not only promotes the development of the medium and large cities and lowers the cost of urbanizing, but also maintains its environment and ecology.[13]

5 Summary

China is a vast country with diverse endowments, historical backgrounds, and geographic, cultural, as well as economic conditions. As such, the mode and extent of urbanization also differs among the provinces. The provinces of Zhejiang and Jiangsu are China's two largest manufacturing bases and the driving force of the Yangtzi River Delta's economic development. The development of TVEs and

---

[13]For detailed analysis of Hainan's urbanization, seeChen (2003a) and Jia and Song (2003).

private enterprises has not only brought considerable vitality to their economies, but also set an example of development for the other provinces. The urbanization mode of the two provinces can thus be considered as a TVE-based model, athough between the two provinces, Zhejiang has a heavier accent of private enterprise development, while Jiangsu is more collectively TVE-based. In fact, Zhejiang has become a model of success for the private enterprises in China.

The urbanization of Hainan, on the other hand, follows the model of developing the coastal plains to attract migration from the central, mountainous areas. In other words, Hainan's is rather a migration model from the central, mountainous areas to the coastal plains. Meanwhile, the special geography of Hainan and its tropical and sub-tropical weather afford the province the most unique tourism resources in China, making tourism a pivotal industry of the province. Moreover, Hainan can afford the unique approach of urbanizing the rural sector through developing agricultural tourism.

Urbanization in Fujian, however, possesses characteristics of both rural industrialization and migration toward central cities. The advanced development of TVEs in Fujian shares the same pattern as Zhejiang and Jiangsu, while the mountainous northern region of Fujian can benefit more from migrating its rural surplus labor to other parts of the province.

In Inner Mongolia, urbanization differs from the other four provinces because of its inland geographical conditions, long and cold winters, and history of state-enterprise dominance. As discussed earlier, while putting emphasis on the development of specialty agriculture and trade with central Asian nations, Inner Mongolia is most in need of capital investment and talented human resources.

The fieldtrip research in the five provinces has afforded us with the valuable observations and thoughts on the situations, models, and development prospects of urbanization in the provinces. We must, however, point out that the five provinces in this study are by no means the poorest provinces in China's western region where the "Three Agriculture Problems" are most severe and urbanization needs most urgent. The case of Inner Mongolia serves as one example but not a typical one, leaving room for better future study.

References

Chen, A., 'Urbanization and disparities in China: Challenges of growth and development', *China Economic Review*, 13 (2002): 407-411.

———, 'Assessing China's Economic Performance Since 1978: Material Attainments and Beyond', *Journal of Socio-economics*, vol. 34, Issue 4 (August, 2005): 499-527.

———, 'Urbanization in Fujian: the Case of Fujian Province', *Modern China* (January, 2006).

———, 'Characteristics of Economic Development and Urbanization in Hainan Province', in A. Chen (eds), *Urbanization in China: Field Research and Case Studies of Provinces (Chinese)* (China Economic Science Press, October 2003a).

————, 'A Comparative Analysis of Economic Conditions and Urbanization in Five Chinese Provinces', in A. Chen (eds), *Urbanization in China: Field Research and Case Studies of Provinces (Chinese)* (China Economic Science Press, October 2003 b).

Chen, A. and Coulson, E., 'Determinants of Urban Migration: Evidence from Chinese Cities', *Urban Studies*, vol. 39, No. 12 (2002): 2189-2198.

Chen, Y. and Chen, A. (eds), *An Analysis of Urbanization in China (in Chinese)* (Xiamen University Press, June 2002).

Chen, A. and Song, S., 'The Development of Service and Tourism Industries in Hainan: Observations and Policy Suggestions', in A. Chen (eds), *Urbanization in China: Field Research and Case Studies of Provinces (Chinese)* (China Economic Science Press, October 2003).

China Statistical Yearbook, various years.

Hong, C. and Song, S., 'Urban Construction with Private Capital: the Experience of Taizhou', in A. Chen (eds), *Urbanization in China: Field Research and Case Studies of Provinces (Chinese)* (China Economic Science Press, October 2003).

Jia, Y. and Song, H., 'Strategies of Hainan's Urbanization', in A. Chen (eds), *Urbanization in China: Field Research and Case Studies of Provinces (Chinese)* (China Economic Science Press, October 2003).

Part 4
The Role of Government in Rural Development

Chapter 15

The Caring Hand of a Local Government in China

Wenbo Wu

1 Introduction

One critical and profound component of China's reform programs launched in the late-1970s is fiscal decentralization. Under a centrally planned economy, China's fiscal system was correspondingly centralized. As agents of the central government, local governments collected all taxes and profits from state-owned enterprises, which were remitted to the center. Local governments received transfers from the central government to cover their mandated spending responsibilities. They were responsible for providing most of the social services with funds allocated by the central government.

The fiscal system under the command economy was highly redistributive, at least at the provincial level. Rich provinces remitted a high percentage of their GDP, and poor provinces received larger subsidies. Through several waves of fiscal reforms since the 1980s—especially the radical reforms in 1994—a decentralized fiscal system characterized by a tax assignment system has been established.

Many scholars identify China's evolving decentralized fiscal system as a *de facto* fiscal federalism and regard it as an institutional foundation for China's rapid economic growth (e.g. Lin and Liu, 2000). In models of "market-preserving fiscal federalism" (Montinola, Qian and Weingast, 1995: Jin, Qian and Weingast, 2001), a Chinese local government is characterized as using its helping hand to promote local economic growth. The main engine for local prosperity is township village enterprises (TVEs).

A local government's helping hand is motivated by fiscal incentives. However, the local government may use both its helping hand and its grabbing hand at the same time. The helping hand promotes local economic growth, enlarging the total surpluses that are available for redistributions. To enhance its revenues, a local government is also motivated to use its grabbing hand to seize a larger portion of the surpluses. China's decentralized fiscal system not only motivates local governments to use their helping hands but also enables them to use their grabbing hands since the central controls are much weaker. As discussed below, a local government can grab revenue from TVEs under its direct control as well as households. The revenue is outside of the formal fiscal system.

This chapter analyzes the "third" hand of a local government in China: the caring hand, which is largely ignored in the literature on the behavior of local governments in a decentralized fiscal system. A local government in China is mandated with responsibilities for financing many basic social services such as primary education and rural health care. The incentive for a local government to lend its caring hand is quite different from the motivation to help TVEs and provide other public goods. The helping hand is strongly justified from the perspective of local governments because it ultimately helps the local government itself by enlarging the size of the local economy and thereby the potential revenue for the local government.

A caring hand, however, does not directly enhance the local economy. It is redistributive and costly. In other words, a caring hand leads to reduced revenue for the local government, while the helping hand enhances its tax base. We speculate that a local government is motivated to lend its caring hand because it needs political support from its superiors as well as its local constituency. After all, the local government operates in a political environment in which it must accomadate the demands from both above and below. The local government's helping hand may enhance the efficiency of the local economy and hence enlarge the "pie" that is available for distribution among different stakeholders. However, these stakeholders can realize their own utilities only after the "pie" is distributed. The local government's caring hand plays in the politics. We illustrate the essential characteristics of the redistributive politics and the role played by the local government as it pertains to the case of rural health care financing in China. A simple model is built to analyze local government behavior in choosing its consumption and expenditure in health care.

This chapter is organized as follows. Section 2 describes townships and villages in China's fiscal system, focusing on the lowest government level. Basic problems in financing rural health care are described in Section 3. We present the model and related discussion on policy implications in Section 4, and we conclude with some brief remarks in Section 5.

2 Townships and Villages in China's Fiscal System

While technically a unitary state, China is a highly decentralized country with a high degree of autonomy enjoyed by local governments. China's local governments consist of provinces—including centrally administered municipalities and autonomous regions—prefectures, counties, and townships.

Townships officially replaced people's communes in 1983 as the lowest level of public administration and were incorporated into the fiscal system. As agents of the township government, village committees, which are not in the government system, manage village affairs. Local governments at the township levels have a significant degree of autonomy from the higher authorities. They have their own regulations in regard to how their localities operate, and they are influential in personnel matters of local government employees.

To complement such a high degree of administrative independence, these local governments have substantial control over their fiscal resources. However, a high portion of their fiscal resources is outside of the formal fiscal system. To a large degree, the township finances operate in a "black box," which is beyond any regulation or control by higher-level governments.

Under the new fiscal regime (after the radical fiscal reforms in 1994), the central government controls a substantial portion of lucrative tax bases—75 percent of the VAT and all consumption tax. Local governments at the provincial level and below compete for other taxes, such as agricultural, industrial, and commercial taxes, which are less lucrative and much more difficult to collect. In the nested hierarchy of government in China, the lower level can only get less meaningful tax bases in the formal fiscal system, tending to rely more on extra-budgetary and non-budgetary funds. At the township level, main extra-budgetary items encompass five *tongchou* (unified and planned) fees: education supplements, social assistance, family planning, collective transportation, and militia exercises. Similarly, villages impose three *tiliu* (retained) fees: a public accumulation fund, a collective welfare fund, and administrative fees. These extra-budgetary revenues are allowed and supervised by higher-level governments, and these funds are supposedly used to cover administration costs incurred by townships and villages and provide social services. In most cases, they are levied as fixed quotas on each household. Essentially, rural residents pay for the "social services" they receive at a much inflated price.[1]

Besides these quasi-taxes, townships and villages collect numerous types of non-budgetary charges such as *xingzheng shiye xing shoufei* (charges for administrative and institutional purposes), *jizi* (fund collection), and *tanpai* (apportionments). These off-budget funds have ballooned into a major revenue source for townships and villages.[2] According to several surveys, the total amount of off-budget revenues for townships and villages is about the same as the sum of state agricultural taxes and extra-budgetary charges (*tongchu* and *tiliu*) (Li, 2001; Fu, 2001; Xu and Ren, 2002). Since the latter two categories of revenues are remitted to the central government and regulated, townships and villages are motivated to expand and control the base for off-budget revenues.

The incentive to enlarge their revenue bases also drives township-level governments to control, or collude with, local enterprises within their territories. In areas where TVEs are more developed, township and village officials play a significant role in the operation of firms they exercise ownership rights and effectively control the financial resources of these firms. When local governments

---

[1] Collective welfare fund is relevant to our discussions below on the rural health care system. The fund is used for cooperative health insurance and other welfare services such as the provisions for the *wubaohu* (five types of protected families).

[2] China Agricultural Yearbook (1991) already recognized 148 types of unofficial payments by farmers.

cannot directly control local businesses, they still have considerable power to impose *ad hoc* charges and fines in a variety of ways.[3] As a consequence, TVEs have enormous financial burdens imposed upon them by local governments. Ody (1992) found that taxes, profit remittances, fees, and contributions absorbed 65 to 75 percent of the pre-tax profit of TVEs in the Jiangsu province, 35 to 45 percent in the Guangdong province, and 53 percent nationwide. Although these burdens may seem high, they are the price paid for the development of these native businesses.

When the legal system and other market institutions are not well established, local government ownership of TVEs is an effective second-best institution. Developing, privately owned enterprises are also motivated to collude with local governments in order to maintain their effective private ownership and face challenges in a competitive environment.

The collusive relationship between local governments and local enterprises works as a mechanism to keep the information of local businesses hidden from higher-level governments. Local governments are able to access the books and accounts of local enterprises, receiving portions of the profit unobserved by higher levels of government. Therefore, this collusive relationship serves as a credible mechanism for tax evasion (Taubman, 1998). Taxes that are evaded are then shared between local governments and enterprises—completely hidden from higher-level governments.

As many argue (e.g., World Bank, 2002), local governments find it inevitable to search for off-budget revenue to meet shortfalls since a large portion of revenue in the formal fiscal system is retained by the higher-levels of government. Meanwhile, local governments are required to take on more expenditures and responsibilities as the higher levels would mandate at will whenever the assignment of public expenditures is not rule-based, or negotiated among the different levels of government.

A local government cannot borrow or develop new sources of taxes on its own when its spending exceeds its tax revenue. The rigidity in local public finance exists because of strict central regulations on borrowing as well as the imposing of new taxes by local government—after the tax assignment is negotiated and settled among the different levels of government. The only choice for local government is to find off-budget sources of revenue, which is by definition flexible and unregulated.

Off-budgetary charges may be a necessity for local governments under the current fiscal system in China. It is reasonable to assume that a local government attempts to maximize its revenue, which is used to meet its expenditure responsibility as assigned by the central government.

---

[3] Local governments in China have numerous "creative" ways to collect revenues from local enterprises and enrich their own *xiao jinku* (small treasury). For example, they may require local businesses to attend fairs and pay high registration fees. Furukawa (1990) found that TVEs in Hunan Province were subjected to more than 100 different types of fees, paid to 60 odd administrative units and agencies.

According to many studies, the most important spending item is its own administrative costs, particularly, personnel costs. Local governments in China seem to be typical Leviathans. Yang (1996) indicates that the ratio of township-level cadres to farmers increases from 1.2 to 1,000 in 1978, to 2.1 in 1984, and further to 3.4 in 1989. According to Zhu and Li (2001), there are about 13 million cadres (including school teachers and health workers) for 48,000 townships and 800,000 villages in rural China. All the revenue a local government controls is often either just enough or even inadequate in many cases for the salaries of cadres and administrative expenses (Li, 2002). In many relatively poor areas, there is either very little or no revenue available for social services, including rural health care as described below.

3 Rural Health Care Financing in China

China's rural health care system, established under a centrally planned economy, was widely regarded as a success. This system was decentralized and based on a three-tier structure. By the mid-1970s, about 90 percent Chinese villages had a health station with several so-called "bare foot" doctors, who participated in agricultural production and were paid additional shares of collective output to compensate for their medical services.

These part-time health workers provided basic health services and organized public health campaigns. The communes (now townships) had health centers, which coordinated and supervised public health programs among villages and provided medical care. The doctors and other health workers at these centers were paid a government salary or a share of collective output. The performance of these health stations and health centers was monitored by the county health bureau, which managed the annual government budget allocated to rural health care. The county had hospitals which supervised commune and village health facilities and provided referral services.

Under the so-called Rural Cooperative Medical System (RCMS), the costs of rural health care were covered by a pre-payment scheme, which collected revenue from three sources: premiums paid by rural households, a collective welfare fund, and subsidies from higher-level governments. Subsidies were mostly used to compensate health workers and purchase medical equipments. These funds made it possible to provide rural populations with some medical services free of charge and reimburse some of the other medical costs, mostly drugs and other consumables. Rural residents had reasonable access to basic health services either for free or at small cost.

In the 1980s, most RCMS schemes with some exceptions in rich coastal areas collapsed with communes, which were replaced by townships. Responsibility for the financing and management of township and village health facilities was devolved to township governments (Bloom and Gu, 1997). Some estimate that overall self-payment by the rural population accounted for 88.3 percent in 1998

(Gao, Qian, Tang, Ericsson and Blas, 2002). Public sources are very limited. The World Bank (2002) estimates that more than 90 percent of the rural populace, or 700 million rural residents, do not receive any coverage from these risk-pooling schemes. Without adequate public assistance, the methods for poor rural households to finance costly treatments for serious illnesses are limited.

Rural households may use their limited funds, borrow from family or neighbors, who are similarly poor, reduce expenditure, sell some assets, seek fee discounts, and so on, but all these alternatives are very insignificant. With the double squeeze of escalating costs and declining public supports, the rural poor become less likely to use health services and more likely to seek earlier discharge from hospitals or use self-medication or more inexpensive forms of treatment through unqualified village "doctors." The dysfunctional rural health care system has become a significant contributor to problems relating to poverty and thereby threatens the policy goal of equitable health care for all (Liu and Hsiao, 1995; Li, 2002).

The central government has repeatedly acknowledged serious problems in the rural health care system and issued policy statements on establishing a reconstructed RCMS. The first policy initiative was announced in 1996 when the central government held China's first national health policy conference. It was proposed that voluntary RCMS schemes be established and improved as a major strategy to provide rural health insurance coverage (MOH, 1997). National policies have been evolving ever since.

As these policies envision, the government will take major responsibility in financing rural health care. Local health insurance schemes will be established to protect rural families against serious illnesses, and the poor will have access to essential health services. Under the current conditions of China's fiscal system and public administration structure, however, the implementation of these broad national policies is largely determined by strategic actions of local stakeholders and particularly local government officials.

To meet the need of establishing an effective local health insurance scheme and a rural health care system, local governments definitely need to increase expenditure by re-allocating their budget or obtaining fiscal transfers from higher-level governments. Bloom and Gu (1997) argue that pre-payment schemes such as RCMS can only have limited success when they are self-funded and they compete for scarce resources in townships and villages. Before we can go further to derive a better financial scheme, however, we need to address a fundamental question about why local governments should be motivated to pursue policy objectives that might not bring immediate benefits.

In the following section, we build a simple model to analyze a local government's decision regarding financing essential social services, such as health care. These social services are most likely redistributive in nature and only bring about long-term social benefits. In particular, a health insurance system is an income-protection mechanism, which is essential for efforts in poverty reduction in rural China. Transfers to the poor through the insurance scheme are critical in protecting the poor from being trapped in chronic poverty when they need medical treatments that require large expenses.

How will local governments balance the interests of the poor against their own when they allocate budgetary funds that are largely under their control? The question is valid and significant since local governments are at a powerful position to independently decide its budgetary priorities. The following simple model attempts to shed light on the "black box," which is the fiscal behavior of local government.

4 Local Government Behavior: Lending Its Caring Hand

We consider a local government whose utility function is determined by its own consumption (C) and the political support it receives. The consumption by a local government may take the forms of an enlarged government employment beyond a reasonable level, better perks for government officials, and so on.

There exist two distinct sources of political support for local government: its supervising governments in a nested government hierarchy (A), as well as its constituency (B). There exist many channels for rural residents to influence local government officials: election of village committees, a public petition to higher-level government about local corruption, and increased access to the courts (Zweig, 2000). In the centralized political system in China, higher-level governments have the authority in personnel matters, which can be effectively used to control officials in lower-government (Blanchard and Shleifer, 2000).

4.1 The Model

The utility function for the local government is:

$$U = U(C, A, B),$$

where:

$$\partial U / \partial C, \partial U / \partial A, \partial U / \partial B > 0 \text{ and}$$
$$\partial^2 U / \partial C^2, \partial^2 U / \partial A^2, \partial^2 U / \partial B^2 < 0.$$

The local government spends S_H and $S_{\bar{H}}$ on financing rural health care and all other social service, respectively. Thus, the local government's total expenditure is: $S = S_H + S_{\bar{H}}$. We focus on analyzing S_H and take $S_{\bar{H}}$ as fixed. These two spending items are redistributive in nature. For example, in the rural health insurance scheme, the poor are subsidized. The costs for these social services include the amount of transfers, related administrative costs and possible leakage. Social spending is different from local expenditures (G) in providing legitimate public goods, which enhance local economic growth—including investments in infrastructures and human capital. For simplicity, we assume G is fixed. Furthermore, we assume local total output (Y) as fixed. Therefore, the local government's total expenditure is

$G + C + S$.

The local government obtains its revenue from two distinct sources: budgetary as well as off-budget revenue. Local government must share the former with upper-level government and controls the latter. After a local government collects its off-budget revenues, T_o, the total government revenue is $t(Y - T_0)$, where t is the effective overall tax rate, and $0 < t < 1$. If the share of the local government revenues in the formal fiscal system is τ, supervising governments collect $Y_A = (1 - \tau)t(Y - T_o)$. The local government collects a total of $Y_L = \tau t(Y - T_o) + T_o$. After-tax income for the locality is $Y_B = (1 - t)(Y - T_0)$. An assumption of a local balanced budget gives:

$$G + C + S = \tau t(Y - T_0) + T_0 \tag{1}$$

Rearranging the equation (1) yields $T_0 = (G + C + S - \tau t Y)/(1 - \tau t)$. Therefore, we have:

$$Y_A = \frac{(1 - \tau)t}{1 - \tau t}(Y - G - C - S),$$

$$Y_B = \frac{1 - t}{1 - \tau t}(Y - G - C - S).$$

The local government wins support from the above because it submits taxes to its supervising government in the formal fiscal system, establishes and operates a rural health care system as mandated by the supervising government.[4] Political support received by the local government from the above is:

$$A = A(Y_A, S_H),$$

where

---

[4] To please its supervising governments, the local government may also implement public projects and campaigns which are mandated by supervising governments but provide little or no benefits to local residents. For example, a township government may spend a huge amount in building a grandiose square and gardens, which scores high in a campaign for "Township Images" but does not meet the needs of local populace. Moreover, local government officials may invest in building up and maintaining *guanxi* (connection) with supervising government agencies to win their favors. However, we do not analyze these spending here.

$\partial A / \partial Y_A > 0, \partial^2 A / \partial Y_A^2 < 0, \partial A / \partial S_H > 0$, and $\partial^2 A / \partial S_H^2 < 0$.

To gain political support from its constituency, local government needs to perform well in managing the local economy and local redistributive politics. In particular, citizens give more political support (B) when they receive more after-tax income (Y_B) and a higher level of spending for health care (S_H):

$$B = B(Y_B, S_B),$$

where

$$\partial B / \partial Y_B > 0, \partial^2 B / \partial Y_B^2 < 0, \partial B / \partial S_H > 0 \text{ and } \partial^2 B / \partial S_H^2 < 0.$$

The objective of the local government is to maximize its utility, U, by choosing the level of its own consumption, C, and its expenditures in health care, S_H. We substitute for A and B in U, and sequentially, Y_A and Y_B in A and B, respectively. Then, we maximize U with respect to C and S_H, and obtain:

$$\frac{\partial U}{\partial C} = \frac{\partial U}{\partial C} - \frac{(1-\tau)t}{1-\tau t} \frac{\partial U}{\partial A} \frac{\partial A}{\partial Y_A} - \frac{1-t}{1-\tau t} \frac{\partial U}{\partial B} \frac{\partial B}{\partial Y_B} = 0 \tag{2}$$

$$\frac{\partial U}{\partial S_H} = -\frac{(1-\tau)t}{1-\tau t} \frac{\partial U}{\partial A} \frac{\partial A}{\partial Y_A} + \frac{\partial U}{\partial A} \frac{\partial A}{\partial S_H} - \frac{1-t}{1-\tau t} \frac{\partial U}{\partial B} \frac{\partial B}{\partial Y_B} + \frac{\partial U}{\partial B} \frac{\partial B}{\partial S_H} = 0 \tag{3}$$

Rearranging equation (2) yields

$$\frac{\partial U}{\partial C} = \frac{(1-\tau)t}{1-\tau t} \frac{\partial U}{\partial A} \frac{\partial A}{\partial Y_A} + \frac{1-t}{1-\tau t} \frac{\partial U}{\partial B} \frac{\partial B}{\partial Y_B} \tag{4}$$

Equation (4) indicates that the local government chooses a consumption level in such a way that the marginal utility from the last revenue spent on its own consumption just equals the marginal utility from increased marginal political support from its supervising governments

$$\frac{(1-\tau)t}{1-\tau t}\frac{\partial U}{\partial A}\frac{\partial A}{\partial Y_A}$$

and from its constituency

$$\frac{1-t}{1-\tau t}\frac{\partial U}{\partial B}\frac{\partial B}{\partial Y_B}$$

if the revenue was not raised by the local government and flowed to the two other agents instead.

Rearranging equation (3) yields:

$$\frac{\partial U}{\partial A}\frac{\partial A}{\partial S_H}+\frac{\partial U}{\partial B}\frac{\partial B}{\partial S_H}=\frac{(1-\tau)t}{1-\tau t}\frac{\partial U}{\partial A}\frac{\partial A}{\partial Y_A}+\frac{1-t}{1-\tau t}\frac{\partial U}{\partial B}\frac{\partial B}{\partial Y_B} \qquad (5)$$

Equation (5) shows that the local government faces a tradeoff between increasing (decreasing) expenditures in health care and decreasing (increasing) income flows to both supervising governments and the constituency since both options enable the local government to win political support from the other stakeholders, but they compete for the revenue under the local government's control. The local government devotes its revenue to health care up to the point where the marginal utility from an extra dollar spent on health care is equal to the marginal utility from that extra dollar which is returned to its supervising governments and constituency.

We can substitute equation (4) in equation (5), and have

$$\frac{\partial U}{\partial C}=\frac{\partial U}{\partial A}\frac{\partial A}{\partial S_H}+\frac{\partial U}{\partial B}\frac{\partial B}{\partial S_H} \qquad (6)$$

Equation (6) demonstrates a tradeoff relationship between the consumption and spending of the local government in the rural health care system. It chooses a level of spending for health care such that the marginal utility from the last dollar of spending is equal to the marginal utility from an increase in its consumption if that dollar is spent on its own consumption instead.

4.2 Discussion

The above model describes a local government balancing its grabbing hand (C) and caring hand (S_H). The incentive for local government to provide essential social services, such as helping the rural poor in health care, depends on the institutional environment in which it operates. In the environment as depicted in the model, local government is able to control a substantial portion of fiscal resources that are unregulated by any supervising governments. These resources can be devoted to pure consumption as it directly benefits the local government. As a rational agent, the local government lends its caring hand only when its own utility is enhanced by doing so.

The model does not analyze the social optimality of the level of S_H since it would involve detailed analyses of the behavior of the supervising governments and local populace in regard to that level. Intuitively, however, we understand that the equilibrium level of S_H is unlikely to be socially optimal since the two other stakeholders do not appreciate the level of C as much as the local government does, and C is competing with S_H. The local government cannot be trusted to provide a socially optimal level of S_H on its own. In an ideal institution, the level of C and S_H should be legally sanctioned and regulated. More fundamentally, the unrestricted fiscal autonomy enjoyed by local governments should be brought under the control of laws. In other words, the local government's grabbing hand should be tied up. All in all, the ideal institution is a rule-based fiscal system characterized by proper assignments of spending responsibilities and tax bases at different levels of government and a system of intergovernmental transfer (World Bank, 2002).

Under such a system, the level of S_H is decided by a political process in which different interest groups legitimately compete for the benefits of S_H. In the process, a rational local government would still strive for its own direct benefits. However, the incentive to provide a higher level of S_H would be much stronger than the incentive demonstrated in the model where the level of S_H is mostly decided by the local government with a strong grabbing hand.

The move toward a better fiscal system first requires controlling off-budget revenues by local governments. Recent attempts by the central government in this direction appear to be difficult. So-called "peasant burdens," which are fundamentally driven by the off-budget activities of local government, become a serious social problem (Bernstein and Lu, 2000). The central government has made several serious attempts to reduce "peasant burdens." For example, the central government tried to integrate *ad hoc* charges and fees into the tax system. The measure alone, however, did not change the incentive of the local government. Local government responded by further reducing funds available for providing social services. Then some argue that higher-level government, especially the central government, is obliged to provide equalizing subsidies to local governments in order to provide social services to the poor.

When a locality receives subsidies that are earmarked for health care or otherwise, the local government may not reduce its own consumption to increase the level of S_H when other parameters are unchanged. The exogenous increase in funds available is equivalent to a "windfall." As a result, local government may be able to devote less of its revenue to win political support. Effectively, $\partial A / \partial Y_A$ and $\partial B / \partial Y_B$ fall. Then equation (3) implies that local government will devote more resources to its own consumption. In other words, the local government is able to control subsidies and divert some portion of it for its own benefits. Less than the full amount of the subsidies will be used in health care.

The basic premise of the model is that a local government is motivated to provide S_H because it needs political support from the supervising government as well as its local constituency, which is affected by the sensitivities of these two stakeholders to the level of S_H. Equation (5) implies that the local government will cut the level of its consumption (C) if political support from its supervising government ($\partial U / \partial A$) and constituency ($\partial U / \partial B$) becomes more important. It will then increase the level of S_H to re-balance the two sides of the equation (when Y_A and Y_B are unchanged). Therefore, strengthening the importance of political support in the utilities of local government is fundamental in motivating them to increase their efforts in providing social services. Mechanisms for politically controlling local government officials need to be strengthened. However, it might be a difficult task to achieve intended objectives.

Zhang, Fan, Zhang and Huang (2004) demonstrate that village elections do not improve the allocation of expenditures on public goods. They further argue that the level of public investment is higher when local decision-making power is shared between cadres and villagers. At the village level, power-sharing and community decision-making may be equally important in improving social services. In regard to the health care system, a reform proposal may be to assign the major responsibility to a higher-level local government, such as a provincial government. At such a level, political support becomes more important for government officials, and the pool for risk-sharing becomes significantly larger.

5 Conclusions

Failures in the rural health care system present a daunting challenge for China's policymakers. Spectacular economic growth over several decades will be less spectacular if inequality between the rich and poor, the urban and rural areas, and the coastal and inland areas persists. To improve the situation, policymakers need to take into account the incentive of local governments to lend their caring hands. The decentralized fiscal system motivates local governments to use their helping hands to promote local economic growth and use their grabbing hands to keep a substantial portion of revenue off-budget. The fiscal system, however, has failed to motivate local governments to lend their caring hands to the poor.

A fundamental dilemma in reforming China's fiscal system is the balance between preserving the incentive of local governments to promote local prosperity and motivating them to provide meaningful social services. The current fiscal system needs to be fundamentally reformed, and ultimately, a rule-based fiscal system needs to be established. Under such a system, a local government's incentive to provide social services is more closely aligned with people's needs.

References

Bernstein, T.P. and Lu, X., 'Taxation without Representation: Peasants, the Central and Local States in Reform China', *The China Quarterly*, 163 (2000): 742-763.

Blanchard, O. and Shleifer, A., 'Federalism with and without Political Centralization: China versus Russia' (NBER Working Paper 7616, 2000).

Bloom, G. and Gu, X., 'Health Sector Reform: Lessons from China', *Social Science and Medicine*, 45(3) (1997): 351-360.

China National Statistic Bureau, *China Agricultural Yearbook* (Beijing, China: China Statistical Publishing House, 1991).

Fu, G., 'Survey Report on the Taxes and Fees Shouldered by Farmers in Seven Counties in Hubei Province', *Problems of Agricultural Economy* (in Chinese), 4 (2001): 40-41.

Furukawa, K., 'Rural Enterprises under Reconsideration', *JETRO China Newsletter*, 88 (1990).

Gao, J., Qiang, J., Tang, S., Eriksson, B. and Blas, E., 'Health Equity in Transition from Planned to Market Economy in China', *Health Policy and Planning*, 17 (Suppl.1, 2002): 20-29.

Jin, H., Qian, Y., and Weingast, B.R., 'Regional Decentralization and Fiscal Incentives: Federalism, Chinese Style' (Working Paper, Hoover Institution, Stanford University, 2001).

Li, C., 'Four Challenges Facing the Reform of Rural Taxes and Fees', *China Reform* (in Chinese), 10 (2001): 33-34.

Li, H., 'Strengthen Reforms in the Health Sector with Innovative Spirit', *Chinese Health Policy* (in Chinese), 12 (2002): 15–18.

Li, Y., 'Causes of Financial Difficulties in Counties and Townships and Countermeasures', *Chinese Finance* (in Chinese), 1 (2002): 36-37.

Lin, Y. and Liu, Z., 'Fiscal Decentralization and Economic Growth in China', *Economic Development and Cultural Change*, 49(1) (2000): 1-22.

Liu, X. and Hsiao, W.C.L., 'The Cost Escalation of Social Health Insurance Plans in China: Its Implication for Public Policy', *Social Science and Medicine*, 41(8) (1995): 1095-1101.

Ministry of Health, PRC., *Proceedings of the 1996 National Health Confrence* (Beijing, China: The Peoples Publishing House, 1997).

Montinola, G., Qian, Y. and Weingast, B.R., 'Federalism, Chinese Style: The Political Basis for Economic Success in China', *World Politics*, 48(1) (1995): 50–81.

Ody, A., 'Rural Enterprise Development in China, 1986-90' (World Bank Discussion Papers, China and Mongolia Department Series, 162, 1992).

Taubman, W., 'The Finance System and the Development of Rural Towns in China', in F. Christiansen and Zhang J. (eds), *Village Inc. Chinese Rural Society in the 1990s* (Richmond: Curzon Press, 1998), pp. 48-65.

World Bank, 'China: national development and sub-national finance' (Washington, D.C.: World Bank, 2002).

Xu, Z. and Ren, B., 'Reform of Rural Taxes and Fees: Where is the Bottleneck', *The World of Surveys and Research* (in Chinese), 3(0) (2002): 31-32.

Yang, D., *Calamity and Reform in China: State, Rural Society and Institutional Change since* the *Great Leap Famine* (Stanford, CA: Stanford University Press, 1996).

Zhang, X., Fan, S., Zhang, L. and Huang J., 'Local Governance and Public Goods Provision in Rural China', *Journal of Public Economics*, 88(12) (2004): 2857-2871.

Zhu, Z. and Li, D., 'The Innovative Reform of the System of Peasant Burden', *Problems of Agricultural Economy* (in Chinese), 9 (2001): 35-37.

Zweig, D., 'The Externalities of Development: Can New Political Institutions Manage Rural Conflict', in Elizabeth J. P. and Mark S. (eds), *Chinese Society: Change, Conflict and Resistance* (London: Routledge, 2000), pp. 120-142.

HS4   RS3
518   RS8   275-87
P25
R11

Chapter 16

Infrastructure and Regional Economic Development in Rural China[*]

Shenggen Fan

Xiaobo Zhang

1 Introduction

Rapid growth in Chinese agriculture after the reforms has triggered numerous studies to analyze the sources of the rapid growth. These studies include McMillian *et al.* (1989), Fan (1990 and 1991), Lin (1992), Huang and Rozelle (1995), Zhang and Carter (1997), and Fan and Pardey (1997). Most of these studies attempted to analyze the impact of institutional changes and the increased use of inputs on production growth during the reform period from the end of the 1970s to the beginning of the 1990s.

Fan and Pardey (1997) and Fan (2000) were among the first to point out that omitted variables such as research and development (R&D) investment would bias the estimate of the sources of production growth. To address this concern, they included a research stock variable in the production function to account for the contribution of R&D investment to rapid production growth, in addition to the increased use of inputs and institutional changes. They found that, ignoring the R&D variable in the production function estimation, the effects of institutional change would be overestimated to a large extent.

In addition to R&D investment, government investments in roads, electrification, education, and other public investment in rural areas may have also contributed to the rapid growth in agricultural production. It is highly likely that omitting these variables will bias the estimates of the production function for Chinese agriculture as well.

One of the most important features in rural China is the rapid development of rural non-farm economies since the economic reform in 1978. But very few have analyzed the sources of growth in this sector. The only exception is Fan, Zhang,

[*] Reprinted from China Economic Review, 2004, Vol. 15, No. 2, page 203-214. The funding from FAO to the first author for his travel to Beijing to participate the International Seminar on Chinese Census Results September 19-22, 2000, Beijing, and the funding from ACIAR for all the authors in data collection, data compiling and paper preparation are acknowledged.

and Robinson (2003), who decomposed the growth in the non-farm sector into growth in labor and capital. But they failed to include public capital as an input in their source accounting, partly due to the lack of reliable public capital data.

Associated with the rapid economic growth, regional disparity in productivity has also increased for China for the last two decades. The regional difference in productivity is a major determinant of income disparity, an increasing concern by policymakers and many scholars alike. The uneven regional development in non-farm activities, in particular in the non-farm sector, in the rural sector has been regarded as one major driving force behind the changes in rural regional inequality (Rozelle, 1994; Zhang and Fan, 2003). However, despite large body of literature on the sources of growth, few studies have attempted to account for the sources of regional difference in productivity of both the agricultural and non-farm sectors (one exception is Fan (1990)), and no studies have systematically assessed the roles of public investment in such differences in regional development.

The motivation of this study is to include these public investment variables that are newly available from the Census to estimate the production functions for both agricultural and non-agricultural economies in rural China and to decompose the sources of difference in productivity among regions. In particular, the specific role of infrastructure in explaining the difference in productivity among regions will be evaluated. There are several advantages in using the Agricultural Census data. First, the census reports detailed infrastructure information at the country level, which is more disaggregate than the provincial level data commonly seen in the official statistical yearbooks. Second, the arable land area and labor force data are more accurately measured than the previous official sources (Ash and Edmonds, 1998; Smil, 1999).

The chapter is organized as follows: Section 2 reviews the regional distribution of public capital in rural China. Section 3 develops a conceptual framework and model for the purpose of our analysis. Section 4 describes the data, and Section 5 discusses our estimated results. We conclude the chapter, and point out the limitations of the current study and future research directions in the final section.

2 Regional Dimension of Rural Infrastructure

The Agricultural Census provides a unique opportunity to analyze the regional dimension of rural infrastructure in China. Table 16.1 presents the selected infrastructure indicators by province in 1996 when the census was conducted. First, we compare the newly available Census data with the official data which are published previously in various *China Statistical Yearbooks* by the State Statistical Bureau (SSB) or other government agencies. For road density, the Census reported 1,679 kilometer per 10,000 square kilometers, which is 34 percent higher than the official data, released from the Ministry of Transportation. Therefore, the data from the Ministry of Transportation may have understated the road density in rural areas. With respect to rural telephones, the Census reported 283 sets per 10,000 rural residents, which is 43 percent higher than the 197 sets reported by SSB *Statistical Yearbook*. For rural electricity consumption, the Census reported 260 kw per person for 1996, while the SSB *Statistical Yearbook* reported 200 kw per person in rural China, a 30 percent difference.

Table 16.1 Regional difference in rural infrastructure (1996)

Province	Road Density			Electricity Use	Rural Telephone		
	km/10,000 km²	km/10,000 labor	km/10,000 person	kw per person	Set per 10,000 labor	Set per 10,000 People	
Beijing	6310	48	28	709	1024	933	
Tianjin	5258	27	17	844	625	555	
Hebei	3021	18	11	252	222	207	
Shanxi	3578	40	24	309	205	183	
Inner Mongolia	484	64	42	150	229	199	
Liaoning	2985	31	21	375	502	487	
Jilin	2136	48	29	184	286	266	
Heilongjiang	1200	54	35	177	388	345	
Shanghai	17676	36	26	1771	2767	2760	
Jiangsu	6863	19	13	453	604	573	
Zhejiang	3505	15	10	525	596	582	
Anhui	4905	20	13	113	160	156	
Fujian	4305	35	21	383	735	594	
Jiangxi	3529	29	19	115	109	102	
Shandong	6358	21	14	287	242	206	
Henan	4382	15	9	195	111	106	
Hubei	4199	31	20	182	319	296	
Hunan	4633	30	20	129	171	160	
Guangdong	3843	25	14	625	1258	1222	
Guangxi	2287	24	15	114	97	91	
Hainan		51	29	63	163	158	
Chongqing		22	16	159	121	111	
Sichuan	2050	25	17	165	88	74	
Guizhou	3172	29	18	78	54	42	
Yunnan	2840	51	32	268	108	96	
Tibet	344	339	199	22	65	54	
Shaanxi	3210	37	23	172	101	95	
Gansu	1300	42	26	190	81	71	
Qinghai	207	72	46	273	247	244	
Ningxia	1082	32	19	161	104	103	
Xinjiang	277	90	52	159	172	166	

Notes: 1. When calculating road density, Hannan and Chongqing are included in Guangdong and Sichuan, respectively.
Sources: Calculated from the Agricultural Census.

In terms of the illiteracy rate, the Census data reported 14 percent for the rural population over the age of 7 years. This percentage is comparable to 11 percent in

1996 for agricultural labor reported by SSB's *Rural Statistical Yearbook, 1997*. The higher rate for the general population than agricultural labor may be due to the fact that general population may have higher illiteracy rate than the total labor force.

With respect to R&D spending and personnel, the data are not easily comparable. The Census reports such data only for the township level, while official SSB or Ministry of Science and Technology reports the data above the county level. Nevertheless, the Census data provides unique and valuable information about science and technology at the lower level which has never been reported before by other official sources.

The regional data reveals that the infrastructure development is highly correlated with the economic development level. Road density measured as length of rural town roads per 10,000 square kilometers has very large regional variation. If we exclude Beijing, Shanghai, and Tianjin in our analysis, Jiangsu has the highest road density, and Shandong has the second. Not surprisingly, Inner Mongolia, Tibet, Qinghai, and Xinjiang have the lowest road densities among all provinces. However, if we use the length of roads per rural resident, it is the western provinces or regions that per capita length of roads are the highest due to their relatively lower population density.

In terms of rural electricity, again it is the coastal region that has the highest per capita consumption. For example, Guangdong, Jiangsu, and Zhejiang have more than 400 kW per person per year, while in Inner Mongolia, Tibet, Xinjiang, Guizhou, and surprisingly some central provinces such as Anhui, Jiangxi, and Guangxi, per capita electricity consumption is less than 200 kW in 1996.

The difference in rural telephone possession is the largest among all types of rural infrastructure. In Guangdong, Jiangsu, Zhejiang, and Fujian, for every 10,000 residents, there are more than 500 telephone sets. But in Gansu, Tibet, Guizhou, Sichuan, and Guangxi, less than 100 sets are possessed for every 10,000 rural residents.

The education data reveals that in the western region the Census reported much higher illiterate rate than the official SSB *Rural Statistical Yearbook, 1997* (Table 16.2). For example, in Tibet and Qinghai, the Census recorded 76 percent and 45 percent for Tibet and Gansu, compared to 61 percent and 34 percent reported by *Rural Statistical Yearbook*, respectively. The gap in the education level between the Eastern and Western regions may have been higher than previously believed.

The Census data on science and technology personnel and spending uncovers a striking phenomenon (Table 16.3). It is the Western region, for example Xinjiang, and Inner Mongolia, that have the highest ratios of science and technology personnel to rural population or labor. But in terms of science and technology spending, the region has the lowest. This implies that the science and technology personnel in less-developed areas experience a severe shortage of operation funds compared to their Eastern cohorts.

Table 16.2 Percentage of rural population with different education levels (1996)

	Illiterate and semi-illiterate	Primary school	Junior middle school	Senior middle school	Special secondary school	College and above
National	14.01	42.15	38.04	5.07	0.57	0.16
Beijing	6.28	21.04	59.08	10.67	2.23	0.70
Tianjin	7.15	37.54	48.30	6.21	0.64	0.16
Hebei	10.03	39.11	43.87	6.45	0.44	0.09
Shanxi	8.81	35.74	48.41	6.20	0.62	0.22
Inner Mongolia	17.26	39.66	36.54	5.66	0.70	0.18
Liaoning	6.31	41.29	47.22	4.08	0.79	0.30
Jilin	8.27	45.47	40.75	4.56	0.77	0.19
Heilongjiang	8.67	43.54	41.95	4.77	0.84	0.24
Shanghai	13.83	28.39	49.38	6.37	1.44	0.60
Jiangsu	12.53	36.94	42.49	7.12	0.63	0.29
Zhejiang	13.85	44.26	36.30	5.07	0.37	0.15
Anhui	16.32	42.52	37.18	3.28	0.55	0.14
Fujian	7.01	51.53	35.83	4.86	0.61	0.16
Jiangxi	11.67	48.90	34.29	4.51	0.52	0.12
Shandong	9.80	40.65	43.09	5.63	0.66	0.15
Henan	13.57	33.41	46.26	6.13	0.49	0.14
Hubei	14.63	40.97	38.21	5.49	0.60	0.10
Hunan	9.65	43.76	39.42	6.37	0.65	0.15
Guangdong	7.93	42.87	41.39	6.81	0.75	0.24
Guangxi	10.42	47.98	35.77	5.00	0.71	0.12
Hainan	17.73	35.60	38.76	7.20	0.59	0.12
Chongqing	11.87	52.03	32.44	3.20	0.37	0.10
Sichuan	15.67	48.60	32.42	2.88	0.35	0.08
Guizhou	29.95	45.47	22.23	1.76	0.50	0.08
Yunnan	28.09	49.11	20.25	2.12	0.38	0.06
Tibet	75.71	22.93	1.21	0.09	0.05	0.01
Shaanxi	16.35	35.21	40.88	6.90	0.50	0.15
Gansu	35.57	34.40	24.12	5.25	0.51	0.15
Qinghai	46.04	31.82	19.10	2.77	0.21	0.06
Ningxia	31.16	33.37	29.68	4.70	0.86	0.22
Xinjiang	15.73	53.69	25.24	3.78	1.18	0.39

Sources: Calculated from the Agricultural Census.

Table 16.3 Sciences and technology personnel and expenses (1996)

	Number of ST Personnel per 10,000 Rural Labor	Number of ST Personnel per 10,000 Rural Residents	ST Spending in Yuan per Rural Labor	ST Spending in Yuan per Rural Residents
National	90.89	58.41	0.81	0.52
Beijing	200.16	115.69	0.90	0.52
Tianjin	253.67	155.73	0.38	0.23
Hebei	147.87	90.82	0.33	0.20
Shanxi	81.39	48.94	0.47	0.28
Inner Mongolia	344.24	224.39	0.24	0.16
Liaoning	88.93	58.88	1.38	0.92
Jilin	126.34	77.55	0.43	0.26
Heilongjiang	166.80	107.64	0.40	0.26
Shanghai	150.28	107.68	5.93	4.25
Jiangsu	81.50	55.64	1.12	0.77
Zhejiang	57.80	39.10	1.11	0.75
Anhui	54.56	35.04	0.46	0.30
Fujian	92.89	55.40	1.62	0.97
Jiangxi	47.77	30.90	0.22	0.14
Shandong	92.89	61.33	1.26	0.83
Henan	123.86	79.42	0.25	0.16
Hubei	84.61	54.11	0.77	0.49
Hunan	79.70	52.38	0.88	0.58
Guangdong	80.93	45.99	2.76	1.57
Guangxi	66.82	42.16	0.38	0.24
Hainan	143.37	82.08	1.10	0.63
Chongqing	37.32	26.49	0.39	0.28
Sichuan	64.45	44.86	0.91	0.64
Guizhou	27.10	17.12	0.43	0.27
Yunnan	35.05	22.32	0.61	0.39
Tibet	44.86	26.41	0.02	0.01
Shaanxi	104.83	64.08	0.15	0.09
Gansu	104.42	64.93	0.07	0.04
Qinghai	68.40	43.59	0.00	0.00
Ningxia	48.42	28.99	0.14	0.08
Xinjiang	345.98	199.60	0.24	0.14

Sources: Calculated from the Agricultural Census.

In summary, the Census data reveals a higher level of rural infrastructure development than previously thought. But it also uncovers a larger regional difference, not only in the development of rural infrastructure, but also in the development of education and science and technology. This may explain why the

Western region has lagged behind despite rapid economic growth for the nation as a whole.

3 Conceptual Framework and Model

There have been numerous studies on the estimation of production functions for both agricultural and non-farm sectors. One significant feature in these previous studies is the use of a single-equation approach. There are at least two disadvantages to this approach. First, many production determinants are generated from the same economic process. In other words, these variables are also endogenous variables, and ignoring this characteristic leads to biased estimates of the production functions. Second, certain economic variables affect the rural economy through multiple channels. For example, improved rural infrastructure will not only contribute growth in agricultural production, but also affect non-farm production. It is very difficult to capture these different effects in a single equation approach.

This study uses a simultaneous equations model to estimate the effects of rural infrastructure on both farm and non-farm production.

$$AY = f\left(LAND, AGLABOR, FERT, MACH, IR, RD, SCHY, ROADS, RTR\right) \tag{1}$$

$$NAY = f\left(RILABOR, ELEC, SCHY, ROADS, RTR\right) \tag{2}$$

Equation (1) models the agricultural production function. The dependent variable is gross agricultural output value (AY). Land (LAND), labor (AGLABOR), fertilizer (FERT), machinery (MACH) are included as conventional inputs. We include the following variables in the equation to capture the impact of technology, infrastructure and education on agricultural production: percentage of irrigated cropped area in total cropped area (*IR*); number of agricultural researchers and extension staff (RD), road density (*ROADS*), number of rural telephone sets per thousand rural residents (*RTR*), and average years of schooling for population over the age of 7 years old (SCHY).[1]

Equation (2) is a production function for non-agricultural activities in rural areas. The dependent variable is gross value of the township and village enterprises (NAY). Labor input used in the non-farm sector (RILABOR), infrastructure, and the labor education level are independent variables included in the function.[2] The electricity consumption (ELEC) is used to proxy for fixed and current capital used in the non-farm sector.

---

[1] The electricity variable is excluded mainly because it is highly correlated with road and telephone variables.

[2] Ideally, the capital variable should also be included in the function. But there is no such data available at the county level.

Following Fan (1991), Lin (1992), and Fan and Pardey (1997), we use the traditional Cobb-Douglas form for both agricultural and non-farm equations. In this form, the coefficients of independent variables are simply their elasticities with respect to the dependent variable. Regional dummies are also added to capture the impact of other factors that are not included in the equations.

To account for the sources of difference in productivity, we choose labor productivity in our analysis. Labor productivity is one of the most important indicators in economic development and is one of the major determinants of rural income. Following Hayami and Ruttan (1985) and Fan (1990), we use the following accounting formula:

$$\frac{\Delta \frac{Y}{L}}{\left(\frac{Y}{L}\right)_0} = \sum_i a_i \frac{\Delta \frac{X_i}{L}}{\left(\frac{X_i}{L}\right)_0} + \sum_i b_i \frac{\Delta P_i}{P_{i0}} \tag{3}$$

We use the average productivity at the national level $(Y/L)_0$ as our base for comparison, i.e., we try to explain the difference in productivity between each region and the national average.[3] In (3), labor productivity difference is explained by the difference in the use of conventional inputs X_i such as labor, land, fertilizer, machinery all measured on a per labor basis, and the difference in rural infrastructure, education, and science and technology capacity, denoted by P_i. If we divide every term on the right hand side by the productivity difference (on the left hand side), then the difference in productivity can be explained by right hand side variables in terms of percentages.

4 Data Explanations

Our analysis is based at the county level. Most of infrastructure, education and technology variables are available in the Agricultural Census. However, Agricultural Census does not report detailed information on agricultural and non-farm output. Input uses are also not available. Therefore, in this analysis, we combine the Census data with the data from other SSB sources such as *China Statistical Yearbooks* and *China's Rural Statistical Yearbooks*.

Agricultural output—Agricultural output is measured as gross agricultural production value. The data is taken from the SSB official statistical source.

---

[3] This decomposition implicitly assumes a constant return to scale, i.e., $\sum ai = 1$. This assumption is not too realistic, as evidenced by Fan (1991) and Zhang and Carter (1997).

Non-farm output—Non-farm output is measured as gross output value of township and village enterprises. The sources of the data are official SSB and Ministry of Agriculture publications

Agricultural labor—Agricultural labor is measured in stock terms as the number of persons engaged in agricultural production at the end of each year. They are taken from the Census.

Non-farm labor—Non-farm labor is measured as number of employees in the township and village enterprises reported by the Agricultural Census.

Land—land is total arable land used for agricultural production. The data is taken form the Census.

Machinery—Machinery input is measured as horsepower of machinery used in agricultural production. Since the Census does not report horsepower of machinery, we use the data from the SSB *Statistical Yearbook*.

Irrigation—Irrigation services used in agriculture are proxied by the ratio of irrigated area. Since the published Census data do not report irrigated areas by county, we use the data from official sources of SSB and Ministry of Agriculture.

Fertilizer—It is measured as pure nutrients of chemical fertilizer. The data are taken from official sources of SSB and Ministry of Agriculture.

Roads—The length of township roads is reported by the Census. We divided the road length by the geographic areas to obtain the road density variable for our analysis.

Rural telephone—Number of rural telephone sets is available from the Census. We use the number of telephone sets per 10,000 rural residents as our telephone variable.

Education—For the education variable, we use the percentage of population with different education levels to calculate the average years of schooling as our education variable, assuming 0 year for a person who is illiterate and semi-illiterate, 5 years with primary school education, 8 years with junior high school education, 12 years with high school education, 13 years with professional school education, and 16 years with college and above education. The Agricultural Census reports the percentages of population with different education levels who are above the age of 7.

Electricity consumption—Electricity consumption in the non-farm and agricultural sectors are reported by various issues of *China Rural Statistical Yearbooks*.

Science and technology—We use the number of science and technology personnel per 10,000 rural labor at the township level to represent the capacity of science and technology. The data are taken from the Census.

5 Results

Table 16.4 presents the estimated results of production functions for agriculture and non-farm economies. Only 15 provinces or regions reported county level data in recent SSB provincial publications on the Agricultural Census. They are:

Beijing, Tianjin, Shanxi, Heilongjiang, Shanghai, Jiangsu, Zhejiang, Fujian, Jiangxi, Shandong, Hunan, Sichuan, Tibet, Shaanxi, and Ningxia. Although they cover roughly half of the provinces, the number of observations covers only 45 percent of the total number of counties. Therefore, the sample we used in our regression may not represent the whole of China.

Table 16.4 Estimation of the equation system

	Agricultural Output	Non-Farm Output
Labor	0.262	0.510
	(3.14)*	(16.84)*
Land	0.228	
	(8.47)*	
Fertilizer	0.150	
	(4.55)*	
Machinery (or electricity)	0.115	0.480
	(6.34)*	(15.89)*
Research	0.104	
	(3.42)*	
Irrigation	0.260	
	(9.48)*	
Roads	0.032	
	(2.25)*	
Years of Schooling	0.275	0.792
	(1.81)*	(1.94)*
Telephone	0.056	0.119
	(6.41)*	(6.51)*
R^2	0.865	0.813

Notes:
1. Regional dummies are added to capture the provincial fixed effect, but the coefficients are not reported here. Total number of observations is 1,104.
2. The subscript * indicates statistically significant at the 5 percent level.

Most coefficients in both agricultural and non-farm production functions are statistically significant. The coefficients for conventional inputs in the agricultural production function such as those for labor, land, fertilizer, and machinery are in the same ranges of other studies (Fan 1991, Fan and Pardey 1997, Zhang and Carter 1997). The labor and electricity variables (as a proxy for both fixed and current capitals) are also statistically significant. One notable feature is that the coefficients for infrastructure and education variables are more significant in the non-farm production equation than those in the agricultural production function. The fitness of both equations is exceptionally good with R^2 of 0.865 for the agricultural production function, and 0.813 for the non-farm production function, despite the fact that cross-sectional data are used. The road variable in the non-farm sector is insignificant due to its high correlation with the telephone variable, therefore we drop it in the final estimation.

Table 16.5 presents the results of accounting. The numbers in the parentheses below the first row are the difference in labor productivity level between each region and the national average. By assuming this difference as 100 percent, we can explain the productivity difference in terms of the percentages by various factors shown in the rest rows in the table. [4] The sources of difference in agricultural labor productivity vary sharply among regions. The higher labor productivity in the Eastern region is primarily explained by higher fertilizer use, better infrastructure and the residual, which accounts for other missing variables. This residual is particularly large, implying that other factors rather than those included in the equation may have played even bigger role in explaining its higher productivity. For the Central region, higher productivity is mainly explained by more use of land per labor together with more fertilizer, machinery and irrigation use. In the Western region, the lower productivity is due to lower land use per labor (and therefore lower fertilizer use), poorer infrastructure and human capitals, and more limited science and technology capacity. The residual that has not been accounted by the variables included is also quite large, indicating other factors may have also contributed to lower productivity in the region.

Table 16.5 Accounting for the sources of labor productivity difference among regions

| | Agriculture | | | Non-farm | | | Total Rural | | |
	Eastern	Central	Western	Eastern	Central	Western	Eastern	Central	Western
Productivity	100.00	100.00	100.00	100.00	100.00	100.00	100.00	100.00	100.00
	(47.06)	(2.35)	(-35.29)	(38.08)	(17.22)	(-47.35)	(41.32)	(10.82)	(-40.08)
Land	-0.96	230.35	15.36				-0.35	99.08	9.26
Fertilizer	7.45	46.27	10.63				2.69	19.90	6.41
Machinery	0.72	121.43	9.87	-11.46	3.62	-5.92	-7.07	54.29	3.60
Irrigation	-3.44	103.20	7.45				-1.24	44.39	4.50
S&T	-0.08	4.58	0.16				-0.03	1.97	0.10
Roads	-2.16	-30.85	-4.25	0.00	0.00	-0.00	-0.78	-13.27	-2.56
Telephone	20.50	-210.14	10.66	53.83	-61.02	16.88	41.82	-125.16	13.13
Education	1.57	21.04	6.35	5.68	8.41	13.84	4.20	13.84	9.32
Residual	76.39	-185.88	43.78	51.95	148.99	75.20	60.76	4.95	56.25

[4] Because the development level in the Central region is close to the national average, the absolute difference in labor productivity is rather small. However, the decomposition analysis is based on relative percentage terms. Therefore, the results for the Central regions could be very sensitive.

For labor productivity in the non-farm economy, roads and telephone together explained more than 60 percent of the difference between the regional and the national average in the Eastern region. For the Western region, nearly 40 percent of the productivity difference (lower than the national average) can be attributed to the physical infrastructure and lower education level. Large residual in the accounting for non-farm productivity indicates that many other factors may also play a very important role in the non-farm economy.

For the overall rural economy (aggregation of both agricultural and non-farm economies), public capital such as roads, telecommunication, and education explained about 45 percent of the higher productivity in the Eastern region. In the Western region, lower public capital accounted for 26 percent of the lower productivity. In the Central region, however, since its productivity is very close to the national level, it is not obvious how public capital has affected its productivity difference when compared to the national average.

6 Conclusions

The 1996 Agricultural Census provides a unique dataset to analyze various issues on rural development in China. In particular, it provides very detailed data on rural infrastructure, education, and science and technology. This chapter is an early attempt to use this data set. Partly due to the limited access, the data we have is not complete, covering only 45 percent of the country. We will pursue more detailed and more thorough analyses once we have a complete data for all counties.

Despite the crudeness of the data and model we used, the results do shed new lights. First, rural infrastructure and education play a more important role in explaining the difference in rural non-farm productivity than agricultural productivity. Since the rural non-farm economy is a major determinant of rural income, investing more in rural infrastructure is key to increase overall income of rural population. Second, the lower productivity in the Western region is explained by its lower level of rural infrastructure, education, and science and technology. Therefore, improving both the level and efficiency of public capital in the West is a must to narrow its difference in productivity with other regions.

This research merely serves as a touch stone for future research. One of the urgent future research topic is to search different policy options to mobilize resources to support public investment provisions for the less developed western region. Under the current fiscal decentralization scheme, financing infrastructure in regions with a small non-farm sector faces a great challenge. Lack of local revenues causes under-investment in the less developed Western region.

References

Ash, R.F. and Edmonds, R.L., 'China's Land Resources, Environment and Agricultural Production', *China Quarterly,* 156 (1998): 836–879.

Fan, S., *Regional Productivity Growth in China's Agriculture* (Boulder: Westview Press, 1990).

———, 'Effects of technological change and institutional reform on production growth in Chinese agriculture', *American Journal of Agricultural Economics*, 73(2) (1991): 266-275.

———, 'Research investment and the economic returns to Chinese agricultural research', *Journal of Productivity Analysis,* 14 (92) (2000): 163-180.

Fan, S., Zhang, X. and Robinson. S., 'Structural change and economic growth', *Review of Development Economics,* 7(3) (2003): 360-377.

Fan, S. and Pardey, P., 'Research, Productivity, and Output Growth in Chinese Agriculture', *Journal of Development Economics*, 53 (1997):115-137.

Hayami, Y. and Ruttan, V., *Agricultural development: An international perspective* (Baltimore: John Hopkins University Press, 1985).

Huang, J. and Rozelle, S., 'Environmental stress and grain yields in China', *American Journal of Agricultural Economics*, 77 (1996): 853-864.

———, 'Technological change: rediscovering the engine of productivity growth in China's agricultural economy', *Journal of Development Economics*, 49 (1997): 337-369.

Kanbur, R. and Zhang, X., 'Which regional inequality? The evolution of rural-urban and inland-coastal inequality in China 1983-1995', *Journal of Comparative Economics,* 27 (1999): 686-701.

McMillan, J., Whalley, J. and Zhu, L.G., 'The Impact of China's Economic Reforms on Agricultural Productivity Growth', *Journal of Political Economy*, 97 (1989): 781–807.

Rozelle, S., 'Rural Industrialization and Increasing Inequality: Emerging Patterns in China's Reforming Economy', *Journal of Comparative Economics*, 19(3) (1994): 362-391.

Smil, V., 'China's Agricultural Land', *China Quarterly,* 158 (1999): 414–429.

Lin, J.Y., 'Rural reforms and agricultural growth in China', *American Economic Review*, 82(1) (1992): 34-51.

Zhang, B. and Carter, C.A., Reforms, 'The weather, and productivity growth in China's grain sector', *American Journal of Agricultural Economics*, 79 (1997):1266–1277.

Zhang, X. and Fan, S., 'Public Investment and Regional Inequality in rural China', *Agricultural Economics* (forthcoming 2003).

Chapter 17

Local Government Indebtedness in China: What is the Role for the Municipal Government Bond Market?

Ligang Liu
Shaoqiang Chen

016   P34

H74   018   017   P25

1 Introduction

Despite China's impressive economic growth, its fiscal sustainability has increasingly become one of the most watched risk indicators facing the economy. Although China's explicit national debt to GDP ratio is rather manageable by the OECD standard, at about 20 percent of GDP—given its small share of tax revenue to GDP currently at 18.5 percent of GDP—this fiscal system may stumble upon major challenges in the medium- to long-term if China's large contingent fiscal liabilities are also taken into consideration. The contingent liabilities—unpaid pension debt, non-performing loans (NPLs) at the financial institutions, local government debt, publicly guaranteed debt, and so on—mostly resulted from its gradualist approach to economic transition and have reached close to 100 percent of the 1997 GDP,[1] thus giving rise to a serious question on whether China can maintain fiscal sustainability.

Indeed, the small revenue base and a large interest payment in the expenditure of the central government budget (see Figure 17.1) have already substantially weakened the ability of the central government to conduct effective and redistributive fiscal transfers to poor provinces as well as to disadvantaged groups. As a result, the regional disparity and income gap have worsened substantially. Presently, the urban-rural income gap is close to 6; coastal-inland region per capita income difference is 3; and the Gini coefficient is close to 0.5 (Chan-Lee et al., 2002). These indicators depict a dangerous trend that the country is increasingly growing apart, rather than growing together.

While the public sector is facing large fiscal liabilities, the private sector as a whole has already accumulated a large stock of savings, which is also about the

---

[1] A consistent estimate put forward by the World Bank put China's contingent fiscal liability to about 75 percent of China's 1997 GDP (Krumn and Wong, 2002). However, their study does not include the estimates of local government debt.

size of GDP in addition to the nation's large foreign exchange reserves. Thus, how to transform this stock of wealth into future productive capital is what the government will need to address urgently.

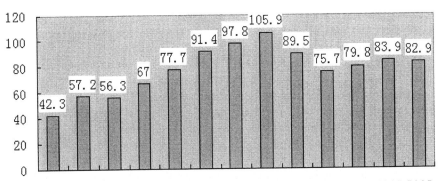

Figure 17.1 Debt dependency of the central government budget

This chapter suggests that the key to reducing fiscal risks of the central government as well as resolving the regional income gap is to first sort out a mismatch between the responsibilities of local governments for their economic development at this stage and the necessary financing tools at their disposal to finance large and long-term development projects. Although China's private sector has developed rapidly, some major provincial development projects are too large in terms of the funding required. They are difficult to organize, implement, and finance privately. Thus, the local government involvement in long-term, local economic development is inevitable. Provincial governments, similar to the central government, also face the problem of how to effectively smooth their expenditures inter-temporally or inter-generationally because of unexpected business cycles, technology shock, and demographic changes. Without long-term financing, local governments would have to rely on their tax revenues and borrowing from banks to finance these investments. These financial instruments, however, suffer from another mismatch problem, maturity mismatch. That is when long-term investment is financed by short-term financing.

One obvious way to resolve these mismatch problems is to allow provincial governments in China to have the right to issue long-term and development-related bonds, but this solution will also involve another risk: local governments may have a tendency to issue excessively, which in turn may lead many of them to default.[2] If there are no laws or regulations governing the default of local governments, the

---

[2] Indeed, in the 1840s, nine state governments (Louisiana, Florida, Maryland, Mississippi, Arkansas, Illinois, Michigan, Pennsylvania, and Indiana) in the United States defaulted. The most recent case is in 1995 when Orange County of California also defaulted (Sylla and Wallis, 1998).

central government may eventually have to take over local government debts, inducing moral hazard and increasing its own fiscal risks. If the debts of local governments are then monetized, price stability of the entire economy will also be undermined.

Recognizing these potential risks, we propose a "Carrot and Stick" approach to developing China's local government debt market. The "Carrot" is to grant provincial governments the right to issue debt. The "Stick" is that provincial governments will have to adopt stringent fiscal rules governing balanced budget and debt limit requirements so as to prevent excessive debt issuing and debt default. In order to be able to tap into the domestic bond market, Chinese provinces would have to disclose their finances to credit rating agencies, the general public, and the central government. Such disclosure, meanwhile, will also allow the provincial-level People's Congresses to decide and approve debt issues of provincial governments. Before effective market mechanisms emerge to credibly discipline local government bond issues, it is suggested that the market, the local legislature, and the central government jointly play the disciplining role to complement the inadequacy of markets at the initial stage.

This chapter proceeds as follows. Section 2 surveys the debt problem of local governments in China. Section 3 discusses the balanced-budget rules of the United States and the implications of these fiscal rules on U.S. macroeconomic management. Section 4 assesses the credit worthiness of Chinese provinces. Based on the results of Section 4, we spell out preconditions and a sequencing strategy to develop China's municipal bond market in Section 5. Finally, Section 6 offers our conclusions.

2 How Big Is Local Governments' Debt Problem in China?

China's national governance structure can be categorized as a unitary system in which the power is mostly held by a central authority with local and regional governments having limited autonomy. At the local government level, it has a four-level administrative system in charge of 1.28 billion people: municipal/provincial, regional, county, and township. At the provincial level, there are four municipality governments whose status is equivalent to province (Beijing, Shanghai, Tianjing, and Chongqing), five autonomous regions (Guangxi, Inner Mongolia, Ningxia, Tibet, and Xinjiang) and 22 provinces, two special administrative regions (Hong Kong and Macao). At the regional level, there are 333 regional districts, 275 of which are regional municipalities. At the county level, there are 2,861 counties, 381 of which are county-level municipalities and 830 municipal administrated counties. At the bottom level of the national governance structure, there are 44,067 townships (National Bureau of Statistics, 2004). China's legal system is based on continental law.

The central government has the right to appoint and replace government officials at the provincial level. Since 1983, however, the central government has been less involved in personnel appointment at the sub-provincial level. For other provincial officials, for example, the heads of the fiscal and tax bureaus at the province level are often recommended by the provincial branch of the Communist Party, nominated by the local government, endorsed by the local People's Congress (Huang, 1996).

Across the country, a vast difference exists in geography, ethnicity, and per capita income. The average population of each province is about 40 million, equivalent to that of a mid-sized country. The regional disparity is also large. At the end of 2003, the poorest province in Southwest, Guizhou province, had an annual per capita income of about 3,504 *yuan* or \$424.20. On the other hand, the richest municipality, Shanghai, has a per capita income of 36,556 *yuan* or \$4,310 (see Table 17.1).

Fiscal decentralization is considered one of the key features of China's economic transition and a factor for rapid economic growth.[3] The devolution of fiscal authority from the central to local governments has greatly enhanced the incentives for local governments to actively participate in local economic development.

Both *de facto,* though not *de jure,* fiscal and monetary decentralization took place before 1995. *De facto* fiscal decentralization was able to take place because of the central government's limited information on the fiscal activities of local governments (Qian and Weingast, 1997). Therefore, local governments are able to maintain various "extra-budget" and "off-budget" accounts. *De facto* fiscal decentralization provides good incentives for local governments to generate revenues for the needs of local economic development. On the other hand, it gives incentives to local governments to preserve wealth at the local level, which makes the central government difficult to acquire its legally deserved shares of tax revenues in order to conduct fiscal transfers from rich to poor provinces. The participation of local governments in local economic development complements the ill-developed market institutions at the initial stage of economic transition and has acted as a substitute institution for China's rapid economic growth (Qian, 1999).

Under *de facto* fiscal decentralization, an ill-adopted tax system further exacerbated revenues of the central government. China's tax system has gone through two major stages with a tax contract arrangement between the central and local governments for the period of 1978 and 1994 and a tax-sharing system from 1994 on. However, greater local autonomy over tax collection and a strong element of central-local bargaining in the fiscal process, together with a growth in off-

---

[3] Zhang and Zou (1998) find that the degree of fiscal decentralization in China is negatively related to economic growth. However, such a result is difficult to be rationalized with provincial growth figures, which are very high. Qian (1999) theorizes that decentralization gives incentives for local government to develop local economies under the circumstance that formal institution is ill-developed, though he does not provide an empirical test on the causation between growth and decentralization as in the Zhang and Zou article.

Table 17.1 Summary information of Chinese Provinces (2003)

Provinces	GDP Size (Billion of Yuan)	Total Population (year-end) (million)	Per Capita Provincial Income (Yuan)	Government Revenue (Billion of Yuan)	Revenue-GDP Ratio
Anhui	397.2	64.1	6196.5679	22.1	5.5639476
Beijing	366.3	14.6	25089.041	59.3	16.188916
Chongqing	225.1	31.3	7191.6933	16.2	7.1968014
Fujian	523.2	34.9	14991.404	30.5	5.8295107
Gansu	130.5	26	5019.2308	8.8	6.743295
Guangdong	1362.6	79.5	17139.623	131.6	9.6580068
Guangxi	273.5	48.6	5627.572	20.4	7.4588665
Guizhou	135.6	38.7	3503.876	12.5	9.2182891
Hainan	67.1	8.1	8283.9506	5.1	7.6005961
Hebei	709.9	67.7	10485.968	33.6	4.733061
Helongjiang	443	38.2	11596.859	24.9	5.6207675
Henan	704.9	96.7	7289.5553	33.8	4.7950064
Hubei	540.1	60	9001.6667	26	4.8139233
Hunan	463.9	66.6	6965.4655	26.9	5.7986635
Inner Mongolia	215	23.8	9033.6134	13.9	6.4651163
Jiangsu	1246.1	74.1	16816.464	79.8	6.4039804
Jiangxi	283	42.5	6658.8235	16.8	5.9363958
Jilin	252.3	27	9344.4444	15.4	6.1038446
Liaoning	600.2	42.1	14256.532	44.7	7.4475175
Ningxia	38.5	5.8	6637.931	3	7.7922078
Qinghai	39	5.34	7303.3708	2.4	6.1538462
Shandong	1243.6	91.3	13621.03	71.4	5.7413959
Shanghai	625.1	17.1	36555.556	88.6	14.173732
Shannxi	239.9	36.9	6501.355	17.7	7.3780742
Shanxi	245.7	33.1	7422.9607	18.6	7.5702076
Sichuan	545.6	87	6271.2644	33.7	6.1766862
Tianjing	244.8	10.1	24237.624	20.5	8.374183
Tibet	18.5	2.7	6851.8519	0.8	4.3243243
Xinjiang	187.8	19.3	9730.5699	12.8	6.8157614
Yunnan	246.6	43.8	5630.137	22.9	9.2862936
Zhejiang	939.5	46.8	20074.786	70.7	7.5252794
Memorandum					
Maximum	1362.6	96.7	36555.556	131.6	16.188916
Minimum	18.5	2.7	3503.876	0.8	4.3243243
Average	*437.22903*	*41.410968*	*11139.703*	*31.787097*	*7.2544677*

Source: Chinese Statistical Yearbook (2004).

budget activities, have contributed to the sharp decline of central government's fiscal revenues as a share of the GDP (Ma, 1997; Arora and Norregaard, 1997)

The 1994 tax reform has significantly reversed the central government's revenue decline, but to some extent, the reform has also contributed to the indebtedness of local governments as steady tax revenue sources have been taken over by the central government. Local governments were left with limited fiscal resources to fend themselves. At the same time, expenditures on education and health—the two major items of expenditure of local government—account for an average of about 20 percent of the total expenditures of the local government. Although the central government's revenue share has increased to 55 percent of the total revenue collected, provincial governments have seen their revenue fall to 45 percent (see Figure 17.2).

This sharp decline of provincial tax revenues with the same or even increasing fiscal obligations has forced local governments to run deficits. In recent years, the aggregate deficits of provincial governments as a whole reached 6.3 percent of the 2003 GDP (see Table 17.2), even though the 1995 Chinese Budget Law clearly prohibits provincial governments from running deficits. Based on Table 17.2 and the assumption that the deficits accumulated since 1994 have not been repaid, the debt of provincial governments could run as high as 32 percent of China's 2003 GDP. Some survey results reveal that governments at the county level are encountering the most severe fiscal difficulties. They are rapidly accumulating debts (Wei, 2004).

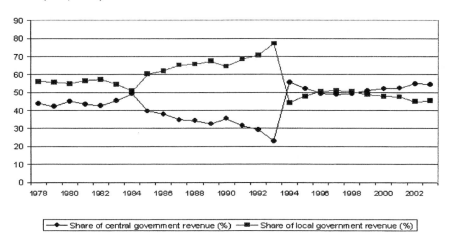

Figure 17.2 Central and provincial revenue share in total revenues

Presently, most local governments have debts. Primary forms of local government debt are as follows: (1) guarantees via the "decisions" issued by the local People's Congress for the local government's loans from banks to local government-owned enterprises. It is estimated that guarantees are the largest segment of the explicit contingent liabilities; (2) the social security fund used for current expenditure due to short falls of tax revenues, which is implicit but direct debt; (3) losses due to state-owned, grain-related enterprises or grain debt, which are implicit but direct liabilities; (4) salaries owed to school teachers, which is explicit debt; and 5) the construction debt owed to construction companies, which is also explicit debt.

Table 17.2 Provincial level of revenues and expenditures 1993-2003
(billions of *Yuan*)

	1993	1994	1995	1996	1997	1998	1999	2000	2001	2002	2003
Revenue	339.1	231.2	298.6	374.7	442.4	498.4	559.5	640.6	780.3	851.5	985
Share of total government Revenue	78%	44.3%	47.8%	50.6%	51.1%	50.5%	48.9%	47.8%	47.6%	45%	45.40%
Expenditure	333	403.8	482.8	578.6	670.1	767.3	903.5	1036.7	1313.5	1528.1	1723
Share of total government Expenditure	71.7%	69.7%	70.8%	72.9%	72.6%	71.1%	68.5%	65.3%	69.5%	69.3%	69.9%
Fiscal Gap	6.1	-172.6	-184.2	-203.9	-227.7	-268.9	-344	-396.1	-533.2	-676.6	-738
Share of GDP	0.2%	-3.7%	-3.1%	-3.0%	-3.1%	-3.4%	-4.2%	-4.4%	-5.5%	-6.4%	-6.3%
Memorandum:											
GDP		3463.4	4676.9	5847.8	6788.5	7446.3	7834.5	8206.8	8946.8	9731.5	10517.2	11725.2

Source: China Statistical Yearbook (2004).

Among these debts, the construction debt was the second largest local government debt. According to National Bureau of Statistics (NBS) surveys, the construction debt owed by local governments amounted to 90 billion—close to 1 percent of GDP (Wei, 2004).

At the county level, the problems with debt are even worse. Although statistics on such debt is sparse and inconsistent, regional surveys and analyses indicate the problems have been rather widespread. Generally, the poorer the region, the higher the debt is. According to an audit done by the National Bureau of Audit, 37 out of 49 counties in ten provinces in the middle and western regions have deficits of 1 billion *yuan*, or 13.8 percent of their 7.2 billion allowed budget. The accumulative debt of the 49 counties exceeds 16.2 billion *yuan* or 2.1 times that of their total tax revenue (NBS, 2003). At the township level, it is estimated that the total debt is nearly 222 billion *yuan* or about 4 million *yuan* per township, which is 1.89 percent of the average township GDP in 2003, or 25.7 percent of the average tax revenue at the provincial level.[4]

Three factors have contributed to the indebtedness of local governments. First, their fiscal responsibilities remained—or even increased—after the 1994 tax

---

[4] Calculated by the authors based on Table 17.1.

reform, but their tax revenues have declined sharply. The central government's revenue has increased rapidly in 2003 to 55 percent from 22 percent in 1993. However, the revenue growth of local governments has been rather stagnant, only 4 percent. In addition, the 1994 tax reform has left local governments with an uncertain and smaller revenue base, which is costly to collect and has low revenue potential.

Second, the speed of local bureaucracy expansion is much faster than its tax revenue increase, reflecting the fact that local governments in China are under little check and balance from their local taxpayers. For example, the population of ten provinces in the mid-west region has increased by only 4.6 percent since 1994, but their numbers of government employees have increased by 22 percent (Wei, 2004). The lack of accountability of local governments to local taxpayers clearly exacerbates their debt problem.

Third, because local government officials are not yet directly accountable to local taxpayers—but are to their superior officials—they may attempt to maximize their achievements during their tenure at the expense of future generations. This incentive system has led to the investment in projects (grand municipal government buildings, for example) that have immediate short-term but little long-term impact on sustained long-term economic growth in their region, causing serious misallocation of productive capital. Because of the biased incentive system, the interests of local taxpayers are often ignored.

The Chinese experience has shown that local governments have been running increasingly large debts in spite of the fact that they are prohibited from accumulating debt. Both economic theory and empirical evidence indicate that price stability and fiscal disciplines are closely linked. Fiscal profligacy needs to be reined in by disciplined monetary policy. However, without the central bank's independency, monetary policy can be easily overrun by a large volume of government debt (at both the central and local government levels) when high interest rates resulted from tight monetary policy may cause the default of local governments. This, in turn, requires the monetary authorities to provide loans to provinces in a fiscal crisis. Under the circumstances, where local government debts are not properly recorded or even accounted for, the financial institution that lends them is in danger.

An alternative is to grant local governments the legal right to issue debt so that at least their indebtedness can be made transparent. However, without proper fiscal rules or regulations to constrain their spending, local governments can easily run into insolvency. This is why fiscal rules—such as those specified by the Maastricht Treaty that bound the deficit of EU members to 3 percent of the GDP and the debt level to 60 percent of the GDP—are needed to guard against fiscal profligacy. Because of the limited history of the fiscal rules stipulated by the Maastricht Treaty, it is difficult to evaluate how effectively they have performed to discipline the EU members. However, the balanced-budget rules have been used extensively in the United States for a relatively long period of time, and so far, these budget rules have proven to be quite effective in disciplining U.S. fiscal spending as there have been few defaults in the U.S. municipal bond market since the 1840s.[5]

3 Would Debt Issuing by Local Governments Necessarily Lead to Excessive Debt?—The U.S. Experience

3.1 Budget Rules in U.S. States

The United States provides the best test ground on whether fiscal rules and institutions are effective in curbing excessive state government spending. Nearly all of the states within the United States have balanced-budget rules stipulated either by their state constitutions or statutes on their operating budgets. These rules require state governors to submit, state legislatures to pass, and state governors to also sign balanced-budget rules (see Table 17.3) adopted from the National Association of State Budget Officers (NASBO) (2002). Most of these rules were enacted in the 19th century and have clearly stood the test of time.

Forty-five states—with the exception of Indiana, Texas, Vermont, Virginia, and West Virginia—require their governors to submit balanced budgets to the state legislature annually.[6] Out of these 45 states, 15 are required by both the state constitution and the state statute to do so. The remaining 30 states are required by either the state constitution or the state statute. In general, the state constitution requirement is stronger than the state statute because of the difficulty to change the state constitution.

The weakest requirement for a balanced budget is that the governor of a state must submit a balanced budget at the beginning of a fiscal year—also known as the *ex ante* rule. However, if unexpected events during the fiscal year cause fiscal imbalances and the state is not required by its constitution or statutes to take a corrective action, the state is allowed to run a deficit because neither constraints at the end of year nor an adjustment to the unexpected deficits, or surplus, are necessary (Advisory Council on Intergovernmental Relations (ACIR), 1987).

The next level of restriction requires the state legislature to enact a balanced budget, and 41 states require such a rule, 11 of which have it stipulated in both their state constitutions and statutes. If unforeseen economic events lead to deficits, the state can borrow to carry the deficit forward to future years. Because there is no fiscal discipline at the end of a fiscal year, these states are legally allowed to run deficits. This is also an *ex ante* balance-budget rule. There are eight states currently adopting such a practice.

---

[5] See footnote 2.

[6] Although the State of Idaho does not specify it, the governor always submits a balanced budget; it is politically unpopular if not to do so.

Table 17.3 Balanced budget rules in U.S. states

States	Governor Must Submit Balanced Budget	Nature of Require ment	Legislature Must Pass Balanced Budget	Nature of Require ment	Governor Must Sign Balanced Budget	Nature of Require ment	May Carry Over Deficit	Credit Ratings
Alabama	Y	C,S	Y	S	n.a.	n.a.		AA
Alaska	Y	S	Y	S	Y	S		AA-
Arizona	Y	C,S	Y	C,S	Y	C,S		AA-
Arkansas	Y	S	Y	S	Y	S		AA
Califonia	Y	C	n.a.	n.a	Y	S	Y^1	A
Colorado	Y	C	Y	C	Y	C		AA-
Connecticut	Y	S	Y	C,S	Y	C		AA
Delaware	Y	C,S	Y	C,S	Y	C,S		AAA
Florida	Y	C,S	Y	C,S	Y	C,S		AA+
Georgia	Y	C	Y	C	X	C		AAA
Hawaii	Y	C,S	n.a.	n.a	Y	C,S	[2]	AA-
Idaho	[3]	n.a.	Y^3	C	n.a.	n.a.		NR
Illinois	Y	C,S	Y	C	Y	S		AA
Indiana	n.a.	n.a.	n.a.	n.a	n.a.	n.a.		AA+
Iowa	Y	C,S	Y	S	n.a.	n.a.		AA+
Kansas	Y	S	Y	C,S	n.a.	n.a.		AA+
Kentucky	Y	C,S	Y	C,S	Y	C,S		AA-
Louisiana	Y	C,S	Y	C,S	Y	C,S		A+
Maine	Y	C,S	Y	C	Y	C,S		AA+
Maryland	Y	C	Y	C	[4]	C^4		AAA
Massachusetts	Y	C,S	Y	C,S	Y	C,S		AA-
Michigan	Y	C,S	Y	C	Y	C,S		AAA
Minnesota	Y^5	C,S	Y^5	C,S	Y^5	C,S		AAA
Mississippi	Y	S	Y	S	n.a.	n.a.		AA
Missouri	Y	C	n.a.	n.a	Y	C		AAA
Montana	Y	S	Y	C	n.a.	n.a.		AA-
Nebraska	Y	C	Y	S	n.a.	n.a.	NO	NR
Nevada	Y	S	Y	C	Y	C		AA
New Hampshire	Y	S	n.a.	n.a	n.a.	n.a.		AA+
New Jersey	Y	C	Y	C	Y	C		AA
New Mexico	Y	C	Y	C	Y	C		AA+
New York	Y	C	n.a.	n.a	[6]	n.a.		aa
North Carolina	Y	C,S	Y^7	S	n.a.	n.a.		AAA
North Dakota	Y	C	Y	C	Y	C		AA-
Ohio	Y	C	Y	C	Y	C	NO	AA+
Oklahoma	Y	S	Y^8	C	Y^8	C		AA
Oregon	Y	C	Y	C	Y	C		AA
Pennsylvania	Y	C,S	n.a.	n.a	Y	C,S	Y^9	AA
Rhode Island	Y	C	Y	C	Y	S		AA
South Carolina	Y	C	Y	C	Y	C		AAA
South Dakota	Y	C	Y	C	Y	C		NR
Tennessee	Y	C	Y	C	Y	C	NO	AA
Texas	n.a.	n.a.	Y	C,S	Y	C		AA
Utah	Y	C	Y	C,S	Y^{10}	n.a.		AAA
Vermont	n.a.	n.a.	n.a.	n.a	n.a.	n.a.		AA+

Continued

Virginia	11	n.a.	11	n.a	11	C	NO	AAA
Washington	Y	S	n.a.	n.a	n.a.	n.a.	S[12]	AA+
West Virginia	n.a.	n.a.	Y	C	Y	C	n.a.	AA-
Wisconsin	Y	C	Y	C	Y	C,S		AA-
Wyoming	Y	C	Y	C	n.a.	n.a.		AA+
Total	45 STATES		41 STATES		35 STATES			

Notes: 1. X: Yes ; C: Constitutional : S: Statutory ;   "n.a." means not apply. The highest rating is AAA and investment grade is BBB-.

2. California: May carry over deficit from current year to budget year. The budget for any year must be balanced when enacted.

Hawaii: A Fiscal may have deficit if prior years' surpluses can be sued to balance it.

Idaho: Not required. But in practice governor always submits balanced budget.

Maryland: When the budget is passed by both houses, it shall become a law immediately without further action of the governor.

Minnesota: The state constitution limits the use of public debt, which requires balanced budget.

New York: Governor is not technically required to sign a balanced budget, but the governor must certify the budget in balance in order to meet borrowing requirement.

North Carolina: the Governor is not required to sign a bill for the bill to become a law. If a bill is not returned by 10 days after it is presented to the governor, it becomes a law.

Oklahoma: legislature could pass and the governor could sign a budget when appropriation exceed cash and estimated revenues, but constitutional and statutory provisions reduce the appropriations so that the budget is balanced.

Pennsylvania: The deficit must be paid from the next fiscal year's revenue.

Utah: Governor may allow balanced budget to go into law without signature.

Virginia: Requirement applies only to budget execution. The governor is required to insure that actual expenditures do not exceed actual revenues by the end of appropriation period.

Washington: Ability to carry over a deficit in any account must be approved by the Office of Financial Management for a specific period.

Source: Budget Process in the States, January 2002 and S&P's (2004).

The third level of strictness allows for deficits at the end of a year, but the deficit has to be explicitly budgeted for the next fiscal year. This means that the deficit can be carried over from one year to the next, but the state must provide funds to repay the deficit incurred in the previous year. This is an *ex post* rule, and ten states are using this fiscal rule.

The most restrictive type of balanced-budget rule stipulates that the legislature can enact a balanced budget with a prohibition on deficit carry-forward. Deficits incurred during the budget year have to be reduced to zero by the end of the year. Borrowing is only allowed within the budget cycle. This is a strict version of the *ex post* rule, and 35 states have adopted the no-carry-over, balanced-budget rules (ACIR, 1987).

When discussing these budget rules, we have to be mindful about other components of the state budget. Other than its operating budget or general fund, a U.S. state budget also includes a capital fund and an insurance trust, or the rainy-day fund. In general, the balanced-budget rule only applies to the general fund. Thus, even with a stringent balanced-budget rule, it still allows for fiscal flexibility because general funds are often linked with capital and rainy-day funds. The proceeds of the general fund are usually allocated to the two funds, and the magnitude is subject to overall economic cycles. For example, the rainy-day fund is filled with the surplus of the general fund and is used for future deficits. However, some states also use fiscal rules for funds that are earmarked by tax revenues or particular programs. Thirty-four states have such programs, and 33 have rules on capital spending funds. These rules tend to limit the fiscal flexibility of these states (NASBO, 1987).

In addition to putting limits on expenditures, some U.S. states also have rules on the revenue side—the so-called tax limitation rules. For example, some states have specific tax limitations on property tax. Besides the tax limitations, some states also put explicit restraints on borrowing, either by specifying the allowed amount of debt or by stipulating the percentage of debt over the total state revenue. In general, most states impose debt limits in nominal dollar terms as a percentage of state revenue, taxable property, state property, or budget funds. When debt limits are reached, states will be required to enact state constitutional amendments in order to issue additional debt. In some other states, when debt limits are reached, only special legislative processes that require a qualified majority or a public referendum can approve additional debt spending.

Similar to the situation in any other government, off-budget activities are also possible among U.S. states, which can bypass the debt limit by engaging in off-budget activities, such as creating public corporations and creating special authorities that administrate specific projects. These off-budget activities reduce the restrictiveness of the debt-limit rules.

3.2 Effectiveness of U.S. State Fiscal Rules

The effectiveness of fiscal rules depends on the strength of the enforcement capability, the ability to overturn fiscal rules, the budget process, and voter preferences.

Empirical evidence has indicated that the combination of the deficit rule and the debt-limit rule will help reduce state indebtedness (Von Hagen, 1996). On the strength of the budget rules of the U.S. states, empirical studies have convincingly shown that no-carry-over rules have a statistically significant effect in reducing a state's general fund deficits (Bohn and Inman, 1996; Poterba, 1996). In addition, the U.S. municipal bond market also takes state budget rules into account when determining the risk of state government bonds.

Concerning municipal bond yields and budget rules, Bayoumi, Goldstein, and Woglom (1995) and Poterba and Rueben (1997) find that U.S. municipal bond yields are significantly lower in states with strong balanced-budget rules than in those with weaker rules. The market does punish those states with loose budget rules. Specifically, Poterba and Rueben (1997) estimate that the interest rate differentials paid on state bonds are about 15 to 20 basis points between states with strong anti-deficit rules and those without.

This is also verified by looking at state credit ratings. States with a no-carry-over rule in general have higher ratings than those without (see Table 17.3). Similarly, states with strong balanced-budget rules tend to use tax increases or spending cuts to reduce deficits, rather than accounting changes. Empirical evidence also shows that states with weak anti-deficit rules reduce spending by only 17 percent in response to unexpected deficits while states with the no-carry-over rule reduce spending by 44 percent (Poterba, 1994).

As for the enforcement capability, state budget rules are enforced by the state Supreme Court. So far, however, an event has yet required the state court's intervention, attributing to the effectiveness of the enforcement procedure.

With regard to the ability of overturning fiscal rules, U.S. states usually use its constitutional budget and statutory rules to overturn fiscal rules as shown in Table 17.3. Constitutional budget rules require a two-thirds super majority to overturn a law while statutory rules demand only a simple majority to repeal a law. Thirty-two U.S. states with a no-carry-over rule require a constitutional rule to overturn the balanced budget rule. Only four states use a statutory rule to overturn the budget rule (ACIR, 1987).

A typical budget process is divided into three stages: the government/parliamentary stage, the implementation of the budget, and the *ex post* control process. In general, the effectiveness of fiscal rules is higher when the budget process is centralized. Also, transparency in the budget process helps enforce fiscal discipline and control the state expenditure especially. Off-budget funds and other accounting manipulations often reduce transparency (Milesi and Gian, 1996; Von Hagen, 2002). The rating process by market participants, such as rating agencies, provides additional information to investors and thus reduces information asymmetry. As a result, such information reduces the borrowing cost by four basis points (Peng, 2002).

In addition to these determinants that effectively enforce budget rules, other factors, such as the accounting system, the political system, and the rules approved by the legislature—or voters—to borrow, also affect the effectiveness of fiscal rules (Von Hagen, 2002).

3.3 Fiscal Rules and Cyclical Fluctuations

Although fiscal rules can safeguard against fiscal profligacy and unsustainable fiscal conditions, do such rules mean a loss of short-term fiscal flexibility when local economies are subject to adverse shocks?

Barro (1979), in a seminal paper, points out that tax rates should change as little as possible in order to minimize the excess burden of taxes. Also, changes in tax rates are unpredictable and follow a random walk. To maximize welfare, the budget surpluses should be allowed to fluctuate over the business cycle. However, as shown by Bohn and Inman (1996), changes in tax rates in the U.S. states do not follow a random walk. Thus, there is no evidence that U.S. states follow a tax-smoothing policy. Indeed, almost 90 percent of the reduction in fiscal revenues due to fiscal rules requires the reduction of the cyclical sensitive expenditures in U.S. states (Bayoumi and Eichengreen, 1995), but how do fiscal rules affect the volatility of state outputs?

Alesina and Bayoumi (1996) show that the balanced-budget rules of U.S. states have no costs in terms of increased output variability. In fact, tighter fiscal rules are associated with a larger than average surplus and lower cyclical variability of the balanced budget. However, the lower flexibility of the budget's balance does affect state output variability.[7]

However, the adverse impact of the fiscal rules is further mitigated by the following three factors. First, U.S. states usually spend and raise funds outside the general fund, such as capital funds and the rainy-day fund as mentioned above. These funds enable states to run effective deficits during recessions (Bohn and Inman, 1996). Second, a reduction of state expenditures due to budget restraints, or rules, will lead a state to change the composition of the state budget. Fiscal constraint will also give an incentive for states to reform its social welfare system. Third, and perhaps the most important, fiscal stabilization in the presence of fiscal rules is also provided by the federal government through fiscal transfers. Forty percent of income volatility is reduced by fiscal transfers in the U.S. states (Sachs and Sala-i-Martin, 1992). However, this effect does not consider the fact that the labor market in the United States is very flexible, and people can move freely from one state to another based on job opportunities. The efficient U.S capital market also helps short-term adjustment that a state is facing by providing access to the capital market.

The U.S. experience has demonstrated that through carefully designed budget rules and credible enforcement mechanisms, the potential problem of excessive local debt can be contained. Indeed, the default probability of U.S. state bonds is almost zero. Even in rare occasions where states did default, creditors were asked to wait for their payments.[8] Eventually, all debts were still paid as governments have longer horizons than individuals and corporations. In addition, its revenue base is generally steady over time. Relatively speaking, the risks are lower than the risks involved in a corporate default case.

---

[7] Fatas and Mihov (2004), in a recent paper, show that strict budgetary restrictions lead to less discretion in conducting fiscal policy and therefore less output volatility. However, fiscal restrictions reduce the responsiveness to fiscal policy and therefore more output volatility. Overall, the first effect, less output volatility, dominates the second effect, more output volatility, due to lack of fiscal responsive to shocks.

[8] For example, the 1995 Orange County default case recently. During the defaults of nine states in the 1840s, Mississippi and Florida repudiated their debt in 1842. Arkansas stopped paying debt and finally repudiated its debt after the Civil War. Louisiana never officially reputed its debt and it finally settled its defaulted bonds until the 20th century (Sylla and Wallis, 1998).

4 Are Chinese Provinces Fiscally Sound Enough to Issue Debt?

This section assesses whether Chinese provinces are fiscally sound enough to issue provincial government bonds.[9] We adopt a rating methodology developed by the Moody's Investment Services (2000) on emerging market sub-national governments but with substantial modifications to the realities of Chinese provincial governments because of the availability of data. There are five categories of qualitative and quantitative indicators: (1) central and local government fiscal relations and oversights; (2) fiscal institutional quality at the provincial level; (3) economic fundamentals of provinces; (4) financial conditions; and (5) indebtedness of local government and fiscal risks. These five categories are used in the rating process. Within each of the five categories, we use both qualitative and quantitative indicators with a numerical scale of 1 to 10.[10] Using some weighting schemes based on some recent empirical literatures on determinants of long-term growth,[11] we come up with the following ratings for Chinese provinces.

Given our assumption that only domestic currency local government debt is allowed to issue in China, our ratings on Chinese provinces start from the lowest scale of the investment grade of ratings—Baa. The reason is that although some governments have started to run deficits and accumulate local government debt, their deficits and debt levels are still manageable if we allow inter-temporal smoothing of their expenditure against their existing tax revenues. Although we emphasize that some Chinese provinces have large fiscal liabilities, they also have even larger assets, such as land, SOEs, public infrastructure, and rent from licensing and fees, among other assets. At this stage, our quantitative and qualitative indicators show that all Chinese provinces can issue domestic currency debt.

Table 17.4 presents credit ratings for all 31 Chinese municipalities, provinces, and autonomous regions. Our results show that Shanghai and Beijing have the highest ratings—Aaa. Provinces or municipalities, such as Guangdong, Tianjin, Zhejiang, Jiangsu, and Liaoning, have the second highest credit ratings in the range from Aa1 to Aa3. Most other provinces fall into a rating scale of A1 to A3.

---

[9] Please see Liu and Chen (2004) for technical details of the rating methodology.

[10] See Liu and Chen (2004) for a detailed discussion of indicators chosen to do the exercise.

[11] For example, please see Barro (1996). Our perturbation shows that weights attached on these five categories are not that significant.

Table 17.4 Domestic currency ratings of Chinese provinces using Moody's rating scale

Province Name	Code Name	Numerical Rating	Letter Rating Scale
Shanghai	SH	8.9	Aaa
Beijing	BJ	8.4	Aaa
Guangdong	GD	7.6	Aa1
Tianjin	TJ	7.3	Aa2
Zhejiang	ZJ	7.2	Aa2
Jiangsu	JS	7.0	Aa2
Fujian	FJ	6.7	Aa3
Liaoning	LN	6.4	Aa3
Shandong	SD	6.2	A1
Hainan	HA	6.1	A1
Hebei	HB	5.8	A2
Hubei	HE	5.6	A2
Helongjiang	HL	5.4	A2
Shanxi	SHX	5.4	A2
Guangxi	GX	5.3	A2
Jilin	JL	5.2	A3
Jiangxi	JX	5.2	A3
Hunan	HU	5.2	A3
Anhui	AH	5.1	A3
Shaanxi	SX	5.1	A3
Xinjiang	XJ	5.1	A3
Inner Mongolia	IM	5.0	A3
Sichuan	SC	4.9	A3
Henan	HN	4.9	A3
Yunnan	YN	4.9	A3
Ningxia	NX	4.9	A3
Chongqing	CQ	4.8	A3
Gansu	GS	4.7	Baa1
Qinghai	QH	4.6	Baa1
Guizhou	GZ	4.3	Baa2
Tibet	XZ	3.7	Baa3

Notes: 1. Moody's Rating Scales are Aaa, Aa1, Aa2, Aa3, A1, A2, A3, Baa1, Baa2, Baa3, Ba1, Ba2, Ba3, B1, B2, B3, Caa1, Caa2, Caa3, Ca, C. Ratings bellow Baa3 are Speculative Ratings, i.e., bellowing estimate grade.
Source: Calculated by the Authors.

However, Gansu, Qinghai, Guizhou, and Tibet have the lowest grade of credit ratings. In general, economically developed and coastal provinces obtained a relatively high rating compared with those from the inland, western, and southwestern regions.

However, how do our ratings reflect the economic reality of Chinese provinces? We can see from Figure 17.3 that our ratings are highly correlated to per capita income, the most important indicator of economic development. The R-square from the ordinary least square (OLS) is .85, which means that our ratings can explain an 85 percent variation of the per capital income of Chinese provinces. In other words, our ratings do a relatively good job in assessing the creditworthiness of Chinese provinces.

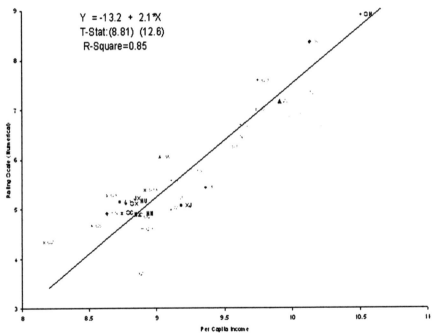

Figure 17.3 Relationship between assigned ratings and log provincial per capita GDP

5 Sequencing China's Sub-national Debt Market Development

5.1 Stage I: Building Necessary Institutions

1 The immediate action that the central government can take in order for Chinese provinces to issue debt is to revise Article 28 of the 1995 Budget Law to explicitly grant local governments—not only at the provincial level but also at the regional

and county levels—the right to issue debt. In addition, a local government bankruptcy law should be promulgated to deal with local government default. The bankruptcy law will provide the legal basis to allow an orderly handling of the default.

2 In exchange, local governments should be required to adopt some version of the fiscal rules governing a balanced budget and the debt-limit requirement, similar to the U.S. states. To start the process, the central government should first set some benchmarks on deficits and debt limits and require each province to adopt a version of fiscal rules compatible to the local development's stage and conditions. In addition, provincial People's Congresses should be heavily involved in approving these fiscal rules and in designing mechanisms to enforce the rules.

3 Given that effective institutions to enforce such rules take time to emerge, during the initial stage of market development, the enforcement of fiscal rules can be done collectively by the central government, the market, and the provincial People's Congress.

4 In addition to these fiscal rules, other institutions must be there to help monitor the fiscal conditions of local government. They include independent accounting and auditing agencies to monitor the local government's fiscal accounts, using a unified framework. To ensure the budget forecast for all provinces is done in an objective manner, an independent budget analysis and forecast agency (similar to the U.S. Congressional Budget Office) should be established.

5 All provincial governments should be required to adopt a transparent budget process. Other institutions—such as intergovernmental relations agencies (Advisory Council on Intergovernmental Relations), national provincial governors associations for information exchange and provincial collaboration, and provincial budget officer associations for training, information disclosure, and promulgation of best practices—should also be established.

6 Independent rating agencies should be encouraged to participate in local governments' rating process. Given that it takes time for domestic rating agencies to gain reputation to give credible assessment of the financial and default probabilities of local governments, reputable foreign rating agencies should be allowed to enter the market. In addition to rating agencies, other issuing and underwriting agents should also be encouraged to facilitate the provincial debt issues.

7 The central government, together in consultation with the provincial governments, should—based on best practices—promulgate a set of minimum criteria, which each province needs to satisfy before it is allowed to enter the debt market at the initial stage of the local government bond market. As long as a province meets the criteria and is rated by a rating agency with an investment grade, it should be able to issue debt regardless of its stage of economic development or region.

5.2 Stage II: Implementation Stage

1 The Japanese local government debt model as an intermediate step:[12] Given that market and institutional development takes time to build, at the initial stage—say five to ten years—China could learn from the Japanese local debt market experience by assigning both market forces and the central government to discipline debt issues of local governments.[13] Such an arrangement can prevent excessive debt issuing by local governments when market discipline is weak. The debt issuing process can be first initiated from provincial governments. However, their proposed debt issues have to be within the stipulation of the fiscal rules established by local governments and with the approval of the local People's Congress. In addition, the amount of debt issues needs to satisfy the guidelines set by the relevant agencies of the central government, such as the Ministry of Finance (MOF), together with the State Reform and Planning Commission.

2 The U.S. model as a final stage: Once institutions and markets have become fully developed and matured in the sense that they can effectively monitor and discipline the finances of local governments, the central government should then withdraw from the local government debt-issuing process. The withdraw of the central government from the debt markets of local governments will send strong signals to investors that the perceived guarantees of the central government due to the approval procedures will be gone. Provinces should be solely responsible for their debts. The market by then will be able to adequately price the potential default risks because the probability of local governments to go default is real. For those poor provinces that may suffer from high market interest rates because of their relatively low ratings, the central government can nevertheless provide certain guarantees for the purpose of credit enhancement. However, even this function can eventually be taken over by some market-based financial institutions to provide insurance and guarantees.

6 Concluding Remarks

The indebtedness of local governments in China is serious and needs to be addressed urgently. In this chapter, we propose a "Carrot and Stick" incentive mechanism to allow local governments to issue debts but remain subject to stringent fiscal rules. To prevent excessive debt issuing, this chapter advocates that some effective fiscal rules, which are akin to those adopted by the United States, be required for Chinese provinces as well.

---

[12] See Wei (2004) for a detailed analysis of the Japanese system.

[13] However, the Japanese system may rely too much on the administrative approach but with limited role given to the market. This is perhaps the reason why local government rating scales are quite similar.

In addition to fiscal rules, there should also be a local government bankruptcy law to allow orderly resolution of local government debt. Also, some parallel institutions must be built to promote an efficient local government bond market. They include a transparent budget process and budget monitoring institutions, intergovernmental agencies to analyze and forecast the budget of local governments, independent credit rating agencies, a credible accounting and auditing process, and a set of intergovernmental agencies that can reduce information asymmetry of local government finances.

These institutions, together with a well thought-out sequencing strategy, will help defuse the fiscal risk that is largely concentrated at the central government level at this time. Meanwhile, the local government debt market will also help speed up the provincial infrastructure development, investment in rural education and health, and other urgent rural economic development needs in China. Furthermore, the sub-national bond market will likely enhance the sophistication of other segments of China's capital markets, especially the stock market, since the provincial government bonds can also be used as hedging instruments for risk management.

A vibrant domestic bond market will also help alleviate the "Original Sin Problem" facing all emerging market economies. That is when their inability to issue either long-term domestic debt or domestic-currency debt internationally. A deep domestic bond market will also mitigate the risks of currency mismatches that often arise from international borrowing.

Perhaps the most far-reaching effect of the sub-national bond market development in China is that it will make local governments accountable to local taxpayers, expand the power of the local People's Congress, and build necessary institutions to facilitate the firm establishment and effective enforcement of rule of law, which ultimately will help China's eventual transformation to a market economy that is governed by effective and democratic institutions.

References

Alesina, A. and Bayoumi, T., 'The cost and benefits of fiscal rules: evidence from U.S. States' (NBER Working Papers: No. 5614, 1996).

Advisory Council on Intergovernmental Relations (ACIR), *Fiscal Discipline in the Federal System: National Reform and Experiences of the States* (Washington D.C.:ACIR, 1987).

Barro, R., 'On the determination of public debt', *Journal of Political Economy*, Vol. 87 (1979): 940-971.

———, 'Determinants of Economic Growth: A Cross-Country Empirical Study' (NBER Working Papers: No. 5698, 1996).

Bayoumi, T. and Eichengreen, B., 'Restraining yourself: the implication of fiscal rules for economic stabilization', *IMF Staff Papers*, Vol. 42(1) (1995): 32-48.

Bayoumi, T., Goldstein, M. and Woglom, G., 'Do credit markets discipline sovereign borrowers? Evidence from US States', *Journal of Money, Credit and Banking*, Vol. 27/4 (1995): 1046-1058.

Bohn, H. and Inman, R., *Balanced Budget Rules and Public Deficits: Evidence from the US States* (Discussion Paper *10-96*, University of Pennsylvania, 1996).

Chan-Lee, J., Liu, L. and Yoshitomi, M., *Policy Proposals for Sequencing the PRC's Domestic and External Financial Liberalization* (Tokyo: Asian Development Bank Institute, 2002).

Fatas, A. and Mihov, I., 'The macroeconomic effects of fiscal rules in the US states' (CEPR Discussion Papers: No. 4372, 2004).

Huang, Y., 'Central-local relations in China during the reform era: the economic and institution dimensions', *World Development*, Vol. 24, No. 4 (1996): 655-672.

Krumn, K. and Wong, C., 'China's contingent fiscal liabilities', in H.Brixi and A.Schick (eds), *Government at Risk: Contingent Liabilities and Fiscal Risk* (Washington D.C.: World Bank Publications 2003).

Liu, L., *A Credit Rating Approach to Assessing China's Provincial Government Creditworthiness: Implications on the Development of China's Municipal Bond Market* (Mimeo, School of Public Policy, George Mason University 2004).

Ma, J., *The Chinese Economy in the 1990s* (London: Macmillan Press 2000).

Milesi, F. and Gian, M., 'Fiscal rules and the budget process', *IMF Working Papers*, 96/60 (1996).

Moody's Investment Services, *Moody's Credit Rating Methodology* (New York: Moody's Global Credit Services, 2000).

National Association of State Budget Officers (NASBO), *Budget Process in the States* (Washington D.C., 2002). (It is in quoted in table 17.3)

——, *State Balanced Budget Requirements: Provisions and Practices* (Washington D.C., 1987).

National Bureau of Statistics (NBS), *China Statistical Yearbook* (2003, 2004).

Arora, V.B. and Norregaard, J., 'Intergovernmental Fiscal Relations: The Chinese System in Perspective', *IMF Working Paper*, WP/97/129 (1997).

Peng, J., 'Do investors look beyond insured triple-A rating? An analysis of Standard and Poor's underlying rating', *Public Bugeting and Finance,* Fall 22(3) (2002): 115-131.

Poterba, J. M., 'State responses to fiscal crises: the effects of budgetary institutions and politics', *Journal of Political Economy*, Vol. 104(4) (1994): 799-821.

——, 'Budget Institutions and Fiscal Policy in the US States', *Ameircan Economic Review*, Vol. 86(2) (1996): 395-400.

Poterba, J.M. and Rueben, K.S., 'State fiscal institutions and the U.S. municipal bond market' (NBER Working Papers, No. 6237, 1997).

Qian, Y., 'The institutional foundations of market transition in the People's Republic of China' (ADBI Working Paper, No. 9, May 1999).

Qian, Y. and Weingast, B.R., 'Federalism as a commitment to preserving market incentives', *Journal of Economic Perspectives*, 11(4) (1997): 83-92.

Sachs, J. and Sala-i-Martin, X., 'Fiscal federalism and optimum currency areas: evidence from the United States' (*CEPR Discussion Paper*, 1992: 632).

Sylla, R. and Wallis, J.J., 'The anatomy of sovereign debt crises: lessons from the Ameircan state defaults of the 1840s', *Japan and World Economy*, 10 (1998): 267-293.

Von Hagen, J., 'Budget Processes and Commitment to Fiscal Discipline', *IMF Working Paper*, 96/78 (1996).

——, 'Fiscal rules, fiscal institutions, and fiscal performance', *Economic and Social Review*, 33(3) (2002): 263-284.

Wei, J., *Problems of Chinese Local Government Debt and Some Thoughts on the Resolution Strategy ('Guang Yu Zhong Guo De Di Fang Zhai Wu Wen Ti Ji Qi Du Ce Si Kao'*) (Conference Report of Development Research Center of the State Council, China, 2004).

Chapter 18

Fiscal Decentralization and Political Centralization in China: Implications for Regional Inequality

Xiaobo Zhang

P35 023
P25 018 017 R12 P26

> All nations have endeavoured, to the best of their judgment, to render their taxes as equal as they could contrive; as certain, as convenient to the contributor, both in the time and in the mode of payment, and in proportion to the revenue which they brought to prince, as little burdensome to the people.
>
> Adam Smith, *The Wealth of Nations* (p. 1046)

1 Introduction

Transferring authority to lower level governments, which have better knowledge of local conditions and preferences and are under closer scrutiny by their constituencies, may improve the provision of goods and services to the public (Dethier, 1999; Bardhan, 2002). Tiebout (1956) argues that under fiscal decentralization and inter-jurisdictional competition, citizens can vote with their feet to allocate themselves to a package of local public goods and taxes according to their preference. In other words, fiscal decentralization can prompt more efficient provisions of local public goods if individuals can freely move across localities.

In addition to the sorting and matching role, Qian and Roland (1998, QR for short hereafter) emphasize that fiscal decentralization can also serve as a disciplinary device to preserve market incentives. These theories highlight the positive role of fiscal decentralization and inter-jurisdictional competition on the efficiency of public goods provision. In the past two decades, decentralization has become a global trend. However, empirical evaluation on the impact of decentralization on growth and distribution in developing countries is still in its infancy (Bardhan, 2002).

China, like many developing countries, has undergone a process of fiscal decentralization.[1] The sheer size of China provides a good ground to test the predictions of decentralization theories in the context of development. Using

---

[1] For detailed description on China's fiscal decentralization, see Tong (1998), Zhang (1999) and World Bank (2002).

provincial data up to 1993, Lin and Liu (2000) provide empirical evidence that decentralization is conductive to growth. Zhang and Zou (1998), however, have found a negative relationship between growth and decentralization, while Jin, Qian, and Weingast (2005) reach a more optimistic finding that decentralization is not only good for growth but also good for equity based on data up to 1992. Using data at more of a micro level, a few other studies (West and Wong, 1995; Park *et. al.* 1996; Knight and Li, 1999) show that decentralization has a negative distributional effect. These studies are all based on data up to the early 1990s. Since then, more in-depth fiscal reforms have taken place and more comprehensive data have become publicly available. Therefore, it is important to extend the work to cover a longer period and more spatial units so as to reconcile the differences.

A recent World Bank study (2002) warned that the fiscal reforms could exacerbate regional disparity in fiscal public spending largely because of the mismatch between local fiscal revenues and responsibilities. The finding is primarily based on case studies in several counties. In this study, we use a nationwide panel data set at the county level to more systematically investigate the distributional impact of decentralization. To our knowledge, this study is one of the first attempts done with panel data at the county level.[2] The more recent panel data set at the county level provides a vehicle to reconcile the differences of empirical research on China's fiscal decentralization. The work is also a contribution to the literature. As Bardhan (2002) points out, few studies have empirically examined performance of fiscal decentralization at the micro level in developing countries.

The next section discusses the major theoretical arguments on decentralization. Section 3 provides empirical analysis and shows why the results seemingly conflict with theoretical predictions. The last section ends with a conclusion that includes policy implications.

2 Theoretical Consideration

Much of the literature on fiscal federalism, represented by Tibout (1956) and QR (1998), focuses on the economic efficiency aspect of market competition. In essence, the Tiebout model assumes full factor mobility. Bardhan (2002) comments that the assumptions underlying the Tiebout model are often too stringent in regard to developing countries. In the case of China, despite loosening control of migration in recent years, there still exist obstacles to labor movement, particularly from rural to urban areas.

Another implicit assumption of the Tiebout model is that local governments are responsive to the needs of voters. However, in China, local government officials are generally not elected and their preferences may not be consistent with those of their constituents. In addition, the size of local governments is mainly determined

---

[2] Shih and Zhang (2004) examine the issue of transfers and subsidies using the same data set.

by higher level government and has little to do with local needs. Therefore, all these factors may make the Tiebout model inapplicable.

The QR federalism model has a crucial assumption that all the regions are identical. Within the more developed coastal areas, such as Zhejiang province, many counties share similar initial conditions, and this assumption may hold. Considering China as a whole, however, the regional difference—particularly between inland and coastal counties—is substantial, making this assumption inappropriate.

Moreover, neither of these theories takes the transaction costs of tax collection and its consequences into account. As shown in the quote above, Adam Smith regards fairness and economy in tax collection as fundamental principles. Regarding collection cost, he states explicitly:

> Every tax ought to be so contrived as both to take out and to keep out of the pockets of the people as little as possible, over and above what it brings into the public treasury of the state. (p. 1044)

In particular, Smith opposed levying a tax if it involves employing a great number of people whose salaries would eat up a large share of that tax.

In a less perfect world, labor migration involves costs as do tax collection and policy implementation. In China, regions differ greatly in economic and taxation structures. As a result, the assumptions underlying the two theoretical models above may not be valid, and their predictions may not bear out in reality.

Let us begin with a thought experiment. Suppose there are two regions: A (coast) and B (inland). Before the fiscal decentralization, Region A is endowed with a large share of non-farm economy, while Region B relies on agriculture as the major source of revenue. The administrative structures in the two regions, however, are the same.[3] In addition, the average cost of collecting each unit of tax from a firm is much lower than from a rural household. Consequently, both regions prefer to levy taxes on enterprises than on households if possible. After decentralization, both regions must be responsible for collecting their own revenues and fulfilling the same responsibilities or mandates.[4]

In Region A, because of the large industrial base, the local government can obtain most revenues from the industrial sector. Moreover, a large industrial base means high opportunity cost of labor, making collecting taxes from rural households rather costly. If the incurred tax collection cost from households outweighs the revenue, it is more cost-effective for the local government to forego tax obligations of farmers and pay the agricultural taxes to upper level governments using other revenue sources. When there are many local enterprises, the implicit taxation burden to each firm is relatively lower, which in turn help

---

[3] Xu (2003) has documented the evolution of administrative units in rural China and shown how excessive they are.

[4] Liu and Tao (2004) list a set of central mandates and policy burdens.

attract more business and enlarge the tax base. Because the government size is mainly related to population instead of economic development level, the government in this region has more local revenue at its disposable for productive public investment after covering the salary of public employees. Better infrastructure and lower tax burdens can offset the relatively higher labor and land cost in Region A. All these help create an enabling investment and form a virtuous cycle.

In contrast, there are few non-farm enterprises in Region B. Because of the lower tax collection cost on firms relative to agricultural taxes on households, the existing firms are more prone to be the predatory targets of their local government's excessive taxes and fees. Therefore, the implicit industrial tax rate tends to be high, which will discourage the entry of potential investment and drive away existing business enterprises, hampering the growth in the non-farm sector over the long run.

However, in China the size of local governments is rather fixed. After paying the salaries of public employees, local governments in poor regions often have little resources remaining to provide public investment. Low levels and quality of public infrastructure and service often result in an unfavorable investment environment. Obviously, it is difficult for any factory to operate normally and efficiently in an area plagued with irregular power outages and unpaved roads. Consequently, Region B may have a worse investment environment despite its lower wage rate and land rent. The large share of the agricultural sector means a higher collection cost of taxes on average because more significant manpower is required in the collection activities.

All in all, the transaction cost of tax collection and economic structure may affect the outcome of decentralization. It is an empirical question to examine whether, under fiscal decentralization, the heterogeneous revenue structure and homogenous government structure matter to the growth patterns.

3 Empirical Analysis

3.1 Descriptive Analysis

In this study, we mainly make use of a county-level public finance data set for our analysis. Since 1993, the China Statistical Bureau has published the *China County Public Finance Statistical Yearbook*, which contains detailed revenue, expenditure, gross value of industrial and agricultural output (GVIAO), population, and size of the public sector at the county level information. There are over 2,000 rural counties in China. Between 1993 and 2000, several hundred counties have changed their names or judiciary boundaries. We make an effort to match these counties, relying mainly on the official declarations of judiciary changes posted in the Ministry of Civil Affairs website. Because data for Tibet are largely missing, we drop Tibet in our analysis. In total, we have a panel of 1,860 observations in 1993 and 2000.

Following Jin, Qian, and Weingast (2005), we regress local expenditures on local revenues in 1993 and 2000, respectively, and use the coefficient β for revenues to measure the degree of hardness of budget constraints. The larger the value, the harder the budget constraint and the more decentralized the fiscal system. As shown in Table 18.1, the coefficient β has increased significantly in only seven years, indicating that China's fiscal system has indeed become more decentralized. This result confirms the findings by Jian, Qian and Weingast (1999) and the World Bank (2002).

Table 18.1 The correlations between local revenue and expenditure, 1993 and 2001

	1993	2000
	0.815**	1.144**
β	(0.018)	(0.031)
R^2	0.808	0.812
No. of observations	1860	1860

Notes:
1. The figures in the parentheses are standard errors;
2. Each regression includes a full set of prefecture dummies;
3. Tibet is excluded due to missing data;
4. The symbol ** represents a significant level of 1%.

To examine the dynamics of regional distribution, we further calculate the Gini coefficient of per capita GVIAO, per capita productive public expenditure (total expenditure minus salaries and operating cost), and the share of productive investment in total public expenditure, respectively, based on data at the county level and present them in Table 18.2. All the three indicators show rising regional disparity. The Gini coefficient of per capita GVIAO rises from 46.47 to 48.39. Figure 18.1 graphs the density distributions of logarithmic per capita GVIAO in 1993 and 2000 and clearly shows a spread out during the period. Noticeably, inequality in the level and share of productive investment has increased by 7 and 26 percent, respectively, during the seven-year period, much higher than that in per capita GVIAO.

To provide more information relevant for the policy debates in China, we first aggregate the public finance data set at the county level into coastal and inland categories.[5] Table 18.3 presents per capita GVIAO, the real annual growth rate of

---

[5] The coastal zone includes Hebei, Liaoning, Shandong, Jiangsu, Zhejiang, Fujian, Guangdong and Guangxi provinces; the inland zone comprises of all the remaining provinces. Kanbur and Zhang (1999; 2005) have used the same classification.

Table 18.2 Gini coefficient of three indicators, 1993 and 2001

Year	Per capita GVIAO	Per capita productive public expenditure	Share of productive investment in total public expenditure
1993	46.47	68.28	33.04
2000	48.39	73.34	41.61
Rate of change (%)	4.13	7.41	25.94

Notes:
1. Calculated by the author based on China County Public Finance Statistics Yearbook;
2. GVIAO stands for the gross value of industrial and agricultural output.

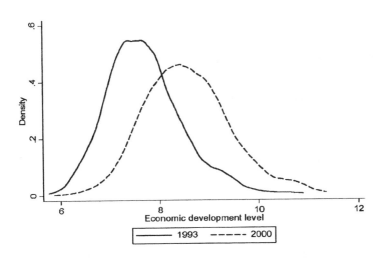

Figure 18.1 The density function of per capita gross industrial and agricultural output (log form)

per capita GVIAO, taxation structures, and the fiscal dependent burdens for the two regions in 1993 and 2000. The agricultural tax rate in the third column is defined as the ratio of agricultural tax revenue to the gross agricultural output value, while the implicit industrial rate is measured as the ratio of tax revenues from the industrial sector relative to the gross industrial output value. Land rents include city construction tax and land user fees. Fiscal dependent burden is denoted as the number of public employees per 10,000 *yuan* (1993 value) of local revenue. We use the national GDP deflator (1.977) to adjust the growth rate of per capita GVIAO, per capita land rent, and the fiscal dependent burden to ensure they are comparable between the two years.

Several features are apparent from Table 18.3. First, although both regions have experienced fast growth, the eastern region has grown at an annual rate of 3.81 percent—compared to 3.71 percent in the inland region—indicating a widening regional gap. Second, the tax rates in both agricultural and rural industrial sectors are regressive because the better-off coastal regions enjoy lower tax rates than the less developed inland regions. This finding is consistent with Lin *et al.* (2002). Third, the coastal region benefits more from the rising land value. The local revenue from the city construction tax and land development in the coastal region is much higher than that of the inland region. With a lower industrial tax rate, the rich region can attract more investments and migrants, which certainly boosts the land value. Fourth, the fiscal burden of supporting the local government is unevenly distributed across the regions. The number of people on public payroll per unit of local revenue in the coastal region is almost double that in the inland region. Moreover, the ratio has increased for all the regions from 1993 to 2000, indicating an inflating government size.

Table 18.3 Economic development, taxation structure and fiscal burdens, 1993 and 2000

Year/Region	Per capita GVIAO (current *yuan*)	Agricultural tax rate (*yuan* per 100 *yuan*)	Industrial tax rate (*yuan* per 100 *yuan*)	Fiscal burden (public employee per 10,000 *yuan*)	Land rent (*yuan* per capita)
1993					
Coast	6,062	0.81	2.74	1.33	4.50
Inland	2,050	1.15	5.95	2.41	2.60
China	3,569	0.99	3.67	1.86	3.32
2000					
Coast	7,876	1.06	0.80	1.83	8.01
Inland	2,646	1.72	1.30	3.54	3.89
China	4,612	1.40	0.94	2.67	5.44
Annual growth rate (%)					
Coast	3.81	3.83	-16.07	4.75	8.60
Inland	3.71	5.90	-19.48	5.64	5.95
China	3.73	5.06	-17.63	5.28	7.33

Note:
1. Calculated by author based on *China County Public Finance Statistics Yearbook*;
2. GVIAO stands for the gross value of industrial and agricultural output;
3. Per capital growth rate of GVIAO, per capita land rent, and fiscal burden are calculated using comparable national GDP deflator using 1993 as a base year.

Figure 18.2 presents the implicit industrial tax rate against the logarithmic per capita GVIAO in 1993 and 2000. The downward straight line in the figure clearly demonstrates that the industrial tax rate is regressive. The richer a county, the lower its industrial tax rate is. Figure 18.3 illustrates that land revenue is positively related to the level of economic development, which is inconsistent with the results for the two regions in Table 18.2. The rich regions can capitalize more from the rising land value than the poor regions.

Figure 18.4 further highlights the correlation between the fiscal dependent burden and economic development. The negative relationship reveals that the revenue capacity to support the public payroll in poor counties is much weaker than in more developed ones. The government size—which is to a large extent in proportion to the total population—is largely determined by the higher level government. The top priorities for local government are collecting taxes, maintaining social order, and carrying over various tasks, such as agricultural industrialization and urbanization, which is assigned from upper level governments. In the poor regions, the local government has little financial resources to carry over to the task of public goods provision after covering the salaries of public employees.

The uneven regional development in non-farm activities in the rural sector has been regarded as one of the major driving forces behind the changes in rural regional inequality (Rozelle, 1994; Fan, Zhang, and Zhang, 2004). Wan, Lu, and Chen (2003) and Zhang and Fan (2004) further show that the growing regional disparity in public capital significantly attributes to the rising regional inequality in non-farm development largely because public capital is complimentary to private capital. The evidence here offers an additional explanation: regions with a higher implicit industrial tax rate have more difficulty attracting capital inflows than those with lower tax rates, thereby resulting in more fragmentation in the capital markets and higher regional disparity.

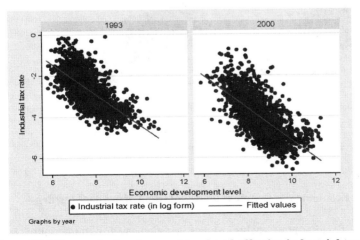

Figure 18.2 Economic development level and effective industrial tax rate

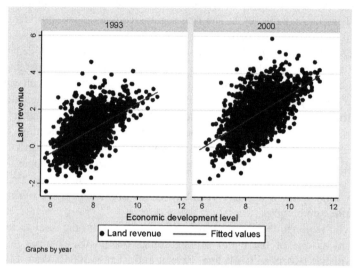

Figure 18.3 Economic development level and rent from land development

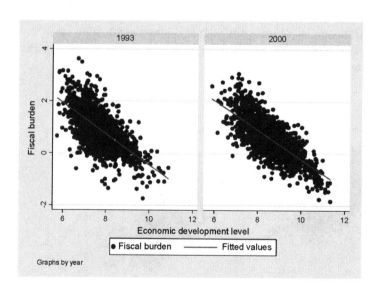

Figure 18.4 Economic development level and fiscal dependent burden

In short, the descriptive analysis shows that along with fiscal decentralization, regional distribution in public finance—particularly in productive public spending—has greatly deteriorated, contrary to what Jin, Qian and Roland (2005) observed up to 1992. The results seem to be inconsistent with the theoretical predictions by Tiebout (1956) and QR (1998). In the next section, we provide a more thorough and quantitative examination of decentralization's impact.

3.2 Quantitative Evidence Based on County Data

Now we use a more quantitative method to examine the impact of initial economic structures and fiscal dependent burdens on subsequent local economic growth. Following Barro and Sala-I-Martin (1995) on growth convergence, we model the growth rate of per capita GVIAO as a function of its initial value, the initial economic structure, the fiscal dependent burdens, and a set of other variables:

$$\log(y_{it}/y_{it-1}) = a + \beta \log(y_{t-1}) + \gamma Z + \delta D + \varepsilon_i \qquad (1)$$

where y_{it} is per capita GVIAO. The subscripts t and $t-1$ refer to 2000 and 1993, respectively. The left-hand side variable represents the growth rate of per capita GVIAO over the period. The coefficient β stands for the speed of convergence of per capita GVIAO. A negative value for this coefficient indicates convergence while a positive value implies divergence. It provides useful information on understanding how initial conditions contribute to long-term growth and whether there is convergence or not. Because of diminishing returns to capital, the returns to capital and labor will equalize across regions and lead to convergence in a perfect market. Z includes the share of the gross value of agricultural output in GVIAO, the ratio of public employee to total local revenue.

These two variables are in logarithmic form. γ is the corresponding coefficients for the two variables. D is a set of dummy variables. If a county is nationally designated as a poor county, it is assigned a value of 1 and zero otherwise. In different specifications, we also include prefecture and provincial fixed effects. δ is a vector of coefficients for these fixed effects.

Table 18.4 reports regression results under four specifications. The first three regressions include the prefecture, provincial, and regional fixed effects, respectively. The last column excludes any dummy variables. The second to the last row presents the Akaike's information criterion (AIC) for model selection. The model with the smallest value is preferred. The AIC criterion suggests that the first regression with the prefecture fixed effects dominates the other three. Because we do not have county-specific price information, the fixed prefecture effects serve as a good proxy to eliminate the price effect inherent in the nominal growth of per capital GVIAO in the period. Moreover, they may capture other shocks common to a prefecture.

The table also presents the p-values of the regression specification error test (RESET) for omitted variables. Only the first specification with prefecture dummies accepts the null hypothesis that there are no missing variables. The other three regressions all reject the null hypotheses. As a result, the first specification is preferable.

Table 18.4 The effect of initial economic structure and government size on economic growth

Variables	R1	R2	R3	R4
Initial value in 1993	-0.467**	-0.423**	-0.384**	-0.313**
	(0.030)	(0.027)	(0.026)	(0.025)
Economic structure in 1993	-0.340**	-0.209**	-0.211**	-0.244**
(Agricultural gross output value/GVIAO)	(0.084)	(0.083)	(0.080)	(0.081)
Fiscal dependent burdens in 1993	-0.125**	-0.171**	-0.165**	-0.161**
(No. of employee on public payroll /Total local revenue)	(0.025)	(0.025)	(0.023)	(0.023)
Nationally designated poor county status in 1993	-0.227**	-0.243**	-0.233**	-0.233**
	(0.028)	(0.028)	(0.030)	(0.031)
Regional dummies	Prefecture**	Province**	Region**	None
Omission variable test (p-value)	0.336	0.037	0.086	0.046
AIC	1681.5	2220.1	2598.8	2653.1
Adjusted R^2	0.536	0.290	0.117	0.090

Notes:
1. Coefficients for dummies are not reported here;
2. The figures in the parentheses are standard errors;
3. The symbol ** means a significance level of 1%.

The coefficient for the initial value of per capita GVIAO in all the three regressions is negative, suggesting the existence of a mean convergence. The coefficient for the share of agricultural output in the initial year of 1993 is statistically significant in all the three regressions, indicating that the heterogeneous economic structure is an offsetting divergent force. For a region primarily relying on agricultural revenues, the subsequent growth in productive spending is slower than a region endowed with a large non-farm tax base.

The negative and significant coefficient for the fiscal dependent variable in 1993 suggests that oversized bureaucracy can be a real burden for local economic growth in poor regions. In an ideal Tibout world where local governments are responsive to the needs of their constituents, lower revenues mean lower levels of public service and smaller government. Because of the nature of political centralization in China, the government size is rather inflexible, which leads to relatively heavier burdens in the poorer regions than in the richer regions under the arrangement of fiscal decentralization.

Table 18.5 The effect of initial economic structure and government size on economic growth by region

Variables	Coast	Inland
Initial value in 1993	-0.418**	-0.503**
	(0.062)	(0.036)
Economic structure in 1993	-0.153	0.406**
(Agricultural gross output value/GVIAO)	(0.160)	(0.099)
Fiscal dependent burdens in 1993	-0.198**	-0.106**
(No. of employee on public payroll /Total local revenue)	(0.060)	(0.028)
Nationally designated poor county status	-0.229**	-0.238**
	(0.070)	(0.031)
R^2	0.690	0.580

Notes:
1. Coefficients for prefecture dummies are not reported here;
2. The figures in the parentheses are standard errors;
3. The symbol ** means a significance level of 1%.

The table also shows that those nationally designated poor counties are growing slower than other counties. This is consistent with the findings of Fan, Zhang, and Zhang (2004) on the performance of China's poverty alleviation program. There are several possible explanations. First, local governments in the poor countries may be more likely to understate their performance indicators so as to retain the "designated-poverty" status and qualify for transfers. Second, in the presence of central transfers, local officials may spend more time building up connections with upper level governments rather than developing the local economy.

The coefficients for the dummy variables are not presented in the table to save space. They are jointly significant in the first three specifications. In the third specification, the coefficient for the inland coefficient is statistically negative. To check the robustness of the results, Table 18.5 lists the separate regression results for the coastal and inland regions. Except for the economic structure variable, the coefficients for other variables are rather robust. Within a prefecture in a coastal region, the economic structure is more homogenous. This is probably why the coefficient for this variable in the first regression is insignificant.

In short, fiscal decentralization may bring about detrimental distributional consequences when the economic structure differs and government sizes are excessive.

4 Conclusions and Policy Implication

Considering the sheer size of China, fiscal decentralization is imperative for the government to tackle the information and incentive problems inherent in the relationship between central and local governments. However, decentralization is a complex process involving not only fiscal aspects but also governance and mandates. When government sizes are largely independent of the demand of constituencies, the standard Tiebout sorting model is not applicable anymore.

Under the current local-central fiscal arrangement, the large regional variation in production patterns and revenue structures makes the underlying assumption of the QR fiscal federalism model invalid. Moreover, the transaction costs of tax collections become a more serious issue under fiscal decentralization.

The high collection cost of agricultural tax plus the excessive government size makes local governments in regions endowed mostly with agricultural production barely able to provide the necessary public goods and services. Farmers and firms in poor regions are paying heavy taxes, while those in rich regions enjoy generous support and lower tax burdens. The regressive nature of the rural taxation system plays a significant role in explaining the divergent regional growth patterns even after controlling for the initial value. Overall, the fiscal decentralization is in favor of the rich localities, exacerbating the regional gap.

In his famous article, Oates (1968) has argued that to ensure the functioning of fiscal federalism, the central government should carry over the functions of stabilization and distribution, while the local government should be mainly responsible for performing the allocation role, such as a more efficient provision of public goods and service. In the case of China, however, the local government has to perform the functions of both distribution and allocation. By nature, it is almost impossible for local governments to equalize the fiscal capacity across regions in such a diverse country.

The large and inflexible size of local governments is another major impediment. Without a large reduction in the number of local public employees, especially in areas with agriculture as the major means of revenue, fiscal decentralization alone is not sufficient to deal with the distributional problem. Most theories on federalism assume that the size and service of local government are responsive to the needs of local residents. In a democratic society, voters endogenously determine local government size. However, under the current system in China, if the central government grants more power to the local government and lets it determine the staffing level, it is likely that local government sizes in less-developed regions will increase rather than diminish.

In a region lacking non-farm job opportunities, entering the government payroll is one of the most attractive options, which may create a large rent-seeking behavior for officials to hire relatives and friends. Consequently, the size of local government is more likely to rise provided that the constituents do not have much say on local affairs.

Therefore, how to control and reduce government sizes under the current political system poses a dilemma for policymakers. Economic decentralization in the reform period has undoubtedly helped prompt China's growth, but under the regime of political centralization, regional disparities have widened significantly. How to achieve balanced regional growth is a delicate task. Considering that China has been rather successful in engineering institutional innovations based on existing institutions, the challenge may induce more institutional innovations on fiscal decentralization and governance.

References

Bardhan, P., 'Decentralization of Governance and Development', *Journal of Economic Perspective*, 16 (4) (2002): 185-205.

Barro and Sala-I-Martin, *Economic Growth* (McGraw-Hill Inc, 1995).

China State Statistical Bureau, various years. *China County Public Finance Statistical Yearbook* (Beijing: China Statistical Publishing House).

Dethier, J., 'Governance and Economic Performance: A Survey' (ZEF Discussion Paper on Development Policy, 1999).

Fan, S., Zhang, L. and Zhang, X., 'Reform, Investment and Poverty in Rural China', *Economic Development and Cultural Change*, 52 (2) (2004): 395-422.

Jin, H., Qian, Y. and Weingast, B.R., 'Regional decentralization and fiscal incentives: federalism, Chinese style', *Journal of Public Economics*, 89 (9-10) (2005): 1719-1742.

Kanbur, R. and Zhang, X., 'Which Regional Inequality: Rural-Urban or Coast-Inland? An Application to China', *Journal of Comparative Economics* 27 (1999): 686-701.

———, 'Fifty Years of Regional Inequality in China: A Journey Through Central Planning, Reform and Openness', *Review of Development Economics* (2005).

Knight, J. and Shi, L., 'Fiscal decentralization: incentives, redistribution and reform in China', *Oxford Development Studies*, 27 (1) (1999): 5-32.

Knight, J. and Song, L., 'The spatial contribution to income inequality in rural China', *Cambridge Journal of Economics*, 17 (1993): 195-213.

Lin, J.Y. and Liu, Z., 'Fiscal decentralization and Economic Growth in China', *Economic Development and Cultural Change*, 49 (1) (2002): 1-21.

Lin, J.Y., Tao, R., Liu, M. and Zhang, Q., 'Urban and Rural Household Taxation in China: Measurement and Stylized Facts' (CCER Working Paper, 2002).

Liu, M. and Tao, R., 'Regional Competition, Fiscal Reform and Local Governance in China' (paper presented in the conference 'Paying for Progress. Public finance, Human Welfare, and Inequality in China', Oxford: Institute for Chinese Studies, May 21-23, 2004).

Oates, W., 'The theory of public finance in a federal system,' *Canadian Journal of Economics*, 1 (1) (1968): 37-54.

Park, A., Rozelle, S., Wong, C. and Ren, C., 'Distributional Consequences of Reforming Local Public Finance in China', *China Quarterly*, 147 (September 1996): 751-778.

Qian, Y. and Roland, G., 'Federalism and the Soft Budget Constraint', *American Economic Review* 88 (5) (December 1998): 1143-1162.

Rozelle, S., 'Rural industrialization and increasing inequality: emerging patterns in China's reforming economy,' *Journal Of Comparative Economics*, 19 (1994): 362-391.

Shih, V. and Zhang, Q., 'Who Receives Subsidies: A Look at the County-level before and after the 1994 Tax Reform' (paper presented in the conference 'Paying for Progress. Public finance, Human Welfare, and Inequality in China', Oxford: Institute for Chinese Studies, May 2004), pp.21-23.

Smith, A., *The Wealth of Nations*, Bantam Classic Edition (Bantam Dell: New York, March 2003).

Tiebout, C., 'A pure theory of local expenidures', *Journal of Political Economy*, 64 (1956)4: 16-424.

Tong, J., 'Fiscal Regimes in China, 1971-1998', *Chinese Economy*, 31 (3) (May-June 1998): 5-21.

Wan, G., Lu, M. and Chen, Z., 'Globlization and Regional Inequality in China' (World Institute of Development Economic Research (WIDER) working paper, 2003, http://www.wider.unu.edu/conference/conference-2003-3/conference-2003-3-papers/wan-chen-3-9-03.pdf).

West, L.A. and Wong, C., 'Fiscal decentralization and growing regional disparities in rural China: some evidence in the provision of social services', *Oxford Review of Economic Policy*, 11 (4) (1995): 70-84.

World Bank, *China National Development and Sub-national Finance: A Review of Provincial Expenditures* (Washington DC: World Bank, 2002).

Xu, Y., 'Xiangcun zhili jiegou gaige de zouxiang', (Direction of reforms on rural governance), *Zhanluo Yu Guanli (Strategy and Management)*, 4 (2003): 90-97.

Zhang, L., 'Chinese Central-Provincial Fiscal Relationships, Budgetary Decline and the Impact of the 1994 Fiscal Reform: An Evaluation', *China Quarterly*, 157 (May 1999): 115-141.

Zhang, T., and Zou, H., 'Fiscal decentralization, public spending and economic growth in China,' *Journal of Public Economics*, 67 (1998): 221-240.

Zhang, X. and Fan, S., 'Public Investment and Regional Inequality in Rural China,' *Agricultural Economics*, 30(2) (2004): 89-100.

Chapter 19

On the Institutional Arrangements of Farmer Cooperatives in China

Zuhui Huang
Xu-chu Xu
Yu Song

Φ13 Ō13
P32

1 Introduction

Since the 1990s, China's agricultural economy has experienced profound changes. These changes result from the following two factors: one is the sharp transition of China's agricultural products market; the other is the urgent need for the international agriculture practices after China's accession into the WTO. In such a background, farmers will be facing more risks and uncertainty during their production and operation, and the desire of farmers to unite and strengthen their market competitiveness becomes strong.

Being a major form of farmer-specialized, cooperative economic organizations, cooperatives are the fruit of such desire and have been developing very rapidly. This paper describes the development of farmer cooperatives in China and analyzes the farmer cooperatives in the costal areas in China based on the case study of Zhejiang.

2 Overall Development of China's Farmer Cooperatives

If the campaigns for farmer cooperatives in China—during the Mao Zedong Era or even earlier—were neglected, we can say that China's modern campaigns for farmer cooperatives began in the mid-1980s and have developed rapidly since the 1990s. According to the statistics of China Agriculture Ministry, the number of farmer cooperatives and agricultural products associations in China is over 150,000, and the number of comparatively standardized cooperatives is over 140,000.

However, the development of farmer cooperatives in different areas is not balanced. They develop quickly in areas such as Zhejiang, Shangdong, Jiangsu, Beijing, Sichuan, Anhui, Hebei, Shaanxi and Shanxi (see Table 19.1). The business activities of cooperatives include production, processing, storage, transportation, and sale. Cooperatives provide their members with various services such as purchase and sale, techniques, information, loan guarantee, and so on.

There are three cooperative forms: specialized associations, which provide techniques information, and purchase and sales services; specialized cooperatives, which sign purchase and sales contracts with their members and provide unified production materials, unified technical services, unified purchase and sales services, and unified prices; and cooperative economic organizations, which have entities, such as shareholding cooperatives. Cooperatives are established by farmers themselves or by organizations, such as agricultural technique service departments and agricultural enterprises.

Table 19.1 The number of farmer cooperatives in some provinces of China

Province	Zhejiang	Jiangsu	Chong-qing	Heilong-jiang	Hebei	Hubei	Shangdong	Jilin
Number	2,335	5,167	1,590	2,816	2,689	985	18,840	2,850
Time of Statistics	Dec. 2003	Dec. 2002	Jun. 2003	Jun. 2003	Dec. 2003	Oct. 2003	Dec. 2003	Jun. 2003

In recent years, the government of China at all levels is taking a more active attitude towards—and consequently making more efforts on the development of—farmer cooperatives. The central government emphasizes the importance of developing farmer cooperatives in its yearly governmental reports, and the National People's Congress has been making new relevant laws. The local governments in Zhejiang, Shangdong, Jiangsu, and so on advocate and support the development of local farmer cooperatives. Zhejiang province has promulgated the first local law on the farmer cooperatives in China.

Generally speaking, farmer cooperatives in China develop at a comparatively low level. Most cooperatives are still of small scale, loose structure, non-standardized management, and weak market competitiveness. What's more, they lack the protection of related laws.

3 Restrictive Factors of Development of Farmer Cooperatives in China

As a developing country in East Asia, China's agricultural economy develops in a totally different environment than European and American countries. Such an environment affects not only the birth and development of farmer cooperatives in China but also their future.

3.1 Land Fragmentation

Farmland fragmentation is a big obstacle to the development of China's agriculture. It prevents the use of agricultural machines, decreases production efficiency, and consequently hinders agricultural modernization. Land fragmentation in China is much more serious than in other countries (see Table 19.2). Land fragmentation makes it difficult for farmers to pursue scale economies through cooperatives, and this situation will also definitely affect the competitiveness and bargaining ability of China's farmer cooperatives in the market and hence affect the enthusiasm of farmers to organize and join cooperatives.

Table 19.2 Comparison of land fragmentation in different countries

Nation/Year	Average size of land (hectare)	Average number of land owned by every household (piece)	Household operation scale (hectare)
India/1960-1961	0.46	5.7	2.6
Netherlands/1950	2.3	3.2	7.4
Belgium/1950	1.1	6.8	7.5
West Germany/1949	0.7	10.0	7.0
Roumania/1948	0.9	6.6	5.9
Greece/1950	0.5	5.6	2.8
Spain/1945	1.6	7.0	11.2
China/1929-33	0.38	5.6	2.1
China/1999	0.087	6.1	0.53

3.2 Stratification of Farmers

Market-oriented reform, which began in the 1980s in China, is not only a fierce economic reform but also a profound social reform. With the development of industrialization and a market-oriented economy, the stratification of farmers in the rural society is unavoidable. Unlike the equal allocation of income in the Mao Zedong Era, the gap between the rich and the poor in rural China is now becoming much wider (see Table 19. 3). Taking the Zhejiang province in 2003 as an example, the net per capita income of the richest 20 per cent of families was 11,693 *yuan,* while that of the poorest 20 per cent of families was only 1,704 *yuan.* The income ratio of the rich to the poor was 6.86:1—higher than the ratio of 6.16:1 a year earlier. Rich people are usually the "rural elite" with certain political, economic or cultural resources; poor people usually come from families living on a small fragment of land with no social or economic resources. The stratification of farmers results in diversified property owners in the rural areas and consequently diversified property and governance structures of the cooperatives.

Table 19.3 Income difference among farm households in five provinces in 2002

Provinces	Jiangsu	Zhejiang	Guangdong	Shangdong	Fujian
Highest and lowest income ratio	5.80	6.16	5.12	5.10	5.72
Difference between the highest and lowest incomes (*yuan*)	7,204	8,766	6,841	4,934	6,482

3.3 Lack of Cooperative Entrepreneurs and Knowledge on Cooperatives

There is no doubt that the cooperative entrepreneurs are the key to the success of cooperatives. Creative cooperative entrepreneurs are usually from a rural social and economic background. They are usually the "rural elite" with a cooperative consciousness and knowledge. Rooted in the complex rural social relations, they have better communication with local farmers and hence easier access to the factors of production. China's campaign for agricultural cooperatives in the Mao Zedong Era didn't cultivate entrepreneurs. Therefore, rural China is facing a severe shortage of cooperative entrepreneurs. Most farmers, rural entrepreneurs, and government officials lack the basic ideas and knowledge of the real cooperative systems. It seriously restricts the formation and development of farmer cooperatives in China.

3.4 Worries of the Governments

The Chinese government at all levels has a strong influence on social and economic affairs. The market-oriented economy will not necessarily lead to the birth and development of cooperatives, which is also determined by the political environment. Even when there are no suitable, objective conditions, powerful government intervention can also lead to the birth of cooperatives.

All levels of government in China still have some concerns about farmer cooperatives. On the one hand, they are still afraid of the recurrence of the inefficient cooperatives; on the other hand, they worry that the vigorous development of various farmer cooperatives will bring about negative effects. They worry that farmer cooperatives will become a powerful political force, challenging the national decision-makers. All these concerns and worries have a subtle yet important influence on the birth and development of farmer cooperatives in China.

3.5 The Developing Path of Agricultural Economy in China

Since the beginning of a market-oriented economy, China's agricultural economy has developed along a different path in comparison to European and American countries—where the horizontal integration of the primary agricultural products' purchase and sale comes before the vertical extension of the value chain. In China, however, the vertical integration comes before the development of cooperatives.

After implementing the Household Contract Responsibility System for about a dozen years, China started a campaign of agricultural industrialization towards the end of the 1980s and beginning of the 1990s in which cooperatives were developed in the mid- and late-1990s.

This different development path suggests that farmer cooperatives in China have shareholding features from the very beginning. Such a feature is very distinct in the coastal areas where industrialized operation is developed.

4 Organizational Forms of Farmer Cooperatives in China

4.1 Organizational Types

Farmer cooperatives in China can be classified into three types: classical cooperatives (Type A), cooperatives with the tendency of shareholding (Type B), and specialized associations (Type C).

Conforming to the principles of mainstream farmer cooperatives, Type A farmer cooperatives have standardized management and a close relationship with members. Their members usually pay a certain sum of money for shares and receive dividends at the bank interest rate at the end of every year. In addition, the members can get the return profits according to the quantity of products they've sold. Type A farmer cooperatives are usually registered as legal representatives in the business administration departments. Such type of cooperatives accounts for about 10 per cent of total cooperatives in China, and they are mainly distributed throughout East China where there are many produce-processing enterprises.

Type B farmer cooperatives combine the stock system and the cooperative system. Compared to Type A, Type B farmer cooperatives are like integrated enterprises rather than pure cooperatives. Shareholders of Type B farmer cooperatives include: agricultural enterprises, agriculture-technology extension departments, grassroots supply and marketing cooperatives, and the "rural elite" (with entrepreneur qualities). They also get some share of capital from their members. Type B farmer cooperatives usually have their own enterprises and are registered as legal representatives in the business administration departments. The number of Type B farmer cooperatives accounts for about 5 per cent of the total number in China.

Type C farmer cooperatives are usually called specialized associations in China. They are the earliest specialized service organizations established by farmers at their own will since the reform and opening-up of the rural areas. They mainly provide agricultural technology extensions and technical services. In the beginning, they were not genuine cooperative, economic organizations. With the improvement of their strength, however, they begin to provide other pre-production and post-production services. They are now showing more and more characteristics of farmer cooperatives. Therefore, they can be regarded as farmer cooperatives with loose structures. Most Type C farmer cooperatives are registered as mass organizations in the civil administration departments. They account for about 85 per cent of total farmer cooperatives in China.

Various types of farmer cooperatives in China can facilitate the establishment of relations among the economic entities of the agricultural industry. However, such relations might be either loose or close. The difference between the two lies in whether the cooperative bodies are within the same entity. It is even more important that the maintenance of such relations should be based on common property rights. That is the basic difference between Types A and B cooperatives and Type C cooperatives. The former are trade cooperation-based on the combination of property rights, while the latter are service union-based on anything but the combination of property rights. That is also the reason why some people think Type C cooperatives (specialized associations) are not real cooperatives.

4.2 Membership

Members are the basic components of farmer cooperatives. Different cooperatives have different regulations on membership. Most cooperatives (usually those of Type C) have loose regulations. Farmers can be admitted as members if they apply. Other cooperatives (usually those of Type A or B) have a strict requirement for membership. Their members must buy some shares as well as meet certain requirements for production scale. Only those who are up to the standards are accepted as members. Some cooperatives (usually Type B) classify their members into two groups: "core members," or "owner members," and then "common members," also known as "user members." The former are required to buy shares, while the latter are not. They sell agricultural products or pay some membership fees to the cooperatives. Although quite a number of cooperatives have no restriction on membership in their written regulations, they do tend to accept farmers from the same community, of a certain production scale, or with some operational skills.

In most cooperatives, members can join and quit at will. However, some cooperatives make regulations to restrict a member from quitting, especially core members of the organizations. For example, some cooperatives stipulate that their council members and working staff cannot quit during their tenures, and the founders of cooperatives can never quit. When no specific laws on cooperatives exist, the phenomenon of a few members having many more shares than the rest of the shareholders is not uncommon, especially in Type B.

4.3 Explanation of Cooperatives of Type B

A phenomenon, which is also common along the Chinese coast, can be observed in Zhejiang in which there are very few Type A cooperatives, some Type C cooperatives with loose structures, and many Type B cooperatives. The shareholding—or capitalization—tendency of cooperatives is very distinct from the beginning.

In fact, the most vigorous enterprise systems are not those capable of making the minimal transaction cost, but rather those capable of attracting the owners who usually own the key production factors. In the current rural economy of China, there is a scarce supply of capital yet a sufficient supply of labor. With high marginal productivity, capital deserves a high return. In practice, capital still takes a controlling position in most farmer cooperatives. It is difficult to make the owners of capital equal with the common members. Even if they look like equals, the small sum of capital that the common members own cannot ensure an equal say within the cooperatives. Secondly, the farmer entrepreneurs or those with entrepreneurial qualities are the most precious human resources in the countryside. Creative and capable, they are the people who are most likely to possess capital.

Therefore, these key members (usually initiators, heads, or large shareholders) have more currency, capital, and human resources than common farmers in the cooperatives. They usually do not engage in production. Instead, they start their business with the purchase and sales activities in the industry chain, and they are intended to gain private benefits by establishing the cooperative organizations. Thus, they view cooperatives like enterprises. As the regulation makers and real controllers of cooperatives, they have powerful influence on the initial property right construction, system design, and routine decision-making. Thirdly, unlike many cooperatives in western countries that are initially derived from horizontal cooperation, the cooperatives in China—since most of them appeared on the demand of the agricultural-industrialized operation—are characterized by vertical cooperation from the very beginning.

The vertical cooperation, featuring the combination of various production factors, will easily lead to a shareholding system rather than to traditional cooperation. Fourthly, farmers in China who join cooperatives often have a distinct purpose. They are usually pursuing pure benefits instead of pure equity status. Their main concern is whether the benefits can be derived from the cooperatives and how much they may pay. In other words, they pursue Pareto improvement rather than Pareto Optimality. Therefore, they aren't concerned about the tendency of shareholding of the cooperatives, at least for a short run. Lastly, Zhejiang is where the shareholding systems were first applied prevalently in China, and therefore, when the farmer cooperative was established, it is not odd that people tend to follow the existing paths and systems.

5 Benefit Mechanism of China's Farmer Cooperatives

The benefit mechanism of farmer cooperatives may refer to two aspects: one is the benefit relation between the cooperatives and their members; and the other is the benefit allocation mechanism within the cooperatives.

5.1 Benefit Relations

5.1.1 Relation Based on Service

This type of cooperatives mainly provides farmers with services, such as technical training and extension, information exchange, young fowls, and production materials purchasing. This is a very common practice for most Type C cooperatives, or specialized associations.

For example, Gaibei Township Grape Technical Association in Shangyu and Edible Fungus Association in Kaihua are both Type C. Often, these organizations have neither powerful economic strength nor economic entities. They charge membership fees or depend on the limited financial aid from local government, functional departments, or some agricultural enterprises. Farmers can enjoy the services provided by the associations as long as they pay their membership fees and abide by the regulations. Such organizations do not have many requirements of, or responsibilities for, the farmers.

Presently, this type of cooperative organization accounts for the majority of farmer cooperatives in China. However, it is predictable that such cooperative organizations with loose structures would evolve into cooperatives with more stable contract relations, closer property right relations, or die out if the competition of the agricultural market becomes more competitive or agricultural industrialization becomes more profound.

5.1.2 Relation Based on Contract

Usually, this type of cooperative (mainly Type B) signs purchase and sales contracts with their members at stable or protective prices. For example, Tonglu County Meat Rabbit Breeding Cooperatives and Xianju County Guangdu High-mountain Vegetable Cooperative are Type B cooperatives, and they are usually established by major producers, agricultural enterprises, or supply and marketing cooperatives. Therefore, they are usually of a large scale and have a strong marketing ability and smooth sales channels.

In such cooperatives, "core members" and "common members" are treated quite differently. They deal with their common members based on the purchase and sales contracts as well as with their shareholders' dividends according to their shares. Such cooperatives tend to be shareholding-oriented, and their relations with the common members are not very close but still stable. This type of cooperative and their members are sharing mutual benefits to some extent. At present, most Type B cooperatives purchase agricultural products at the protective prices. They settle accounts with members every month and give them dividends according to their share capital at the end of year. Fewer Type B cooperatives return profits to their members according to the transactional volume at the end of year instead of the dividends on the share capital.

5.1.3 *Relation Based on Property*

The closeness of the relationship between cooperatives and members depends on whether the cooperative is in the same economic entity and whether they form a relationship based on common property rights. This type of cooperative can be found from the standardized Type A or Type B, which are not in accord with the international cooperative standards. The members of these cooperatives are both shareholders and traders, and they gain dividends on shares and returned profits according to their volume of trade. However, few of those cooperatives follow the principles of "limitation of capital reward" and "return profits according to trade volume." Some cooperatives in Taizhou City of Zhejiang province determine the share proportions of their members—user members—according to production scales or sales volume. To a certain extent, they can be regarded as "the new generation cooperatives" in North America and in EU.

5.2 *Benefit Allocation*

Benefit allocation is the key to the benefit mechanism of farmer cooperatives. Farmer cooperatives are the organizations that pursue the maximum benefits for their members, and farmers' requirements for the system of cooperatives arise from their hope of maintaining as well as increasing the benefits of members.

The cooperative core's benefit allocation is to what extent it can help members, especially common members, receive a profit return. Furthermore, it improves the organization situation of farmers in addition to maintaining and increasing farmers' benefits.

The two basic principles of cooperatives are "limitation of capital reward" and "return profits according to trade volume." Only a few farmer cooperatives in Zhejiang, however, now follow these important principles because most farmers care more about the contribution income than the capital and more about the contribution income than the trade volume. The reason for this behavior can be attributed to four aspects.

First of all, farmers are fully aware of the value of capital scarcity and understand that only a high return can attract capital. Second, agricultural products in China are generally in surplus now, and for individual farmers, they are very difficult to sell. Cooperatives can provide sales channels, solving this problem. Moreover, the more products that are sold, the more benefits farmers can receive. Therefore, quite a few farmers expect a profit return according to their trade volume, and it is not important if the cooperatives return a much smaller profit to the farmers. Thirdly, most cooperatives currently provide techniques, information, delivery, and sales services free of charge, or at preferential prices. These services can also be seen as a kind of profit return. In fact, a service, such as selling goods on a commission basis, implies the meaning of return according to trade volume. Fourthly, many farmers do not have clear ideas about the allocation of trade volume, while allocation based on shareholding is easy to understand and consequently more accepted and well-known.

What's more, many cooperatives have already provided their members with preferential pricing or profits when they purchase production materials or sell agricultural products. In addition, because of the traditional culture, benefits received beforehand are much more substantial than those promised to most Chinese farmers.

6 Decision-making Mechanism of Farmer Cooperatives in China

As an economic organization that is established, managed, and benefited by farmers themselves, farmer cooperatives should attach great importance to the democratic decision-making in order to ensure farmers such positions as controllers, owners, and benefit recipients. The key here is the voting mechanism and the controlling right.

Theoretically, the principle of making decisions for the grassroots cooperatives should be "one member, one vote." However, due to the tendency of shareholding in farmer cooperatives, this principle actually gives way to the system of "one share, one vote." The biggest difference between the two systems is that "one member, one vote" emphasizes the rights of members, embodying the principle of equity—maximum benefits of members. In contrast, "one share, one vote" stresses the rights of capital, embodying the principle of efficiency—maximum benefits of capital. The emphasis of capital naturally leads to a system arrangement, such as giving dividends according to shares, and in some cooperatives, the members are classified as either "core members" (shareholders) or "common members" (non-shareholders). There are significant differences when it comes to the rights and obligations of these two types of members. The core members are usually initiators, leaders, and owners of the key production factors. They have great influence on initial property right construction, system design, routine management, and decision-making, and they hold the real controlling rights of the cooperatives. Since core members, or shareholders, bear more obligations, they are naturally entitled to more rights.

Therefore, even though many cooperatives stipulate that the member, or representative, congress is the supreme power department and that the system of "one share, one vote" has to be enforced, in the most situations, members are under the great influence of "core members." At times, the vote is only a confirmation. Discussion seems like a notification, and supervision looks like a passive reception. Obviously, it is a controlling system of "core members," but to a certain extent, it can also be regarded as a form of expert management.

7 Conclusions

1. The organizational forms of farmer cooperatives in China are diversified and still in a beginning phase.

2. Affected by various restrictive factors, the principles and forms of farmer cooperatives in China have differed from traditional ones since the 1990s. The institutional arrangement and development trend of cooperatives in Zhejiang province are quite similar to those of the "new generation cooperatives."

3. Farmer cooperatives in China will be more and more closely organized. In the future, most Type C cooperatives (specialized associations) may develop into the comparatively standardized Type A and B cooperatives with their distinct features of shareholding. Type A and B may become the mainstream in China, but in the coastal areas, such as Zhejiang, Type B cooperatives may become mainstream.

4. It might be a trend that farmer cooperatives in China will gradually merge. Some cooperative societies, such as cooperative unions, trade associations, and agricultural associations, may emerge in certain areas.

5. The Chinese government—and some functional departments—at all levels should continue in the cultivation and development of farmer cooperatives as well as pay more attention to the combination tendency of farmer cooperatives.

6. The process and operation of legislation on farmer cooperatives will greatly influence the development trend of farmer cooperatives in China.

References

Chen, X., 'Construction of Rural Specialized Cooperative Economic Organizations', *Farmer's Daily* (February 14, 2003).

Du, Y., *Cooperative: Modern Enterprise Systems in Agriculture* (Jiangxi People's Press, 2002).

Huang, Z., Xu, X. and Feng, G., 'An Analysis of Factors Affecting the Development of Farmer cooperatives', *China Rural Economy*, (3) (2002): 13-21.

Tan, S., Qu, F. and Harrik, N., 'Causes of Land Fragmentation and Determinants', *China Rural Observation*, 6 (2003): 24-30.

Yuan, P., 'A Study of Farmer Cooperatives in the Course of Rural Market Process', China Social Sciences, 6 (2001): 63-76.

Chapter 20

Government Regulations, Legal-Soft-Constraint and Rural Grassroots Democracy in China

Qi Zhang
Mingxing Liu
Wei Shan

1 Introduction

Recently, two stylized facts in rural China have drawn attention among researchers and policy-makers at home and abroad. One is that competitive elections for grassroots offices have become prevalent in the countryside; the other is that social conflicts between peasants and local officials—primarily resulting from tax burdens—have been growing since the mid-1990s. Since village elections are supposed to improve peasant-cadre relations and thus far most villages have experienced at least one election, the coexistence of the village direct election and the uprising tensions in the countryside advances a puzzling problem in rural political economy.

Several authors provide explanations for this inconsistency. O'Brien and Li (2000) cast doubt on the effect of implementation of *the Organic Law*. They argue that even in places where village elections are seemingly free and fair, there isn't yet democracy in village governance.

Ray (2002) believes that the insufficient resources for effective governance could explain the gap between democracy and governance. Fiscal reforms in the last decade have made local governments less and less financed so that they have to finance themselves via informal charges on peasants. In his recent paper, Kennedy (2002) tries to explain the coexistence problem mentioned above by arguing that the implementation of village elections is uneven across different regions, which has led to uneven outcomes in the practice of grassroots governance. A common assumption underlying these arguments is that local governments are one of the most important factors in determining the development of rural democracy.

However, the difference among the behaviors of local governments can only partially explain the various developments in village governance, because such explanation itself is something that needs to be explained.

Table 20.1 Definition of variables

	Definition
DEMO	Defined as the way of candidate nomination in the election. DEMO=0, if there is no election after 1987; DEMO=1, if candidates are nominated by the upper-level government; DEMO =2, if candidates are nominated by the upper-level government and the election council of village jointly; DEMO =3, if candidates are nominated by the election council of village; DEMO=4, if candidates are freely nominated by the villagers (any one in the village can be nominated if certain conditions are met).
VLAND	Defined as the area of operating arable land (*Mu*) per capita.
VFOOD	Defined as the government grain procurement quota (Kg) per capita at village level.
VFEE1	Defined as all formal state taxes plus all local levies as a share of household income. Local levies include the charge legitimated and not legitimated by the center.
VFEE2	Defined as local levies as a share of household income. Local levies include the charge legitimated and not legitimated by the center.
VINC	Per capita net income for the village measured by the price level in 1986.
VOUT	Defined as the percentage of migrant labor to the total labor.
VEDU	Defined as the percentage of the labor who have or have a higher than primary school education to the total labor.
VINCSTR	Defined as the percentage of household income from the collective enterprise to the total household income
VAGRSTR	Defined as the percentage of household income from the grain planting to the total household income
T	Defined as the dummy variable for enforcement of the Organic Law of Village Committee. T=1, if year>=1998; T=0, if year<1998.

Here we argue a "legal-soft-constraint" (LSC) problem between the center and its local agents. We benefit from the concept of budget-soft-constraint (BSC) in economics. Kornai (1980 and 1992) first uses Budget-Soft-Constraint to explore the reason why firms in traditional planning economic systems can get sustainable cash injections from the government despite their long-term deficit. Then more and more researchers reveal that as long as one organization can successfully finance its partial or even entire deficits by relying on support from other organizations, which are called supporting organizations such as the government, banks, and enterprises, to evade bankruptcy, BSC will exist. Even in mature market economies, we can still see the BSC phenomena. For example, despite their poor performance, chaebols in Korea can maintain their operation under the aegis of the government rather than go bankrupt.

Unlike early researchers (Kornai, 1979 and 1980; Hillman, 1987; Goldfeld and Quandt, 1988; Schaffer, 1989; Schleifer and Vishny, 1994) who view BSC as exogenous, current researchers consider BSC as an endogenous variable (Qian, 1994; Dewatripont and Maskin, 1995; Li, 1992 and 1998□Bai and Wang, 1998a and 1998b; Qian and Roland, 1998; Dong and Putterman, 2002). The research of Dewatripont and Maskin (1995) is worth noting. In their model, the agent in one economic system has less incentive in making efforts to improve efficiency even when facing the danger of bankruptcy because he/she knows he/she won't get punished, despite the poor performance, because the supporting organizations will come to rescue. Their conclusion is incisive: not until the institutions causing BSC are abandoned is a commitment to harden the budget constraint to be considered credible.

Lin and Tan (1999) and Lin and Li (2003) have furthered the research of BSC. They notify in many cases firms are assigned with the so-called "policy burdens" when the government assigns policy missions to firms. Since these policy burdens lead to distorted technology choice of firms and in turn the deviation from the comparative advantage of the economy, the government should be responsible for firms' bad performance because of the information asymmetry problem between the government and firms. Even in market economy, BSC wouldn't disappear if policy burdens continue to exist.

Similar logic helps to explain why the seemingly contradictory phenomena we mentioned at the beginning of this chapter, exists. In China, the central government assigns a lot of mandates to local governments without plenty of funding. As a result, local governments have to finance themselves to implement the regulation tasks.

Because there are severe information asymmetry between the central government and local governments, local authorities can levy taxes and fees higher than the level that is necessary to implement regulations. The free-rider levy behaviors of local governments will be largely constrained if village elections are fully implemented. So for their self-interests, local governments tend to be slack in the enforcement of village democratic reforms.

Moreover, in order to enforce the mandates smoothly, the center has to tacitly permit the non-democratic behaviors of local-level governments. In such case there exists the LSC situation since local governments don't need to worry about the punishment for violating the village election law.

LSC and BSC are quite similar in many aspects. In both cases there are entities (local government in the case of LSC and enterprises in the case of BSC) for certain reasons whose behaviors are not restricted by rules (*the Village Committee Organization Law* in the case of LSC and *the Bankruptcy Law* in the case of BSC). What LSC differs from BSC is that, in the context of LSC, local governments will not collapse due to financial strain; instead, they only subject to the administrative constraints from the center and need the center's connivance when conducting illegal activities.

Therefore, the logic of BSC can be employed to analyze the LSC phenomenon, in which the credibility of the commitment of the center of carrying out THE ORGANIC LAW will play a pivotal role in affecting the behaviors of local governments, much the way the credibility of the commitment on hardening the budget plays its role in structuring BSC.

Based on the LSC theory, we develop a local equilibrium model to explore the association between the center's regulations, free-ride charges of local governments on peasants, and their strategies in implementing elections. We argue that due to LSC, local governments will levy more tax and fees than necessary to implement the mandates and will resist implementing the Law.

In the following, we will first briefly describe the history and the practice of village democracy in rural China and the mandatory tasks assigned by the center. In Section 2, we will try to explain the reason why great differences exist in implementing the Law across different regions from the perspective of the regulation argument. In Section 3, we will set up a local equilibrium model to explore the phenomena of LSC. Section 4 provides an empirical analysis, and we will draw a conclusion and discuss implications in Section 5.

2 Village Democracy Practice and Government Regulations in Rural China

After the end of the commune system in the early 1980s, politics in the countryside has experienced significant changes. In order to maintain the political order in the grassroots within a new institutional environment, the Standing Committee of the National People's Congress approved a trial *Organic Law* of village committees in November 1987 that regulates how village polities should be organized. The law was made permanent in 1998.

The law grants village committees a broader autonomy. According to the law, the villagers' committee is a community administration to manage village affairs. In addition, elections must be held every three years for positions in the village committee. Every adult has one vote. Candidates are not required to be members of the Communist Party. The *Organic Law* reflects the political and economic interests of peasants.

The law also specifically states that the township (*xiang*) and town (*zhen*) government "may guide, help and support village committees, but must not intervene in affairs that in the purview of the villagers' committee" (The Organic Law of Village Committee, Article 2).

In other words, village committees are no longer the administrative subordinate of the county or the township government. The reality, however, is much more complicated. Local governments have remained a dominating influence on the political lives of rural residents, including an influence on the committee election.

For example, Xiao (2001) reports in a survey on 40 villagers' committee elections that "... Except balloting by themselves or being as candidate in person, the impacts of the county and township governments are omnipresent during the elections. The governments involved in elections not only as legislator, but also as executor and supervisor in devising and interpreting the rules, releasing and transferring related information, and so on. They are also responsible for organizing and supervising elections, arbitrating disputations, and maintaining election order". Zhang (1998) reaches a similar conclusion in his survey on Villagers' Committee election of Lishu village of Jilin province.

Local governments can influence or manipulate the process of village democracy through several strategies. Firstly, they can appoint or remove village cadres via administrative mandates. This is their last choice because according to the *Organic Law* this practice is illegal. Secondly, because local governments usually control the allocation and usage of most political, economic, and social resources that are needed for villages' development, they can induce village cadres to subordinate to them by preferentially distributing these resources. Moreover, according to the Article 3 of the *Organic Law* on village committees, "the rural grassroots unit of the Chinese Communist Party (CCP) should work under the Charter of CCP and play a core role in leadership". Because village CCP secretaries are usually appointed by the township party, local governments can control village committees via the village party branch, but the situation varies greatly from place to place (Hu, 1998; Li, 2002). Finally, local governments usually have the authority for interpreting the *Organic Law* so that they may manipulate the law for their own interests (Zhang, 1998).

However, in most cases local governments do not fully act on the Law. It's common for them to ignore villagers' legitimate demand for self-governance, to intervene in internal issues within villages, and to manipulate or sometimes even reject the elections by using traditional administrative methods.

Ke (1997), O'Brien and Li (2001) vividly describe how local-level governments publicly comply with the Law but covertly oppose village election. Xiao (1999) finds in a survey on township cadres that they are laden with misgivings and fears about villagers' self-governance. Zhang (1998) concludes in her survey that although the center and provincial governments have a positive view of the rural grassroots democracy, the county and township governments are likely to oppose villagers' self-governance. We will analyze the reasons in this section.

In the case that local governments ignore peasants' legitimate democratic rights and interests, the tension between cadres and villagers is inevitable. Once the conflicts break out, "peasants will resort to letters of complaint (*xinfang*), to individual and collective petition (*qingyuan*), or even to litigation for retrieving their rights and interests."... "In recent years, peasants resort more and more to litigation to safeguard their rights and interests" (Li, 2002: pp. 10-48).

Under these circumstances, the attitudes of the central government toward rural grassroots democracy have played a key role in determining what has been going on. Given China's authoritarian regime, the center has various ways to make local governments meet its political and policy-related requirements. The case of village democracy is also no exception.[1] If the center is willing to push local governments

---

[1] No direct evidences to bear out this judgment. However, this conclusion is consistent with a great deal of empirical evidences, such as the implementation of the basic policies of the state and the administrative control of the spread of SARS in 2003.

to comply with the election law as its leaders declare in public, then the implementation of the law would be much smoother.

However, in practice when there's a conflict between local governments and villagers on village democracy, the center usually sides with the former, putting the development of village democracy in an awkward position.

We hold that the insufficiently funded regulation tasks assigned by the center constitute the key to the understanding of the unbalanced development of village democracy and the center's failure to reduce rural tax and fee burdens.

To be more specific, the most important mandates in rural China are:

1. The compulsory sale of grain to the government at below-market prices. Depending on the region, the grain may be in the form of rice, maize, or wheat. Once the government is involved in grain distribution, grain production and grain's selling prices are also under the government's control. The amount purchased in each region is collected from households in proportion to the cultivated land which is operated under the Household Responsibility System. From the late 1980s to the early 1990s, the mandatory quota procurement system was relaxed, the procurement quantity was reduced, and the grain market gradually developed.

Despite the heavy financial burdens and administrative costs in managing the food procurement system, the government policy still persisted, although the degree of mercerization went up and down during the 1990s. In 1995, after the market prices of grain rose sharply following several rounds of market liberalization in the early 1990s, the government resumed again to administrative intervention in the grain market. The center's policies in 1995 held each provincial governor responsible for the balance of grain demand and supply within that province, and hence intensified the local government's intervention in grain production and marketing.[2]

2. Family planning. Defined as a national policy, birth control is another major task for local cadres. The current policy in rural areas is that if the first child of a household is a boy, no second birth is allowed. If it is a girl, then, three or more years later, a second birth can be permitted.

Given the current under-development of the rural social security system, low education and low employment for rural women, and the cultural factors at work, the difference between the number of children that the current family planning policy permits and the number that peasants want is very large. It is unusually difficult and expensive for local cadres to carry out the policy; very high administration costs and large staffing numbers are required.

3. Politically motivated developmental mandates. After the economic reform in the late 1970s, local cadres are not mainly evaluated by their ideological intention, but instead by their ability to achieve economic and social targets. The local leaders must try to reach certain "hard targets" to stay in power or get promoted. For example, the state law mandates that all children must receive the nine-year compulsory education.

---

[2] It should be noted that after 2002, grain procurement policy was gradually abolished in many provinces, especially in those coastal provinces.

However, in contrast to urban residents, whose education is heavily subsidized by municipal governments, rural residents must pay for most of their education. Since the central government cannot provide sufficient resources for the mandate, local governments must try to finance the expenditures by spending a large part of their budgets, and in many cases, the local public schools also join this financing process by charging various fees in addition to tuition to fill the financial gap.

In many cases, the fees are charged on an arbitrary basis, such as charging excessive electric and water fees, experiment fees, library fees, school policing fees, and examination fees.

Compared with the center, local governments have an obvious advantage over the information about the cost of implementing the center's policies.[3] As we have pointed out, the cash-deprived local governments have to finance themselves in all ways.[4] Since the central regulations should rely on local governments for implementation and an information asymmetry exists between the two (i.e., higher-level governments cannot perfectly monitor the regulations' implementation), local governments may easily find good excuses to seek their self-interests in the name of implementing the regulation tasks.

In other words, because of the information asymmetry, local governments can levy taxes and fees higher than the level that is necessary to offset the implementation costs of regulations.[5] As a matter of fact, local governments use their administrative power to charge fees on peasants usually in the name of state regulations and policies.

Moreover, the regulations will influence the attitudes of the center and local governments toward village democracy. As for local governments, these policy burdens, especially the tax and fee levy as well as birth control, must be implemented through village cadres. However, once the village democracy is fully realized, local governments would be faced with organized and legitimate defiance against the implementation of the regulations.[6]

Therefore, local governments naturally have the tendency to inhibit, control, and manipulate the villagers' committee and its election (Hu, 1998). Therefore, at the beginning of the implementation of the law, the seed of conflict between local governments and villagers was planted, which would eventually burst out. In other

---

[3] Generally speaking, all modern states have to face the asymmetric information problem between tiers of governments, and between tiers of administrative bureaucrats. For a detailed discussion, see Weingast, Barry and Banks (1992).

[4] Apart from levying taxes and fees, negotiating for huge fiscal transfers from higher tiers of government is also an important way for local governments. For details, see Liu, Shih and Zhang (2004).

[5] Another representative way is to expand local bureaucracy. However, without imposing more taxes and fees on peasants, it's impossible for local level governments to do that. In addition, local governments also engage in rent-seeking activities in developed areas, especially in villages with collectively-owned factories or enterprises.

[6] Tao et al (2004) discusses how mandatory regulations from the center hurt rural development in the long run.

words, the central government has been carrying a contradictory policy combination: on one hand it endows villagers with the right of self-governance; on the other hand, it requires local governments to enforce various unpopular regulation tasks. These contradictory policies push local governments to the front line of the conflict with peasants. Local governments in turn have to face the conflict directly and make decisions favoring their own interests. Some researchers also note that the regulations can affect the attitude of local governments toward village democracy (Ray, 2002).

On the other hand, the center still gives priority to the implementation of regulations over others, including the implementation of the Law. In order to ensure that the regulations are implemented, the central government will give tacit consent to or permit the anti-democracy behaviors of local governments when a conflict between local governments and villagers emerges.

In other words, if village democracy and tax burdens reduction have to be reached at the cost of failing to fulfill the central government's regulations, the center would rather sacrifice the interests of peasants (O'Brien and Li, 1999). If local governments fully anticipate the above behavioral mode of the center, they will bravely levy extra tax and fees and openly resist village democracy in spite of the stipulations by the Law. In such case there exists an LSC problem.

However, if the center promotes the regulation homogeneously across the country, why are there heterogeneous implementation outcomes of the *Organic Law* across regions in the 1990s?

We argue that although the center mandates the regulations to be implemented across the country, the difficulty of enforcing such regulations is heterogeneous across different regions (Tao, Liu and Zhang, 2002). For example, the center implemented the grain procurement policy in almost all provinces. However, the quantities of grain procurement and the ratio of government procurement to total grain output are very different across provinces, counties, townships, villages, and even households. The quantity of grain procurement and its ratio to total grain output for every province, county, township, and village are determined by upper-level governments according to a set of rules which take into account such factors as natural conditions, historical factors, and even political concerns.

Apparently, these factors are not controlled by the villages or peasants who sell grains to the government; thus they can be viewed as relatively exogenous. The fact is that sufficient differentiation exists in grain procurement regulation enforcement across regions and even across households. For the birth control regulation, the central policy is much more homogeneous across regions. However, the difficulties in implementing the relatively homogeneous regulation differ significantly across regions. In poor areas where income is low, non-agricultural employment limited, and education underdeveloped, peasants usually want to have more children than their counterparts in richer regions. Therefore, the difficulties in implementing the relatively homogeneous birth control policy in poorer regions are much bigger, which may entails higher administrative costs and more staffing.

With this "homogeneous regulations with heterogeneous enforcement" controlling other factors, the regions with a higher degree of regulations will have less developed village democracy and more tax and fee burdens because of more mandates from the central government and the existence of information asymmetry between the central government and local governments, while the regions with a lower degree of regulations will have more developed village democracy and less tax and fee burdens.

3 A Partial Equilibrium Model

In this part, we develop a simple partial equilibrium model to describe the relationship between regulation and LSC. We assume that the level of regulations that a local government must implement is F, the level of village democracy stipulated by the law is D^*. The cost local governments should pay for implementing regulations is R^*, and in practice, local governments will levy R because of the problem of information asymmetry. $R-R^*$ is the profit of the local government.

Although the central government doesn't know how much the level of R^* is, it will place a cap on the local government's levy so that it wouldn't be higher than the level of Y^*, which represents the necessary level to maintain simple reproduction of villagers. Therefore, the objective function of the center is $Min\{R, Y^*\}$.

As for the local government, given the level of democracy D, the higher R is, the more cost it will incur, which will also draw the attention of the center. Therefore, the local government will limit R to a level lower than Y^*. The objective function of the local government can be written as:

$$MAX : b(R-R^*) - d\left[(R-R^*)^2\right] \bullet D + e \bullet D$$

$$s.t. \qquad R^* \leq R < Y^* \tag{1}$$

$$D \leq D^*$$

In equation (1) D, b, d, e are parameters. $b, e \in (0,1]$, $d \in (1, \infty]$, $D^* \in [0,1]$.

$b(R-R^*)$ and $d(R-R^*)^2 \bullet D$ are income function and cost function, respectively, of the local government. The local government's cost function has a positive first-order derivative of D, which represents that given the level of D, the local government will pay more when it levies more from peasants. Here we see D as a continuous variable.

However, keeping a certain level of democracy may also be helpful for the local government in carrying out its work in the village.[7] We use $e \cdot D$ to reflect this effect. In addition, we also assume that the local government has a higher marginal utility from levying extra fee than from providing a higher level of democracy. Thus, $b > e$.

The envelop form of equation (1) is:

$$b\left(R-R^*\right)-d\left[\left(R-R^*\right)^2\right] \cdot D+e \cdot D+\lambda_1 \cdot \left(R-R^*\right)+\lambda_2 \cdot \left(Y^*-R\right)+\lambda_3 \cdot \left(D^*-D\right) \quad (2)$$

$$\Rightarrow F.O.C: b-2d \cdot D \cdot R+2d \cdot R^* \cdot D+\lambda_1-\lambda_2=0 \quad (3)$$

$$-d(R-R^*)^2 +e-\lambda_3=0 \quad (4)$$

Which simultaneously satisfies the Kun–Tucker Condition:

$$\begin{cases} \lambda_1 \cdot \left|R-R^*\right|=0 \quad (5) \\ \lambda_1>0, R-R^*=0 \quad (6) \\ or \, \lambda_1=0, R-R^*>0 \quad (7) \end{cases} \quad \begin{cases} \lambda_2 \cdot \left(Y^*-Y\right)=0 \quad (8) \\ \lambda_2>0, Y^*-Y=0 \quad (9) \\ or \, \lambda_2=0, Y^*-Y>0 \quad (10) \end{cases} \quad \begin{cases} \lambda_3 \cdot \left|D^*-D\right|=0 \quad (11) \\ \lambda_3>0, D^*-D=0 \quad (12) \\ or \, \lambda_3=0, D^*-D>0 \quad (13) \end{cases}$$

As for equation (5) ~ (7):

If A: $\lambda_1>0 \Rightarrow R=R^* \Rightarrow \lambda_2=0, D=D^*$ the value of objective function is $e \cdot D^*$ (O-1)

If B: $\lambda_1=0 \Rightarrow R>R^*$; now if $\lambda_2>0, Y^*=R$, this result contradicts constraint condition R<Y*.

If C: $\lambda_1=0 \Rightarrow R>R^*$; now if $\lambda_2=0, Y^*>R$; and if $\lambda_3>0 \Rightarrow D=D^*$ (14)

Put the result of equation (14) into equation (3) and equation (4), and we have

---

[7] Li (2004) found that self-governance by villagers will in effect facilitate the implementation of the center's mandates, for instance, the food procurement targets assigned by the center. These stylized facts in a large part show what villagers strongly oppose is not the center's mandates but instead the predatory behaviors of local cadres.

$$\Rightarrow R = \frac{b}{2dD^*} + R^*, \lambda_3 = e - d \bullet \left(\frac{b}{2dD^*}\right)^2 \tag{15}$$

Now the value of objective function is $\dfrac{b}{2dD^*} \bullet \left(1 - \dfrac{b}{2}\right) + e \bullet D^*$ (O-2)

If D: $\lambda_1 = 0 \Rightarrow R > R^*$; now if $\lambda_2 = 0, Y^* > R$ and $\lambda_3 = 0 \Rightarrow D^* > D$ \hfill (16)

Put the result of equation (16) into equation (3) and equation (4), and we have

$$\Rightarrow D = \frac{b}{2d\sqrt{\dfrac{e}{d}}}, R = \sqrt{\frac{e}{d}} + R^* \tag{17}$$

Now the value of objective function is $b\sqrt{e/d}$ (O-3).

When constraint condition (16) is satisfied, we have $D^* > \dfrac{b}{2d\sqrt{e/d}}$. Because under this circumstance (O-2) is a descending function so that we have $\dfrac{b}{2dD^*} \bullet \left(1 - \dfrac{b}{2}\right) + e \bullet D^* < b\sqrt{e/d}$. As far as the interest of local governments is concerned, the result (O-3) is better than the result (O-2).

The optimal strategy of local governments is ($D = \dfrac{b}{2d\sqrt{e/d}}, R = \sqrt{e/d} + R^*$).

That is, there is a *legal-soft-restraint* ($\lambda_3=0$) problem because of the regulation tasks of the center, and the actual democracy level is under the natural level (D<D*).

The above analysis can be viewed as a strategic game between the center and local governments. First, when facing regulations from the central government and the Organic Law of Villagers' Committee, local governments should decide how much democracy it will provide in the village and how much it will levy on villagers. If local governments decide not to levy extra fees, which means local governments only levy fees to cover the implementation costs of the regulations, it's not necessary for them to resist self-governance of villagers. Second, if the local government chooses to resist village democracy, which will partly be detected by the center, the center should decide whether or not it should force the local governments to comply with the law or to ensure the implementation of the regulations.

If the central government gives higher priority of the latter over others, it will connive or admit posthumously the anti-democratic behaviors of local governments. Local governments can anticipate well the response mode of the center, and they will levy extra fees and resist village democracy openly (or secretly).

4 Empirical Analysis and Results

On the basis of previous analysis, we propose two hypotheses, H1: There is a U-shape relationship between the level of village democracy and the center's regulations.

In general, the more the center's mandates, the more the center will depend on local government to implement them, and in turn the negotiation power of local governments will be stronger, which gives local governments more opportunities to levy taxes and fees on peasants.

However, in case regulations come to a certain level where cost surpasses the interests from regulation implementation (for instance, rigorous regulations tamper the vigor of rural economy or even make it unsustainable), the center might turn to support village democracy to relieve social tensions ($R<R^*$).

H2: There is a U-curve relationship between village democracy level and tax and fee burdens on peasants.

As revealed by Tao etc al. (2004), higher degree of regulations will lead to heavier burdens, legally or illegally, on peasants levied by local governments. There is nearly a linear relationship between governmental regulations and tax and fee burdens over peasants. H1 predicts that there's a U-curve relationship between regulations and village democracy level. If H1 holds, then logically we will also see a similar U-curve relationship between tax and fee burdens and village democracy level.

We measure the intervention of local governments through candidate nomination in an election, which is categorized as five possible processes: no election, nomination by the upper-level government, nomination by both the upper-level government and villager representatives, nomination by villager representatives, and free nomination by all villagers (any one in the village can be nominated if certain conditions are met). Table 20.2 and Table 20.3 show the frequency of village election and the distribution of nomination means in our sample.

Besides, for the years without the election, we assign them the values equal to the last elections, which makes the nomination means a continuous variable with annual information.

Peasants' tax burden is defined as the state taxes plus the legitimate and illegitimate rural fees as a percentage of rural net income. The state tax should be shared by the town-level government and its upper-level government, and various fees might mainly feed the fiscal needs of the town-level government or are indirectly controlled by it; for example, the fees are shared by the cadres at the village level.

To some extent, to collect the state tax can be viewed as one kind of policy burdens from the upper-level government. For the other policy burdens, since we cannot find a good proxy to represent the strength of birth control policy, we will only test the hypothesis related to the grain procurement policy represented by the government grain procurement per capita.

Table 20.2 The frequency of elections in terms of villages (1987-2002)

Number of elections in a village	Number of villages	Percentage (percent)
1	1	2.13
2	10	21.28
3	3	6.38
4	6	12.77
5	18	38.3
6	8	17.02
7	1	2.13

Source: Fixed-Point Rural Survey, Ministry of Agriculture, P. R. China.

Now we consider the following econometric specifications for H1 and H2 respectively,

$$DEMO_{it} = \alpha \cdot REGU_{it} + \beta \cdot REGU_{it}^2 + \phi \cdot VINC + \varphi \cdot VINC^2 + \rho \cdot t + \gamma \cdot X_{it} + \varepsilon \qquad (18)$$

$$DEMO_{it} = \alpha \cdot VFEE_{it} + \beta \cdot VFEE_{it}^2 + \phi \cdot VINC + \varphi \cdot VINC^2 + \rho \cdot t + \gamma \cdot X_{it} + \varepsilon \qquad (19)$$

where i and t subscripts indicate village and year respectively. And, the variable *REGU* in equation (18) represents the policy burden where we use *VFOOD*, the grain per capita procurement. *VFEE* in equation (19) represents the tax burden of farmers. *VINC* is the net per capita income, T is the time dummy for the enforcement of the Organic Law of Village committee in 1998, and X represents the other control variables. In addition, we separately test the impacts of total tax burden *VFEE1* and fee burden *VFEE2* (*VFEE1* minus state tax). So we can check how differently local governors control rural election to collect state taxes and fees. The detailed information for the variables in the regression can be found in Table 20.1 and 20.4.

Table 20.3 The frequency of elections in terms of years (1987-2002)

Year	Number of elections	Percentage (%)	Candidate nomination			
			Elect = 1	Elect = 2	Elect = 3	Elect = 4
1987	12	6.03	4	4	4	0
1988	4	2.01	1	2	0	1
1989	8	4.02	2	5	1	0
1990	14	7.04	3	4	7	0
1991	4	2.01	1	2	0	1
1992	13	6.53	4	7	2	0
1993	17	8.54	2	9	6	0
1994	5	2.51	1	1	1	2
1995	11	5.53	2	8	1	0
1996	18	9.05	2	7	8	1
1997	7	3.52	2	3	0	2
1998	15	7.54	0	13	1	1
1999	24	12.06	0	6	15	3
2000	4	2.01	0	1	0	3
2001	13	6.53	0	7	2	4
2002	30	15.08	1	6	11	12

Source: Fixed-Point Rural Survey, Ministry of Agriculture, P. R. China.

Since the intervention of village elections, collections of rural tax and fee, and enforcement of various policies are all of the behaviors simultaneously determined by local governments, the explanatory variables in the above regressions, such as *VFOOD* and *VFEE*, are likely to be endogenously determined. To address this endogeneity problem, we use a two-stage instrument approach for estimation. In the first stage, the arable land per capita is adopted as the instrument variable. On one hand, the quantities of government grain procurement are very different in different regions, and they are determined by upper-level governments according to a set of rules that take into account such factors as natural conditions, historical factors, and even political concerns (e.g. local food self-sufficiency).

Table 20.4 Statistical description of the variables

	Observations	Mean	Standard deviation	Min.	Max.
VFOOD	1,312	70.45	118.639	0	988.785
VFEE1	1,304	0.065	0.05	0	0.374
VFEE2	1,304	0.069	0.067	0	0.493
VINC	1,299	696.255	567.864	39.905	6,884.048
VOUT	1,263	0.131	0.136	0	0.927
VEDU	1,171	0.407	0.127	0.026	0.903
VINCSTR	836	0.134	0.224	0	1
VAGRSTR	1,312	0.458	0.23	0	0.982
VLAND	1,312	1.534	1.551	0.006	13.096

Obviously, the per capita arable land in the category of natural conditions should be one of important determinants among them; secondly, the cost in implementing the food policy in different regions is unobservable to the upper-level government, which may create excuses for local governments to increase administrative costs and staffing, and then to collect more taxes and fees as extra-budgetary revenue.

Therefore, the implementation of the policy entails high social costs, not only in policy implementation and administration but also in corruption, because local officials can impose charges on peasants in the name of implementing these central government policies and the central government cannot effectively monitor the behaviors of local cadres due to significant information asymmetry. Table 20.5 presents the results for the first stage regression. As expected, *VLAND* has significantly positive impact on *VFOOD*, *VFEE1*, and *VFEE2*.

In the second stage, since the dependent variable is a categorical variable, we use Ordered Logit model to estimate equation (18) and (19). As shown in Table 20.6, when controlling all other factors, there is a stable U relationship between grain procurement and intervention to election, which means when policy burden increases, the intervention to election might be strengthened. However, as long as the policy burden becomes heavier, the cost of enforcing the policies will be higher, and the social conflicts will be more serious.

Table 20.5 The regression results for the first stage

Dependent variables	(1)	(2)	(3)
VFOOD	0.177***		
	(0.053)		
VFEE1		0.004***	
		(0.001)	
VFEE2			0.005***
			(0.002)
Observations	1312	1304	1304
Adj-R^2	0.31	0.13	0.34
Prob.>F	0.00	0.05	0.06

Notes:
1. The independent variable in the above regressions is the arable land per capita in the village level. The yearly and provincial dummies are controlled in the regressions.
2. Figures in parentheses are robust standard errors; the symbols *, ** and *** indicate statistical significance at the 10 percent, 5 percent, and 1 percent level, respectively.
3. VFOOD is in logarithmic form.
4. Other exogenous are also included in the first stage regressions.

Local governments might improve village elections if they incorporated more villager opinions in decision making to alleviate villagers' dissatisfaction. We also find that the fewer rural labors migrate out of one area and the bigger a role agriculture production plays in that economy, the less political control would be on the local election. It might be due to the fact that farmers care about their election rights when they stay in the village and agriculture is their main source of income. For the migrant labors, they might ignore the development of democracy, and choose to migrate, which is known as voting by foot. In addition, the education level and the development of collective firms have no influence in the regressions.

In Table 20.7 and 20.8, we also find the U-relationship between *DEMO* and *VFEE1*, while *VFEE2* only has a negative influence, which means that, to some extent, rural democracy might be helpful to enforce the policies from upper-level government and to collect state tax. In contrast, informal fees always stand for the detrimental factor against rural democracy, which in turn indirectly confirm the general belief that more democracy will lead to the resistance to the levy of informal fees, no matter whether or not they are legal or illegal.

Table 20.6 The regression results for the second stage (I)

Independent variables	(1)	(2)	(3)	(4)	(5)
VFOOD	-2.988***	-2.919***	-4.409***	-4.613***	-3.619***
	(0.884)	(0.885)	(1.169)	(1.060)	(0.925)
$VFOOD^2$	0.260***	0.249***	0.334***	0.342***	0.280***
	(0.068)	(0.067)	(0.099)	(0.074)	(0.069)
T	-0.177	0.195	1.808***	-4.070	-1.459
	(1.974)	(1.985)	(0.656)	(2.553)	(2.031)
VINC	-2.148	-1.853	-4.057	-8.068**	-3.127**
	(1.695)	(1.633)	(2.609)	(3.249)	(1.492)
$VINC^2$	0.145	0.131	0.264	0.551**	0.222**
	(0.124)	(0.119)	(0.186)	(0.230)	(0.109)
VOUT		-1.903***			
		(0.673)			
VEDU			1.325		
			(1.521)		
VINCSTR				-0.696	
				(0.710)	
AGRSTR					2.551***
					(0.657)
Pseudo R^2	0.20	0.21	0.21	0.21	0.21
Prob($>Chi^2$)	0.00	0.00	0.00	0.00	0.00
Observations	569	564	448	362	569

Notes:
1. DEMO is the independent variable in the above regressions. The yearly and provincial dummies are controlled in the regressions.
2. Figures in parentheses are robust standard errors; the symbols *, ** and *** indicate statistical significance at the 10 percent, 5 percent, and 1 percent level, respectively.
3. VFOOD and VINC are in logarithmic forms.

In both tables, labor migration, education level, status of collective firms, and agriculture industry in the economy play similar roles as in Table 20.6. The dummy variable for 1998 is positively significant in most cases in our regressions. In other words, the central initiative to promote rural democracy after 1998 did matter in the micro level. But, its impact could be limited if the center does not reduce the policy burden of local governments.

Table 20.7 The regression results for the second stage (II)

Independent variables	(1)	(2)	(3)	(4)	(5)
VFEE1	-144.399***	-147.668***	-162.496***	-188.811**	-171.805**
	(53.999)	(56.931)	(69.836)	(83.835)	(54.878)
VFEE1^2	554.534**	560.764**	483.704	507.831	613.719**
	(255.929)	(272.419)	(343.535)	(475.480)	(257.687)
T	4.902***	5.244***	6.203***	4.671***	5.075***
	(0.567)	(0.565)	(1.101)	(0.725)	(0.576)
VINC	-2.062	-1.899	-4.074	-7.952**	-2.832*
	(1.740)	(1.656)	(2.803)	(3.429)	(1.545)
VINC^2	0.150	0.145	0.278	0.552**	0.217**
	(0.126)	(0.121)	(0.198)	(0.240)	(0.112)
VOUT		-2.170***			
		(0.646)			
VEDU			1.392		
			(1.543)		
VINCSTR				-0.783	
				(0.687)	
AGRSTR					1.706***
					(0.567)
Pseudo R^2	0.19	0.20	0.2	0.19	0.2
Prob(>Chi^2)	0.00	0.00	0.00	0.00	0.00
Observations	569	564	448	362	569

Notes:
1. DEMO is the independent variable in the above regressions. The yearly and provincial dummies are controlled in the regressions.
2. Figures in parentheses are robust standard errors; the symbols *, ** and *** indicate statistical significance at the 10 percent, 5 percent, and 1 percent level, respectively.
3. VINC is in logarithmic form.

Table 20.8 The regression results for the second stage (III)

Independent Variables	(1)	(2)	(3)	(4)	(5)
VFEE2	-17.460	-20.891	-42.235	-48.401	-29.137
	(21.390)	(22.339)	(30.878)	(52.193)	(21.910)
VFEE2^2	-122.134**	-106.338*	-114.380*	-236.095***	-125.240***
	(56.778)	(57.915)	(71.037)	(70.897)	(57.489)
T	6.489***	6.896***	8.584***	8.438***	7.239***
	(1.061)	(1.106)	(2.500)	(2.747)	(1.094)
VINC	-2.124	-1.892	-3.872*	-8.185**	-2.898**
	(1.537)	(1.481)	(2.348)	(3.863)	(1.412)
VINC^2	0.151	0.142	0.259	0.563**	0.219**
	(0.111)	(0.107)	(0.166)	(0.267)	(0.102)
VOUT		-2.089***			
		(0.666)			
VEDU			1.310		
			(1.501)		
VINCSTR				-0.532	
				(0.705)	
AGRSTR					1.639***
					(0.566)
Pseudo R^2	0.19	0.20	0.20	0.20	0.2
Prob(>Chi^2)	0.00	0.00	0.00	0.00	0.00
Observations	569	564	448	362	569

Notes:

1. DEMO is the independent variable in the above regressions. The yearly and provincial dummies are controlled in the regressions.

2. Figures in parentheses are robust standard errors; the symbols *, ** and *** indicate statistical significance at the 10 percent, 5 percent, and 1 percent level, respectively.

3. VINC is in logarithmic form.

5 Conclusions

Many researchers try to reconcile the conflicting facts of the increasing unrest in rural areas and the growing village democracy. Since the formal enacting of the Village Committee Organic Law in 1998, peasants have had the right to elect their leaders. Such rights, as many observers predicted, will inevitably set restrictions against the predatory behaviors of local governments.

Therefore, local cadres will be unwilling to accept or even oppose to the full implementation of the self-governance by peasants. Because in practice local governments usually are in command of various resources, they can interfere in village election to get their preferred election outcomes.

In contrast to the traditional wisdom that views local governments as the major obstacle to village democracy, we hold that the regulations from the central government may be the primary culprit. We argue in this chapter that as long as the center gives higher priority to regulations over other policy targets, the LSC situation is inevitable. Fearing that more democracy in the countryside will hinder local governments from implementing the regulations, the center will favor local governments' anti-democracy behaviors.

Local officials predict the priority sequences and the possible responses of the center, and thus resist the full implementation of the Organic Law, and continue their rent-seeking behaviors in the name of carrying out the center's policies. A policy implication of this chapter is that to change the priority sequences in the center's policy basket and to further remove the regulations are two necessary conditions of promoting the development of village democracy.

References

Bernstein, T.P. and Lu, X., 'Taxation without Representation: Peasants, the Central and the Local States in Reform China', *The China Quarterly* (2000): 742-763.

Dewatripont, M. and Maskin, E., 'Credit and Efficiency in Centralized and Decentralized Economies', *The Review of Economic Studies* 62 (4) (1995): 541-555.

Dong, X. and Putterman, L., 'Investigating the Rise of Labor Redundancy in China's State Industry', http://www.econ.brown.edu/fac/Louis_Putterman/working/, 2002.

Edin, M., 'State Capacity and Local Agent Control in China: CCP Cadre Management from a Township Perspective', *China Quarterly* (2003): 35-52.

Goldfel, S., and Quandt, R., 'Budget Constraints, Bailouts and the Firm Under Central Planning', *Journal of Comparative Economics*, 12(4) (1988): 502-520.

Huang, Y., 'The Institutional Roots of Peasant Burden and Its Solution', *Zhongguo Nongcun Jingji* (*China Agricultural Economy*), No.5 (1994).

Kennedy, J.J., 'The Face of 'Grassroots Democracy' in Rural China', *Asian Survey*. Vol. 42 (3) (2002): 456-482.

Kornai, J., *Economics of Shortage* (Amsterdam: North-Holland, 1980).

Kornai, J., Maskin, E. and Roland, G., 'Understanding the Soft Budget Constraint', *Journal of Economic Literature*, Vol. XLI (December 2003): 1095-1136.

Lampton, D.M., 'Chinese Politics: Bargaining Treadmill', *Issues & Studies* Vol. 23 (1987): 11-41.

———, 'A Plum for a Peach: Bargaining, Interest, and Bureaucratic Politics in China', in K. Lieberthal and D.M. Lampton (eds), *Bureaucracy, Politics, and Decision-Making in Post-Mao China* (Berkeley: University of California Press, 1992).

Lawrence, S.V., 'Democracy, Chinese Style', *Australian Journal of Chinese Affairs*, No. 32 (1994): 61-68.

Li, D., *Public Ownership as the cause of a soft budget constraint* (mimeo, Harvard University, 1992).

Li, L., 'The Empowering Effect of Village Elections in China', *Asian Survey* Vol. 43 (4) (2003): 648-662.

————, Political Trust in Rural China (Presentation at Midwestern Political Science Association Annual Meeting at Chicago, USA, April 18, 2004).

Lieberthal K., 'Introduction: The 'Fragmented Authoritarianism' Model and Its Limitations', in K. Lieberthal and D.M. Lampton (eds), *Bureaucracy, Politics, and Decision-Making in Post-Mao China* (Berkeley: University of California Press, 1992).

Lin, J.Y. and Tan, F., 'Accountability, Viability, and Soft Budget Constraint', *American Economic Review*, Papers and Proceedings, Volume 89 (2) (May 1999): 426-431.

Lipset, S.M., 'Some Social Requisites of Democracy: Economic Development and Political Legitimacy', *American Political Science Review*, Vol. 53 (1959): 69-105.

Liu, M., Shih, V. and Zhang, Q., '"Eating Budget": Credible Information and Fiscal Transfers under Predatory Fiscal Federalism' (Unpublished paper, 2004).

Lu, X., 'Politics of Peasant Burden in Reform China', *Journal of Peasant Studies*. Vol. 25 (1) (1997): 113-138.

O'Brien, K.J., 'Implementing Political Reform in China's Village', *Australian Journal of Chinese Affairs*. No 32 (July, 1994): 33-59.

O'Brien, K.J. and Li, L., 'Selective Policy Implementation in Rural China', *Comparative Politics*, Vol. 32 (January, 1999): 167-186.

————, 'The Struggle over Village Elections', in M. Goldman and R. MacFarquhar (eds), *The Paradox of China's Post-Mao Reforms* (Cambridge, MA: Harvard University Press, 1999).

————, 'Accommodating "Democracy" in a One-Party State: Introducing Village Elections in China', *China Quarterly*, Vol. 162 (June, 2000): 465-89.

Qian, Y., 'A Theory of Shortage in Socialist Economies Based on the Soft Budget Constraint', *American Economic Review*, 84 (1994): 145-156.

Qian, Y., and Roland, G., 'Federalism and The Soft BUDGET Constraint', *American Economic Review*, 88(5) (1998): 1143-1162.

Schleifer, A., Lakonishok, J., Vishny, R.W., 'Contrarian Investment, Extrapolation and Risk', *Journal of Finance*, vol. 49 (1994): 1541-1578.

Tao, R., Lin, J.F., Liu, M. and Zhang, Q., 'Rural Taxation and Government Regulations in China', *Agricultural Economics* (forthcoming).

Weingast, B. and Banks, J., 'The political control of bureaucracies under asymmetric information', *American Journal of Political Science* 36 (2) (1992): 509-524.

Xiao, T., et al, 'Elections in the Chinese Rural Society: A Comprehensive Survey of 40 Elections of Villagers' Committee in Jiangxi Province', *Strategy and Management* (*Zhanglue yu Guanli*), 5 (2001).

Yep, R., Maintaining Stability in Rural China: Challenges and Responses (Unpublished paper, 2002).

Zhang, J., 'Observing an Election of Villagers' Committee in Lishu County', *The 21st Century* (*Ershiyi Shijie*). (Winter, 1998).

Zhang, X., et al, 'Local Governance and Public Goods Provision in Rural China', *Journal of Public Economics* 2305 (2003): 468-483.

Zhao, Y. and Zhou, F., 'Local Fiscal System, Land Rights, and Peasant Burden', *Carter Dynamics* (*Kate Dongtai*), 4 (2002): 1-15.

Zhong, Y., 'Withering Governmental Power in China? A View from Below', *Communist and Post-Communist Studies*, Vol. 29 (4) (1996): 363-375.

———, 'The Township Fiscal Predicament: Its Causes and Solutions', *Zhongguo Nongcun Guancha* (*China Agricultural Review*), 3 (2003).

Appendix: Fixed Point Rural Survey

We used a panel data set drawn from the "Fixed Point Rural Survey" carried out annually by the Ministry of Agriculture of China. The survey began in 1983 in nine provinces. After 1984, it was extended to 28 provinces (only Tibet is excluded), covering 37,422 households, 93 townships, and 71 counties.

Starting in 1986, the Fixed Point Rural Survey System was established and institutionalized.

The survey covers not only rural households but also villages and rural enterprises. All household samples are selected randomly. For villages, the rural areas are first divided into different categories, such as mountainous area, hilly area, and plain area; urban (shizhen), suburbs (shizhen jiaoqu) and non-urban suburbs (xiangcun); rich areas and poor areas. Then the villages are randomly selected within these areas according to certain guidelines.

The survey questionnaire was revised after 1991, 1993, and 2003 to include more questions.

The household survey covers information on population, labor force, land, fixed assets, area of agricultural plantation, output of main agricultural products, sales of agricultural products, purchase of production materials, family revenue and expenditures, consumption of major food items, and the durable goods consumption.

The village-level survey covers information on total population, labor force, households, community organization, fixed assets, output and sales of major agricultural products, operating revenue and expenditure of the whole village, and revenue and expenditures of community organization.

The data we obtained are for eight provinces, covering about 1,400 households and over 48 villages from 1986 to 2002, and the data set on village elections used in this article comes from a 2003 survey jointly conducted by the Ministry of Agriculture and the China Center for Economic Research in Peking University.

Based on the same sample as above, this survey reveals the information of village election and medical expenditure of farmers from 1987 to 2002.

Index